C ACTIVE

Ja   se
La   eople
W EDITION

D1493729

23 JUN 2022

WITHDRAWN

ABOUT JAPAN

Brian Moeran

Copenhagen Business School, Denmark

Editorial C   rry Doyle

Educational Publishers LLP trading as BBC Active
Edinburgh Gate, Harlow
Essex CM20 2JE
England

BBC logo © BBC 1996. BBC and BBC ACTIVE are trademarks of the British Broadcasting Corporation

First published 1991. New edition published 2006.

The right of Richard Smith and Trevor Hughes Parry to be identified as authors of the Language Course, and Brian Moeran to be identified as author of the About Japan units, has been asserted by them in accordance with the Copyright, Designs and Patents Act, 1988.

ISBN-10: 0-563-51949-5
ISBN-13: 978-0563-51949-2

Cover designed by Gary Day-Ellison
Cover photograph: © Bruce Burkhardt/ Corbis
Illustrations by Lucy Su
Calligraphy by Yukki Yaura
Maps by Technical Arts Services
TV producer: Terry Doyle
Audio producer (first edition): Terry Doyle

Acknowledgements The authors gratefully acknowledge the creative contributions of Miyuki Shioya and Sumiko Okada, and the constructive comments of Terry Doyle, Akiko Motoyoshi and Stefan Kaiser. Thanks are also due to Robert Cooke, Naomi Takama, Miki Yoroizuka and Mayumi Nakamura for their help with particular parts of the book, as well as to our editors, Suzanne Webbe and Martha Caute, and designer Sarah Amit. Initial advice: John Collins.

Printed and bound by Ashford Colour Press Ltd, Hants.

The Publisher's policy is to use paper manufactured from sustainable forests

Also available: CD pack (six audio CDs) ISBN-10: 0-563-51951-7   ISBN-13: 978-0563-51951-5

CONTENTS

CD TRACK LIST

CD TRACK LIST

CD TRACK LIST

HOW TO USE THIS BOOK

The *Japanese – Language and People* course consists of:

- this book;
- six CDs;

The course aims to take the beginner – alone, with a friend or in a class – to a stage where he or she can communicate at a basic level in spoken Japanese, in a variety of everyday situations. As a glance inside the book will show you, there are many practice activities designed to encourage you to *use* the language from the very beginning, often in conjunction with the CDs. The book and CDs then, are closely integrated, and may be used independently of the television programmes.

STRUCTURE OF THE COURSE

Learning a language like Japanese involves not only a mastery of grammar, vocabulary and pronunciation, but also an understanding of the cultural context in which the language is used. In this course, language and culture are closely linked, with the ten units of the book (corresponding to the ten television programmes) focusing on distinct themes such as family and home, work, education, travel and leisure. Units 1 to 8 provide the beginner with a solid grounding in basic spoken Japanese, Unit 9 invites the learner to progress to a still higher level through mastery of a variety of useful verb forms, while Unit 10 consists of a comprehensive review of language presented in the book. Although complicated grammatical explanations are kept to a minimum in the body of the text, a reference section at the end of the book contains useful supplementary information on Japanese grammar for the interested learner. At the end of the book you will also find a key containing answers to exercises, and Japanese–English and English–Japanese glossaries of the words used in the book.

WORKING YOUR WAY THROUGH A UNIT

Each unit is divided up in the following way:

- About Japan
- (Language 1)
- (Language 2)
- About Japan
- (Language 3)
- (Language 4)
- About Japan
- (Language 5)
- About Japan
- What you'll hear
- Written Japanese
- Language summary

About Japan sections provide insights into present-day Japanese society and culture, relating both to the overall unit theme and to the language presented elsewhere in the unit.

Language sections should each take approximately one to one and a half hours to complete. We strongly recommend that you try to set aside this amount of time at each sitting, and do not stop until you reach the end of a section. This way, you will begin each unit with the confidence that five sessions will see you through the new language presented. These two symbols will help you recognise where one language section ends and another begins:

means 'Keep going!'   means 'Rest here!'

Language sections consist of dialogues (entitled 'Japanese live'), simple explanations ('Take note'), vocabulary lists ('Build-up'), pronunciation exercises ('Soundcheck') and a variety of other practice activities. Shaded boxes contain the central language points to be practised and learned in a particular section.

The symbol @ in the left-hand margin next to an exercise indicates that you will find answers in the key at the end of the book.

What you'll hear sections, and the corresponding CD items, provide extra practice in *listening* to Japanese. The aim of these sections is to reproduce something of the situation in which you will find yourself in Japan – where you will certainly not understand every word you hear – and to help you practise concentrating on what you *do* know and getting the gist of what is being said. You will be doing well enough if you can complete the listening tasks suggested in these sections. Try not to worry about not understanding every word; you're not expected to!

Written Japanese sections provide a basic introduction to the way Japanese is written by the Japanese themselves. Although Japanese is often referred to as a 'difficult' language, what is really difficult is not so much the language itself as the way it is written. The aim of these sections is to show that even reading Japanese is neither as impossible nor as tedious as might at first appear. In other parts of the course, however, Japanese is presented in a more familiar form, in Roman alphabet, to help you gain immediate access to the spoken language.

Language summary pages conclude the units; use these pages to remind you of the language you've studied, and as a reference point for revision.

USING THE AUDIO CDS

You may be tempted to miss out some of the activities connected with the CDs, but try not to! Remember that speaking and understanding a language are skills which can only be developed through practice. To get the most out of the audio, take account of the following features:

- Audio items are numbered consecutively, from 1 to 307. If an activity in the book requires you to use the CD, you'll see a symbol like this:

  CD☐232

  This means play item 232 on your CD, following instructions given there and in the book.

- To find out which CD and track number this item is on, consult the CD track list on pages iv–vi.

- In some activities, you are asked to speak during a pause on the CD. However, when the question or response to be formulated is longer than a few words, you will hear a musical tone, and you will be asked to pause the CD at the tone in order to speak. Try to make sure, then, that you have a CD player with a pause button which is easy to operate.

- In many cases, the CD will follow up with one possible way you could have responded. As a result, you may gradually get into the habit of opting out: failing to pause the tape and going straight on to hear the answer. Try to avoid this; far more important than producing a perfect answer is struggling to work it out for yourself.

- Some of the activities may appear rather complicated, but persevere! The more challenged by or involved in a task you are, the better you are likely to learn the language you are practising.

- Some of the exercises on the CDs require you to use a large number of new vocabulary items. So as not to overwhelm you, we have often chosen Japanese words which are borrowed from English. It is important, however, that you try to pronounce these words in a Japanese way, and avoid pronouncing them as in English – otherwise you quite simply won't be understood.

- Although some of the dialogues on the are very similar in content to conversations in the television programmes, they are not exactly the same. Also, although people who appear in the television programmes are mentioned in the book, the voices on the tapes are those of actors.

OPTIONS IN FOLLOWING THE COURSE

For reasons of time or interest, you might wish to consider these alternatives to following the course straight through from cover to cover:

- Although both the 'What you'll hear' and the 'Written Japanese' sections relate in theme and language content to the rest of the unit, you do not have to attempt them at the same time as the other language sections. If, for example, you are above all concerned with developing an ability in spoken Japanese, or do not have time to complete a whole unit between transmissions of the television programmes, you may decide either not to attempt the 'Written Japanese' sections at all, or to return to them at some stage after you have completed the core language course. Similarly, you might wish to come back to the 'What you'll hear' sections after completing the course, or to work through them at a slower pace than the rest of the course.

- If you have access to video recordings of the television programmes, you might like to try the following approach: first watch the programme, treating it as an introduction to the cultural information and language presented in the book, then work through the corresponding unit in the book, and finally watch the programme again to review what you've studied.

KEEPING GOING

You will probably have heard at least one story of someone who started a language course with good intentions and then just ran out of energy after the first month or so. Recent research has identified some of the most common reasons learners have for stopping. Here are some suggestions for countering them:

Stay motivated. Having a concrete reason for learning is a greater guarantee of success than a general interest. If you already have a concrete reason, then you are at an advantage (for example, if you have to go to Japan in three months, or a knowledge of Japanese will improve your promotion prospects). If, however, like many people, you have a more general interest, you might like to try and give yourself some specific aim to work towards. This may be ambitious (to understand a favourite Japanese film without the subtitles) or more modest (to make contact with Japanese people in the community). Alternatively, persuade a friend to start the course with you, or join a class; learning with others can be a motivating experience in itself.

Organise your time. Try to create specific times each week when you can be sure you will be able to devote yourself to learning Japanese. Create firm objectives for yourself (for example, to get through a unit by a particular date). Record them in a diary or on a calendar, and refer to them frequently to keep yourself on course.

Try not to 'overlearn'. Don't get bogged down in a particular language section, even if you are having difficulties. The design of this course is such that words and language patterns will recur later on, and you may well find that things fall into place at a later stage, in a different context. Don't set yourself things to do which aren't specified in the instructions (don't try to transcribe 'What you'll hear' dialogues, for example): if you find that even after two or three hours on a particular language section you still haven't dealt with it to your satisfaction, you may be being unrealistic. If you're not sure what to learn by heart, the summary page at the end of each unit provides a list of all important items. You might like to write these items down in a vocabulary book, so that you can memorise them at spare moments during the day.

Review. Revision is essential, and yet it is often the least appetising aspect of learning. Research seems to show that learning is most effective if revision takes place after one day, again after a week, then after a month, six months, and a year. Apart from re-reading, try the following revision methods:

- Go back to speaking activities you have already attempted. Unless it is necessary to the task, try to interact with the CD without looking at the book.
- Also, return periodically to listening exercises – in particular those contained in 'What you'll hear' sections: you should find that you can understand them better, the further you have advanced through the book. (Note that it is advisable to write answers in the book in pencil, so that you can later erase them and attempt exercises again.)
- Review with a friend or classmate: quiz one another on material in the book, or act out a situation such as asking directions, a shopping sequence, etc.
- Once you have completed the course, it may be some time before you get a chance to make full use of what you have learned. To prevent your forgetting everything in that time, return to Unit 10, which contains the complete language course in microcosm. A week spent immersed in this unit should bring everything back to you.

Finally, *ganbatte!* ('stick with it!'). We hope you enjoy the course!

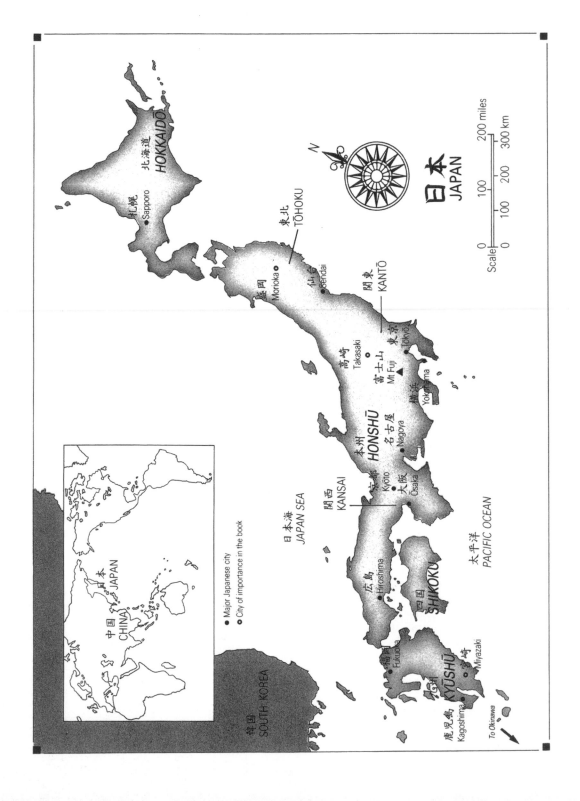

1
INTRODUCTIONS

日
本

About Japan

When we think of Japan, most of us conjure up an image of a land of contrasts: of Mount Fuji, geisha and cherry blossoms, on the one hand, and of crowded homes making up an endless urban sprawl, fashion-conscious school girls, and wide-eyed manga cartoon characters, on the other. Japan seems to be a country where nature and technology, tradition and modernity, coexist in harmony. But how true are these images? In the About Japan sections of this book, we will try to disentangle reality from clichéd stereotypes, and present the Japanese as they really are.

The Japanese often describe their land as a small 'island country' (*shimaguni*). About the size of France or California, Japan in fact consists of four main islands and dozens of smaller ones. These range from Hokkaidō in the north, through Honshū, Shikoku and Kyūshū in the southwest, down to Okinawa and the Ryūkyū Islands in the far south. Altogether, this small 'island country' stretches from 46 to 24 degrees latitude, ranging over an area equivalent to that from central France to Morocco. It is, however, sufficiently separated from Korea and the Asian continent to have resulted in some feelings of isolation.

In spite of the varied environmental conditions and the cultural differences that accompany them, the Japanese often say that they are a 'homogeneous race' of people. In fact, their origins are diverse. The original inhabitants of Hokkaidō were the 'hairy' Ainu, a race of people totally distinct from the Japanese and more akin to those living in eastern Siberia, while the inhabitants of Okinawa are equally different from 'mainland' Japanese, since their racial and cultural origins are probably closer to the Chinese than to the Japanese.

Still, in the course of everyday conversation, it soon becomes clear that most Japanese do not readily admit among themselves to being 'the same'. For example, people born and brought up in Kyūshū will argue that they are different from those living on the largest island of Honshū, while the inhabitants of Kyōto (which literally means 'capital city') will insist that they are by no means the same as those inhabiting Tōkyō (meaning 'eastern capital', since it took over from Kyōto as the capital in 1868) and vice versa.

Right above **Mount Fuji**
Right below **Shikoku and the Inland Sea**

History suggests that a number of different peoples came together to make up the race now referred to as 'the Japanese'. Some of these came to the Japanese archipelago by way of Siberia; others arrived via the Korean peninsular; yet others made their way up through the islands that dot the China Sea. There are thus a number of racial, cultural and linguistic differences dividing the Japanese into select groups which often owe primary allegiance to the geographical area in which they were born and brought up.

SAYING WHO YOU ARE, WHERE YOU'RE FROM, WHAT YOU DO

- 'How do you do?':
  Hajimemashite.

- 'I'm ...': ... **desu.**
  (E.g. 'I'm American': *Amerikajin desu.*)

JAPANESE LIVE 1   `CD ▶ 1`

Listen as two visitors to Japan introduce themselves.

Robert
Hajimemashite.
Robāto Hōpu desu.
Igirisujin desu.
Bijinesuman desu.

Elizabeth
Hajimemashite.
Erizabesu Guriin desu.
Amerikajin desu.
Dezainā desu.

igirisujin	British (lit. 'Britain person')
amerikajin	American (lit. 'America person')
bijinesuman	businessman
dezainā	fashion designer

SPOTCHECK 1

@ How would you write their surnames in English? (You can find the answer in the key at the back of the book.)

TAKE NOTE

'I AM'

Desu in the above self-introductions means 'am'; as in Italian or Spanish, you don't have to use a word for 'I' when it's clear you're talking about yourself. Note that *desu* comes last of all; verbs in general come at the end of the sentence in Japanese.

FOREIGN WORDS AND NAMES

One thing the Japanese have imported in vast quantities is vocabulary. Foreign – in particular, English – words like *bijinesuman* and *dezainā* are to be seen and heard all around, especially in the media and in younger people's speech. However, foreign words (and names) are always adapted to the Japanese sound system, so you may have some difficulty in recognising them at first.

- 'I': **watashi**

- 'As for me, I'm ...': **Watashi wa ... desu.** (to contrast yourself with another person)

- 'I'm ..., too': **Watashi mo ... desu.** (to emphasise your similarity with another person)

JAPANESE LIVE 2 `CD ▶ 2`

Our Japanese guides introduce themselves.

Yuka
Hajimemashite.
Nukina Yuka desu.
Nihonjin desu.
Repōtā desu.

Kyōko
Hajimemashite.
Watashi wa Matsumoto
 Kyōko desu.
Nihonjin desu.
Watashi mo repōtā desu.

| **nihonjin** | Japanese (lit. 'Japan person') |
| **repōtā** | TV/radio reporter |

SPOTCHECK 2
@ What does Kyōko emphasise as being similar about herself and Yuka?

TAKE NOTE

NAMES
In Japan, as in other Asian countries such as China and Korea, family names come first (Nukina Yuka, Matsumoto Kyōko, Ono Yōko); however, Western names are not altered to fit this order (Erizabesu Guriin, Robāto Hōpu, Jon Renon).

'I'
There are several words for 'I' in Japanese in addition to *watashi*: you may hear, for example, *watakushi* (more formal than *watashi*). More informally, men may say *boku* or *ore*. However, remember that saying 'I' isn't usually necessary at all, except for emphasis or to avoid confusion.

'WA' AND 'MO'
Wa has no exact equivalent in English. Its function is to indicate that the word which comes before it is a new topic for discussion. Think of it as meaning 'regarding ...' or 'as for ...'; e.g. *Watashi wa Matsumoto Kyōko desu*: 'As for/regarding me, I'm Matsumoto Kyōko'. *Wa* can be replaced with *mo* when you want to emphasise a similarity; e.g. *Watashi mo repōtā desu*: 'I'm a reporter, too'.

SOUNDCHECK

On the whole, Japanese pronunciation isn't very difficult, and these hints and exercises will take you a long way towards 'sounding Japanese'.

THE SOUND SYSTEM | CD ▸ 3 |

Look at the sound chart on page 325.
Japanese words are made up of these syllables alone; *hajimemashite*, for example, is formed like this: *ha/ji/me/ma/shi/te*. Try to find these sounds in the chart.

Now listen to the sound chart being read line by line, and repeat each line. In particular, try to pronounce correctly:

● the five vowel sounds (*a – i – u – e – o*)
● *r* (as in *ra – ri – ru – re – ro*)
● *f* (as in *fu*).

NO STRESS

The main barrier to 'sounding Japanese' isn't the pronunciation of the syllables themselves, but the relative absence of stress and intonation as compared with English. Whereas we tend to say 'SUshi', 'karAte' and 'TOkyo', for example, the Japanese themselves say these words more monotonously, giving equal weight to each syllable. Practise this by saying some more Japanese names.

| CD ▸ 4 |

A First, listen to the names being spoken slowly. Using the pause button, repeat each name, taking care to give each syllable an equal beat.

E.g. **Yamamoto Kimiko:**
Yá/má/mó/tó/Kí/mí/kó
(not 'YamaMOto KImiko')

Women's names:

Yamamoto Kimiko	(Ya/ma/mo/to/Ki/mi/ko)
Suzuki Noriko	(Su/zu/ki/No/ri/ko)
Tanaka Akiko	(Ta/na/ka/A/ki/ko)
Nakamura Mayumi	(Na/ka/mu/ra/Ma/yu/mi)
Kamikawa Ariko	(Ka/mi/ka/wa/A/ri/ko)

Men's names:

Watanabe Tatsuo	(Wa/ta/na/be/Ta/tsu/o)
Hasegawa Yoshio	(Ha/se/ga/wa/Yo/shi/o)
Nakajima Yasuo	(Na/ka/ji/ma/Ya/su/o)
Yamada Masahiro	(Ya/ma/da/Ma/sa/hi/ro)
Kimura Shinji	(Ki/mu/ra/Shi/n/ji)

| CD ▸ 5 |

B Now practise saying each name on your own, gradually building up speed. (Continue to pronounce each syllable clearly, and don't emphasise any of them more than others: try to speak 'monotonously'!) Then listen to and repeat after the CD, where this time the names are spoken at normal speed.

LONG VOWELS

Long vowels, written ā, ii, ū, ē, ō, take roughly twice as long to say as short vowels. To pronounce a long vowel, make the vowel sound last for two 'beats' rather than one.

E.g. **dezainā: dé/zá/í/ná/‒**
Here are some more words borrowed from English and adapted to the Japanese sound system. Practise saying them after the CD, and try to guess what they @ mean:

| CD ▸ 6 |

1	sofā	(so/fa/‒)
2	kurisumasu kādo	(ku/ri/su/ma/su/ka/‒/do)
3	biifu shichū	(bi/‒/fu/shi/chu/‒)
4	takushii	(ta/ku/shi/‒)
5	konpyūta	(ko/n/pyu/‒/ta)
6	pūru	(pu/‒/ru)
7	kēki	(ke/‒/ki)
8	karēraisu	(ka/re/‒/ra/i/su)
9	kōhii	(ko/‒/hi/‒)
10	chokorēto	(cho/ko/re/‒/to)

Right **Miyajima Shrine, near Hiroshima**

DISAPPEARING VOWELS

Although in general every syllable is pronounced clearly and distinctly in Japanese, there are some exceptions where vowels tend to disappear. For example, when the words *hajimemash(i)te* and *des(u)* are spoken at normal speed, the bracketed (*i*) and (*u*) sounds are hardly pronounced at all. This happens very commonly with the syllables *shi* and *su*, and sometimes with other *-i* and (especially) *-u* syllables; e.g. *Erizabes(u) G(u)riin, Robāto Hōp(u).*

@ Practise saying the following names with a Japanese pronunciation. Can you recognise them?

CD ▶ 7

1	Adamu Sumisu	(A/da/m(u)/S(u)/mi/s(u))
2	Kāru Marukusu	(Ka/–/r(u)/ Ma/r(u)/k(u)/s(u))
3	Uinsuton Chāchiru	(U/i/n/s(u)/to/n/ Cha/–/chi/r(u))
4	Ronarudo Rēgan	(Ro/na/r(u)/do/Re/–/ga/n)
5	Pōru Nyūman	(Po/–/r(u)/Nyu/–/ma/n)
6	Meriru Sutoriipu	(Me/ri/r(u)/ S(u)/to/ri/–/p(u))
7	Kāru Ruisu	(Ka/–/r(u)/Ru/i/s(u))
8	Ringo Sutā	(Ri/n/go/S(u)/ta/–)
9	Ibu San Rōran	(I/b(u)/Sa/n/Ro/–/ra/n)
10	Bābara Sutoraisando	(Ba/–/ba/ra/ S(u)/to/ra/i/sa/n/do)

REWIND

CD ▶ 1   CD ▶ 2

Now that you've learned how to 'sound Japanese', go back to 'Japanese live 1'. Listen once more and repeat, using the pause button at the end of each line. Then do the same for 'Japanese live 2'. Later you'll get the opportunity to introduce yourself, but first for some training in the essential art of bowing ...

About Japan

Language learning is not just an intellectual, but a cultural exercise. For example, one of the difficulties in learning a foreign language is how to acquire the 'nonverbal' and 'paralinguistic' features that accompany speech. In Japan people often make a number of sounds like *hō, hā* or *hē* to show the speaker that they are paying attention to what is being said. These sounds help establish communication between speaker and listener and are referred to as *aizuchi*, or 'chiming in'. They are used in much the same way as, but much more frequently than, such words as 'really' or 'I see' in English.

A very important form of nonverbal communication is the way in which the body is used to articulate a conversation. The Japanese have a range of hand or finger signals with which to communicate certain meanings to others. For example, a chopping motion of the hand means 'excuse me', while the concept of 'lover' is signified by the raising of a little finger (for girlfriend) or of the thumb (for boyfriend). Sometimes, indeed, these signals will take the place of words entirely.

One form of body language that anyone learning Japanese should try to acquire is that of bowing. The Japanese seem to spend a lot of time bowing. They bow when they greet someone, and bow when they say goodbye. They bow when they receive applause, and again when accepting an order. They bow when they wish to express their gratitude, to say that they are sorry about something, and even when they are being criticised.

Bowing is so ingrained in the Japanese mind, so much a part of the Japanese language, that Japanese will bow even when on the telephone. On the face of it, bowing would seem to come as naturally to a Japanese as, say, shaking hands to a continental European, but in both cases such habits are of course taught. Indeed, one of the first things a Japanese mother teaches her new-born baby is how to respond to greetings or to say goodbye; she does this by pushing down its head and saying the necessary phrases.

Given the importance of bowing, it is as well to learn how to do it. Basically, the angle to which the torso is lowered depends on the formality of the occasion. Fifteen degrees is very informal; forty-five degrees very formal. Most of the time, Japanese bow at an angle of about thirty degrees.

This in itself is not too difficult. What the beginner has to learn, however, is not to let the neck flop forward so that he or she looks like a prawn! The backbone should be straight from the head to the hips. Men should place their hands down the seams of their trousers. Women should lightly place one palm over the other in front of their bodies. In theory at least, one should bow to a count of eight: three to go down, one for a pause, and four to return to the vertical position.

Elementary school baseball team bowing to opponents (incorrectly!)

That this is an ideal not always adhered to by younger people today can be seen in the fact that the 'proper' way of bowing often has to be taught to new employees in large companies, and we shall see in later units how quite a lot of Japanese etiquette – from respect language to serving tea – is consciously perfected. Indeed, in some respects, it is this conscious creation of a set of shared ways of behaviour that has marked Japan's transition over the past century from a 'feudal' system to a modern state, and helped to make it such a great economic power.

ASKING QUESTIONS; SAYING YES; EXPRESSING INTEREST

- 'Mr' or 'Ms Suzuki': **Suzuki-san**
- 'He/She/It is ...', 'You/We/They are ...': ... **desu**
- 'Is he/she/it ...?', 'Are you/we/they ...?: ... **desu ka?**

JAPANESE LIVE 3   `CD ▸ 8`

Ms Yamaguchi and Mr Tanaka both work for Marubeni (a large trading company) in Tōkyō. Tanaka-san has just asked Yamaguchi-san to meet Robert Hope, a visiting businessman, at his hotel.

Tanaka   (*showing Ms Yamaguchi a photograph*)
             Hōpu-san desu.
Yamaguchi Ā, sō desu ka. Amerikajin desu ka?
Tanaka   Iie, igirisujin desu.
Yamaguchi Ā, sō desu ka. Rondon kara desu ka?
Tanaka   Hai, sō desu.

ā, sō desu ka	oh, really? (lit. 'is that so?')
iie	no
Rondon kara	from London
hai, sō desu	yes, that's right (lit. 'that is so')

SPOTCHECK 3
@ Where's Robert Hope from?

TAKE NOTE

SAYING YES

If you're asked a question to which the answer is 'yes', say *hai* or less formally *ē*. However, leaving it at that can sound rather abrupt to Japanese ears. It's common to add *sō desu* or to repeat the content of the question in a reply: *Amerikajin desu ka?* → *Hai, sō desu/Hai, amerikajin desu.*

'Ā, SŌ DESU KA'

Continually showing you're listening carefully is very important to communication in Japanese, and you'll hear this expression much more often than, for example, 'oh, really' in English. Other signs of 'enthusiastic listening' (*aizuchi* in Japanese) include frequent nodding and repetition of *hai*: these do not necessarily imply agreement with what's being said. *Hai* – on its own – can mean 'I hear you'/'I understand you', as well as 'yes (that's right)'.

SOUNDCHECK   `CD ▸ 9`

When you ask a question, your voice should rise on *ka?* (listen and repeat):

Amerikajin desu ka ↗ **?**	**Igirisujin desu ka** ↗ **?**
Nyū Yōku kara desu ka ↗ **?**	**Rondon kara desu ka** ↗ **?**

But when you show interest by saying *Ā, sō desu ka*, you aren't really asking a question, so intonation falls on *ka* (listen and repeat):
Ā, sō desu ka ↘ **.**

REWIND   `CD ▸ 8`

Rewind to 'Japanese live 3' above. Listen again and repeat, pausing the CD after each line.

BUILD-UP

In 'Japanese live 3', it's clear to both Mr Tanaka and Ms Yamaguchi that they're talking about Robert Hope, so Ms Yamaguchi simply asks *Amerikajin desu ka?*, *Rondon kara desu ka?* However, when it's necessary to make clear who's being talked about, you can ask, for example:
Hōpu-san wa amerikajin desu ka?: 'Is Mr Hope American?'

ASK

CD ▶ 10

Write some questions and answers about the people introduced on pages 4 and 5, using the cues below and following the example given in 1.

1 Nukina-san   ...nihonjin?

Nukina-san wa nihonjin desu ka?
Hai, sō desu.

        ...dezainā?

Dezainā desu ka?
Iie, repōtā desu.

2 Guriin-san   ...igirisujin?
                 ...dezainā?

3 Matsumoto-san ...amerikajin?
                 ...repōtā?

4 Hōpu-san   ...bijinesuman?
                 ...Rondon kara?

Now play the CD. On hearing a cue, ask the question you wrote (the CD will follow up with the correct question), check the answer you wrote is correct by listening to the CD's response, then 'show your interest' by saying *Ā, sō desu ka.*

Next, rewind and try again without looking at what you've written, this time forming questions simply by listening to the cues on the CD.

BUILD-UP

CD ▶ 11

Here are some more names of countries. As with *igirisu/igirisujin, amerika/amerikajin* and *nihon/nihonjin,* you can add *jin* to any of these country names to talk about a person's nationality, e.g. *chūgokujin desu, doitsujin desu.* Practise doing this now. The CD will say the country names in order. You add *-jin desu,* then the CD will follow up with what you should have said.

	kuni	*country*
1	**chūgoku**	China
2	**doitsu**	Germany
3	**nyūjiirando**	New Zealand
4	**furansu**	France
5	**burajiru**	Brazil
6	**kankoku**	South Korea
7	**ōsutoraria**	Australia
8	**kanada**	Canada
9	**airurando**	Ireland
10	**indo**	India

ANSWER

@ Here are some more people's names. Try to work out who they are and check your answers in the key.

1 Sutefi Gurafu (Germany) **5** Aran Doron (France)
2 Sanjitto Ganji (India) **6** Gureggu Nōman (Australia)
3 Erizabesu Tērā (UK) **7** Ben Jonson (Canada)
4 Pere (Brazil) **8** Tina Tānā (USA)

CD ▶ 12

The CD will ask you about these people's nationality.
  E.g. (1) **Sutefi Gurafu wa furansujin desu ka?**
  Answer with either **Hai, sō desu** or **Iie, ... -jin desu.** The CD will follow up with the correct answer.

SAYING NO;
FIRST MEETINGS

- 'I'm not ...', He/She/It isn't ...',
  'You/We/They aren't ...': ... **ja arimasen**.

- As you bow when you first meet someone, say
  dōzo yoroshiku or, more formally, **yoroshiku
  onegai shimasu** (both mean literally 'please look
  kindly on me').

JAPANESE LIVE 4 | CD ▶ 13

Ms Yamaguchi (eventually) meets Robert Hope in the lobby of his hotel.

Yamaguchi	(*going up to the wrong man*) Shitsurei shimasu. Hōpu-san desu ka?
Smith	Iie, chigaimasu. Hōpu ja arimasen.
Yamaguchi	Ā, sō desu ka. (*bowing slightly*) Dōmo sumimasen.
Smith	Iie, iie.
Yamaguchi	(*going up to Mr Hope*) Shitsurei shimasu. Hōpu-san desu ka?
Hope	Hai, sō desu.
Yamaguchi	Hajimemashite. Marubeni no Yamaguchi Keiko desu.
Hope	Hajimemashite.
Yamaguchi	(*bowing*) Yoroshiku onegai shimasu.
Hope	(*bowing*) Dōzo yoroshiku.
	Rewind and repeat!

shitsurei shimasu	excuse me (lit. 'I'm being rude')
iie, chigaimasu	no, I'm not (lit. 'it is different')
dōmo sumimasen	sorry
iie, iie	don't mention it
Marubeni no Yamaguchi Keiko desu	I'm Keiko Yamaguchi of Marubeni

TAKE NOTE

'MANSPEAK'/'WOMANSPEAK'
Women often tend to use more polite, formal expressions where men might use more familiar language. There are even some words which only men or women use (such as the 'men's words' *boku* or *ore* to mean 'I'), but don't worry – everything you'll learn to say in this book is unisex!

SAYING NO
Say 'no' too abruptly and you risk hurting people's feelings; if you're asked, for example, *Amerikajin desu ka?* and the answer is 'no', you shouldn't just say *Iie*. Instead, you could say 'No, I'm not American': *Iie, amerikajin ja arimasen* – more formally *dewa arimasen*, less formally *ja nai (desu)* – but commonly the short and less direct expression *chigaimasu* is used: *Iie, chigaimasu*. Of course, it's usually best to be constructive and provide the correct answer! For example, *Iie, igirisujin desu*. Note that, just as *hai* doesn't always mean 'yes', *iie* or *iie, iie* can also mean 'don't mention it'/'it's nothing' in response to an apology or to an expression of thanks.

BUILD-UP | CD ▶ 14

Here are some more names of occupations. Listen to how the words are pronounced on the tape, and each time form a question using the word, as if you were asking someone about their work.

E.g. (1) *CD:* **moderu**
You: **Moderu desu ka?**

shigoto	job
1 **moderu**	model
2 **puro gorufā**	golf pro
3 **enjinia**	engineer
4 **OL (ōeru)**	'office lady'
5 **shufu**	housewife
6 **kaishain**	company employee
7 **kōmuin**	civil servant
8 **ginkōin**	bank employee
9 **sensei**	teacher
10 **gakusei**	student

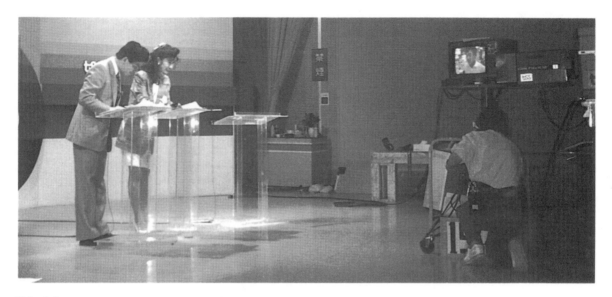

Television newscasters bowing

INTRODUCE YOURSELF

CD ▶ 15

You're about to take part in a panel discussion at an international conference in Tōkyō. The first panel member (John Smith, American bank employee) introduces himself:

Hajimemashite. Jon Sumisu desu. Amerikajin desu. Ginkōin desu. Dōzo yoroshiku.

@ Write down similar self-introductions for the other panel members.

1 Karl Graf, German civil servant
2 Barbara Green, Irish engineer
3 Meryl Johnson, Canadian model
4 Yves Delon, French company employee
5 Elizabeth Norman, Australian student
6 Now introduce yourself!

GUESS WHO

A This is a guessing game. The woman on the CD is thinking of a particular person (one whose name has already appeared in this book). You have to find out who she's thinking of by asking her questions, but she can only answer with 'yes' or 'no'. Ask whether the person she's thinking of is . . .

1 Japanese (*nihonjin desu ka?*)   2 French
3 Canadian   4 American   5 Australian
6 a bank employee   7 a teacher   8 a model
9 a professional golfer

B Try again, this time saying *Ā, sō desu ka* when you hear the replies. Guess who this second person is by asking whether he or she is . . .

1 Chinese   2 South Korean   3 German   4 British
5 a student   6 a civil servant   7 an 'office lady'   -
8 a businessman   9 from London

@ Now check you guessed correctly by looking at the answer key in the back of the book.

C Now it's your turn to answer the questions. The person you're thinking of is Yuka Nukina. Answer with *Hai, sō desu* or *Iie, chigaimasu.*

13

About Japan

The Japanese occasionally suggest they have something in common with the British because both are island nations. One thing the two nations certainly share is an enthusiasm for talking about the weather. People in Japan always seem to be commenting on some aspect of the climate during the daily conversations – even in the opening paragraphs of their letters or e-mails. They are also rather proud of the fact that 'Japan has four seasons'.

There is a reason for this. The seasons in Japan are, for the most part, clearly marked. Spring, for example, arrives when the cherry trees (*sakura*) blossom and ends with the beginning of the monsoon-like rainy season (*tsuyu*) which extends to most of Honshū, Shikoku and Kyūshū in June. The hot and humid summer months are finally brought to a close by a succession of typhoons which sweep up from the southern Pacific and hit the Japanese coastline in September. There then follows a period of warm, dry weather, during which the green foliage slowly takes on its autumn colouring and people flock to see the bright red maple trees (*momiji*). Finally, there are the winter months, when hoards of young Japanese go to the Japan Alps or to Hokkaidō to ski.

Of course, given the extended geography of Japan, the seasons vary considerably depending on where you happen to be. Hokkaidō, for example, does not have a rainy season. This means that its summers are pleasantly cool, and hence attractive to tourists eager to escape the sticky confines of cities like Tōkyō and Ōsaka, where the temperatures hover in the nineties Fahrenheit (mid-thirties Centigrade) during late July and August. In Okinawa, on the other hand, the climate is subtropical, so that the distinction between 'seasons' as such is much less clearly marked.

Even so, there has been a tendency for Japanese scholars and writers to suggest that the 'Japanese climate' is responsible for, even determines, the Japanese character. In particular, the fact that the rainy season enables the country's (dwindling number of) farmers to grow rice encourages certain intellectuals to suggest that the Japanese are a 'monsoon people', as opposed to the 'pastoral peoples' who live in Europe and the Middle East. Monsoon people are characterised as being 'group oriented', for the nature of their irrigation agriculture obliges them to work together. Pastoral people, on the other hand, work with herds of animals primarily on their own. Hence they are 'individualistic'.

This kind of wild generalisation is – believe it or not – quite popular among Japanese, who are fond of reading books about why their society and culture might be different from those of other peoples. The philosophy underlying this literature – *nihonjinron*, or

Cherry blossom (*sakura*)

'discussions about the Japanese' – unfortunately extends to much of the writing and media reporting on Japan by Westerners, who tend to be taken in by Japanese ideology on the one hand and to indulge in an exoticisation of Japan on the other. The Japanese are indeed different from us in many respects, but they are also quite similar in many others.

GREETINGS; COMMENTING ON THE WEATHER

> - How to say 'hello' varies according to the time of day:
>
> | until about 10 or 11 a.m. | **ohayō gozaimasu** |
> |---|---|
> | from then until early evening | **konnichi wa** (pronounced *kon-nichi wa*) |
> | in the evening | **konban wa** |
>
> - Greetings are often followed by small talk about the weather.
>   E.g.   'It's hot, isn't it?'   **Atsui desu ne.**
>   'It is, isn't it?'   **Sō desu ne.**

JAPANESE LIVE 5   CD ▶ 16

Jun Sakai greets people at different times of the day.

(arriving at work in the morning)

Jun	Ohayō gozaimasu.
Mr Ueda	Ohayō.

(greeting an acquaintance during the day)

Jun	Fukuda-san, konnichi wa.
Mr Fukuda	Konnichi wa. Atsui desu ne.
Jun	Sō desu ne.

(greeting an acquaintance in the evening)

Jun	Yamada-san, konban wa.
Ms Yamada	Ā, Sakai-san, shibaraku desu ne.
Jun	Sō desu ne. O-genki desu ka?
Ms Yamada	Ē, okagesama de.

(saying good night to his mother)

Jun	Oyasuminasai.
Mrs Sakai	Oyasuminasai.

Rewind and repeat!

ohayō	less formal than **ohayō gozaimasu**
atsui	hot
shibaraku desu ne	it's been a long time, hasn't it?
o-genki desu ka?	how have you been? (lit. 'are you well?')
ē, okagesama de	fine, thank you (lit. 'yes, thanks to you')
oyasuminasai	good night (lit. 'please rest')

SPOTCHECK 4

@ Who hasn't seen Jun for a long time?

TAKE NOTE

NAMES

Japanese people almost always address each other and refer to others, even colleagues and friends, by family name. Only close friends, in informal situations, use given names, and in such cases *-san* still tends to be added; e.g. *Jun-san*. Note that *-san* implies respect for another person, and you should never attach it when saying your own name. An even more respectful replacement for *-san* is *-sensei*, used when addressing or talking about teachers, doctors or politicians. You may also hear *-kun* (a rather familiar term for men younger than the speaker) and *-chan* (also familiar, added to the given names of younger women and small children).

GREETINGS

Japanese people don't usually ask *O-genki desu ka?* ('Are you well?') unless someone has been ill or (as in 'Japanese live 5') when two people haven't seen each other for a long time. Instead, greetings are often followed by a comment on the weather plus *desu ne* (*ne*, or *nē*, pronounced with falling intonation, turns a statement into an exclamation).

BUILD-UP

You can use any of the words below to make a comment on the weather, simply by adding *desu ne*. Practise doing this now: the CD will give you the cue. and you add *desu ne*. (Be careful to pronounce this *desu ne* ↘.)

    E.g. (1) *CD:* **ii tenki**
           You: **Ii tenki desu ne.**

    The CD will follow up each time with what you should have said.

CD ▶ 17

1	**ii tenki**	good weather
2	**iya na tenki**	horrible weather
3	**mushiatsui**	hot and humid
4	**samui**	cold
5	**atatakai**	warm
6	**suzushii**	cool

LISTEN

CD ▶ 18

@ Listen to the short conversations (numbered 1 to 8) on the CD and match them with the pictures (A to H) below, by writing a number in each box:

RECREATE

Try to recreate the conversations you've just heard, simply by looking at the pictures. Take both parts if you're on your own, and don't worry about remembering the people's names. (Use any names you like, or none at all.) Check how you did by rewinding the CD.

IMAGINE

Imagine (and speak aloud) the conversations you might have in the following situations:

1 It's early in the morning and very cold. You see your neighbour, Mrs Yamamoto, walking down the street towards you.
2 It's a humid afternoon in August. You meet your friend, Mr Honda.
3 It's a warm evening. You meet an acquaintance, Ms Iida.
4 You meet a friend, Mr Kamiyama, whom you haven't seen for a long time.
5 You're feeling tired: say good night!

A

B

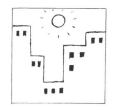
C

D

E

F

G

H

About Japan

All languages have ideologies built into their usage. Even though we have noted that there are several underlying differences between the people of, say, Hokkaidō on the one hand and Kyūshū or Shikoku on the other, most Japanese are convinced that, all in all, they are the same. One important means of anchoring this belief in their national identity has been the Japanese language (*nihongo*).

For a long time, both ordinary people and scholars believed that the Japanese language was 'unique'. It was true, they said, that the Chinese characters (*kanji*) in which much of the language is written had been imported from the Asian continent; true, also, that many words had been borrowed – first from China (during the Nara [710-94] and Heian [794-1192] periods), and later (from the Meiji Period [1868-1912] in particular) from the West. But the grammar and overall structure of the Japanese language, they insisted, were unique.

This attitude is changing – partly because of Japan's overall internationalisation since the mid-1980s, partly because of the scepticism of foreign linguists who counter-argued that, structurally, the Japanese language is very similar to Korean, and so grouped Japanese among the Altaic languages (which include Mongolian and Turkish). Even so, to those of us who are used to speaking only Indo-European languages, Japanese has some unusual features.

For example, there is a fairly clear distinction between men's speech and women's speech. Certain vocabulary items and phrases are used only by women, and vice versa, so be aware of this. This is not to suggest that there are two totally separate languages for men and for women: only that you should be careful in the early stages of language learning to use neutral forms that are available to everyone regardless of gender. It is this 'unisex' language that is presented in the book.

Another unusual feature of Japanese is the use of various levels of speech. The Japanese tend to adopt what are referred to as 'honorific', 'respect' or 'humble' forms, depending on whom they are addressing or talking about, and in what context they are doing so. Again, it is possible during the early stages of language learning – as here – to make use of neutral, but polite, forms so that nobody will be offended. Nevertheless, respect language is something to which we shall return later on in this book.

Finally, like almost all languages, Japanese has a number of dialects. Most of these are readily understood, but some (like those of Tōhoku in the north of Honshū and Kagoshima in the south of Kyūshū) are fiendishly difficult. However, there is a 'standard language' (*hyōjungo*) – equivalent to 'BBC English' in the United Kingdom – and it is this that is presented in this book.

Street scene, Tōkyō

WHAT YOU'LL HEAR

In this section, you'll be developing your ability to cope with the kind of language you'll hear around you in Japan. Just like in real life, you won't understand every word, but concentrate on picking out the information necessary to complete the tasks suggested; if you can do so, you'll be understanding the essentials, and therefore doing well enough.

WHERE'S HOME?

CD ▶ 19

@ You're going to hear some short interviews about where people are from. Seven of the interviews are with foreigners and seven with Japanese. Your task depends on who is being interviewed:

- If the person is a foreigner, listen out for his or her name and write it next to the letter corresponding to the country he or she is from.

- If the person is Japanese, write his or her occupation next to the letter corresponding to where he or she is from in Japan.

o-namae wa?	(what's) your name?
o-kuni wa?	(what's) your country?
o-shigoto wa?	(what's) your job?
Itaria kara kimashita	I come from Italy (lit. 'I came from Italy')
IBM ni tsutomete imasu	I work for IBM (lit. 'I'm employed at IBM')

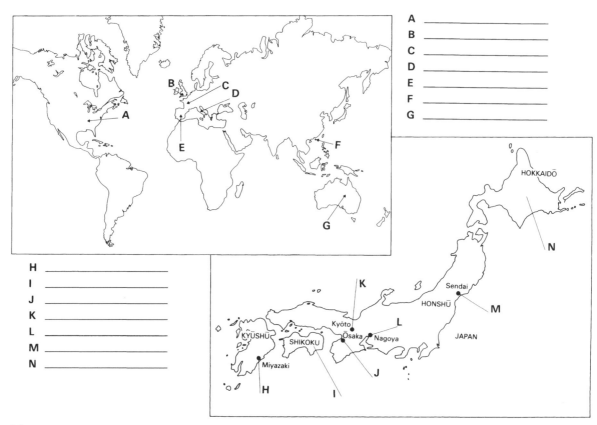

A _____
B _____
C _____
D _____
E _____
F _____
G _____

H _____
I _____
J _____
K _____
L _____
M _____
N _____

UNACCUSTOMED AS I AM ...

Any of the more intimate parties you go to will usually have one thing in common: that at some stage all the newcomers present will be called upon to make a short speech of self-introduction (*jiko shōkai*). Being formally introduced is much more important to Japanese people than it is in the West, and you'll find that strangers become much less reticent once you've made your speech.

Some rather formal expressions you'll hear in self-introductions are:

(Jon Sumisu) to iimasu.
'I'm called (John Smith).'

(Jon Sumisu) to mōshimasu.
(same meaning, more formal)

Dōzo yoroshiku onegai shimasu.
'Please look kindly on me.'

Dōzo yoroshiku onegai itashimasu.
(same meaning, more formal)

@ Listen to five non-Japanese (1 to 5) introducing themselves. You'll hear many expressions you're unfamiliar with, but just concentrate on filling in the table below with their names, nationalities and jobs:

	Name	Nationality	Job
1			
2			
3			
4			
5			

@ Rewind the CD and write out speech number 5 word for word. Then try to write a similar speech for yourself, and learn it off by heart – you won't regret it!

A LOVELY DAY FOR IT ...

@ Listen to the five conversations, and match a picture to each one. (Write the number of the conversation in the appropriate box.)

A 　　**B**

C 　　**D**

E

WRITTEN JAPANESE

Until the 9th century AD, Japanese had no fixed writing system. Chinese characters, known as *kanji* in Japan, had been imported previously, but were found to be wanting in coping with Japanese, a totally different language from Chinese in terms of grammar. Two sound-related so-called *kana* syllabaries – *hiragana* and *katakana* – were gradually evolved to solve this problem.

Even today, Japanese is still written in a mixture of kanji, hiragana and katakana. Generally speaking, kanji are used to represent the core of many words, hiragana for word endings and words with no equivalent in Chinese, and katakana to represent imported (non-Chinese) words and foreign names. Here's an example of how these different kinds of writing work together: *Amerikajin desu ka?*

a / me / ri / ka / jin / de / su / ka

KATAKANA   KANJI   HIRAGANA

Two things to notice about this are the lack of spaces between words and the lack of punctuation, apart from the '。' signalling the end of the sentence. In the Japanese you've been reading so far (in *rōmaji*, i.e. Roman script), we've been trying to make things easier for you by including capital letters, hyphens, question marks and spaces between words, none of which are there in Japanese writing.

Both katakana and hiragana represent the sounds (syllables) of Japanese, and you'll be able to find the symbols for *a, me, ri, ka* (katakana), *de, su* and *ka* (hiragana) in the chart on page 326. In this book, however, we're going to concentrate mainly on kanji, which serve to represent the core components of many words. Let's see how a few kanji are written and how they may have acquired their shape over the years:

Character and main meaning	Derivation	Stroke order
person 人	彳 彳 几	𠆢 人
tree 木	🌳 米 朩 木	一 十 才 木
origin 本	🌳 米 本 本 roots of a tree trunk	一 十 才 木 本
sun 日	☉ ⊙ ⊖ 日	丨 冂 月 日

Practise writing these kanji, making sure you follow the traditional stroke order (developed over the centuries to result in legible writing!). In general, as you'll notice, the movements involved are from top to bottom and from left to right.

Here are four more kanji for you to recognise:

woods	forest	east	capital
林	森	東	京

The origins of some kanji seem clear: 'woods' and 'forest', for example, are obviously related to the symbol for 'tree', which is also to be found in the character for 'east' – often explained as the sun rising behind a tree. However, identifying the origins of most kanji isn't so easy; for example, the character for 'capital' could originally have been a picture of a stone lantern (such as those placed at the entrance to the emperor's palace), or it might represent a building on high ground. In this book we've chosen the interpretations which seem most likely to help you remember the kanji – don't be surprised, though, if you find other explanations elsewhere.

Now you're ready to read some Japanese!

日 本	日 本 人	東 京	京 都
ni hon	ni hon jin	Tō kyō	Kyō to

For the ancient Chinese, Japan was the place where the sun rose, the 'origin of the sun' (what we know as the 'land of the rising sun'): *nihon* or, more formally, *nippon*.

Previously known as 'Edo', Tōkyō acquired its present name when the emperor Meiji moved there from Kyōto in 1867–8. Both Kyōto, capital for over a thousand years, and Nara (capital from 710 to 794) are further to the west, near Ōsaka (Japan's second biggest city). Edo was therefore renamed 'eastern capital': *Tōkyō*. As you can see, the kanji meaning 'capital' appears in both *Tōkyō* and *Kyōto*. (The rather complicated character pronounced *to* in *Kyōto* means 'metropolis'.)

@   Finally, try to read and answer aloud these questions:

1 日本人ですか。	HIRAGANA で　す　か　ら **de su ka ra**
2 アメリカ人ですか。	
3 東京からですか。	KATAKANA ア　メ　リ　カ **a me ri ka**
4 京都からですか。	

An important train station . . .

LANGUAGE SUMMARY

Countries

Nihon	Furansu
Igirisu	Burajiru
Amerika	Kankoku
Chūgoku	Ōsutoraria
Doitsu	Kanada
Nyūjiirando	Airurando
Indo	

- *For people from these countries, add* -jin

Jobs

bijinesuman	shufu
dezainā	kaishain
repōtā	kōmuin
moderu	ginkōin
puro gorufā	sensei
enjinia	gakusei
ōeru	

Weather words

ii tenki	suzushii
iya na tenki	samui
mushiatsui	atatakai

I

watashi	watakushi
ore	boku

Main language structures

I am, you are, she is, etc.: ... desu
Nukina-san wa nihonjin desu.
Watashi mo nihonjin desu.
Repōtā desu.

Negative statement: ... ja arimasen
Iie, chigaimasu.
Hōpu ja arimasen.

Question: ... desu ka?
Amerikajin desu ka?
Dezainā desu ka?

Greetings
Hajimemashite.
Dōzo yoroshiku.
Yoroshiku onegai shimasu.
Ohayō gozaimasu.
Konnichi wa.
Konban wa.
Oyasuminasai.
Shibaraku desu ne.
O-genki desu ka?
Ē, okagesama de.

Names
- *Surnames first*
- *Suffix* -san *for others but not for your own name*

Yes/No
Hai, sō desu.
Iie, chigaimasu.

Responding
Ā, sō desu ka.

Exclaiming
Atsui desu ne.
Sō desu ne

Apologising
Shitsurei shimasu.
Dōmo sumimasen.
Iie, iie.

At this stage you may like to read the following parts of the Grammar section at the back of the book: 'Some differences between English and Japanese' (1), and 'Saying who' (2).

2
ALL IN THE
FAMILY

The Japanese home
Everyday objects
What, where and whose
My family, your family
Visiting someone's home

About Japan

The family has been one of the pivots around which post-war Japanese society evolved. It acted as the primary group to which almost all Japanese belonged, and it was to the family home that most Japanese – until they were married and set up their own homes – returned at the end of each working day. Some of this has begun to change in recent years, as young people move out of their family homes to live on their own. But what sort of homes do single people and families live in? Are they really 'rabbit hutches', as once described by a critical Western press? Or are people's perceptions of space, and with it their expectations, rather different from our own?

In traditional Japanese households, three or four generations live together under one roof, which means houses can be very big. However, most Japanese homes consist of just parents and one or two children, and can be tiny – by our standards at least.

There are certain other features that make the Japanese house a little different from our own. One of these is the entrance hall (*genkan*). The genkan is always placed below the level of the floor of the dwelling itself (even in high-rise apartments) and in some senses forms part of the 'outside' of the home (even though it can only be entered by opening the front door); for instance, in houses with no doorbell it is standard practice for visitors to slide open the door, stand in the genkan and call for attention with a loud *gomen kudasai!* ('pardon me!'). One is only truly 'inside' the house when shoes have been taken off and left behind in the genkan, for – and this is another main difference from Western homes – Japanese do not wear shoes inside the house. Instead, they put on slippers to walk on wooden floors, although these too are taken off when entering a *tatami* (straw-matted) room.

Why don't the Japanese wear shoes inside the house? One major reason is that they regard it as an extremely dirty and unhygienic habit. It is this sensitivity to dirt and uncleanliness that makes most Japanese place a special pair of slippers or clogs in the toilet. Nobody wears the same footwear in the kitchen and the toilet, because that would be to mix two opposite bodily functions connected with food and drink.

Another aspect of cleanliness that needs to be known concerns use of the bath (*o-furo*). Like the genkan (and, in former times, the kitchen) the bathroom is often set a little lower than the main floor of the house. Japanese use the bathtub to soak themselves in, but wash themselves outside on the floor (which has a drainage system attached). In

Food offering to household gods

this way, the water stays clean and all members of the family can use the same hot bath. Cleanliness is also economical!

Given that the inside of a house is clearly separated from the world outside (including the genkan, where outside shoes are left behind), and that some areas within the house are differentiated from others according to their function, it would seem that the Japanese are conscious of certain ritual or social boundaries which might elude Westerners. To some extent these are connected with cleanliness and dirt, and hence with traditional beliefs about purity and pollution. Also, by distinguishing clearly between the inside (*uchi*) and outside (*soto*) of the home, the Japanese seem to mark a clear boundary between the family unit and people from the 'outside world'. As we shall see, this distinction is also mirrored in language usage.

WHAT IS IT?

If you visit a Japanese home as a guest, you'll probably be shown into the main living room, or *zashiki*, and – in winter – invited to sit on the floor at the **kotatsu**, a low table with a heater underneath, surrounded by quilts. If the room has a **tokonoma** (an alcove traditionally decorated with a hanging scroll and a flower arrangement), your place as guest will be with your back to it and/or your face to the door.

- 'this': **kore**
  'that': **sore / are**

- To ask what something is: ... **nan desu ka?**
  (E.g. 'What's this?': *Kore wa nan desu ka?*)

JAPANESE LIVE 1

CD ▸ 22

Elizabeth is looking for a house to rent. Yōko, her friend, has found one for her and is showing her around.

	(*Yōko slides open the door and they go into the 'genkan'.*)
Yōko	Kore wa 'genkan' desu.
Elizabeth	(*stepping up into the house, where there's a smell of new 'tatami'*) Atarashii tatami desu ka?
Yōko	Hai, sō desu. Ii nioi desu ne.
Elizabeth	Sō desu ne. (*pointing at the 'kotatsu'*) Sore wa nan desu ka?
Yōko	'Kotatsu' desu. (*She turns on the 'kotatsu' heater and gestures for Elizabeth to sit down.*) Dōzo.
Elizabeth	(*sitting at the 'kotatsu'*) Ā, atatakai. (*pointing at an alcove in the wall*) Are wa 'tokonoma' desu ka?
Yōko	Hai, sō desu. (*They get up to go and look at the bathroom.*)
Yōko	O-furo desu.
Elizabeth	Chiisai desu ne!
Yōko	(*opening the door of the toilet*) Kore wa toire desu. (*They go back into the main room. Elizabeth looks around appreciatively.*)
Yōko	Dō desu ka?
Elizabeth	Totemo ii desu ne. Dōmo arigatō.
Yōko	Iie, dō itashimashite. **Rewind and repeat!**

atarashii	new
nioi	smell
dōzo	go ahead!
o-furo	bath
chiisai	small
toire	toilet
dō desu ka?	how is it?/how do you like it?
totemo ii	very good
dōmo arigatō	thank you
dō itashimashite	don't mention it

SPOTCHECK 1
@ What does Elizabeth think of
a the smell of the *tatami*
b the bath
c the house in general?

TAKE NOTE

'THIS' AND 'THAT'
Whereas we divide the world merely into 'this' and 'that', in Japanese there are three divisions: *kore* for things near the speaker, *sore* for things between the speaker and listener or near the listener and *are* for things away from both speaker and listener.

ONE OR MANY

Japanese words stay the same whether you're talking about one of something or several. For example, *kore* can mean 'this' or 'these', and *sore/are* 'that' or 'those'. Whether you're talking about one or more objects, the word to use is exactly the same:

OBJECTS

CD ▸ 23

1 **kakejiku**   hanging scroll(s)
2 **wagashi**   Japanese sweet(s)
3 **shōji**   wood and paper screen(s)
4 **yunomi**   tea cup(s)
5 **(o-)hashi**   chopstick(s)
6 **pasokon**   personal computer(s)
7 **terebi**   television(s)
8 **butsudan**   household shrine(s)

Learn the words in this list by pointing in turn at the numbered objects in the picture below and repeating after the CD.

WHAT IS IT?

Robert (on the left) is asking what the things marked 1 to 8 are. From where he's sitting, decide in each case whether he should say *kore ...*, *sore ...* or *are ... wa nan desu ka?*, and write the questions you imagine he asks.

@   E.g. (1) ***Kore*** wa nan desu ka?

BUILD-UP

CD ▸ 24

Japanese people continually try to put others at ease by making 'appreciative noises'. Flattery can get you far in Japan, and you may find these words very useful:

suteki	great
subarashii	wonderful
sugoi	amazing
benri	convenient/handy
kirei	pretty/beautiful
kawaii	pretty/cute
oishii	delicious
omoshiroi	interesting/funny

Listen to these words on the tape, and in each case use the word to make an appreciative comment (by adding '*desu ne*').
   E.g. *CD:*   **suteki**
      You: **Suteki desu ne!**

TEST YOURSELF

CD ▸ 25

Now cover up the vocabulary above the picture, and test yourself by answering the questions.
   E.g. (1)   *CD:*   **Kore wa nan desu ka?**
           You: **Kakejiku desu.**
Robert will follow up with an appreciative comment, using one of the words from 'Build-up' above: next to that word write the number of the conversation.
   E.g. (1)   *CD:*   **Subarashii desu ne.**
@   →You write '1' next to *subarashii*.

YOU ASK

CD ▸ 26

Imagine you are sitting where Robert is: in order, ask what the things numbered 1 to 8 are. The CD will answer, then you make the same appreciative comment that Robert made.
   E.g. (1)   *You:*   **Kore wa nan desu ka?**
          CD: **Kakejiku desu.**
          You: **Subarashii desu ne.**

WHERE IS IT?
WHOSE IS IT?

- To say whose something is, use **no**.
  E.g. 'It's my house.'   *Watashi no ie desu.*
  'It's mine.'   *Watashi no desu.*
  'It's Mrs Kamikawa's house.'   *Kamikawa-san no ie desu.*
  'It's Mrs Kamikawa's.'   *Kamikawa-san no desu.*

JAPANESE LIVE 2

`CD ▶ 27`

Yuka is looking for Mrs Kamikawa's house.

Yuka	Sumimasen, kore wa Kamikawa-san no uchi desu ka?
Housewife	Iie, chigaimasu. (*pointing*) Kamikawa-san no uchi wa asoko desu.
Yuka	Sumimasen ga dono ie desu ka?
Housewife	Ano ōkii ie desu.
Yuka	A, sō desu ka. Dōmo arigatō gozaimashita.
Housewife	Dō itashimashite.

Rewind and repeat!

sumimasen (ga)	excuse me (but)
uchi	house/home
ie	house
asoko	over there
dono ie?	which house?
ano . . .	that . . .
ōkii	big
dōmo arigatō gozaimashita	thank you very much (more formal than **dōmo arigatō**)

SPOTCHECK 2

@ What is Mrs Kamikawa's house like?

BUILD-UP

This table will help you ask and say where things are:

Do..?	Ko..	So..	A..
dore?	kore	sore	are
dono _____?	kono _____	sono _____	ano _____
doko?	koko	soko	asoko

E.g. *Kamikawa-san no ie wa dore/dono ie/doko desu ka?*
Which/Which house/Where is Mrs Kamikawa's house?
Kore/Sore/Are desu.
It's this one/that one/that one over there.
Kono ie/Sono ie/ Ano ie desu.
It's this house/that house/that house over there.
Koko/Soko/Asoko desu.
It's here/there/over there.

SPOTCHECK 3

@ Translate these questions and answers into Japanese:
a Which is my tea cup? It's this one.
b Which house is Mrs Honda's house? It's that house.
c Where are my chopsticks? They're over there.

ASK

`CD ▶ 28`

Look at the words numbered 1 to 6 below. Imagine you've mislaid your tea cup, chopsticks etc., and practise asking where they've got to. The CD will give you two cues: the name of the object plus the question word you should practise using.

    E.g. (1) *CD:* **Yunomi . . . doko?**
           You: **Watashi no yunomi wa doko desu ka?**

Always follow this pattern: *Watashi no _____ wa do.. desu ka?*

1 yunomi
2 hashi
3 chawan (rice bowl)
4 (o-)sara (plate)
5 oshibori (hand towel)
6 koppu (glass)

MRS UENO   MRS TANAKA

✓LISTEN

CD ▶ 29

Mrs Tanaka and Mrs Ueno were planning to have dinner together, but Mrs Ueno's naughty toddler has played havoc with the table setting! Listen to Mrs Tanaka asking which things are hers. Mrs Ueno will reply with *ko..*, *so..* and *a..* words in relation @ to where she's sitting. Write a 'T' next to the things in the picture which are Mrs Tanaka's. Check your answers in the key.

RECREATE

CD ▶ 30

Now you are sitting where Mrs Ueno is in the picture. Mrs Tanaka will ask you where her things are. Answer with *ko../so../a.. desu*, and then say where your things are, using the pattern *watashi no wa ko../so../a.. desu* ('mine is . . .').

E.g. (1) *CD:* **Watashi no chawan wa dore desu ka?**

You: **Kore desu. Watashi no wa are desu.**

POSSESSIONS

CD ▶ 31

A Some of these things belong to Mr Tanaka and some to his friend Mr Satō. In each case, ask the person on the tape *Kore wa Tanaka-san no _____ desu ka?* If something does belong to Mr Tanaka, write 'T' below the picture, but if it belongs to Mr Satō, write 'S'.

E.g. (1) *You:* **Kore wa Tanaka-san no ie desu ka?**

CD: **Iie, Satō-san no desu.**

@   →You write 'S' under the picture of the house.

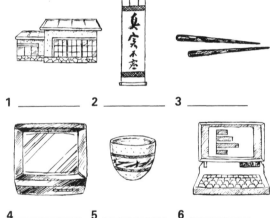

1 _____   2 _____   3 _____

4 _____   5 _____   6 _____

CD ▶ 32

B Now memorise who each thing belongs to, and cover your answers and the pictures above. The person on the CD will ask you *who* each thing belongs to (_____ *wa* **dare** *no desu ka?*). Answer from memory with either *Tanaka-san no desu* or *Satō-san no desu*.

About Japan

Attitudes towards social behaviour in the family are reflected in the architecture of the home. Ideally, the family as a whole is considered to be more important than the individuals of which it consists. In traditional architecture, this ideal is reflected in the fact that there is little division of space into public and private realms. It is true that some rooms are more 'public' than others, but one of the functions of the sliding screen doors (*fusuma*) which separate one living room from another is that they can be removed and separate rooms joined together as and when the occasion arises. In other words, space within the home is flexible.

Similarly, the large windows and wood and paper screens (*shōji*) facing towards the outside of the house allow a family to be more or less exposed to the outside world, and are often opened or left closed according to the seasons. At the same time, rooms are frequently multi-purpose, so that members of a family will use the same room for different activities. While we tend to eat in one downstairs room, watch television in another and sleep in a third (which is often upstairs), Japanese may do all three activities in the same room (usually where the kotatsu table heater is located). When they want to go to sleep, they merely take out mattresses (*futon*) and place them on the *tatami* floor.

The tatami themselves are thick rice straw pallets, covered with finely woven strands of rush. Traditionally, they were 1.80 metres long and 90 centimetres in width, so that one tatami was just right for one person to sleep on. Tatami are still the basic unit of measurement of room size. So people talk about a 'six mat' or 'four and a half mat' room, and all *shōji*, *fusuma*, windows, furniture and fittings are made in proportion to the size of the tatami (which are usually smaller in city apartments).

Whether rooms really are fitted with tatami these days is another matter, for many people prefer to sleep in beds rather than on futon. Younger people also tend to divide up their living space rather like ourselves, with separate rooms for each member of the family. In this respect, the social change from the traditional, multigeneration household to the nuclear family has been accompanied by a corresponding set of architectural changes. These family differences can be seen in the different kinds of house occupied by the Kamikawa and Sakai families in the television series *Japanese – Language and People*.

Right Futons airing on balconies

TALKING ABOUT FAMILY (1)

> • 'my son': **musuko**   'your son': **musuko-san**
> 'my daughter':   'your daughter':
> **musume**   **musume-san/o-jō-san**
>
> (Words for 'my' or 'your' aren't needed when talking about the family; see 'Take note' on the opposite page.)

JAPANESE LIVE 3 | CD ▶ 33 |

Yuka, now at Mrs Kamikawa's, is looking at an English textbook left lying on the 'kotatsu'.

Yuka	Kore wa o-jō-san no tekisuto desu ka?
Mrs Kamikawa	Iie, musuko no desu.
Yuka	Muzukashii desu ne.
Mrs Kamikawa	Sō desu ka.
Yuka	Musuko-san wa kōkōsei desu ka?
Mrs Kamikawa	Hai, sō desu. (*showing her another textbook*) Kore wa musume no desu. Musume mo kōkōsei desu.
Yuka	Ā, sō desu ka. (*pointing at a photograph on the wall*) Are wa o-jō-san desu ka?
Mrs Kamikawa	Hai. Shichi-go-san no shashin desu.
Yuka	Kawaii desu ne.

Rewind and repeat!

tekisuto	textbook
muzukashii	difficult
kōkōsei	senior high school pupil (15–18 years old)
shichi-go-san	lit. 'seven-five-three', a day in November when girls aged seven and three and boys aged five dress up in traditional clothes and visit a shrine
shashin	photograph (**shichi-go-san no shashin** = a photograph of **shichi-go-san**)

SPOTCHECK 4

 Whose textbook does Yuka say is difficult?

A 7-year-old girl dressed in a kimono for *shichi-go-san*

TAKE NOTE

MY FAMILY, YOUR FAMILY

An important aspect of being polite in Japan is to be humble about oneself and members of one's group (family, company, etc.) and to show due respect to 'outsiders'. This distinction is reflected even in the words used to refer to family members: respect is shown for someone else's family through the use of so-called 'honorifics', such as *-san, o-* or *go-*; however, honorifics are not usually applied when talking about one's own family. This use or non-use of honorifics makes it clear whose family you're talking about, so it's unnecessary to say, for example, 'my son' (just say *musuko*) or 'your son' (say *musuko-san*). In some cases there are even different words entirely for 'my family' and 'your family' members.

BUILD-UP

CD ▸ 34

Listen and repeat:

'my family'	'your family'	
kazoku	go-kazoku	family
shujin/otto	go-shujin	husband
kanai/tsuma	oku-san	wife
chichi	o-tō-san	father
haha	o-kā-san	mother
ani	o-nii-san	elder brother
ane	o-nē-san	elder sister
otōto	otōto-san	younger brother
imōto	imōto-san	younger sister

TAKE NOTE

Shujin means literally '(my) master', while *kanai* means '(my woman) inside the house'. You – along with many younger Japanese – may prefer to use the less sexist terms *otto* and *tsuma* to refer, respectively, to your husband or wife.

FAMILY MATTERS

CD ▸ 35

You're talking to Mrs Kaneko about her family. Review the job list on p. 12 before beginning. Ask Mrs Kaneko whether the following things are true (which *three* of them are not true?):

1 Her husband's a company employee.
   (*Go-shujin wa kaishain desu ka?*)
2 Her father's a teacher.
3 Her mother's a housewife.
4 Her daughter's a student.
5 Her son's a senior high school pupil.
6 Her elder brother's a civil servant.
@ 7 Her younger sister's an 'office lady'.

AND YOU?

Write a few lines about your own family. For example, *Chichi wa bijinesuman desu. Rondon kara desu. Igirisujin desu. Haha wa kōmuin desu. Haha mo igirisujin desu*, etc.

TALKING ABOUT FAMILY (2)

- In Japanese there is a special verb – **imasu** – for talking about the existence of people and animals as opposed to things. Here's one of the ways in which it's used:

Musume-san wa doko ni imasu ka?	Where's your daughter?
Uchi ni imasu.	She's at home.

- **Ni**, as in *uchi ni imasu*, corresponds to the English 'at' or 'in' (a place).

WHERE ARE THEY ALL? CD ▶ 36

A The names of some places are listed on the right below. Ask Mr Tanaka where the members of his family listed on the left are at the moment. (Ask: . . . *wa doko ni imasu ka?*) Repeat his replies, and draw
@ lines according to the information he provides. Number 1 has been done for you, so in this first case 'warm up' by simply repeating the question and answer you hear on the CD.

1 daughter	**gakkō**	(school)
2 wife	**kaisha**	(company)
3 father	**sūpā**	(supermarket)
4 older sister	**uchi**	(home)
5 younger brother	**ginkō**	(bank)
6 son	**byōin**	(hospital)

CD ▶ 37

B Now pretend that you're Mr Tanaka, and say where your family members are, using 'my family' words. The tape will give you a cue each time, in the form of one of the numbers on the left above.

   E.g. *CD:* **Number three**
      You: **Chichi wa byōin ni imasu.**

- **Imasu** (or, more respectfully, **irasshaimasu**) is also used in situations where we would say 'Do you *have* (children/brothers and sisters, etc.)?' For example:

Oku-san wa imasu ka?/irasshaimasu ka?
Do you have a wife? (lit. 'Does a wife exist (for you)?')

- The answer to this type of question might be **Hai, imasu** (Yes, I have) or **Iie, imasen** (No, I haven't).

BUILD-UP CD ▶ 38

Here are some more 'my family' and 'your family' words (listen and repeat):

ryōshin	**go-ryōshin**	parents
kyōdai	**go-kyōdai**	brothers and sisters
kodomo	**o-ko-san**	child(ren)

YOUR FAMILY CD ▶ 39

Answer the CD's questions about your family with *hai, imasu* or *iie, imasen.*

   E.g. (1) *CD:* **Go-ryōshin wa irasshaimasu ka?**
      You: (if at least one of your parents is alive) **Hai, imasu.**
      (if not) **Iie, imasen.**

AT MEALTIMES; LEAVING AND COMING BACK HOME

To maintain harmony in human relations is of great importance to most Japanese, and this is reflected in the frequency with which they exchange set phrases, on all sorts of occasions.

> - Before drinking or eating, say **itadakimasu** (lit. 'I humbly receive this').
>
> - After finishing, say **gochisōsama deshita** (lit. 'it was a feast') or, less formally, **gochisōsama!**

JAPANESE LIVE 4   CD ▶ 40

Breakfast time in the Sakai household . . .

Jun	Ohayō.
Mrs Sakai	Ohayō. (*She serves her son rice, 'sakana' and a bowl of 'miso shiru'.*) Dōzo.
Jun	Itadakimasu. (*He finishes his first bowl of rice.*)
Mrs Sakai	Okawari wa?
Jun	(*accepting a second helping*) Arigatō. (*finishing eating*) Gochisōsama! (*getting up to leave for work*) Jā, itte kimasu.
Mrs Sakai	Itte 'rasshai.

Rewind and repeat!

sakana	fish
miso shiru	miso soup (**miso** = soya bean paste)
dōzo	here you are
okawari wa?	how about a second helping?
arigatō	thanks
jā, itte kimasu	well, I'll be off (lit. 'I'll go and come back')
itte 'rasshai	'go and come back (safely)!'

SPOTCHECK 5
@ What does Jun have for breakfast?

TAKE NOTE

'GOING AND COMING BACK'

On leaving home (with the intention of returning!), the person going out uses the set phrase *itte kimasu*, and the people left behind reply *itte 'rasshai*. To signal your return, call out *tadaima!* ('I'm back!'); the response, without fail, will be *okaerinasai!* ('welcome back'). These expressions are also used at work, for short trips into the outside world.

THANKING

Dōmo arigatō ('thank you') and *dōmo sumimasen* ('sorry') are often shortened, to *arigatō* and *sumimasen* respectively. Shortest (and most familiar) is simply *dōmo*, which can sometimes mean 'sorry' as well as 'thank you'. In fact, thanking and apologising are very close in Japanese; often, where we would say 'thank you', Japanese people will say (*dōmo*) *sumimasen*, as if in apology for putting someone to trouble on their behalf. In response to either an apology or an expression of thanks, you can say *iie*, or *iie*, *iie*, or (more formally) (*iie*) *dō itashimashite*.

About Japan

The Japanese language is in many respects a mirror of Japanese society. As we have seen, the family forms its own separate social group, and this social separation is reflected in the way people use different words to talk about somebody else's, as opposed to their own, family and relations. My mother, for example, is *haha*, whereas somebody else's is *o-kā-san*; my father is *chichi*, another's *o-tō-san*. Words like *haha* and *chichi* thus refer to an 'in-group', while *o-kā-san* and *o-tō-san* refer to an 'out-group', to those who are not of one's own kind.

Nevertheless, within the family, as within any social group, a hierarchical ranking system prevails, and this too is reflected in language use. Thus, when you actually address your mother, or talk about her to other members of your immediate family, you will call her *o-kā-san*, not *haha*. Seniors in the family, even older brothers or sisters, are addressed using respectful family role terms (an older brother, for example, will be addressed as *o-nii-san*, or an older sister as *o-nē-san*), and only one's juniors are addressed by given name.

This flexibility of language usage with regard to family – rather like the flexible use of respect language mentioned in the previous unit – indicates that nobody is ever in a fixed social position. It is the 'frame', or social context (who one is talking to, when and where), that determines how the Japanese behave and speak.

This idea of 'frame' is very important to an understanding of Japanese society, and the anthropologist Nakane Chie has argued that whereas Westerners tend to be more concerned with social attributes – with who you are – in Japan it is the social frame – where everyone is and who they are with – which influences the way in which people talk and behave.

The frequency with which Japanese people use set phrases is linked to the habit of setting their daily lives in 'frames', since by using phrases such as *itadakimasu* or *gochisōsama deshita* they mark the beginning or end of one activity (in this case related to eating and drinking), and indicate that the event in question is separate from others which have preceded or will follow it. In the countryside people often greet one another with the phrase, 'We are indebted to you for last time' (*kono mae o-sewa ni narimashita*). By referring to the previous time they were together – cleaning the local shrine, for example, or having a drink together – they cement ongoing social relationships through language.

Other set phrases you've already come across include expressions of greeting, thanks, apology and so on, and the expressions Japanese use to indicate that they are leaving or returning home: *itte kimasu* (replied to with *itte 'rasshai*) and *tadaima* (which meets with the response *okaerinasai*). Use of these phrases reflects a strong sense of physical separation between the 'inside' world of home and family (*uchi*) and the world outside (*soto*), just as the use of different words for 'my family' and 'your family' indicates a differentiation between 'in-group' and 'out-group' members. When you visit someone's home, too, the demarcation between inside and outside is reflected clearly in the almost ritualistic words used as you enter . . .

Shichi-go-san

VISITING SOMEONE'S HOME; TAKING REFRESHMENTS

> • The following phrases are used when entering someone's home:
>
> | | |
> |---|---|
> | **gomen kudasai!** | anyone at home? |
> | **ojama shimasu** | I'm disturbing you |
> | **shitsurei shimasu** | excuse me (lit. 'I'm being rude') |

JAPANESE LIVE 5 CD ▶ 41

Robbie Walker (an American housewife) has invited her friend, Mrs Kaneko, to coffee.

Mrs Kaneko	*(calling from the genkan)* Gomen kudasai!
Robbie	*(appearing from inside the house)* Ā, Kaneko-san, konnichi wa. *(gesturing her in)* Dōzo.
Mrs Kaneko	*(taking off her shoes and stepping up)* Ojama shimasu.
Robbie	*(gesturing to the kotatsu)* Dōzo, okake kudasai.
Mrs Kaneko	*(as she sits down)* Shitsurei shimasu. Soto wa samui desu ne.
Robbie	Sō desu ne. Kōhii wa ikaga desu ka?
Mrs Kaneko	Hai, onegai shimasu.
Robbie	*(pouring)* Dōzo. Bisuketto wa?
Mrs Kaneko	Itadakimasu. *(She takes one.)*

Rewind and repeat!

okake kudasai	won't you sit down? (lit. 'sit down, please')
soto	outside
kōhii	coffee
...wa ikaga desu ka?	how about some ...? (**ikaga?** is a more formal equivalent of **dō?**: 'how?')
hai, onegai shimasu	yes, please (lit. 'I ask (of you) a favour')
bisuketto	biscuit(s)

SPOTCHECK 6

@ What refreshments does Robbie offer Mrs Kaneko?

TAKE NOTE

ENTERING A HOME

The basic stages when entering a home are as follows: (1) ring the bell or open the door and call out *gomen kudasai!* (lit. 'pardon me!'), (2) when invited to do so, take off your shoes and step up into the house, saying as you do so *ojama shimasu* or *shitsurei shimasu*, (3) when you sit down, say *shitsurei shimasu*.

'DŌZO'

Like *dōmo*, *dōzo* is a very useful little word which is used in a variety of situations. Say *dōzo* to mean 'go ahead' when urging someone to do something (for example, sit down or come in); you can also offer or give things to people with a *dōzo*, meaning in this case 'here you are'.

SOUNDCHECK CD ▶ 42

When you come across a so-called 'double consonant' like the *tt* in *bisuketto*, pronounce it as in the English 'sit tight' or 'hot tap' (but not as in 'fitter' or 'rotten'). If you don't, you might sometimes be misunderstood, as the pairs of words below make clear.

A Listen, and practise saying these words. (Don't bother trying to remember them.)

1 a	batā	*(butter)*	**b**	battā	*(baseball batter)*
2 a	kite!	*(come!)*	**b**	kitte	*(postage stamp)*
3 a	shite	*(doing)*	**b**	shitte	*(knowing)*
4 a	kata	*(shoulder)*	**b**	katta	*(won)*
5 a	natsu	*(summer)*	**b**	nattsu	*(nut)*
6 a	mitsu	*(honey)*	**b**	mittsu	*(three)*

CD ▶ 43

@ **B** The second time round, only one of each pair will be pronounced: circle the word you hear.

BUILD-UP

CD ▶ 44

Apart from *kōhii* or *bisuketto*, you might be offered any of the following things as refreshments. Practise receiving them gracefully (with *dōmo (arigatō)* or *itadakimasu* and a slight bow) as your host (the CD) offers them to you:

1 **o-cha**   **(o-)senbei**
   green tea   rice cracker
2 **kōcha**   **kēki**
   (black) tea   cake
3 **biiru**   **(o-)tsumami**
   beer   snack consumed with alcohol
4 **jūsu**   **poteto chippusu**
   fruit juice   crisps

Entrance area (*genkan*)

OFFERINGS

CD ▶ 45

Now you offer the refreshments, in the same way as the CD has just offered them to you (i.e. first offer the drink on the left by saying ... *wa ikaga desu ka?*, then offer the corresponding food on the right with ... *wa?*). Each time, the CD will tell you what you should offer, and will follow up with an expression of thanks.

    E.g. (1) *CD:* ˙ **o-cha**
           You: **O-cha wa ikaga desu ka?**
           CD: **Itadakimasu.**
           CD: **o-senbei**
           You: **O-senbei wa?**
           CD: **Dōmo arigatō.**

STIMULUS–RESPONSE

The mixed-up responses on the right are each likely to follow one of the phrases on the left. Connect the phrases by drawing lines.

1 Itte kimasu.   a Ojama shimasu.
2 Dōzo. (*i.e. 'Come in!'*)   b Iie, dō itashimashite.
3 Okake kudasai.   c Itte 'rasshai.
4 Kēki wa ikaga desu ka?   d Shitsurei shimasu.
5 Dōmo arigatō.   e Okaerinasai.
6 Tadaima.   f Itadakimasu.

JUST IMAGINE!

Imagine the conversations you might have in the following situations. Take both parts if you're on your own.

a You've been invited to a meal at someone's home. You ring the doorbell and are greeted by your friend, asked to come in and invited to sit down.

b Before you start eating, say *itadakimasu*. During the meal, your friend offers you beer and, later, green tea. Accept in both cases. After the meal, say 'It was a feast'.

About Japan

Families everywhere tend to be economic, as well as simply blood-related, social groups. Until the end of the Pacific War, the Japanese used to call their families 'households' (*ie*), a concept which still exists in rural Japan. The household was seen to comprise all people living together under one roof, the house which they inhabited, and any property and assets (such as land, equipment, livestock) that they owned. The household also included all previous members of the family who had lived and died there, but not those (like second sons, or daughters) who had moved out and formed homes of their own. Ideally at least, members of a household were expected to subordinate their personal interests to those of the family as a whole – an attitude that, though fading, still exists to some extent in contemporary Japan.

So the Japanese household exists both in space and in time, because it includes all those who have lived and died there since its foundation. In this respect, the nearest Western equivalent to the Japanese household is probably the British royal family. Regardless of who is actually sitting on the throne, the royal family in a sense includes all those kings and queens, past and present, who have occupied the throne, together with their immediate relations. As is apparent in the phrase 'The king is dead. Long live the king!', the royal household continues through time, and will probably continue to do so for as long as there is an heir to the throne.

One major difference is the fact that the Japanese people venerate their ancestors, and it is they who can be said to be the most important people in traditional rural households, for they still influence decisions taken, for example, in selling land. Indeed, their importance can be gauged by the way in which visitors to a house will often pay their respects to the ancestral shrine (*butsudan*) before greeting their hosts.

And what of the women who tend to look after the shrines to the ancestors (even though not usually related to them by blood?) It used to be thought that, by Western standards, Japanese women were unfairly treated and oppressed. As we shall see later on in this book, women do tend to suffer from numerous male prejudices. But we should realise that they have their own separate spheres of existence, in which they wield quite a lot of power. In the family, for example, the husband is apparently the head of the house, but the wife in practice takes full control of the upbringing and education of their children, and usually domestic finances. It is here that they gain their social identity.

So the idea of the 'downtrodden' woman in Japan needs to be treated with some caution. It is a valid criticism in some areas of Japanese social behaviour, but not in others. This leads to a point which needs to be emphasised: in Japanese society, nothing is ever absolute. While we in the West tend to see our 'selves' as having some essential, absolute quality, regardless of the presence or absence of others, Japanese tend to define their selves in relation to others. Depending on the social context, or frame, in which they find themselves, their sense of self will subtly change. Of course, we ourselves react in a similar way, but because of our fixation on the concept of the 'individual', we prefer not to admit it. The Japanese, for their part, are considerably more honest when it comes to analysing their social behaviour.

Left A family meal

WHAT YOU'LL HEAR

1

FAMILY EXCURSIONS | CD ▸ 46

@ Listen to five interviews (numbered 1 to 5) with people visiting Hakone, a popular area for excursions near Tōkyō. Match each interview with one of the descriptions below and write the number of the interview in the appropriate space.

A ____ It's Mrs Imai's father's seventieth birthday. Mrs Imai is here celebrating together with her father, husband, sister and her husband's sister – five people in all.

B ____ Keiko, her two brothers and Yūko (her younger sister) are playing while their mother and aunt chat together.

C ____ Mrs Yamase, her husband, parents-in-law and three children have come here for a day out.

D ____ Mr and Mrs Igarashi are newly married, and on their honeymoon.

E ____ Mr Satō and his wife, their two children and Mr Satō's mother have come down from Tōkyō for their annual holiday.

2

THIS AND THAT | CD ▸ 47

@ Getting a natural feel for the difference between *kore*, *sore* and *are* will take a while. You might like to try your hand at a little detective work in this exercise. Look at the three pictures of rooms in Mrs Kaneko's house. Robbie and Mrs Kaneko went into each of the rooms (in the order 1 to 3) and Robbie asked about some of the objects in each room. Listen, and *try to guess where they were standing in each room when they had their conversations*. In other words, what objects were Robbie and Mrs Kaneko close to and what objects were they far away from? Mark where you think they were standing with a circle.

3

HAPPY FAMILIES

CD ▶ 48

@ We asked three different people to tell us about their families. They each brought along an old photograph and explained who everyone in the picture was. Listen, and write the numbers of the conversations (1 to 3) next to the appropriate pictures. (One of the photographs was not discussed.)

A

B

C

D

WRITTEN JAPANESE

uchi
(inside)

soto
(outside)

The strong differentiation between *uchi* and *soto* underlying much Japanese thinking extends also to conceptions of roles of men and women. While in Western eyes Japan can seem a very sexist society, many Japanese women still seem happy to accept that their vocation lies 'inside', in the home, and that men's place is in the 'outside' world of work. Westerners are often surprised, if not shocked, to discover how separate the domains of men and women are in Japan; very rarely are wives involved in business entertainment, for example, which almost always takes place outside the home in restaurants

and bars, while husbands (seldom at home anyway) hardly ever help out with housework. Of course, women work outside too, but often in the expectation of giving up their jobs once they have children, whose upbringing and education is seen very much as a mother's responsibilty. Attitudes are changing, but, by and large, husbands are the providers (traditionally handing over all their wages to their wives, and getting pocket money in return), while women are the chief consumers. It has even been suggested that men, with their long working hours, lack of holidays and lack of contact with their children, are equally discriminated against in modern-day Japan!

You'll find the kanji for 'female' and 'male' (below) very useful (if not essential!) when you're called by nature, or looking for the changing room at a public bath (*sentō*).

In ancient China, as well as modern-day Japan, a man's place was thought to be outside, working: the character for 'male' represents 'strength in the paddyfields', men's major occupation until relatively recent times having been the cultivation of rice.

女 female							
子 child							
田 paddyfield							
力 strength							
男 male							

Using *no* (written in hiragana), here's how to say and write 'man', 'woman', 'boy' and 'girl' in Japanese:

man	男の人	**otoko no hito** (male person)
woman	女の人	**onna no hito** (female person)
boy	男の子	**otoko no ko** (male child)
girl	女の子	**onna no ko** (female child)

Remember that kanji primarily represent units of meaning, and not particular sounds as is the case with rōmaji, hiragana or katakana. One and the same kanji can therefore be used in the writing of words or parts of words which sound completely different but share the same meaning: 人, for example, is read as *jin* in 日本人 ('Japanese person'), but as *hito* in 女の人 ('female person', i.e. 'woman'). Similarly, 外 (the kanji for 'outside' at the top of the opposite page) is read as *soto* on its own, but as *gai* when found in a combination like 外人: *gaijin*, meaning 'foreigner' (literally, 'person from outside').

好   安

fondness   restful

Returning to the 'inside', though, it's interesting to note that the character for 'fondness' is derived from the archetypal scene of a woman holding a child, or perhaps carrying one on her back, as you can still see many Japanese mothers doing. Also of interest is the kanji for 'restful', which is said to represent a woman under the home roof – difficult, perhaps, to conceptualise with young children around, but then kanji probably weren't invented by women!

Finally, here are two more family-related kanji for you to recognise:

woman and breasts	mother	母 **haha** お母さん **o-kā-san**
hand wielding stick or axe	father	父 **chichi** お父さん **o-tō-san**

Although the words for one's own and another's parents sound completely different, the kanji remain the same (the only difference in written Japanese being that the honorifics *o-* and *-san*, in hiragana, are applied in the case of someone else's family).

@   Now try to read aloud and translate these sentences (and answer aloud the final question):

1   あの男の人は日本人です。
2   あの人は外人です。
3   あの女の子のお母さんはアメリカ人です。
4   母は東京からです。
5   お父さんのお母さんはアメリカ人ですか。

HIRAGANA

あ	の	は	さ	ん
a	**no**	**wa**	**sa**	**n**

LANGUAGE SUMMARY

Around the house

o-furo	butsudan	tatami
kotatsu	shōji	shashin
tokonoma	kakejiku	tekisuto
toire	terebi	

For eating

chawan	koppu	yunomi
(o-)hashi	(o-)sara	oshibori

Food and drink

sakana	biiru	jūsu
miso shiru	(o-)tsumami	(o-)senbei
kōhii	o-cha	kēki
bisuketto	kōcha	
wagashi	poteto chippu(su)	

Family

kazoku	haha	imōto
go-kazoku	o-kā-san	imōto-san
shujin/otto	ani	ryōshin
go-shujin	o-nii-san	go-ryōshin
kanai/tsuma	ane	kyōdai
oku-san	o-nē-san	go-kyōdai
chichi	otōto	kodomo
o-tō-san	otōto-san	o-ko-san

Places

gakkō	sūpā	ginkō
kaisha	uchi/ie	byōin

Thank you

Dōmo arigatō. → Dō itashimashite.

Entering/Leaving a house

Gomen kudasai! → Dōzo.
  → Ojama shimasu.
Okake kudasai. → Shitsurei shimasu.
Itte kimasu. → Itte 'rasshai.
Tadaima. → Okaerinasai.

Eating

Itadakimasu.
... wa ikaga desu ka? →
  Hai, itadakimasu/onegai shimasu.
Okawari wa?
Gochisōsama deshita.

Adjectives

ii	ōkii
atarashii	kirei
suteki	kawaii
subarashii	oishii
sugoi	omoshiroi
benri	chiisai
muzukashii	

Main language structures

this/that/which?: kore/sore/are/dore?
Kore wa nan desu ka?

this house/that house/which house?:
kono ie/sono ie/ano ie/dono ie?
Dono ie desu ka? Ano ie desu.

here/there/where?: koko/soko/asoko/doko?
Honda-san no uchi wa doko desu ka? Asoko desu.

am/are/is: imasu
Musume-san wa doko ni imasu ka? Uchi ni imasu.
O-ko-san wa irasshaimasu ka? Iie, imasen.

Possessions: (person) no (object)
Watashi no tekisuto.
Tanaka-san no uchi.

To deepen your understanding of some of the
grammar presented in this unit, you may like to
look at the following parts of the Grammar section:
'Saying whose' (3) and 'Saying which or where' (4).

3
ALL IN A DAY'S WORK

The Japanese at work
Telephoning
Understanding business cards
Getting around by taxi and on foot
Business introductions

About Japan

A second pillar of contemporary Japanese society has been the company. This can best be seen, perhaps, in the fact that the word for 'company' *(kaisha)* is the reverse of that for 'society' *(shakai)*. In all industrialised societies, companies are important for a number of reasons. First, they employ a large part of the population and so distribute wealth, making some people rich and others poor. They are also political institutions in that they place some employees above others in a system of authority and subordination, while their decisions to open a factory here and close another there cannot be ignored by either local or national governments. Finally, companies have intellectual, cultural and moral effects in that they pay for research, as well as recruit employees in such a way that a country's educational system is affected; they also directly sponsor art exhibitions, sporting competitions and other media events; and they encourage, through advertising, consumer preferences as well as more profound attitudes and ideas underlying what is generally referred to as 'lifestyle'.

Japanese companies are no different from European or American companies in any of these respects. However, they are marked by certain characteristics that make them slightly different from the latter, and that have given rise to the idea that the kind of welfare capitalism practised by Japan (and Germany) is different from Anglo-American-style free market capitalism. For example, in the West, the three main institutions of industry – management *(keiei)*, trade unions *(rōdō kumiai)* and industries and markets *(shijō)* – are usually kept separate. In Japan this has not always been so. Unions, for example, tend to be individual 'enterprise' rather than across-the-board 'labour' unions, so that a Japanese worker would identify himself first and foremost as an employee of Toyota, for example, not a mechanic.

Another difference is that a Japanese company has usually been narrowly specialised. In the West, larger corporations tend to diversify by merging with, or taking over, other smaller companies. In Japan, they create subsideries *(kogaisha)* – literally, 'child companies'). They also tend to confine their production to part of the manufacturing and/or distribution process; the rest they subcontract to other companies. There are also two benefits to this method of business management. First, subcontracting encourages interdependence between companies; second, it helps reinforce the ideal of a homogeneous workforce. The smaller a workforce is, the easier it generally is to create group consensus and a sense of company identity.

Another interesting feature of Japanese companies is that there has usually been a strong correlation between their size, their productivity, the number of university graduates employed, the stability of the workforce, interest rates charged the companies on loans, and so on. In other words, the larger a company is, the greater its annual output, the more highly educated its employees (who are less likely to move on to other jobs) and the more favourable the rates of interest at which it is able to borrow money from its banks. Because of this it is possible to talk in Japan of what has been called the 'status gradation of industry' (Rodney Clark, *The Japanese Company*), in that companies are classified as 'first class' (*ichiryū* – literally, 'first stream'), 'second class' (*niryū*), 'third class' (*sanryū*), and so on.

Morning meeting at the Honda company

TELEPHONING (1): GETTING THROUGH AND SAYING GOODBYE

Moshi moshi means 'hello' on the telephone, and you'll be saying this a lot if you're in Japan on business. There are some golden rules to follow when telephoning Japanese-style:

- Always say your company and name (without -san) e.g. **OMC no Sakai desu ga ...** (*ga* means 'but', and is used to give an impression of modesty, as if to imply your name isn't all that important).

- To ask to speak to someone, say ... **-san onegai shimasu** (lit. 'Mr/Mrs ... please') or ... **-san wa irasshaimasu ka?** ('Is Mr/Mrs ... there?')

- When you want to sign off, say **dewa** (or less formally *jā*) 'well, then'. Don't be in a hurry to put the phone down, but follow up with any (or all) of these polite expressions: **yoroshiku onegai shimasu** ('please look kindly on me': use this if you're hoping for some kind of favour), **shitsurei shimasu** ('excuse me': 'goodbye' on the telephone), **gomen kudasai** ('pardon me (for any inconvenience)').

JAPANESE LIVE 1   CD ▸ 49

Jun Sakai makes a phone call at work.

Receptionist	IBM de gozaimasu.
Jun	Moshi moshi. OMC no Sakai desu ga eigyōbu no Yamada-san onegai shimasu.
Receptionist	Shōshō o-machi kudasai.
Yamada	(*picking up the phone*) Moshi moshi, Yamada desu.
Jun	OMC no Sakai desu ga ... ... (*fade-out*) ... (*fade-in*) ...
Jun	Dewa, yoroshiku onegai shimasu.
Yamada	Hai, dōmo.
Jun	Shitsurei shimasu.
Yamada	Shitsurei shimasu.
Jun	Gomen kudasai.

Rewind and repeat!

de gozaimasu	a very polite equivalent of **desu**
OMC	name of the advertising agency where Jun works
eigyōbu	sales division (**bu** = division)
shōshō o-machi kudasai	wait a moment, please (very polite)

SPOTCHECK 1

@ What department does Mr Yamada work in?

BUILD-UP   CD ▸ 50

Listen, and then say these words for departments in a company:

jinjibu	personnel
keiribu	accounts
sōmubu	general affairs
kokusaibu	international affairs
kōhōbu	public relations
māketingubu	marketing

LISTEN   CD ▸ 51

@ Listen to the five phone conversations (numbered 1 to 5). Who is calling whom? In each case note down the caller's name (and the name of his/her company), and the other person's name (with the name of his/her department). Listen several times if necessary.

RECREATE   CD ▸ 52

Using 'Japanese live 1' as a model, and consulting your notes from 'Listen' above, recreate the five conversations you've just listened to. Always take the caller's part, rewinding the CD each time (the CD will take the other part).

    E.g. (1) *You:* **Hitachi no Nakamura desu ga ...** etc.

    Finally (6), use your own name, and call up Mr Yamada in personnel.

UNDERSTANDING JAPANESE BUSINESS CARDS (1): TELEPHONE NUMBERS

CD ▶ 53

- To ask someone's phone number: **denwa bangō wa nanban desu ka?** (*denwa* = phone; *bangō* = number; *nanban?* = what number?)

- To say a phone number (listen and say):

1 ichi	2 ni	3 san	4 yon	5 go
6 roku	7 nana	8 hachi	9 kyū	0 zero

  Hyphens are read as **no**, so 03-1246-5789 is *zero san no ichi ni yon roku no go nana hachi kyū*. (*Ni* is often pronounced as *nii*, and *go* as *gō* in phone numbers.)

- To check a phone number, repeat the number and add **desu ne?** (Your voice should rise on *ne?*) For example, *1245-6788 desu ne?*

TAKE NOTE

THE NUMBERS 4, 7, 9

In some situations, such as when numbers are used to count (as when someone counts a stack of paper), the words for 4, 7 and 9 are different from those used in phone numbers: 4 = *shi*, 7 = *shichi*, 9 = *ku*. Interestingly, since another meaning of *shi* is 'death', the number 4 is considered unlucky. (For example, the floor numbering in hotels sometimes jumps mysteriously from 3 to 5; it's also considered unlucky to give four of something as a present.)

JAPANESE LIVE 2

CD ▶ 54

Ueda	OMC no Sakai-san no denwa bangō wa nanban desu ka?
Satō	Ichi ni yon zero no kyū nana hachi ichi desu.
Ueda	Ichi ni yon zero no kyū nana hachi ichi desu ne?

Rewind and repeat!

SPOTCHECK 2

@ Write down Jun Sakai's number.

ASK

CD ▶ 55

The CD will tell you someone's company and name. After the tone, make a question asking for that person's phone number. The CD will then tell you what you should have said. Do this 8 times.

E.g. (1) *CD:* **Hitachi no Yoshida-san**
You: **Hitachi no Yoshida-san no denwa bangō wa nanban desu ka?**

NUMBERS

CD ▶ 56

@ Take the part of Ueda in 'Japanese live 2', and ask for the phone numbers of the ten people below. Write down the numbers the CD tells you. Rewind and try again (without looking at 'Japanese live 2'), this time repeating the number back to the CD as if you were checking it.

1 Suzuki (Fujitsū) _____
2 Kobayashi (Hitachi) _____
3 Tanaka (Nissan) _____
4 Ogawa (NHK) _____
5 Yoshida (Marubeni) _____
6 Yamada (Hakuhōdō) _____
7 Satō (Nihon IBM) _____
8 Ōtsuka (Nikon) _____
9 Saitō (Aiwa) _____
10 Morita (YKK) _____

UNDERSTANDING JAPANESE BUSINESS CARDS (2): ADDRESSES

Here's a map of part of Shinjuku-ku ('Shinjuku ward') in Tōkyō:

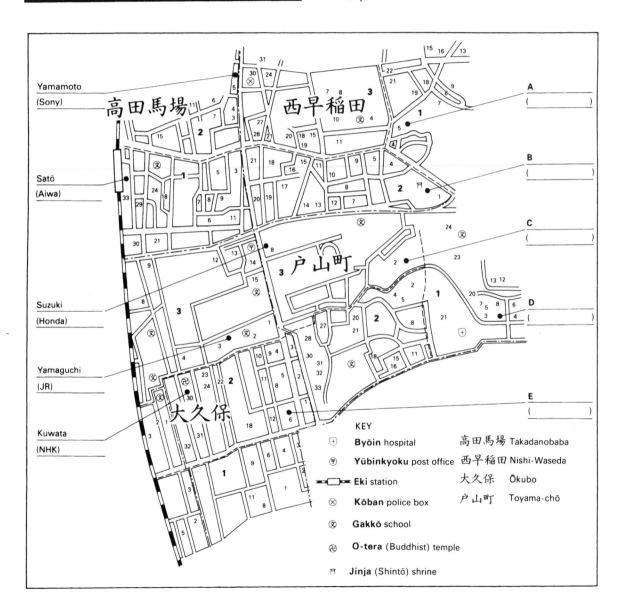

KEY

⊕	**Byōin** hospital	高田馬場	Takadanobaba
〒	**Yūbinkyoku** post office	西早稲田	Nishi-Waseda
▭	**Eki** station	大久保	Ōkubo
⊗	**Kōban** police box	戸山町	Toyama-chō
⊗	**Gakkō** school		
卍	**O-tera** (Buddhist) temple		
⌶	**Jinja** (Shintō) shrine		

The Japanese address system is based not on street names, but on ever-decreasing bounded areas. Thus Tōkyō is divided into 23 wards (*ku*). Each ward is divided into named areas (on the map opposite, these are Takadanobaba, Ōkubo, Nishi-Waseda and Toyama-chō). Each area is divided into *chōme*, which are numbered (Toyama-chō 1, Ōkubo 3, etc.). Then these *chōme* are divided into *banchi* (e.g. Toyama-chō 1–4, Ōkubo 3–5: the hyphen is pronounced *no*, as in telephone numbers).

SPOTCHECK 3

@ Look at the map and the key. What public buildings or facilities are in the following areas?

a Takadanobaba 1–33 **c** Toyama-chō 1–21
b Nishi-Waseda 3–30 **d** Ōkubo 2–30

> - To say where something is located: **... ni arimasu.**
>   E.g. *Byōin wa Toyama-cho ni arimasu:* 'The hospital is (located) in Toyamo-chō.'
>   (Remember that **imasu** is used instead for people or animals.)
>
> - To ask for an address: **Jūsho wa dochira desu ka?**
>   (Japanese say 'where (not 'what') is the address?', *dochira?* being a more polite alternative to *doko?*)

JAPANESE LIVE 3 [CD ▶ 57]

@ Before listening, look at the map and find the address given below. Who lives there? Write in that person's company (first space) and name (second space). Then listen and check.

Ueda	_____ no _____ -san no uchi wa doko ni arimasu ka?
Satō	Ōkubo ni arimasu.
Ueda	Jūsho wa dochira desu ka?
Satō	Ōkubo 3–3 desu.

Rewind and repeat!

SPOTCHECK 4

@ Write down the addresses of the other four people whose names appear to the left of the map.

OMC アドバタイジングエージェンシー
株式会社オーエムシー

第三営業局

酒井　淳

本社　東京都中央区新富1-12-2〒104 第二亜興ビル
電話03-553-6111 (大代表) ファクシミリ03-553-7570

PUBLIC PLACES [CD ▶ 58]

The CD will give you a cue from the list of public places in the key. Find that building on the map, and say in which area it's located. Use the pause button to give yourself time before speaking.

E.g. (1) *CD:* byōin
You: **Byōin wa Toyama-chō ni arimasu.**

ASK [CD ▶ 59]

The CD will give you a cue consisting of a person's company and name. Make a question asking for that person's address.

E.g. (1) *CD:* Yamaha no Tanaka-san
You: **Yamaha no Tanaka-san no jūsho wa dochira desu ka?**

ADDRESSES [CD ▶ 60]

@ Ask the CD for the addresses of the five people below, and listen for the answers. Looking across at the map opposite, find where each person lives and write names on lines A–E.

E.g. (1) *You:* **Daihatsu no Nishida-san no jūsho wa dochira desu ka?**

1 Nishida (Daihatsu) **4** Fukuda (Honda)
2 Satō (NHK) **5** Tanaka (Hitachi)
3 Yamada (Toyota)

DESCRIBING WHERE

Be warned that, without a map, it can be very difficult to find the place you want, since address numbering is area- rather than street-based. The Japanese themselves tend to get around this problem by describing where a place is in terms of nearby landmarks. For example:

1 Gasorin sutando no **tonari** ni arimasu. (*next to*)
   (*It's next to the petrol station.*) ·
2 Yūbinkyoku no **chikaku** ni arimasu. (*near to*)
3 Eki no **soba** ni arimasu. (*very near to*)
4 Kōban no **hantaigawa** ni arimasu. (*opposite*)
5 Byōin no **mae** ni arimasu. (*in front of*)
6 Jinja no **ushiro** ni arimasu. (*behind*)

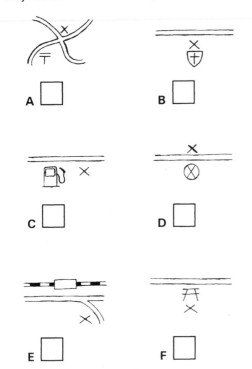

CD ▸ 61

@ Match the descriptions with the pictures below them by writing a number in each box.

Listen to and repeat the descriptions on the CD.

LISTEN

CD ▸ 62

The CD will describe six of the houses on the map on page 54 in terms of the landmarks close to them. Tell the CD who lives in the house being described.

> E.g. (1) *CD:* **Yūbinkyoku no hantaigawa ni arimasu.**
>
> *You:* **Honda no Suzuki-san no uchi desu.**

WHERE?

CD ▸ 63

The CD will ask you where six of the people on the page 54 live. Looking at the map on page 54, answer in relation to the landmarks. Of course there are different ways of describing the same place, but the CD will follow up with one possible answer.

> E.g. (1) *CD:* **NHK no Kuwata-san no uchi wa doko ni arimasu ka?**
>
> *You:* **O-tera no ushiro ni arimasu.**

About Japan

Japanese society is a society of industry, a society that works. It is in the workplace that the great majority of Japanese men seek fulfilment, there that they define their identity. After the family, the workplace is the single most important group to which most Japanese belong. Those white-collar workers who are employed on a regular basis in Japanese companies are called 'salary men' (*sarariiman*), and their way of life *sarariiman no bunka*, or 'the salaried employees' culture'. Every morning they leave their homes to commute to work and only return home quite late in the evenings. Work in Japan is not a 9 to 5 contract, but often a lifetime bond between employer and employee *(shain)*. In major companies, hard work and devotion to the strengthening of this bond were, until the recession, rewarded by security, insurance schemes, leisure facilities and often company housing, as well as favourable borrowing rates.

As one might expect in such a situation, it is the company's welfare that has been seen to be the most important objective for all employees. In other words, individual interests have often been subordinated to those of the company as a whole and of the section to which an employee belongs. This sense of groupness and interdependence is reflected in office layout, where an open-plan system places people together in sections and arrays them in departments, overseen by managers whose importance can generally be gauged by the distance of their desks from the entrance to the office and their proximity to its windows! In other words, at the same time as encouraging a sense of groupness, Japanese companies also clearly demarcate lines of authority and subordination.

Two important points need to be made about Japan's society of industry. First, not all companies practise ideals like 'lifetime employment' which are seen to make up what is popularly called the 'Japanese employment system'. This means that about half the Japanese workforce is employed under conditions that are, on the surface at least, not all that different from those found in Western companies. Second, Japanese companies distinguish between permanent and temporary employees, and it is only the permanent employees, usually male university graduates, who enjoy the perks and privileges mentioned above.

For a long time, women were not usually employed on a regular and permanent basis, as they were expected to get married and raise children at home, but, like much else in Japan, this is changing. An equal opportunities law now obliges companies to treat their male and female employees exactly the same in terms of pay, promotion and career opportunities. As a result, women are starting to think in terms of 'careers' rather than simply 'work', and – to the dismay of young men – are putting off marriage until they are well into their 30s.

Top Tōkyō money market
Above Hiroko Sakai at work in the Tōkyō Gas office

TELEPHONING (2)

JAPANESE LIVE 4

CD ▶ 64

@ Use this conversation to review language work so far in the unit. A is ringing B to discover the address and phone number of the restaurant (*resutoran*) where they've made an appointment to meet. Listen – several times if necessary – and fill in the gaps.

A	Moshi moshi. _____ no
	_____ desu ga,
	_____ no
	_____ -san wa
	irasshaimasu ka?
Receptionist	Shōshō o-machi kudasai.
B	Moshi moshi, _____
	desu ga _____ -san
	desu ka?
A	Hai, sō desu. Kyō no yakusoku desu ga . . .
B	Hai.
A	Resutoran no jūsho wa dochira desu ka?
B	Chotto matte kudasai.
	_____ desu.
	_____ no _____
	ni arimasu.
A	Ā, sō desu ka. Sumimasen ga denwa bangō wa nanban desu ka?
B	_____-_____ desu.
A	Hai, wakarimashita. Dewa, yoroshiku onegai shimasu.
B	Kochira koso yoroshiku onegai shimasu.
A	Shitsurei shimasu.
B	Gomen kudasai.

Rewind and repeat!

kyō no yakusoku desu ga . . .	it's about today's (**kyō no**) appointment . . .
chotto matte kudasai	wait a moment, please (less formal than **shōshō o-machi kudasai**)
wakarimashita	I see (lit. 'I have understood')
kochira koso . . .	for my part, too (lit. 'from here, too') . . .

PUT IT ALL TOGETHER

CD ▶ 65

@ Now practise ringing to check a meeting place and number, using 'Japanese live 4' as a model. Take the parts of the people on the left below, and ring the people on the right. Say exactly what 'A' says in 'Japanese live 4', except for the first two lines, where you'll have to insert the relevant names. (Rehearse this before beginning.) The CD will take the part of 'B'. Listening to B's replies, note down in each case the address and phone number of the restaurant.

1 You are Yamamoto (NHK). Ring Mr Suzuki in public relations.
2 You are Ozawa (Marubeni). Ring Ms Takahashi in accounting.
3 You are Uchiyama (Sony). Ring Ms Nakajima in personnel.

TAKE NOTE

CD ▶ 66

'AIZUCHI'

Look back at what was said on p. 10 about *ā, sō desu ka* and other 'aizuchi'. Nowhere is it more important to give out listening signals than on the telephone, and failure to do so will result in a *moshi moshi* from your opposite number to check you're still there.

@ Listen to the recording of someone explaining a variety of addresses over the telephone, and note down the 'aizuchi' you hear the listener use. Then rewind and say the 'aizuchi' with the listener.

GETTING AROUND
(BY TAXI AND ON FOOT)

Once you've arranged a meeting, you have to get there! Only the largest streets in Japanese cities have names, and the numbering in a neighbourhood isn't much help: number 39 may be a mile away from number 40. So, to all but the best-known places, you may well have to guide the taxi driver, or if you're travelling on foot you'll have to ask for and understand directions in the street.

Police box (*kōban*)

> • Saying 'where' to do something comes before saying 'what' to do there.
> E.g. 'Turn right at the signals (please)': **Shingō de migi e magatte (kudasai)**.
> (*shingō de* = *at* the signals; *migi e magatte* = turn *to* the right)

BUILD-UP

Here are some of the words you'll need:

ano/asoko no ... (that ... over there)	**shingō** (traffic signals)		**migi e magatte** (turn right)
tsugi no ... (the next ...)	**kado** (corner, turning)		**hidari e magatte** (turn left)
	shingō no temae (just before the signals)		**massugu itte** (go straight on)
hitotsume/futatsume/ mittsume no ... (the first/second/third ...)	**kado no saki** (just after the turning)		**tomete** (stop)

WHERE ...?				WHAT TO DO ...?	
(Ano/Asoko no) (Tsugi no) (Hitotsume no) (Futatsume no) (Mittsume no)	shingō kado eki jinja gasorin sutando	(no temae) (no saki)	de	migi e magatte hidari e magatte tomete	kudasai.
				Massugu itte	

LISTEN AND POINT

CD ▶ 67

Get used to using the above chart by listening to the CD and pointing to the words used in the directions you hear. (There are eight different directions.) Then rewind and repeat each direction, using the pause button.

SPOTCHECK 5

Translate these directions into Japanese:
a Go straight on, please.
b Turn right, please.
c Turn left at the next signals, please.
d Stop just after the first turning, please.

TAKE NOTE

To say 'at' or 'in' a place, you've now come across two words: *ni* (as in *byōin wa Toyama-chō ni arimasu*) and *de* (as in the directions above). In general, *de* is used to describe some kind of action happening in or at a place, and *ni* when describing a state of being.

GIVE DIRECTIONS

As far as possible without looking at the chart above, work out how to give directions in the situations pictured on the right.

CD ▶ 68

A First, think how you're going to say *where* the directions are to be carried out (... *de*), and tell the CD.

E.g. (1) *You:* **futatsume no shingō de**
The CD will follow up with what you could have said.

CD ▶ 69

B Now work out *what* direction you should give in each case, and check with the CD.

E.g. (1) *You:* **migi e magatte kudasai**

CD ▶ 70

C Finally, say *where and what*.

E.g. (1) *You:* **Futatsume no shingō de migi e magatte kudasai.**

Again, the CD will follow up with what you could have said.

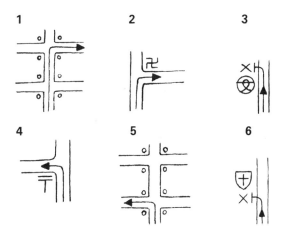

JAPANESE LIVE 5

CD ▶ 71

Robert Hope takes a taxi in Tōkyō.

Robert	Takadanobaba eki no chikaku made onegai shimasu.
Driver	Hai, wakarimashita.
Robert	(*recognising the area*) Massugu itte, o-tera no saki de tomete kudasai . . .
	Koko de kekkō desu . . . (*He pays the fare shown.*)
	Ryōshūsho onegai shimasu.
Driver	Hai, dōzo.
Robert	Dōmo.

Rewind and repeat!

. . . made onegai shimasu	to . . . please (**made** = as far as)
koko de kekkō desu	here is fine
ryōshūsho	written receipt

SPOTCHECK 6

@ Look at the map below. Robert started to recognise the area at point C. What places did they pass on the way to their destination?

LISTEN

CD ▶ 72

@ Three different people took taxi rides from point D on the map below. Listen to their conversations (1 to 3) with the driver, and work out what places they went to.

CD ▶ 73

- Walking around a Japanese city, you're likely to want to ask the way (listen and repeat):

Sumimasen ga *(place)* wa	doko	ni arimasu ka?
	dochira	desu ka?
	dotchi	

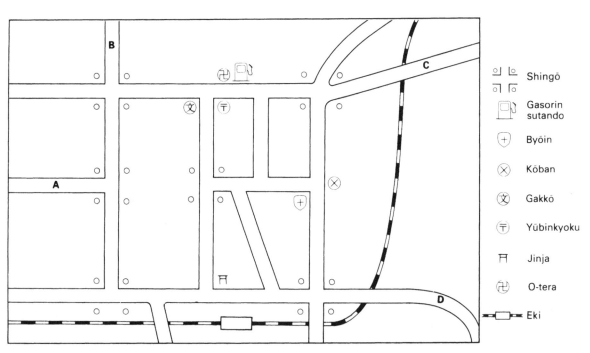

Symbol	Name
Shingō
Gasorin sutando
Byōin
Kōban
Gakkō
Yūbinkyoku
Jinja
O-tera
Eki

TAKE NOTE

Dochira? (less formally, *dotchi?*) was explained earlier as being a polite equivalent of *doko?* Literally, however, it means 'which way?', and might meet with one of these replies:

kochira/kotchi desu   'it's this way'
sochira/sotchi desu   'it's that way'
achira/atchi desu   'it's that way, over there'

REPLIES

Here are some more answers you might hear. Draw lines from the written directions (A to E) to the pictures in the middle. (Ignore the symbols on the right for the moment.)

LISTEN

@ Look again at the map on the opposite page. The CD will direct you to four different places, starting in turn from the places marked A, B, C and D. In each case, draw the route and write down the name of the place you go to in Japanese (*A kara ... made* = from A to ...):

1 A kara _____ made   3 C kara _____ made
2 B kara _____ made   4 D kara _____ made

A Futatsume no shingō de migi e magatte – soko desu. ●	● ⌐⌐⌐ ●	**1** ● ▬◻▬
B Asoko no gakkō de hidari e magatte – soko desu. ●	● ╫╫╫ ●	**2** ● ⊗
C Eki no hantaigawa ni arimasu. ●	● ×╥ ●	**3** ● ⊕
D Hitotsume no kado de migi e magatte – soko desu. ●	● ┘� ⊘ ●	**4** ● ⊤
E Asoko no jinja no temae desu. ●	● × ▬◻▬ ●	**5** ● ⛽

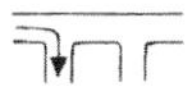

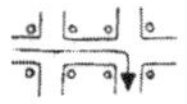

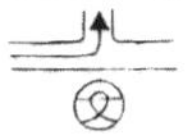

ASK

@ Ask the CD in turn where each of the places numbered 1 to 5 is. Cover up the written directions on the left, and, listening to the answers, draw lines from the symbols on the right to the pictures in the middle.

E.g. (1) *You:* **Sumimasen ga eki wa doko ni arimasu ka?**
CD: **Asoko no gakkō de ...** etc.

TAXI!

Using 'Japanese live 5' on the opposite page as a model, take Robert's part and direct the taxi driver in turn from A, B, C and D to the places you've written down in 'Listen' above. (Your directions should be similar to those you've just listened to, except that finally you should say ... *de tomete kudasai* rather than ... *desu* or ... *ni arimasu*.) Start by saying (*place*) *made onegai shimasu*. The taxi driver's words are the same in each case, so rewind

@ the CD each time. Finally, look at the suggested directions in the key and repeat the exercise if your own directions differed wildly!

About Japan

To Westerners unfamiliar with Japan, all Japanese names tend to sound alike and all Japanese to look alike. This can be embarrassing, for to say 'you' in Japanese it is common to use the other person's name (or rank). One way the Japanese get round the problem of remembering names is by using *meishi* (namecards). All Japanese businessmen carry namecards, regardless of their position in their company, and the first thing that people do if they have not met before is exchange their meishi.

There are important rules of etiquette about namecards which should be observed. Ideally they should be carried in the inside pocket of your suit jacket, and not in the hip pocket of your trousers, for it would be rude to place in someone else's hands something that has been in close proximity with your own buttocks! When about to be introduced, you should have your meishi ready and not have to fumble for them and so keep your associates waiting. Do not deal them out as if they were playing cards, and make sure, too, that when you hand one over it is facing the right way up for your opposite number to read. When introduced, take one step forward and hand over your card, saying your name slowly and clearly as you do so. Then take a step back and bow. (Of course, it is likely these days that a Japanese businessman will expect to shake hands with his Western counterpart, but there is no harm in learning polite Japanese-style procedure.)

You should not immediately put away the namecards that you have just received, but rather examine them carefully, since initial conversation will probably revolve around what is written on them. When you sit down, you can place the meishi on the table in front of you and keep them there until it is time to leave. It helps if you place them in the order in which your associates are sitting opposite you. You can then readily refer to them, should you forget someone's name.

Namecards are important, not only because they provide a very useful means of recalling people's names, but also because they give details of an employee's position in a particular company. Meishi can therefore be used to assess how useful your associate is likely to be in negotiations. One slight complication in Japan's society of industry concerns the exact calculation of ranks in someone else's company vis-à-vis those of your own. For example, a section chief (*kachō*) in an *ichiryū* corporation like Panasonic or the Mitsui Sumitomo Bank may well be considered equal to, or even more senior than, a department chief *(buchō)* in a *niryū* company, who may himself be on an equal footing with a director *(torishimariyaku)* of a *sanryū* company. This means that companies spend quite a lot of time working out who would be the best person to meet you, and you can often gauge your own importance to the company you visit by the rank of the person or people sent to talk to you.

To Japanese business people themselves, the details of company affiliation and position contained on meishi are vital for conversation to start up at all, since – as you are already aware – there are various levels of formality to contend with in the Japanese language, and words are chosen with care according to one's status relative to that of another person. Foreigners, however, are generally excused the need to adapt to these niceties: *any* attempt you make to speak Japanese will meet with approval, and as long as you stick to the relatively polite forms taught in this book, you won't risk offending anyone.

Language reflects the hierarchical structures of Japanese society not only when people of different companies meet, but also within the company itself, where role names are used for all those in positions senior to oneself. Thus one's section chief will be called by his title, *kachō*, rather than by his individual name. The same applies to division heads (*buchō*), managing directors (*jōmu*) and company presidents (*shachō*). You will recall that the same principle applies within the family, where elder brothers and sisters are referred to as *o-nii-san* and *o-nē-san*, but younger ones by name.

Just like in the family, however, group identity comes to the fore when people from different companies meet or talk on the telephone. In the same way as 'humble' words are used to describe one's own and respectful terms applied to another's family, in the presence of outsiders the honorific *-san* is not applied to the name even of someone senior to oneself in the same company. Instead, he or she might be introduced or referred to, for example, as *uchi no Tanaka* (literally, 'Tanaka from inside', i.e. 'from inside my company'). The distinction between *uchi* and *soto* – insiders and outsiders – runs deep in Japan, and, just as if it were a family, the company puts aside its internal hierarchy in favour of group solidarity in all its dealings with the 'outside world'.

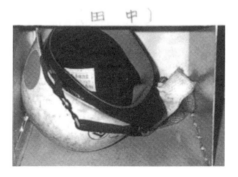

INTRODUCTIONS

Nakajima-san wa?	and you?
go-shōkai shimasu	let me introduce you
	(**shōkai** = introduction)

SPOTCHECK 7

@ What companies do Ms Asano, Robert and Mr Ueda work for?

TAKE NOTE

Japanese people often repeat their name when introduced, perhaps to make it easier to remember; as you'll be reading on the next page, it's important to remember names, since they are often used to mean 'you'.

- To introduce someone from a different company, be indirect (say *kochira* rather than *kore* to mean 'this') and courteous (always use *-san*). E.g. *Kochira (wa) TDK no Asano-san desu.*

- To introduce or talk about someone from your own work group, don't use *-san* (however senior to you your colleague may be). Instead you could mention his or her position in your company. E.g. *Uchi no Ueda-buchō desu:* 'This is (Division Chief) Ueda.'

LISTEN `CD ▸ 78`

@ Listen to four introductions. Decide which of the two people being introduced works for a different company from the introducer, and write his/her name and company on the left below. Write the other person's name and position on the right.

Different company		*Same company*	
1 Tomizawa	(Toyota)	Satō	(shachō)
2 _____	( )	_____	( )
3 _____	( )	_____	( )
4 _____	( )	_____	( )

JAPANESE LIVE 6 `CD ▸ 77`

Robert arrives at an appointment with Mr Nakajima of Fujitsū, who introduces him to two people.

Robert	Ā, Nakajima-san, konnichi wa.
Nakajima	Konnichi wa. O-genki desu ka?
Robert	Hai, okagesama de. Nakajima-san wa?
Nakajima	Watashi mo genki desu. Go-shōkai shimasu. (*indicating Ms Asano*) Kochira, TDK no Asano-san desu.
Robert	Hajimemashite. (*giving his meishi*) Rondon konpyūtāzu no Hōpu desu.
Asano	(*giving her meishi*) Asano to mōshimasu. Yoroshiku onegai itashimasu.
Robert	Kochira koso yoroshiku onegai shimasu.
Nakajima	(*indicating Mr Ueda*) Uchi no Ueda-buchō desu.
Robert	(*giving his meishi*) Hōpu desu. Yoroshiku onegai shimasu.
Ueda	Hajimemashite. (*giving his meishi*) Ueda to mōshimasu. Dōzo yoroshiku.
	Rewind and repeat!

RECREATE `CD ▸ 79`

Now you do the introducing, using the information you've just written down. Each time, start by saying *Go-shōkai shimasu*, and introduce the person on the left first. The CD will take the parts of the people introduced.

SAYING 'YOU'; 'GETTING TO KNOW YOU' QUESTIONS

There are words in Japanese similar to the English 'you' (e.g. *anata*, or more familiarly *kimi*), but these tend not to be used very much (except between partners or very close friends). The less direct alternatives given below are generally preferred.

> - When it's clear you're talking about the other person, it's unecessary to use a word for 'you' (as when Ms Yamaguchi asked Robert Hope *Hōpu-san desu ka?* on p.12). Similarly, it's unnecessary to say 'your' when this is obvious. For example, *Kaisha wa doko ni arimasu ka?*: 'Where's your company?'
>
> - When it's necessary to make clear who you're referring to, for example when there are several people in front of you, use the person's name to mean 'you' or 'your' (*Nakajima-san wa kaishain desu ka?/Nakajima-san no kaisha wa doko ni arimasu ka?*).

SPOTCHECK 8

@ How would you ask Mr Ino 'Are you a teacher (*sensei*)?' in the following situations?

a normally

b when there are several people listening

How would you ask where his school (*gakkō*) is in the same situations?

BUILD-UP CD ▶ 80

Here are some 'honorific' questions you might be asked or want to ask on first meeting someone (listen and repeat):

O-namae wa nan to iimasu ka?	What's your name?
O-shigoto wa nan desu ka?	What's your job?
O-tsutome wa dochira desu ka?	Where do you work?
O-kuni wa dochira desu ka?	Where are you from?
O-sumai wa dochira desu ka?	Where do you live?
Go-jūsho wa dochira desu ka?	What's your address?
(O-)denwa bangō wa nanban desu ka?	What's your phone number?

ANSWER CD ▶ 80

Rewind, and answer the above questions as if they'd been addressed to you. You can say ... *desu* each time.

PUT IT ALL TOGETHER CD ▶ 81

Play one part in a business introduction, following the procedure below. (Go on to the next instruction whenever you hear a tone.) The CD will play the other parts.

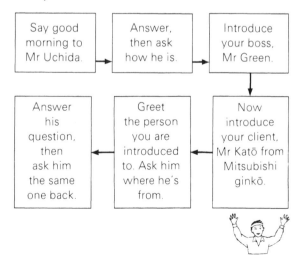

Say good morning to Mr Uchida.	→	Answer, then ask how he is.	→	Introduce your boss, Mr Green.

Answer his question, then ask him the same one back.	←	Greet the person you are introduced to. Ask him where he's from.	←	Now introduce your client, Mr Katō from Mitsubishi ginkō.

About Japan

Like all social types, the 'salary man' is a carefully moulded product. Given that Japan is a society of industry in which corporations are ranked into first, second and third 'streams', each company places considerable importance on what it considers to be the proper training of its employees. As we shall see in Unit 5, the school year starts and ends in the spring, and it is in April of every year that each company takes on its new employees. Although individual corporations will vary the contents of what they teach these recruits, all ichiryū companies tend to put their new employees through a two- to three-week induction programme which, in some cases, is similar to a series of army drilling sessions.

One vital element of this training period is to instil in the minds of the young men and women who were until recently students of one sort or another the fact that they are now full members of society (*shakaijin* – literally, 'society people'). The habits of their student days – including their manner of speaking, their posture and the way in which they wear their clothes – are inexorably criticised, as their new employers try to discipline them into being 'good company members'. A lot of this training includes lectures in all aspects of the company's business; some of it also involves the recruits in practising what they have learned in 'live' business situations.

Part of the induction process almost invariably includes lectures on manners and etiquette, and it is here that new employees learn, for example, how to bow and how to hand over their namecards in the proper manner. They are also taught how to answer the telephone properly and are reminded of the correct ways in which respect language should be used. (That it is not just foreigners who have difficulties using honorifics and so on should be a relief to anyone learning Japanese!)

Another important exercise in training is learning how to receive visitors, and recruits spend a lot of time acting out the parts of hosts ushering guests into a committee room, making sure that they sit in the right places and are served tea properly. Young people these days tend to take such training with the occasional pinch of salt, perhaps, but still women employees find themselves being obliged to learn how to measure tea leaves into a teapot, how full each cup should be (seven tenths), which is the 'front' and which the 'back' of a cup (in accordance with the manufacturer's seal on its base), at what temperature the tea should be (70 degrees Fahrenheit or 21 Centigrade) and how to serve guests in the proper order.

As if this were not enough, in some companies women are also instructed in how to sit in a chair properly, with bottoms half forward on the seat and legs placed together. They are then taught the most ladylike manner in which to stand up and sit down again, in such a way that their knees and ankles are revealed to their fullest perfection. In some organisations – department stores, for example – these lessons in deportment are accompanied by strict instruction in the special tones of voice to adopt on the telephone or in elevators.

In other words, while family life centres on the role of the mother/wife, Japan's society of industry is still male-dominated. Women are now more than mere office decoration, but there is a tendency to employ them to carry out less-important administration tasks that men are unwilling to perform.

Company induction ceremony

WHAT YOU'LL HEAR

WHERE DO YOU WORK?

CD ▶ 82

@ This is a romanised map of the busy Yamanote railway line, which encircles the central part of Tōkyō and connects all the major JR (Japan Railways) termini. Also shown is part of the Chūō line, which traverses central Tōkyō. JR station names are written on platforms in rōmaji as well as in kanji and hiragana, so you shouldn't have any difficulty getting out at the right stop. However, you'll find this kind of rōmaji map invaluable for planning journeys, and they are widely available.

Listen to the interviews on the CD. In each case, circle the place on the map which is mentioned and next to it write the occupation of the person who works there.

'AIZUCHI'

CD ▶ 83

@ Whereas in the West it's quite acceptable to make no noise at all and yet still appear to be a completely interested listener, in Japan people prefer to talk to the enthusiastic accompaniment of different kinds of background noise from people listening. These 'noises' are called 'aizuchi', and vary according to the tone of the speaker or what he or she is talking about. Here are four of the most common kinds of 'aizuchi' (listen to the CD to hear how they sound):

A Urging on
When you're listening to an exciting story and want to maintain the sense of pace: *'n, n'*, *'sō, sō'*, *'sō desu ka, sō desu ka'*.

B Understanding
To show your understanding of an explanation: *'e'*, *'hai'*, *'n'*.

C Showing sympathy
When you want to respond appropriately to something sad: *'ē'*, *'ā, sō desu ka'*, *'sō desu ne'*.

D Showing surprise
At the moment of revelation you can burst out with: *'hē?'*, *'hontō?'* (really?), *'ā, sō desu ka'*.

Now listen to the four conversations (1 to 4) on the CD. Although you won't understand what the speaker is talking about, try to identify what kind of 'aizuchi' the listener is mainly employing (A, B, C or D above). Write one 'aizuchi' letter next to each conversation number below:

1 _____   2 _____   3 _____   4 _____

'MOSHI MOSHI'

CD ▶ 84

@ Listen to six telephone conversations. The people on the left are making the calls; who are they talking to? Draw telephone leads (ordinary lines will do!) from the names on the left to the people on the right.

Sakamoto Eriko	boss
Aizawa Junji	son
Arai Masako	mother
Ogawa Shin'ichi	lover
Saitō Yuri	friend
Suzuki Takeshi	stranger

GETTING THERE ...

CD ▶ 85

@ Bill Green is on an exploratory six-month stay in Japan to assess the viability of setting up a business to market the franchising rights for a chain of computer shops. Not surprisingly, therefore, he has located his office in the heart of Akihabara, the electrical goods centre of Tōkyō. However, on his first working day he is somewhat disconcerted to be unable to find his own office!

Finally despairing, he rings the office and one of his Japanese staff tracks him down and guides him back. Listen to the conversation they have as they walk from Akihabara Station to the office. Draw the route they take, and mark the position of the office with a cross.

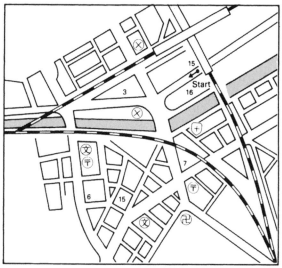

Akihabara, Tōkyō

WRITTEN JAPANESE

China, the country from which the Japanese borrowed their writing system, was the most sophisticated culture in Asia at the time. In China, Korea and Japan it was – and still is – known as the 'middle kingdom'; in Japanese, *chūgoku*.

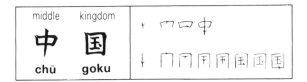

middle **中** **chū**	kingdom **国** **goku**	ʰ 一 口 口 中 ↓ 冂 冂 冃 同 囯 国 国

Along with a writing system, the Japanese borrowed many words from Chinese for which equivalents

didn't exist in their own language. This is the main reason why – as you read in the last unit – the same kanji can be read in different, apparently unrelated ways: *hito* and *jin*, for example, for 人, or *soto* and *gai* for 外. As a general rule, kanji occurring in isolation represent basic concepts, for which native Japanese words have always existed. Kanji were simply borrowed to represent these words, and in such cases are given what is called a 'kun' (native Japanese) reading (*hito* and *soto* are the 'kun' readings of 人 and 外 respectively). Words originally borrowed from Chinese are usually (though not always) more complex, requiring two or more kanji to write them. In these cases, the kanji are given what are known as 'on' (or Chinese-derived) readings (for example, *gai* and *jin* in 外人). To make this point clearer, here are a few new readings and combinations of some kanji you already know:

	国	外	内	中	人
'kun' reading	**kuni**	**soto**	**uchi**	**naka**	**hito**
meaning	country	outside	inside	middle	person

	外国	外(国)人	国内	中国	中国人
'on' reading	**gaikoku**	**gai(koku)jin**	**kokunai**	**chūgoku**	**chūgokujin**
meaning	abroad	foreigner	internal to a country	China	Chinese person

Although most characters in combination are given 'on' readings, Japanese surnames (though usually composed of two kanji) are an exception. The following 'kun' readings of some kanji you already know will serve you in good stead when it comes to understanding Japanese meishi:

木	林	森
ki/gi	**hayashi/bayashi**	**mori**
本	田	
moto	**ta/da**	

Hayashi (林) and Mori (森) are names in their own right, but most Japanese surnames are written with two (usually nature-related) characters, as in the following:

田中	Tanaka	(middle of the paddyfield)
中田	Nakata	(paddyfield in the middle)
内田	Uchida	(inside paddyfield)
森田	Morita	(forest paddyfield)

Paddyfields make frequent appearances in Japanese surnames, as do these two nature kanji:

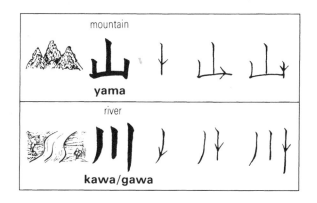

mountain

山

yama

river

川

kawa/gawa

@ Remembering that Japanese surnames are usually read in a 'kun' way, try reading these names aloud, then check your answers in the key and write the names in rōmaji to the right of the kanji. Also try to picture the places the original possessors of these names may have lived and worked in:

1	山川	**7**	川本
2	山田	**8**	山本
3	中川	**9**	中林
4	中山	**10**	内山
5	田山	**11**	木川
6	山中	**12**	本田

You may have got some of the pronunciations slightly wrong – *kawa* instead of *gawa*, for example, or *da* instead of *ta*; these sounds are very close in the Japanese sound system, and switches are made to make the names easier to say. 本田 (Honda), however, is something of an exception where Japanese names are concerned, *hon* (which you've already come across in 日本) being a Chinese-derived 'on' rather than a native Japanese 'kun' reading. Practise writing names 1 to 6 above, following the stroke orders given in this section (and on p. 46 for 田).

Finally, read aloud and translate these sentences:

	HIRAGANA
1 こちらは、本田の田中さんです。 **2** 内の山川です。 **3** あの女の人は、田中さんですか。 **4** 川田さんのお母さんは中国人ですか。	こ ち **ko chi**

LANGUAGE SUMMARY

Numbers
ichi, ni, san, yon (*or* shi), go, roku, nana (*or* shichi),
hachi, kyū, (*or* ku), zero
Hitotsume no ...
Futatsume no ...
Mittsume no ...

Company departments
jinjibu   eigyōbu
kokusaibu   sōmubu
keiribu   kōhōbu
māketingubu

Company positions
shachō
buchō
kachō

Places
byōin   jinja
kōban   gasorin sutando
yūbinkyoku   gakkō
o-tera   eki

Location
tonari   hantaigawa
chikaku   mae
soba   ushiro
saki   temae
e.g. Byōin no mae ni arimsasu

This way/That way
kochira/kotchi   sochira/sotchi
achira/atchi   dochira/dotchi?

Otsukaresama deshita!: 'You must be tired!' This
phrase may be heard at the end of a hard day's
work, often instead of *sayōnara*, to mean 'goodbye'.
If you're not feeling too tired, you may like to look
at these parts of the Grammar section: 'Saying
who' (2), 'Saying which or where' (4), 'Being and
having' (7), and 'Sentence building' (8A, D–J).

Using the telephone
Denwa bangō wa nanban desu ka?
Moshi moshi. OMC no Sakai desu ga ...
Yamada-san onegai shimasu/Yamada-san wa
    irasshaimasu ka?
Shōshō o-machi kudasai.
Chotto matte kudasai.
Yoroshiku onegai shimasu.
Shitsurei shimasu.
Gomen kudasai.

Confirming you have understood
Yūbinkyoko desu ne?
Hai, wakarimashita.

Taking a taxi/Giving directions
Eki made onegai shimasu.
Massugu itte kudasai.
Tsugi no kado de migi/hidari e magatte kudasai.
Asoko de tomete kudasai.
Koko de kekkō desu.

Introductions
Go-shōkai shimasu.
Kochira wa TDK no Asano-san desu.
Uchi no Ogawa desu.

Saying 'you'
• When necessary, use the person's name.

'Getting to know you' questions
O-shigoto wa nan desu ka?
O-tsutome wa dochira desu ka? *etc.*

Main language structures

Statement (describing location): ... ni arimasu.
Ōkubo 2–3 ni arimasu.

Question: ... ni arimasu ka?
Resutoran wa doko ni arimasu ka?

4
SHOPAROUND

The Japanese consumer
Department stores
Numbers
Colours
Shopping

About Japan

Foreigners used to regard Japan's postwar economic development as little short of a miracle. In the space of a mere forty years, the Japanese transformed themselves from a totally ruined and defeated nation to managers of one of the world's major economies. At the time, most commentators stressed the importance of manufactured goods and exports in Japan's economic development even though, as a percentage, exports counted for less of the country's gross national product than they did in the economies of either Britain or the United States. It was in fact as much domestic consumption as 'dumping' goods on foreign markets that kept Japan's economy healthy. Consumerism was the other side of the Japanese economy, the side that helped make the society of industry work.

In 1990, however, the economic 'bubble' built on the stock market and inflated land prices burst. Within a year, Japan found itself entering on its longest period of recession ever. Consumer confidence waned as the homes people had fought so hard to buy, as well as their carefully invested savings, rapidly lost their value. As successive infusions of government money failed to have an effect, politicians and businessmen realised that the country's economic structure needed a radical overhaul to meet new needs induced by the electronic revolution. This overhaul has been a slow and painful process, and has given foreign companies the opportunity to enter the Japanese market and buy up Japanese concerns. Some foreign individuals have even taken over the management of traditional Japanese companies – for example, Carlos Ghosn, who rescued Nissan from bankruptcy in the late 1990s.

Events such as these have encouraged a total re-evaluation among the Japanese of where they are heading in their lives, as well as of their country's position in the world today. Although consumerism may not be quite what it was, the domestic market still depends to some extent on how large corporations are organised. As we have seen, the Japanese company has tended to diversify by creating specialised subsidiaries, rather than through mergers and acquisitions (although this, too, is changing). Over the decades, some of the very largest corporations, originally established in this way, grew to form production, marketing and finance groups known as *keiretsu*. The Mitsui Group, for example, is centred on banking, real estate and trading, and includes 26 members and 171 affiliates in the areas of automobile manufacture, cement, electronics, insurance, mining, optics, paper, petrochemicals, shipping, steel, and so on. It also has loose business and financial relations with such corporate giants as Honda, Sony and Toyota.

What does this mean in terms of consumption? There are eleven of these keiretsu, each of which numbers several tens of thousands of employees; with their families they add up to several tens of thousands more, all of whom tend to consume products and services connected with their keiretsu. A member of the Mitsui Group, for example, will buy his house from Mitsui Homes, drive a Toyota car, and stay at a Mitsui-run hotel while travelling on business. His wife will shop at Mitsukoshi Department Store in Nihonbashi and make use of a Mitsui Sumitomo credit card to pay for her purchases. When they go out together, they will drink Asahi beer and when they buy electronic equipment, their preference may well be for something made by Toshiba. Keiretsu thus act as a simple and very effective method of direct selling in Japan's domestic market.

Keio department store, Shinjuku, Tōkyō

NUMBERS

SUMS
CD ▸ 86

@ Look back at p. 53, where you came across the numbers 1 to 9 and zero. To refresh your memory, try some simple arithmetic. The tape will ask you ten sums, using the words *tasu* (plus) or *hiku* (minus). Write the sums down, work them out, then tell the CD the answer. The CD will follow up with what you should have said. Listen as the CD talks you through the first two. From then on you're on your own.

E.g. (1) *CD:* **6 + 2 = 8**
     (2) *CD:* **4 − 1 = 3**

10	jū	300	sanbyaku
14	jūyon	600	roppyaku
19	jūkyū	800	happyaku
28	nijūhachi	1000	(is)sen
37	sanjūnana	3000	sanzen
46	yonjūroku	8000	hassen
55	gojūgo	10 000	ichiman
64	rokujūyon	20 000	niman
73	nanajūsan	100 000	jūman
82	hacahiūni	1 000 000	hyakuman
91	kyūjūichi	10 000 000	issenman
100	hyaku	100 000 000	ichioku

CD ▸ 87

Listen to some of the numbers above being pronounced on the CD. Point to each number as you practise saying it yourself.

SPOTCHECK 1

@ How would you say the following numbers in Japanese?

a 13 b 56 c 67 d 84 e 99 f 200 g 350 h 999

TAKE NOTE

The easy thing about counting in Japanese is the almost totally regular system and word order. The difficult thing is that, since in large numbers English bases itself on units of a thousand and Japanese on *man* (10 000s), things get very confusing. The only way to familiarise yourself is through practice.

WRITE

@ Write the following words as numbers:

1 sen yonhyaku gojūhachi   **5** rokuman hassen nanahyaku yon
2 nanajūni   **6** nisen hyaku nanajū
3 ichiman gosen   **7** nanajūgoman
4 ichiman yonhyaku ichi   **8** sanbyaku gojūman

LISTEN
CD ▸ 88

@ Listen and write down the numbers you hear. (There will be ten altogether.)

E.g. (1) *CD:* **roppyaku sanjūgo**
         You write 635.

SAY
CD ▸ 89

Say the following numbers. The CD will follow up each time with what you should have said:

1 4205   **2** 54361   **3** 107   **4** 2873   **5** 102491
6 7981   **7** 85   **8** 15032   **9** 575   **10** 450600

MORE SUMS
CD ▸ 90

@ Some more arithmetic! The procedure for this exercise is exactly the same as in 'Sums' above. Write down the problems (there are ten of them altogether), work out the answer, speak that answer, then listen as the CD tells you what you should have said.

PRICES;
COUNTING OBJECTS

Like anywhere else, Japan, despite the universal emphasis on quality, is still a nation full of people who appreciate keen pricing. Shops, especially supermarkets, have to fight hard for custom, and they do this in two ways: first, through the use of advertisements (*kōkoku*) and glossy inserts in the local papers, and second, by bombarding the customer, once in the shop, with announcements about *o-kaidokuhin*: 'special offers'.

> • To say how much something costs (in *yen*):
> **... -en desu.**
> E.g. 'It's ¥100': *Hyaku-en desu.*

JAPANESE LIVE 1   CD ▶ 91

@ Look at this list of *o-kaidokuhin*. All the names of items are derived from English words; try to work out what they are, and check your answers before proceeding.

@   Now listen to the announcements in the supermarket where these things are on offer, and fill in the prices.

bēkon 100g	¥ _____
sarada 100g	¥ _____
tsunakan 1 (ikko)	¥ _____
piza 2 (nimai)	¥ _____
tomato 2 (niko)	¥ _____
kyabetsu 1 (ikko)	¥ _____
banana 4 (yonhon)	¥ _____
jamu 1 (ikko)	¥ _____
painappuru 1 (ikko)	¥ _____
tomatosōsu 1 (ippon)	¥ _____
batā 1 (ikko)	¥ _____
yōguruto 4 (yonko)	¥ _____

yasui desu yo!	it's cheap! (**yo** emphasises the preceding words)
irasshaimase!	welcome! (the standard greeting in any shop you enter)
shinsen desu yo!	it's fresh!

HOW MUCH?   CD ▶ 92

The CD will give you cues to the list of items. Looking at the price you wrote down next to the item, say how much it costs.

E.g. *CD:* **piza**
You: **Piza wa hyaku gojūhachi-en desu.**

TAKE NOTE

COUNTERS

You'll have noticed the words like *ikko, nimai* and *yonhon* to the right of some of the items above. Look now at the first paragraph of part 10 in the Grammar section ('Counters', p. 299) to find out more about these words.

To count any object, the Japanese usually add a so-called 'counter' (*-ko, -mai, -hon* etc.) to the numbers you've been practising; unfortunately there are seemingly countless counters, differing according to the size, shape and other properties of the objects in question. However, you'll be introduced to an easier way of counting later in the unit. For the moment, just concentrate on *understanding* some of the counters.

SHOPPING LISTS   CD ▶ 93

@ Listen to what three different people (1 to 3) are going to buy in the supermarket. Note down which of the items in 'Japanese live 1' and how much or how many of each item they want to buy. Then work out the total cost of each shopping list according to the prices you wrote down in 'Japanese live 1'.

CLOTHES AND COLOURS

Kuniko

kutsushita

baggu

surippa

pansuto

sukāto

O-kā-san

burausu

beruto

bōshi

wanpiisu

bura(jā)

Takeshi

suniikā

sētā

zubon

pantsu

shatsu

O-tō-san

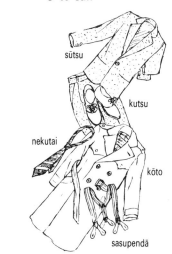

sūtsu

kutsu

nekutai

kōto

sasupendā

CLOTHES

CD ▶ 94

A Look at the picture for one minute, trying to remember who each item of clothing belongs to: is it Kuniko's (*Kuniko no*), Takeshi's (*Takeshi no*), mother's (*o-kā-san no*), or father's (*o-tō-san no*)? Then cover the picture. The CD will give the name of an item of clothing; say (from memory) who it belongs to.

E.g. (1) *CD:* **Sūtsu wa?**

You: **Sūtsu wa o-tō-san no desu.**

B Look at the picture for another minute, then cover it and try to write down the names of all the clothes belonging to each person, in this order: **1** Takeshi, **2** his mother, **3** Kuniko, **4** her father.

Check by looking again at the picture.

COLOURS

CD ▶ 95

Listen and repeat:

nani'iro?	what colour?	**guriin**	green
kuro	black	**burū**	blue
shiro	white	**murasaki**	purple
aka	red	**pinku**	pink
kiiro	yellow	**gurē**	grey
chairo	brown	**orenji**	orange

- To say 'and': **to**
  E.g. 'pink and grey'   **pinku to gurē**
  'pink, grey and purple'   **pinku to gurē to murasaki**

FLAGS

CD ▶ 96

Can you say what colours are in the flags of these nations? As you grow in confidence, cover up the colour words on the left.

1 igirisu   **4** chūgoku   **7** itaria (Italy)
2 nihon   **5** doitsu   **8** airurando
3 burajiru   **6** amerika
  E.g. (1) *CD:* igirisu
    You: **aka to shiro to burū**

TAKE NOTE

Guriin and *burū* are replaced respectively by the Japanese words *midori* and *ao* when describing natural phenomena such as grass or the sky. The 'go!' lamps of traffic lights are also described as *ao* (a rather vague word, which can – as in this case – mean 'green' as well as 'blue').

Shoppers being welcomed by sales staff

COLOURING IN

CD ▶ 97

@ For this activity you'll need crayons in all the colours listed on the previous page. Listen to the descriptions of the three models below, and colour in the appropriate item of clothing with the colour indicated.

E.g. *CD:* **Miyahara-san no wanpiisu wa burū desu.**

→You colour Ms Miyahara's dress blue.

TAKE NOTE

So far you've been saying things like 'it's red' (*aka desu*) or 'it's pink' (*pinku desu*), but what happens when you want to say, for example, '(the) red dress' or '(some) pink shoes'? The colour words divide into two groups, according to whether you have to add *i* before a noun (e.g. *akai wanpiisu*) or *no* (e.g. *pinku no kutsu*):

1 *kuro, shiro, aka, kiiro, chairo, ao → kuroi, shiroi, akai, kiiroi, chairoi, aoi* + noun
2 all the other colours → colour word + **no** + noun

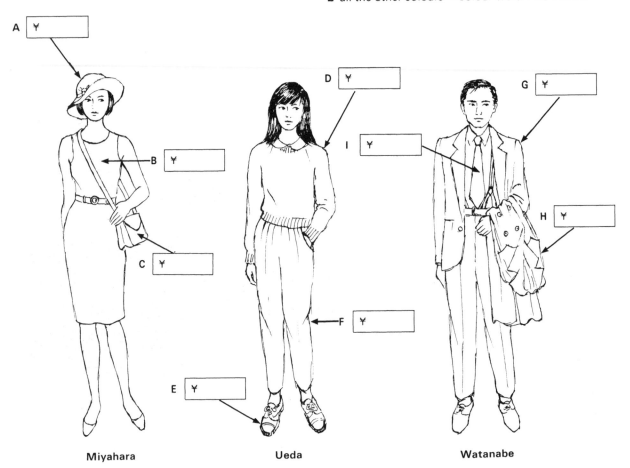

Miyahara　　　　　　Ueda　　　　　　Watanabe

SPOTCHECK 2

@ Translate the following into Japanese:

a (the) black suit
b (a) blue sweater
c (the) brown shoes
d (a) white hat
e (the) green bag
f (some) orange trousers

MEMORY TEST

CD ▶ 98

Memorise who's wearing each piece of clothing in the picture opposite, then cover it. The CD will test your powers of memory by naming items of clothing; you have to say whose that item is.

E.g. (1) *CD:* **Burū no wanpiisu wa?**
You: **Burū no wanpiisu wa Miyahara-san no desu.**

• To ask how much something costs: ... **wa ikura desu ka?**

HOW MUCH?

CD ▶ 99

The bottom line! Ask the CD, in order, how much the items in the picture labelled A to I cost. Always mention the colour of the item.

E.g. (A) *You:* **Akai bōshi wa ikura desu ka?**
CD: **Niman-en desu.**

@ Write the prices on the labels.

Stalls in a shopping street (*shōtengai*)

About Japan

One secret of marketing is the organisation of people, and one of the key factors behind the success of Japanese department chains is their far-reaching organisation and marketing.

One vital part of this organisation is transport. A number of Japanese department stores – like Seibu and Tōkyū, for instance – owe their origins to the private railway lines that these companies operate between the city centre and the suburbs and whose termini are located at the bottom of the department stores themselves. By conveying hundreds of thousands of people every morning and evening through their vast emporia, these stores have been able to build up enormous marketing keiretsu groups.

The end result of shrewd business methods and the clever organisation of people is that those living along the Seibu railway lines, for example, will have bought their land and homes from a member company of the Seibu group, travel by Seibu trains, support the Seibu Lions baseball team, shop in the local Seiyū supermarket and also at the Seibu department store, making use of their Saison credit cards. They may also be members of a Seibu-owned golf club which can only be reached by travelling on a Seibu train to the nearest station and then boarding a Seibu-operated bus or taxi. Day in, day out, from morning to night, therefore, almost all the money a man and his family spend will be going into the coffers of the Saison Group (as the Seibu keiretsu is known).

Of course, not all department stores (or *depāto*, as they are called in Japan) are quite so powerful. Nor do they all owe their origins to private railway businesses. Some of the more traditional stores, like Mitsukoshi and Takashimaya, started out as drapery stores in the Edo Period (1603–1868) and boast a long tradition of service to customers, who often come from far afield to shop at their central Tōkyō stores in Nihonbashi and the Ginza. These stores, too, carefully target their customers and in some cases sell more through direct mailing than in their main stores.

Very sensibly, department stores – like most shops in Japan – make sure that they are open when normal offices are closed. In Japan, there is no equivalent of the Christian Church to influence government regulations and thereby hold back consumerism. By staying open on Saturdays and Sundays every week of the year, retailers invite the invasion of throngs of salary men and their families.

One of the showpieces of every department store is its food hall. Here you can find almost anything, from Japanese *sashimi* (raw fish) and pickled vegetables (*o-tsukemono*) to imported jams and salami sausages, not to mention ready-cooked foods, de luxe chocolates, newly baked breads, roasted coffee, and seemingly endless supplies of locally – and not so locally – brewed sake, whisky and wine (to name but a few of the kinds of alcohol on sale). Not here, however, the staid elegance of Harrods. In the food halls of Japanese department stores there is a cacophony of noise, as male and female assistants vie to outdo one another with their sales cries of *irasshaimase* (welcome!) and *ikaga deshō ka?* (how about this?).

The food hall is invariably located in the basement (*chika*), and – in major cities – almost equally invariably connected both to the nearest underground (or railway) station and to an underground shopping street (*chikagai*), where a whole array of stores can be found, many of them serving food of one kind or another. Of course, a lot of housewives shop at local supermarkets (*sūpā*) and greengrocers (*yaoya*), where the personal touch is still considered important. Often these family-run stores are located in covered shopping streets (*shōtengai*) lined with large sprays of plastic pink and yellow flowers and loud-speakers broadcasting a discreet combination of orchestral music and advertisements to entertain shoppers.

Of these there are usually plenty. There is something about shopping centres with their milling throngs that encourages people to spend their money, even during an extended recession. Men and women, old and young, walk in and out of fashion boutiques (*butikku*), coffee shops (*kissaten*), bookshops *(honya)*, jewellery shops (*hōsekiya*) and chemist's (*kusuriya*). For the Japanese, shopping is a major leisure pursuit.

Sake barrels

SHOPPING (1): ASKING WHETHER SOMETHING'S IN STOCK

- To attract the attention of a shop assistant: **onegai shimasu!** or **sumimasen!** (often pronounced **suimasen!**)

- To ask whether something's in stock: **... wa arimasu ka?**: 'Do you have/Are there any ...?'

- Very polite equivalents of **arimasu** ('there is/are') or **arimasen** ('there isn't/aren't') are, respectively, **gozaimasu** and **gozaimasen**. Shop assistants usually reply using these polite forms.

JAPANESE LIVE 2

CD ▶ 100

Tomoko Sakai goes shopping.

Tomoko	Onegai shimasu!
Shop assistant	Hai, irasshaimase.
Tomoko	Sumimasen, sukāto wa arimasu ka?
Shop assistant	Hai, kochira ni gozaimasu.
Tomoko	Beruto mo arimasu ka?
Shop assistant	Beruto wa chotto gozaimasen ga ...
	Rewind and repeat!

kochira ni gozaimasu	there are some here/here are some/they're here
chotto gozaimasen ga ...	I'm afraid there aren't any (**chotto** and **ga ...** have the effect of softening the bad news)

SPOTCHECK 3
@ **a** What kind of shop are they in?
b What isn't in stock?

TAKE NOTE

Since the 'honoured' customer (*o-kyaku-sama*) is not merely king or queen but a 'god' in Japan (*o-kyaku-sama wa kami-sama desu*, as the saying goes), shop assistants tend to use extremely formal language. You'll be greeted with a polite *irasshaimase!* (to which no reply is necessary) almost everywhere you shop, and you'll often hear the formal equivalents of *desu* (*de gozaimasu*), *arimasu* (*gozaimasu*) and *arimasen* (*gozaimasen*).

ASK

CD ▶ 101

The CD will tell you the names of some items of clothing. Practise asking whether that item is in stock.
E.g. (1) *CD:* **zubon**
You: **Zubon wa arimasu ka?**

BUILD-UP

Here are some items you might want to ask for in a chemist's (*kusuriya*):

shanpū	handokuriimu
rinsu	rippukuriimu
sutairingu rōshon	hea burashi
tisshu	firumu

SPOTCHECK 4
@ Those words are all derived from English. Can you guess what they mean?

WHAT'S IN STOCK?

CD ▶ 102

@ In the *kusuriya*, ask whether each of the items in 'Build-up' above is in stock. Make a question with the word the CD supplies and listen for the reply. If the item is in stock, put a tick next to the name of the item above. If it isn't, put a cross.
E.g. (1) *CD:* **rinsu**
You: **Rinsu wa arimasu ka?**
CD: **Chotto gozaimasen ga ...**
→ Put a cross next to **rinsu**.

SHOPPING (2): GETTING JUST WHAT YOU WANT

If you're shown something you like, you can say *ii desu ne*, or use one of the other appreciative words you came across on p. 29. But what happens when the goods you're offered aren't quite what you were hoping for?

JAPANESE LIVE 3

CD ▸ 103

Tomoko Sakai is in a shoe shop (*kutsuya*).

Tomoko	Sumimasen, <u>burū no surippa</u> wa arimasu ka? *A*
Shop assistant	Hai, gozaimasu. Kore wa ikaga desu ka?
Tomoko	Chotto ōkii desu ne. *B*
Shop assistant	(*showing her another pair*) Kore wa dō desu ka?
Tomoko	(*trying them on*) Ā, chōdo ii desu ne.

Rewind and repeat!

ikaga desu ka?	how about these? (more polite than **dō desu ka?**)
chotto ōkii	a little big
chōdo ii	just right

SPOTCHECK 5

@ What's wrong with the first pair of slippers?

BUILD-UP

To describe something in Japanese is usually quite easy: most adjectives (descriptive words) are simply placed before the word they describe, as in **akai** *sētā* ('a red sweater'). However, the linking word *no* needs to be inserted after some words (**burū no surippa**, for example), and after certain other adjectives *na* is required (for example, **kirei na** *wanpiisu*: 'a pretty dress'). Apart from colours (listed on p. 83), here are all the adjectives you've encountered so far, together with some useful new ones. Review the old, remembering which ones take *na*, and learn the new.

OLD			
ii	mushiatsui	subarashii	ōkii
atsui	atatakai	omoshiroi	chiisai
samui	suzushii	muzukashii	sugoi
oishii	atarashii	kawaii	yasui
iya (na)	suteki (na)	benri (na)	kirei (na)

NEW	
takai (*expensive/high*)	omoi (*heavy*)
nagai (*long*)	karui (*light*)
mijikai (*short*)	furui (*old*)
kantan (na) (*easy*)	fuben (na) (*inconvenient*)

SPOTCHECK 6

@ Translate into Japanese:

a a new house   **d** delicious cake
b a handy bag   **e** a great (*suteki*) dress
c a difficult textbook   **f** a grey skirt

GET WHAT YOU WANT!

CD ▸ 104

@ Take the part of Tomoko in 'Japanese live 3', and at the point marked *A* replace her underlined words with the Japanese for one of the items below. At point *B*, give the reason you're unhappy with the sample offered. (The reason is on the right below.) Rewind the CD each time: the shop assistant's words are always the same.

1 a cheap radio (*rajio*)   – too expensive
2 a handy camera (*kamera*)   – too inconvenient
3 some long socks (*kutsushita*)   – too short
4 a light TV set (*terebi*)   – too heavy
5 an easy book (*hon*)   – too difficult

89

SHOPPING (3): DECIDING TO BUY

> • To say you'd like to buy something:
> **... (o) kudasai.** (lit. 'Please give me ...')
> E.g. *Kore (o) kudasai*: 'I'd like this'.
>
> • To ask for more than one of something:
> **... (o)** (quantity) **kudasai.**
> E.g. *Banana (o) nihon kudasai*: 'I'd like two bananas.'

BUILD-UP
CD ▶ 105

As you'll remember, there are different 'counters' for different sizes, shapes and types of objects; for example, bananas – being long and relatively thin – are counted with *-hon*, whereas flat things like pizzas are counted with *-mai*. However, there is an escape route! Rather than using the words the Japanese borrowed from Chinese (*ichi, ni, san*, etc.), which, as in Chinese, must be associated with a counter, it is possible to use the original Japanese numbers below, on their own, to count *anything*. These numbers only go up to ten, but this should suffice for shopping.

Listen and say:

1 hitotsu	**5** itsutsu	**8** yattsu
2 futatsu	**6** muttsu	**9** kokonotsu
3 mittsu	**7** nanatsu	**10** tō
4 yottsu		

SPOTCHECK 7

@ How would you ask for
  a two hairbrushes
  b four bottles of shampoo
  c three boxes of tissues
  d seven of 'this'?

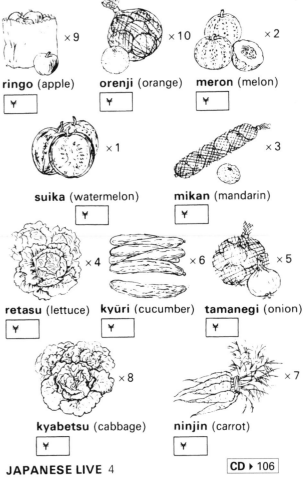

ringo (apple) ¥☐ ×9
orenji (orange) ¥☐ ×10
meron (melon) ¥☐ ×2

suika (watermelon) ¥☐ ×1
mikan (mandarin) ¥☐ ×3

retasu (lettuce) ¥☐ ×4
kyūri (cucumber) ¥☐ ×6
tamanegi (onion) ¥☐ ×5

kyabetsu (cabbage) ¥☐ ×8
ninjin (carrot) ¥☐ ×7

JAPANESE LIVE 4
CD ▶ 106

@ Listen to three different conversations in which people ask for things in a greengrocer's (*yaoya*). Note down what fruit or vegetables, and how many of each, they ask for.

YOUR TURN
CD ▶ 107

@ The CD will say, in turn, the names of the fruit and vegetables in the picture. Ask how much they cost, write the price beside the yen sign, and go on to ask for the quantity indicated next to the picture.

E.g. (1) *CD:* **ringo**
You: **Ringo wa ikura desu ka?**
CD: **Nihyaku-en desu.**
You: **Kokonotsu kudasai.**

SHOPPING (4):
PUTTING IT ALL TOGETHER

> • To ask to be shown something you can say:
> **... (o) misete kudasai.**
> E.g. *Ano akai sētā o misete kudasai*: 'Please show me that red sweater.'

JAPANESE LIVE 5 | CD ▸ 108

@ Robbie Walker goes shopping. Listen and fill in the gaps.

Robbie	Sumimasen!
Shop assistant	Hai, irasshaimase.
Robbie	_____ o misete kudasai. ← wa arimasu ka?
Shop assistant	Hai, dōzo.
Robbie	Ikura desu ka?
Shop assistant	_____ -en de gozaimasu.
Robbie	Jā, _____ kudasai. — —
Shop assistant	Hai, _____ -en de gozaimasu. **Rewind and repeat!**

SPOTCHECK 8

@ What kind of shop is it (in Japanese)?

LISTEN | CD ▸ 109

@ Listen to the CD. What do the three shoppers buy and how much do they spend? Fill in these three charts:

1

Item	Quantity	Price
		¥
		¥
	TOTAL	¥

2

Item	Quantity	Price
		¥
		¥
	TOTAL	¥

3

Item	Quantity	Price
		¥
		¥
	TOTAL	¥

GO SHOPPING | CD ▸ 110

@ With the three shopping lists below, go into **1** a *butikku* (boutique), **2** a *kusuriya* and **3** a *yaoya*. Using 'Japanese live 5' as a model, ask either to be shown the first thing on your list or whether or not it's stocked in the shop. Follow the dialogue down, note down the price for the item, and ask for the required quantity. Then loop back to ask about the next item on your list. When it comes to the final total, check that this tallies with the prices you've noted down:

1	**2**	**3**
red blouse × 2	lipsalve × 2	apple × 8
yellow sweater × 1	film × 4	orange × 5
white underpants × 6	shampoo × 1	lettuce × 9

About Japan

Japanese department stores are not simply places where people spend their money and get nothing in return, apart from the goods that they have purchased. They provide people with 'Culture'. One or two stores, like Seibu for example, have their own 'art museums', in which they display anything from French Impressionist paintings to traditional Japanese arts and crafts. Other stores, such as Mitsukoshi, house their own 'culture centres', where members can attend theatre performances or practise tennis on roof-top courts.

Department stores developed their museums of art and culture centres as a means of competing – and competing successfully – with supermarket chains. Nevertheless, their apparent passion for art has to be seen to be believed. At one stage, every major store used to hold an art exhibition of one kind or another for most weeks of the year. Almost all department stores throughout Japan had at least one – and often two or more – art galleries, in which *sumi-e* brush and ink painters, kimono dyers, textile weavers, potters, calligraphers, sculptors and so on could show their creations to the public.

Naturally, stores do not lend their gallery space for free, but usually charge a commission of 30 per cent (it may be more or less, depending on which store you use and who you are in the art world) on all sales. One craft which Japan's department stores have promoted from early on in this century has been pottery, and in many respects the success of contemporary forms of traditional pottery can be attributed to their clever marketing of the works of such famous potters as Hamada Shōji, Kawai Kanjirō, Tomimoto Kenkichi and the Englishman Bernard Leach. Nowadays, famous potters can expect to make as much as ¥100 million from a one-man show. Indeed, many become famous precisely because of their ability to sell their works, rather than because of any apparent inherent quality therein.

For major exhibitions where works of art are not for sale, the public will usually be required to pay an entrance fee. This in itself is not enough, however, to cover the cost of putting on such a show, and, although exhibitions are sometimes sponsored by a major newspaper like the *Asahi* or *Yomiuri*, it would seem at times as if Japan's department stores are themselves footing the bill for the average person's desire to consume art in all its various forms.

Exhibition of Jill Fanshawe Kato and Yosei Itaka's pottery in the Matsuya Department Store, Tōkyō

That they are not doing so should be made clear, even though department stores will themselves claim that they are performing a cultural role normally taken over by governments in other countries. Although the heyday of the 'blockbuster' exhibition – common in the 1970s – is now over, it should be realised that when a store such as Mitsukoshi puts on a major exhibition of Renoir's work and draws in an average of 10 000 people a day, its daily turnover is said to increase by almost half a million pounds! This is enough to pay for the costs of putting on the exhibition in question and to make a handsome profit into the bargain.

As to whether it is a bargain for the consumer, of course, it is hard to say. But, for better or for worse, Japan's department stores have long been closely involved in the production and consumption of *Bunka* – Culture!

FINDING YOUR WAY AROUND A DEPARTMENT STORE

DEPARTMENTS

CD ▸ 111

@ Below are some words for departments in a *depāto* (department store). To find out what the words mean, listen to the tape. You'll hear each of the words below, followed by the names of three items you'd expect to be able to buy in that department. Using these three words as clues (all of them are words borrowed from English), draw lines from the department names in the middle to the corresponding symbols on the right.

電気製品	denkiseihin	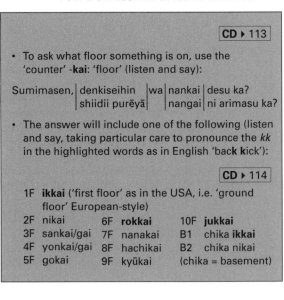
食料品	shokuryōhin	
紳士用品	shinshiyōhin	
婦人用品	fujinyōhin	
化粧品	keshōhin	
アクセサリー	akusesarii	
スポーツ用品	supōtsuyōhin	

BUILD-UP

CD ▸ 111

Above right are the names of the items you've just heard on the CD. However, the words are mixed up. Without listening to the CD again, regroup them (by drawing lines) according to what department they're sold in; if you can't work out what all of the words mean, look them up in the index.

Check you grouped the words correctly by rewinding the CD. This time, repeat the words, using the pause button.

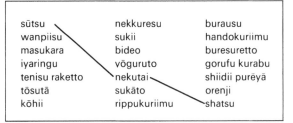

sūtsu	nekkuresu	burausu
wanpiisu	sukii	handokuriimu
masukara	bideo	buresuretto
iyaringu	vōguruto	gorufu kurabu
tenisu raketto	nekutai	shiidii purēya
tōsutā	sukāto	orenji
kōhii	rippukuriimu	shatsu

- To say 'department': **uriba**
  E.g. 'electrical goods department':
  denkiseihin uriba

WHICH DEPARTMENT?

CD ▸ 112

The CD will ask you where some articles from among those listed above (in 'Build-up') can be found. Reply with the name of a department (. . . *uriba ni arimasu*), trying to do so from memory. The CD will follow up with what you should have said.

E.g. (1) *CD:* **Bideo wa doko ni arimasu ka?**
You: **Denkiseihin uriba ni arimasu.**

CD ▸ 113

- To ask what floor something is on, use the 'counter' -**kai**: 'floor' (listen and say):

Sumimasen,	denkiseihin	wa	nankai	desu ka?
	shiidii purēya		nangai	ni arimasu ka?

- The answer will include one of the following (listen and say, taking particular care to pronounce the *kk* in the highlighted words as in English 'bac**k k**ick'):

CD ▸ 114

1F **ikkai** ('first floor' as in the USA, i.e. 'ground floor' European-style)

2F	nikai	6F	**rokkai**	10F	**jukkai**
3F	sankai/gai	7F	nanakai	B1	chika **ikkai**
4F	yonkai/gai	8F	hachikai	B2	chika nikai
5F	gokai	9F	kyūkai		(chika = basement)

READING

@ Below is a store guide from a small department store. Find the kanji which appear in 'Departments' on the opposite page, and create a pictorial guide by drawing symbols for those departments into the chart beneath it.

4	文具、おもちゃ、本、スポーツ用品
3	紳士用品、着物、ジュエリー、電気製品
2	婦人用品、子供服、ベビーウェアー
1	靴、化粧品、アクセサリー
B1	パン屋、酒、食料品、寿司

4F
3F
2F
1F
B1

WHAT FLOOR?   CD ▶ 115

The CD will ask you where certain departments are. Look at the pictorial chart you've just made in order to answer.

E.g. (1) *CD:* **Sumimasen, denkiseihin wa nankai ni arimasu ka?**
You: **Sangai ni arimasu.**

YOUR TURN   CD ▶ 116

This time, you ask the questions. You want to know where to find the departments or items on the left below.

E.g. (1) *You:* **Sumimasen, shokuryōhin wa nankai ni arimasu ka?**

@ On hearing the answers, draw lines from the words on the left to the appropriate floors on the right below.

1 foodstuffs
2 cameras
3 women's goods
4 bags
5 make-up
6 earrings
7 sports goods
8 kimonos (*kimono*)
9 public telephone (*kōshū denwa*)

8F
7F
6F
5F
4F
3F
2F
1F
B1
B2

日本

About Japan

Is it politicians or the leaders of big business who run Japan? Or is it perhaps the large advertising agencies like Dentsū and Hakuhōdō? It is the latter that are involved in the creation of 'events', and Japanese agencies tend to adopt a far broader role than that normally played by their counterparts in the West. By taking an active part in the promotion of marathon races, pop concerts, art exhibitions, opera performances, car rallies, athletics games, film festivals and even a papal visit, advertising agencies in Japan might more properly be called 'total communication agencies'. One of these, Dentsū, is the largest single agency in the world.

Ad agencies are also responsible in one way or another for the vast number of advertisements with which the Japanese are bombarded in their everyday lives. Up to half of the thirty-two pages of each of the five national daily newspapers is devoted to advertising. A similar proportion would seem to be the rule for the 2000 or so magazines published weekly, fortnightly, monthly, quarterly and biannually in Japan. Eight minutes of every hour of television are devoted to the showing of commercials on each of the five private national networks, twenty-four hours a day, 365 days a year (except for a two-day rest from advertising when the Emperor Shōwa died in January 1989).

But advertising in Japan is not limited to four main media of television, radio, newspapers and magazines, as well as the Internet. You can find it on rooftop and roadside billboards, on clothing, calendars, bags, balloons, lighters, ashtrays and station platforms, lining the carriages of suburban and underground trains, and on the inside and outside of city buses. You can also find it in less expected places: in the middle of ricefields, for example, or on bus-stop benches, mountainsides, umbrella stands, trees, lamp posts, telephone cards, concert tickets, bank statements, neighbourhood notice boards, shrine amulets, sewer pipes, fire hydrants, bath mats, in all kinds of free handout (demanded by a society that values high quality service) – the list goes on and on. It is also prominent as part of product placement in television series. It would seem that it is impossible to escape from advertising in Japan.

The fine line that distinguishes information from publicity is blurred by the fact that many of the apparently objective articles in newspapers and magazines are in fact paid for by sponsoring companies. This means that advertisers not only have the opportunity to promote their products, but to influence the average consumer's attitudes towards the world at large by paying for certain kinds of information-publicity. This does not, of course, happen all the time in all the media and it is certainly not only in Japan that we find such advertorials or 'spin'. A lot, too, depends on how buoyant the economy is: when it is strong and advertising demand is high, media can afford to ignore their sponsors' demands; when there is a recession and companies no longer clamour to buy advertising time or space, media organisations are more inclined to cooperate. This means that corporations not only promote cultural events and consumerism in general; they simultaneously control the dissemination of certain types of information to the public.

Left Sunday shopping crowds in Harajuku, Tōkyō

WHAT YOU'LL HEAR

WHAT'S IT LIKE?
CD ▶ 117

@ Listen to five interviews with customers in different types of store. Each customer describes the price, colour and size of the thing he or she has come to buy, without saying precisely what it is. Try to match the customers' descriptions (1 to 5) with the pictures below, writing numbers next to the drawings. (One of the objects is not described; which one?)

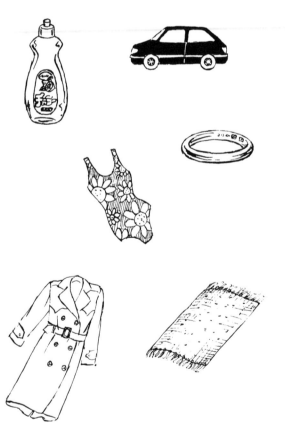

AND IT DOES 190!
CD ▶ 118

@ Listen to three conversations (1 to 3) between a car salesman and potential customers. They come in to look at different models, and have a lot of questions about the specifications of the car they're interested in. Write the figures given in the appropriate boxes below. You'll notice a lot of fashionable Japanese English, which should help you: *supiido, fōdoa, gasorin*, etc.

	1	2	3
Top speed (km/h)			
No. of doors			
Fuel consumption (km/l)			
c.c.			
Price (¥)			

Now match each of the cars described above (1 to 3) with one of the models below:

A ___   B ___   C ___

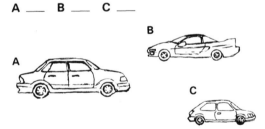

DESIRABLE RESIDENCE (WITH ADJOINING SHRINE!)
CD ▶ 119

@ Estate agents in Japan tend to be small, independently-run businesses mostly dealing with property within a two- to three-mile radius. Since Japanese home-owners rarely sell their homes, the market is almost entirely in rented *manshon* (concrete apartment blocks) or cheaper *apāto* (less solidly constructed blocks of flats). A typical estate agent's window might look something like this:

マンション 西早稲田 2LDK 180,000 **1**	マンション 高田馬場 1ルーム 90,000 **2**
マンション 西早稲田 2DK 130,000 **3**	マンション 大久保 2DK 140,000 **4**
アパート 大久保 1DK 30,000 **5**	アパート 高田馬場 2DK 100,000 **6**
アパート 高田馬場 3DK 150,000 **7**	アパート 高田馬場 2LDK 90,000 **8**
アパート 西早稲田 1DK 75,000 **9**	アパート 西早稲田 3DK 135,000 **10**

Listen to two customers asking about some of the *manshon* and *apāto* on the left. Write the numbers of the flats discussed, in the order they're mentioned. Finally, write the number of the place they ask to be shown around.

1 _____ _____ _____ finally: _____
2 _____ _____ _____ finally: _____

GOING UP ... CD ▶ 120

@ In Tōkyō (less so in the country) shopping in a department store is styled as an 'experience', and part of that experience is the very high level of customer service. As you take a lift, you'll be bombarded with a barrage of information about what the store has to offer by the immaculate, uniformed lift attendant. Listen to a typical trip in a lift and work out on what floors the departments on the left are located. Draw lines from the department names to the appropriate floors on the right.

denkiseihin

shokuryōhin

shinshiyōhin

fujinyōhin

keshōhin

akusesarii

supōtsuyōhin

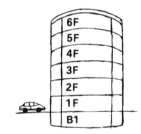

L =	Living room
DK =	Dining room combined with kitchen
2DK =	Two rooms plus dining room/kitchen
1ルーム	= 'One room' (studio flat)
マンション	= *manshon*
アパート	= *apāto*

西早稲田	= Nishi-Waseda
高田馬場	= Takadanobaba
大久保	= Ōkubo

99

WRITTEN JAPANESE

When you're out shopping, some of the most useful kanji are obviously going to be those for numbers. Here are the kanji for 1 to 9, accompanied by Chinese-derived ('on') and native Japanese ('kun') readings with which you're already familiar:

	one	two	three	four	five	six	seven	eight	nine
	一	二	三	四	五	六	七	八	九
'on'	ichi	ni	san	shi	go	roku	shichi	hachi	ku/kyū
'kun'	hito	futa	mi	yo	itsu	mu	nana	ya	kokono

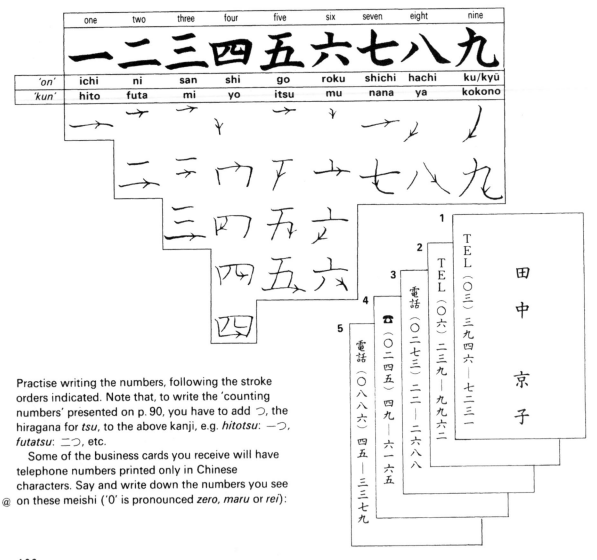

Practise writing the numbers, following the stroke orders indicated. Note that, to write the 'counting numbers' presented on p. 90, you have to add つ, the hiragana for *tsu*, to the above kanji, e.g. *hitotsu*: 一つ, *futatsu*: 二つ, etc.

Some of the business cards you receive will have telephone numbers printed only in Chinese characters. Say and write down the numbers you see @ on these meishi ('0' is pronounced *zero*, *maru* or *rei*):

1

田中 京子

TEL (〇三) 三九四六—七二三一

2

電話 (〇六) 二三九—九九六二

3

電話 (〇二七三) 二二—二六八八

4

☎ (〇二四五) 四九—六一六五

5

電話 (〇八八六) 四五—三三七九

Kanji numbers are hardly ever seen written from left to right; the traditional way of writing Japanese is from top to bottom, as you can see from *kakejiku* (hanging scrolls) or a glance at a Japanese newspaper, book or magazine.

Try writing your own telephone number(s) (and those of your friends) in kanji, proceeding from top to bottom and not from left to right!

When it comes to prices, you'll certainly be dealing with numbers larger than 1 to 9, and understanding these kanji will come in very useful:

10	100	1000	10 000	yen
十	百	千	万	円
jū	hyaku	sen	man	en

Looking back at p. 80, if necessary, try to say, and
@ write in rōmaji, the following prices:

1	2	3	4	5
二千円	八千五百円	一万九千七百円	八十五万七千円	六万四千三百二十円

It would be misleading to suggest that prices are written only in kanji – in fact, in many shops and (especially Western-style) restaurants prices are written in a very familiar way: ¥400, for example, for a cup of coffee. You'll also see combinations of kanji and '0' standing for zero. Try to work out the prices
@ in the photographs on the right:

LANGUAGE SUMMARY

Colours

guriin	ao(i)
midori	aka(i)
murasaki	shiro(i)
pinku	kuro(i)
orenji	kiiro(i)
gurē	chairo(i)
burū	

- pinku **no** kutsu *vs* kuro**i** kutsu

Clothes and accessories

sūtsu	pantsu	nekutai
kutsu	bura(jā)	kutsushita
zubon	burausu	pansuto
baggu	sukāto	kōto
bōshi	surippa	wanpiisu
shatsu	sētā	sasupendā
beruto	suniikā	

Larger numbers

jū	nijū
hyaku	sanbyaku
sen	sanzen
ichiman	yonman

Department stores

denkiseihin	keshōhin
shokuryōhin	fujinyōhin
shinshiyōhin	akusesarii
supōtsuyōhin	kōshū denwa

Fruit and vegetables

ringo	retasu
orenji	kyūri
meron	tamanegi
suika	kyabetsu
mikan	ninjin

Asking about goods in stock

Sumimasen, sukāto wa arimasu ka?
Sumimasen, ano sūtsu o misete kudasai.

Shop assistant language

Irasshaimase!
Hai, gozaimasu.
(Chotto) gozaimasen ga ...
Nanakai de gozaimasu.

Asking about price

Kono beruto wa ikura desu ka?
Gosen-en desu.

Expressing preferences

Chotto chiisai desu ne.
Chōdo ii desu.
Jā, kore (o) kudasai.

Asking about floors

Sumimasen ...
Denkiseihin wa nankai desu ka?
Nikai ni arimasu.

Adjectives

takai ... yasui	kantan (na)
nagai ... mijikai	fuben (na)
omoi ... karui	shinsen (na)
furui	

And

aka **to** shiro
aka **to** shiro **to** burū

Main language structures

Counters

ippon/nihon *etc.*
ikko/niko *etc.*
ichimai/nimai *etc.*
Counters can be avoided by using:

hitotsu	muttsu
futatsu	nanatsu
mittsu	yattsu
yottsu	kokonotsu
itsutsu	tō

e.g. Banana ippon to meron o muttsu kudasai.

There is ..., I've/We've got ...: arimasu

Sūtsu wa arimasu ka?	Hai, arimasu.
	Iie, arimasen.

To deepen your understanding of some of the language presented in this unit, take a look at these parts of the Grammar section: 'Being and having' (7) 'Numbers' (9), 'Counters' (10), and 'Adjectives' (12).

5
SCHOOLTIME

About Japan

The success of Japan's modernisation following the Meiji Restoration in 1868 owed much to its educational system. The fact that a fairly large percentage of the population was literate at that time meant that new information and knowledge could be disseminated quickly. In other words, not only were the Japanese able to learn about new technical developments in the West; they could also carry out written commands sent out by the new centralised government. Literacy was thus a means both of acquiring new knowledge and of enforcing social control.

That the Japanese are highly literate is quite an achievement, given the way in which they have to learn two syllabaries (*hiragana* and *katakana*) as well as approximately 2000 Chinese characters (*kanji*). These latter are divided into 'education' (*kyōiku kanji*) and 'general use' (*jōyō kanji*) characters. *Kyōiku kanji* are the 960 characters which are taught at primary school. *Jōyō kanji* – the normal number used in newspaper articles – are learned less systematically during secondary schooling and university education. Although there is officially a very high literacy rate, we should realise that most people are able to recognise many more kanji than they can write. Kanji need a lot of practice before they are really memorised once and for all.

Literacy and education are – next to the family and the company – the third cornerstone of Japanese society and probably the key to Japan's economic achievement. In Japan, the importance of education has never been doubted. Confucian ideals, imported from China, have long stressed the necessity for learning and emphasised that people who study hard and diligently can raise themselves up the social ladder to positions of authority. Besides this basic moral principle supporting the role of education, however, the Japanese have also believed strongly that education should be useful to society. As a result, Japan's compulsory education system focused right from the beginning on the fact that those who were to run the country's political and economical institutions needed to be well trained in a variety of subjects – including mathematics, economics and law.

There are all kinds of offshoots from the Confucian emphasis on education as a means of 'self-improvement'. In the first place, you will find that Japanese are almost always studying something. Businessmen take classes in a foreign language (usually, but not necessarily, English) – often early in the morning before work – while middle-aged housewives attend cooking, embroidery or aerobics classes (sometimes at a department store's cultural centre). Young women, too, will often practise a Western musical instrument, as well as such traditional arts as flower arrangement (*ikebana*) or the tea ceremony (*sadō*).

This kind of personal study is not entirely without ulterior motivation, of course. Businessmen may well learn a foreign language to improve their chances of being sent abroad and getting promoted; young women, at one stage, would learn the piano or guitar, as well as more traditional Japanese arts, in order to improve their marriage prospects (possibly through the offices of a matchmaker, or *nakōdo*). This kind of learning is useful both to the individual and in a more general social context. As a result, it is probably fair to say that, on average, Japanese have a far greater general knowledge than either Europeans or Americans, although they recognize that the means by which they have acquired that knowledge and attained their present level of education are not entirely satisfactory. Such self-reflection may lead those in charge of the country's education system up the occasional blind alley of failed reform, but it is likely to make Japan and the Japanese economy a force to be reckoned with into the foreseeable future.

Left Kanji lesson at elementary school

TELLING THE TIME

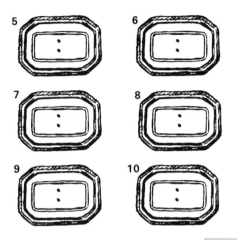

- To ask 'What time is it (now)?':
  (Ima) nanji desu ka?

- The answer will usually take the form
  ... -ji ...-fun/pun desu.
  E.g. Shichiji nijūnifun desu: 'It's 7:22.'

1:00	ichiji	7:00	**shichi**ji
2:00	niji	8:00	hachiji
3:00	sanji	9:00	**ku**ji
4:00	**yo**ji	10:00	jūji
5:00	goji	11:00	jūichiji
6:00	rokuji	12:00	jūniji

0:01	ippun	0:06	roppun
0:02	nifun	0:07	nanafun
0:03	sanpun	0:08	happun
0:04	yonpun	0:09	kyūfun
0:05	gofun	0:10	juppun
		0:30	sanjuppun
			or han (*half*)

SOUNDCHECK CD ▸ 121

@ Repeat the eight times (1 to 8) you hear on the CD, and note them down (in digital form). Be particularly careful to pronounce the *pp* sound, for example in *ippun*, as in the English 'to**p p**layer' (rather than as in 'happy').

JAPANESE LIVE 1 CD ▸ 122

@ Listen to the conversations, and fill in the digital watch faces below with the times you hear:

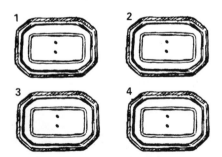

WHAT'S THE TIME? CD ▸ 123

Now the CD will ask *you* for the times shown above, but in a different order. For example, the first question you hear will be as follows:

CD: Number eight: **Sumimasen, ima nanji desu ka?**

You: **Sanji han desu.** (or **Sanji sanjuppun desu.**)

BUILD-UP CD ▸ 124

Listen and repeat:

8 a.m.	**gozen hachiji/asa no hachiji** (**asa** = morning)
8 p.m.	**gogo hachiji/yoru no hachiji** (**yoru** = evening)
about 8 o'clock	**hachiji goro**

A.M., P.M. AND 'ABOUT'

If it's *gogo shichiji* in Tōkyō, it's *gozen jūji* in London (*gozen jūichiji* in summer).

Answer these two questions, without looking at your watch:

1 Ima nanji goro desu ka? (*answer:* ... -ji goro desu.)
2 Tōkyō wa nanji goro desu ka?
   Now look at your watch, and answer more precisely:
3 Ima nanji desu ka?
4 Tōkyō wa?

TALKING ABOUT DAILY ROUTINE

Nanako (right) leads the typically busy life of a **chūgakusei**: junior high school pupil. After lessons, she takes part in club activities, and after that attends a private *juku* (cram school) to prepare for the entrance exams to senior high school. Here's what a typical day entails for her:

Nanako no ichinichi (Nanako's day)

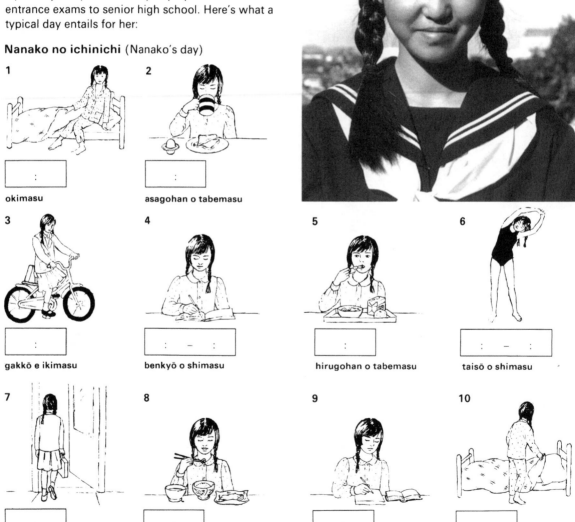

1

:

okimasu

2

:

asagohan o tabemasu

3

:

gakkō e ikimasu

4

: - :

benkyō o shimasu

5

:

hirugohan o tabemasu

6

: - :

taisō o shimasu

7

:

uchi e kaerimasu

8

:

bangohan o tabemasu

9

:

juku e ikimasu

10

:

nemasu

okimasu	get up
tabemasu	eat
ikimasu	go
shimasu	do/make
kaerimasu	go/come back
nemasu	sleep/go to sleep
benkyō o shimasu	study (lit. 'do study')
taisō o shimasu	do gymnastics

SPOTCHECK 1

@ Guess what *asagohan*, *hirugohan* and *bangohan* mean.

TAKE NOTE

Okimasu can mean any of 'I/you/he/she/we/they wake(s) up' (depending on the context), and the same applies to all verbs in Japanese. *O*, for example in *asagohan o tabemasu*, follows the object of an action, i.e. the thing something is 'done to'. (You've come across this *o* before, in *kore o kudasai* and *are o misete kudasai*.)

SOUNDCHECK   CD ▶ 125

Listen to and repeat the words under the pictures opposite. Then try to remember the words. Test yourself by covering the words, replaying the CD and – just by looking at the pictures and listening to the sound effects – trying to say what Nanako does next, before the CD tells you.

- To say 'at ... o'clock': **...-ji ni**
  E.g. 'I get up at 7 o'clock': *Shichiji ni okimasu.*

- To say 'from ... until ...': **... kara ... made**
  E.g. 'I study from 6 until 9 o'clock': *Rokuji kara kuji made benkyō o shimasu.*

JAPANESE LIVE 2   CD ▶ 126

@ Listen to Yuka's interview with Nanako about her daily routine. Concentrating on Nanako's replies, write the times she does the various activities in the small boxes below the pictures opposite.

- To ask 'What time do you (usually) ...?':
  (Itsumo) nanji ni ... -masu ka?

- To ask '(At) about what time do you ...?':
  Nanji goro (ni) ...-masu ka?

- To ask 'From what time to what time do you ...?':
  Nanji kara nanji made ... -masu ka?

REWIND   CD ▶ 126

Listen once more to 'Japanese live 2'. This time, concentrate on understanding the *questions* Yuka puts to Nanako, using the phrases in the box above to help you.

SPOTCHECK 2

@ How would you ask these questions in Japanese?
a 'What time do you usually eat breakfast?'
b 'From about what time to about what time do you sleep?'
How would you answer (according to your usual daily routine)?

YOUR DAY   CD ▶ 127

The CD will ask you six questions, about when you usually get up, eat meals, come back home and sleep. Answer with ... *goro* (*ni*) ... *-masu* or ... *kara ... made ... -masu*.
E.g. (1) *CD:* **Itsumo nanji ni okimasu ka?**
You: ... **-ji goro (ni) okimasu.**

BUILD-UP

Mori-san no ichinichi

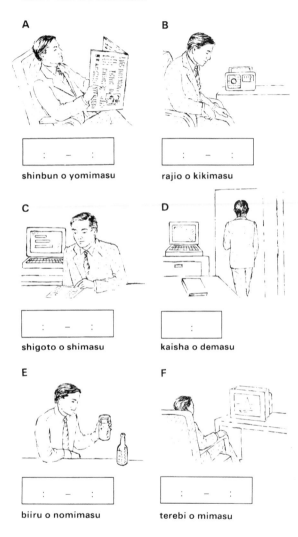

A

: — :

shinbun o yomimasu

B

: — :

rajio o kikimasu

C

: — :

shigoto o shimasu

D

:

kaisha o demasu

E

: — :

biiru o nomimasu

F

: — :

terebi o mimasu

shinbun o yomimasu	read the newspaper
rajio o kikimasu	listen to the radio
shigoto o shimasu	work (lit. 'do work')
kaisha o demasu	leave the company
biiru o nomimasu	drink beer
terebi o mimasu	watch TV

ASK   CD ▶ 128

Practise asking questions with the activity words the CD supplies. From 1 to 4, make questions beginning *Itsumo nanji ni . . .?* From 5 to 8, ask *Itsumo nanji kara nanji made . . .?*

> E.g. (1) *CD:* **okimasu**
> *You:* **Itsumo nanji ni okimasu ka?**

INTERVIEW   CD ▶ 129

@ Help Yuka to interview Nanako's father, Mr Mori, about when (or from when to when) he does the things illustrated in 'Build-up' on the left. Ask in order from A to F and, according to his replies, write times in the boxes.

> E.g. (A) *You:* **Itsumo nanji kara nanji made shinbun o yomimasu ka?**

> - To say what someone doesn't do: change the *-masu* ending of a verb to *-masen*.
>   E.g. A: *Nanako -san wa rokuji ni okimasu ka?*
>   B: *lie, rokuji ni wa* **okimasen**. *Shichiji ni okimasu.*
>   (In the reply, *wa* is added to *rokuji ni* for contrast with the correct answer, *shichiji ni*.)

YES OR NO?   CD ▶ 130

Listen to the ten questions, similar to the one in the box above, about Nanako's day. (Look back at p. 108 to answer.) Some of the answers are 'yes', while others are 'no', in which case you should answer as in the example above.

> E.g. (1) *CD:* **Nanako-san wa shichiji ni gakkō e ikimasu ka?**
> *You:* **lie, shichiji ni wa gakkō e ikimasen. Hachiji ni ikimasu.**

- To ask what someone usually does (at a certain time):
  Itsumo . . . -ji ni **nani** *o shimasu ka?*

SAYING WHAT YOU'RE DOING NOW

Over the last few pages you've been describing regular, routine actions, but how do you describe something happening *now*, at this very moment?

- To say 'I'm/he's/she's (etc.) do**ing** something' use the so-called **-te** (or **-de**) form of a verb plus **imasu**.
  E.g. 'What are you doing now?'
  Ima nani o shite imasu ka?
  'I'm eating breakfast.'
  Asagohan o tabete imasu.
  (You can find the *-te* (or *-de*) forms of all verbs in the book in the chart in part 6 of the Grammar section.)

SPOTCHECK 3

@ Find and note down the *-te/-de* forms of these verbs:

a tabemasu	**e** nomimasu
b mimasu	**f** yomimasu
c nemasu	**g** shimasu
d ikimasu	**h** kikimasu

WHAT'S HE DOING? `CD ▸ 132`

On the CD you'll hear a time, and then a question about what Naoki is doing. Answer by looking at your notes for 'Interview' on this page.

E.g. (1) *CD:* **Ima gozen shichiji desu. Naoki-san wa nani o shite imasu ka?**
You: **Nete imasu.**

On the next part of the CD, there are similiar questions about Mr Mori, Naoki's father. Answer by looking at the times you wrote in 'Build-up' on the opposite page.

IT SOUNDS LIKE . . . `CD ▸ 133`

By listening to the sound effects, guess what Nanako is doing now.

E.g. (1) *CD:* (sound of snoring)
You: **Ima nete imasu.**

INTERVIEW `CD ▸ 131`

@ Nanako's brother, Naoki (above), is a university student (*daigakusei*). His day is altogether different. Ask Naoki what he does at the times below, and note down his answers.

E.g. (1) *You:* **Itsumo gozen jūichiji ni nani o shimasu ka?**

1 11 a.m.	**4** 2:15–4:15 p.m.	**7** 8–11:30 p.m.
2 12:30 p.m.	**5** 5 p.m.	**8** 2 a.m.
3 2 p.m.	**6** 7 p.m.	

(aru)baito o shimasu | do a part-time job (from the German: 'Arbeit')

111

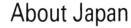

About Japan

For a student, April in Japan can be the cruellest month. It is then that the academic year begins, then that those who have passed their exams are separated from those who have failed them. University graduates and company recruits are forever referred to as the intake of such-and-such a year, and it is their entry into, rather than exit from, an institution which is of prime importance. In this respect, Japan differs from most Western societies, where it is graduation from university or high school which preoccupies people most.

Since the American occupation at the end of the Pacific War, Japanese education has been modelled on the American 6–3–3–4 system. All children start at elementary school (*shōgakkō*) once they are six years old, and go on to junior high (or middle) school (*chūgakkō*) when they are twelve. After spending three years there, their compulsory education is in theory complete, but the vast majority of children proceed to high school (*kōkō* or, more formally, *kōtōgakkō*) for a further three years. Almost 40 per cent of these then enter institutions of advanced education, women often going to two-year junior colleges (tandai or tanki daigaku, 'short-term universities') or, like men, to four-year universities (daigaku).

It is entry to these institutions – especially at the higher levels – that has been the focus of everyone's attention. Examinations have always been hard, since universities had to limit the number of new students they took on every year. So students studied harder and harder to pass examinations that were made correspondingly more difficult – a situation that has been relieved somewhat by the falling numbers of young people going through the education system. Nevertheless, teenagers still spend a lot of time preparing for entrance exams (into senior high school as well as university) in the hope of being admitted to an illustrious academic institution.

This 'examination hell' has fuelled a thriving education industry, for most pupils during the 'grey years' get extra tuition at specialist crammer schools (*juku* or *yobikō*), which teach students how to pass their exams and nothing else. In this respect, education can become little more than an ability to memorise facts, and many of those who fail to get into the university of their choice will resit, year after year, until they pass. These students are known as *rōnin* (a term originally used to describe a masterless *samurai* in feudal times), and every year there are stories in the press about a rōnin who finally passes his entrance exam into Tōkyō university at the sixth or seventh attempt. This spirit of hard work and determination has been much admired in Japan.

And what is the reason underlying it all? Quite simply, that success in life is more or less determined by success at school. Those who get jobs in the Civil Service and the top corporations of Japan are almost invariably those who have gone to its top universities: Tōkyō and Kyōto in the national system, and Keiō, Waseda and Hitotsubashi in the private educational system. Those who get into these universities are for the most part those who have been to the top high schools (i.e. those which get a high percentage of their pupils into prestigious universities).

And so it goes on, right back through junior high school to elementary school. In other words, to get into a good company in Japan, it usually helps if you started your education by going to the 'right' elementary school, or even kindergarten. Indeed, many private universities and colleges (of which there are more than 400 all told) run their own elementary and secondary schools, so that children who enter the system early on get preferential treatment during the selection process for each institution further up the education ladder.

Students sitting university entrance exams in the Tōkyō Dome

DAYS OF THE WEEK AND DATES

- These are the days of the week in Japanese (listen and repeat):

CD ▶ 134

Monday	**getsuyōbi**	Friday	**kinyōbi**
Tuesday	**kayōbi**	Saturday	**doyōbi**
Wednesday	**suiyōbi**	Sunday	**nichiyōbi**
Thursday	**mokuyōbi**	what day?	**nanyōbi?**

- To say on what day of the week you do something:
  ...-yōbi ni ...-masu (*ni* = 'on')
  E.g. A: *Itsumo nanyōbi ni tenisu o shimasu ka?*
  B: *Suiyōbi ni shimasu.*

BUILD-UP

CD ▶ 135

Naoki is a university student living on his own in Tōkyō, and below are some of the things he does apart from studying. Practise forming questions from the words below.
  E.g. (1) *CD:* sōji
  You: **Itsumo nanyōbi ni sōji o shimasu ka?**

1	sōji o shimasu	*do cleaning/housework*
2	sentaku o shimasu	*do the washing*
3	kaimono o shimasu	*go shopping*
4	doraibu o shimasu	*go for a drive*
5	tenisu o shimasu	*play tennis*

TAKE NOTE

Many words can go with *shimasu* to describe different activities, often in cases where in English we'd use words other than 'make' or 'do'; thus, *benkyō o shimasu* = 'study', *doraibu o shimasu* = 'go for a drive', (any sport) *o shimasu* = 'play (any sport)'.

INTERVIEW

CD ▶ 136

@ Ask Naoki on what day(s) of the week he usually does the activities in 'Build-up' above; ask in order from 1 to 5 and note down his answers.
  E.g. (1) *You:* **Itsumo nanyōbi ni sōji o shimasu ka?**

DOUBLE-CHECK

CD ▶ 137

Answer the CD's questions about Naoki's week by referring to your notes.
  E.g. (1) *CD:* **Naoki-san wa itsumo nanyōbi ni kaimono o shimasu ka?**
  You: **Getsuyōbi to suiyōbi to kinyōbi ni shimasu.**

- When saying a date, the order is as follows:
  ...-nen (year) **...-gatsu** (month) **...-nichi** (day)

E.g. '18th June 1955': *sen kyūhyaku gojūgonen* (1955) *rokugatsu* (June) *jūhachinichi* (18th)

'NANNEN?'

With the addition of *-nen*, a year is said exactly as if it were a number: 'one thousand, nine hundred and fifty-five'. Within Japan, there exists a commonly used alternative system for designating years, according to the year of the emperor's reign. 1955, for example, was *Shōwa sanjūnen*, being the thirtieth year of the reign of the Emperor Shōwa (who died in 1989). The era of the present emperor is called *Heisei*, so that 1991, for example, is known as *Heisei sannen*.

'NANGATSU?'

CD ▶ 138

Saying the month in Japanese is all a question of numbers (listen and say):

January	**ichigatsu**	July	***shichi*gatsu**
February	**nigatsu**	August	**hachigatsu**
March	**sangatsu**	September	***ku*gatsu**
April	***shi*gatsu**	October	**jūgatsu**
May	**gogatsu**	November	**jūichigatsu**
June	**rokugatsu**	December	**jūnigatsu**

'NANNICHI?' CD ▶ 139

Mostly, saying the date is just a question of adding -*nichi* to a number, e.g. '15th': *jūgonichi*, '26th': *nijūrokunichi*, '17th': *jūshichinichi*, '29th': *nijūkunichi*. However, there are some exceptions (listen and say):

1st	**tsuitachi**	8th	**yōka**
2nd	**futsuka**	9th	**kokonoka**
3rd	**mikka**	10th	**tōka**
4th	**yokka**	14th	**jūyokka**
5th	**itsuka**	20th	**hatsuka**
6th	**muika**	24th	**nijūyokka**
7th	**nanoka**		

The dates from 2nd to 10th are related to the words for counting you've already come across: *futatsu, mittsu, yottsu*, etc.

SPOTCHECK 4

@ Write out these dates in Japanese words:

a 23 May 1990   **d** 5 November 1998
b 15 December 1812   **e** 1 April 1995
c 4 July 1983

WHAT DATE? CD ▶ 140

@ The CD will tell you eight dates. Write them down like this: '1962/1/22' (year first, then month, then day).

1 _____	5 _____
2 _____	6 _____
3 _____	7 _____
4 _____	8 _____

YOUR TURN CD ▶ 141

Now the CD will tell you the number of one of the dates you've written down, and ask you to say that date (*Nannichi desu ka?*). Use the pause button to give yourself time.

BUILD-UP CD ▶ 142

School holidays are considerably shorter in Japan than in the West, as you can see from the dates of Nanako's holidays this year, on the right below. 'Holiday' is **yasumi** in Japanese, and school vacations are named after the seasons (listen and repeat):

spring	**haru**	spring holiday	**haruyasumi** (3/28–4/6)
summer	**natsu**	summer holiday	**natsuyasumi** (7/26–8/31)
autumn	**aki**		
winter	**fuyu**	winter holiday	**fuyuyasumi** (12/24–1/6)

- To say when something begins: (time/date) **ni hajimarimasu**.

- To say when something ends: (time/date) **ni owarimasu**.

HOLIDAYS CD ▶ 143

The CD will ask you the starting and finishing dates of Nanako's holidays. Answer with the date plus **ni hajimarimasu** or **ni owarimasu**.

E.g. (1) *CD:* **Natsuyasumi wa nannichi ni hajimarimasu ka?**
You: **Shichigatsu nijūrokunichi ni hajimarimasu.**

MEANS OF TRANSPORT

- To say how you go somewhere (i.e. what means of transport you use): **... de ikimasu.**
  E.g. 'I go by train': *Densha de ikimasu.*

- To ask how someone goes somewhere:
  Nan de ... e ikimasu ka?
  E.g. 'How do you go to school?': *Nan de gakkō e ikimasu ka?*

BUILD-UP

CD ▸ 144

@ Listen to six people saying how they go somewhere, accompanied by the sound of the means of transport they use. Draw lines from the words on the left to the pictures on the right:

chikatetsu de

basu de

kuruma de

jitensha de

baiku de

aruite

REWIND

CD ▸ 144

Having checked you got the answers right, rewind the CD and repeat the sentences. The places the people go to are:

1 kaisha
2 sūpā (*supermarket*)
3 pūru (*swimming pool*)
4 ginkō (*bank*)
5 eigakan (*cinema*)
6 daigaku (*university*)

TAKE NOTE

Aruite literally means 'walking', so in this case *de* ('by') isn't necessary. Note that it's possible to say either, for example, *gakkō e jitensha de ikimasu* or *jitensha de gakkō e ikimasu.*

SOUND ONLY

CD ▸ 145

The CD will say the name of a place. Then you'll hear a sound indicating how someone goes there. Make sentences, starting in each case with the name of the place.

E.g. (1) *CD:* **yūbinkyoku** (sound effect of bicycle)
You: **Yūbinkyoku e jitensha de ikimasu.**

- To ask how long something takes: **Dono gurai kakarimasu ka?**

- To answer in hours: **...-jikan kakarimasu.**
  E.g. 'It takes (about) an hour': *Ichijikan (gurai) kakarimasu.*

- To answer in minutes: **...-fun/pun kakarimasu.**
  E.g. 'It takes (about) thirty minutes': *Sanjuppun (gurai) kakarimasu.*

JAPANESE LIVE 3

CD ▸ 146

@ Listen to the interviews with five schoolchildren (1 to 5); they were all asked *Nan de gakkō ni kimasu ka?* (*kimasu* = come; *ni* = an alternative to *e*, meaning 'to' (a place)). Listen, and note down in each case how they come and how long it takes them to get to school.

YOUR TURN

CD ▸ 147

The CD will ask you how the children go to school, and how long it takes, but in a different order.

E.g. *CD:* Number 4: **Nan de gakkō e ikimasu ka?**
You: **Basu de ikimasu.**
CD: **Dono gurai kakarimasu ka?**
You: **Ichijikan han gurai kakarimasu.**

LANGUAGE FOR LEARNING

A lot goes on in Japanese schools besides study: annual events such as sports days, 'culture festivals' and excursions enliven proceedings, as do extra-curricular club activities, to which many students devote a great deal of energy. Such events and activities foster early development of a strong sense of group identity, but the other side of the coin is that individuality and originality often seem to be actively discouraged within the educational system: at high schools and junior high schools, in particular, school uniform and other regulations can be enforced in a rather authoritarian manner, while in lessons themselves the teacher's role tends to be one of imparting information from 'on high', while students ingest facts for the next examination.

To enable you to take a relatively active approach to your own learning of Japanese, the following phrases and questions should come in handy:

> To ask someone to repeat something: **Mō ichido onegai shimasu.** (lit. 'Once more, please.')
>
> To ask someone to speak more slowly: **Mō sukoshi yukkuri onegai shimasu.** (lit. 'A little more slowly, please.')
>
> To ask the Japanese word for something (e.g. 'How do you say "teacher" in Japanese?'): 'Teacher' **wa nihongo de nan to iimasu ka?** (answer: **'Sensei' to iimasu.**)
>
> To ask the meaning of a word (e.g. 'What does "chūgakkō" mean?'): **'Chūgakkō' to iu no wa nan desu ka?** (lit. 'What is the thing called "chūgakkō"?')

SPOTCHECK 5

@ *Eigo de* means 'in English', so how would you ask and answer this question?

'How do you say "**tekisuto**" in English?'

REPEAT `CD ▸ 148`

Listen, and repeat the phrases and questions in the box.

TEST `CD ▸ 149`

The CD will give you a vocabulary test consisting of ten questions about words you've come across in this unit. The first five times you'll be asked to say an English word in Japanese (*nihongo de*), and in questions 6 to 10 you'll be asked how to say a Japanese word in English (*eigo de*). Answer each time with *. . . to iimasu*. The CD will follow up with what you should have said.

> E.g. (1) *CD:* 'April' **wa nihongo de nan to iimasu ka?**
> *You:* **'Shigatsu' to iimasu.**

CLASSROOM WORDS `CD ▸ 150`

@ On the left below are some Japanese words for things in the classroom. Match them with their English equivalents (mixed up on the right) by asking the teacher on the tape: '_____' *to iu no wa nan desu ka?* and listening out for the reply. Each time, the CD will first say the word you should ask about.

> E.g. (1) *CD:* **jisho**
> *You:* **Jisho to iu no wa nan desu ka?**

1 jisho	**a** chair
2 tēburu	**b** window
3 isu	**c** desk
4 tsukue	**d** table
5 mado	**e** dictionary
6 nōto	**f** map
7 chizu	**g** notebook

About Japan

The education system affects Japanese people's relationships to one another in a number of important ways. For example, little distinction is made between the bright and the less bright in class, and individual needs are rarely catered to by teachers, who have to follow a national curriculum laid down by the Ministry of Education. However, because pupils at junior and senior high school are rarely 'streamed', they are able to develop a very close camaraderie with others in their class and year. Not only do they attend classes together; they eat, play games, participate in 'club activities', go on school excursions and even clean their own classroom together. In this way, they learn what it means to be members of a 'group', and so curb the rising tide of self-assertiveness that usually floods the teenage years.

Not all – alas! – is for the good. Although those who can keep up with the pace of study in class survive, a growing number of pupils fail to cope with the examination

Ceremony at the beginning of the school year

pressure. That there is pressure can be seen in the increasing number of incidents of violence and bullying in schools – of and by teachers as well as pupils. Those who have failed at school are also now involved in an increasing incidence of crime (though, to put things in perspective, Japan is probably still one of the least crime-ridden societies in the world, at least where violent crime is concerned).

The authoritarian role adopted by teachers also affects pupils' perceptions of their place in society, as do the relations imposed between children of different ages. The teacher is always right; with experience on his/her side, and expects and is usually given automatic respect. With regard to teachers, then, young people find themselves in the sort of hierarchical relationship that permeates Japanese society as a whole. The fact, too, that children enter school at a fixed point every year, rather than at the moment they individually reach their sixth birthdays, means that among pupils a fairly strict seniority system is enforced.

During their time at these institutions of education, the ages of all children are reckoned not by birth, but by their year of progress through the system. Thus a six-year-old boy or girl will be referred to as a 'first-year elementary school pupil' (*shōgaku ichinensei*), a fourteen year-old girl as a 'second-year junior high school pupil' (*chūgaku ninensei*) and a boy in his early twenties about to graduate from university as a 'fourth-year university student' (*daigaku yonensei*). In this way, not only is each individual placed firmly in a social order; he or she is placed in a strictly hierarchical pecking order, in which seniors expect their juniors to behave in the appropriate subservient manner.

You can see this very clearly in club activities after school. In a tennis club, for example, first-year pupils spend most of their time preparing and tidying up the court, and collecting tennis balls for their seniors to play with. They very rarely get a chance to play themselves, however much ability they may show. Indeed, in some respects, the relationships between seniors and juniors is very much like that found in some private schools in England, where prefects once lorded it over the younger pupils.

The notion of seniority based on age is very important in Japanese society. In most large corporations, for example, it is length of service in the organisation concerned, rather than individual ability, which has tended to determine promotion through the management ranks. Of course, seniority plays a large part in the functioning of different social institutions all over the world, but in Japan the tension between seniority and talent has been particularly pronounced. Nowadays, however, talent is finally being given much greater recognition than previously in large corporations. This is bound to have a knock-on effect in school education.

TALKING ABOUT AGE

NIGHT SCHOOL

They may not look like *kōkōsei*, but these are just some of the thousands of men and women who, for one reason or another, give up school after *chūgakkō* (junior high school) and, much later, struggle to graduate from senior high school by attending evening classes:

Ogawa
Shimada
Hara Yoshida
Uchiyama
Watanabe Yamamoto Kobayashi

In this unit, we've seen how the question pattern *Nan ... desu ka?* can be used to ask about times (*Nanji desu ka?*), days of the week (*Nanyōbi desu ka?*) and dates (*Nannichi desu ka?*). It can also be used to ask someone's age.

- To ask someone's age: **Nansai desu ka?** (or, more politely, *O-ikutsu desu ka?*: lit. 'How many (years) are you?')

- To say your age: **...-sai desu.**
  E.g. 'I'm twenty-five': *Nijūgosai desu.*
  The only irregular forms are:
  1   **issai** (e.g 'I'm twenty-one': *Nijūissai desu.*)
  8   **hassai**
  10 **jussai** (e.g. 'I'm thirty': *Sanjussai desu.*)
  20 **hatachi** (This is the age when young Japanese are considered in law to become adults.)

HOW OLD?　　　　　　　　　　　CD ▸ 151

@ **A** The CD will say the names of some of the students in the photograph. Use the name to ask how old that person is. Listen and write the age under the person's name.

    E.g. (1)　*CD:*　**Ogawa-san**
           You: **Ogawa-san wa nansai desu ka?**
           CD:　**Sanjūgosai desu.**
          → Write '35' under the name.

CD ▸ 152

B Now the CD will ask you the ages of some of the students in the picture. Reply by looking at the answers you've written.

    E.g. (1)　*CD:*　**Yoshida-san wa nansai desu ka?**
           You: **Nijūsansai desu.**

REVIEW

READING

Read these paragraphs about one of the students in the picture, then answer the questions below.

Hara Yōsuke-san wa sanjūnisai desu. Tōkyō no Shinjuku-ku ni sunde imasu. Jūnanasai de kōkō o yamemashita. Ima mō ichido ganbatte benkyō o shite imasu.

Hara-san wa gozen rokuji ni okimasu. Rokuji han ni asagohan o tabemasu. Shigotoba made jitensha de ikimasu. Nishi-Waseda 3-chōme no sūpā ni tsutomete imasu. Shigoto wa hachiji ni hajimarimasu – hachiji kara goji made desu. Hirugohan wa jūniji desu. Goji ni uchi e kaerimasu. Hara-san wa sōji o shimasen! Terebi mo mimasen! Soshite goji han ni bangohan o tabemasu.

Goji yonjūgofun ni uchi o demasu. Jitensha de gakkō e ikimasu. Jugyō wa rokuji ni hajimarimasu. Jūji ni owarimasu. Hara-san wa uchi e kaerimasu. Jūniji ni nemasu. Taihen desu ne! Ganbatte kudasai, Hara-san!

Shinjuku-ku ni sunde imasu	he lives (lit. 'is living') in Shinjuku ward
yamemashita	gave up/stopped (past form of **yamemasu**)
mō ichido ganbatte	trying hard once more
shigotoba	place of work
sūpā ni tsutomete imasu	he works in a supermarket
soshite	and
jugyō	lesson(s)
taihen desu	it's hard

SPOTCHECK 6

@ Answer these questions as if *you* were Yōsuke:
a O-sumai wa dochira desu ka?
b Nanji ni asagohan o tabemasu ka?
c Gakkō wa nanji kara nanji made desu ka?
d Ichiji ni hirugohan o tabemasu ka?

QUESTIONS

@ On the left are some answers taken from the passage on Yōsuke Hara. Write down the questions you would have to ask if you wanted him to answer with that information. (Look back over this unit, and at p. 69.) Write the questions on the solid lines on the right. (Ignore the dotted lines under the answers for the moment.)

1 Hara Yōsuke   *O-namae wa nan to iimasu ka?*
....

2 32
....

3 Shinjuku-ku
....

4 6 a.m.
....

5 6:30 a.m.
....

6 jitensha de
....

7 sūpā
....

8 8 a.m.–5 p.m.
....

9 12 noon
....

10 5:00 p.m.
....

11 6 p.m.–10 p.m.
....

12 12 midnight
....

INTERVIEW   CD ▶ 153

@ Now put the questions, in order, to one of Yōsuke's classmates on the CD. Note down her answers on the dotted lines. One thing which Yōsuke does, this person doesn't do at all. What is it? Put a cross on that line.

WRITING

@ Now write a paragraph about the student you've just interviewed. (Use 'Reading' above as a model.)

About Japan

One feature of the education system in Japan is its perceived 'usefulness'. This extends from what is actually taught to pupils to the friendships and relationships forged in the classroom, which can prove useful in later life. One social use of education in Japan is the formation of school cliques (*gakubatsu*) rather similar to the 'old school tie' networks in the UK or among graduates of Ivy League universities in the USA.

All those going through a particular university in Japan (and sometimes – as in the case of the University of Tōkyō's Law Department – a particular department) are encouraged to maintain contact with one another after they have graduated. There will be annual get-togethers, of course, but students who have shared life at university (being members of the same tennis club, for example, or choir) will often arrange monthly meetings where they can share drinks and reminisce about the past. At the same time, they will make use of these contacts to further their business interests.

The 'usefulness' of education can also be seen in the organisation of family, as well as business, life – particularly in the distinction between male and female roles in Japan. A salary man's life, as we have seen, makes great demands on the head of a household. Fathers find themselves working the best part of every day and night, almost every day of the week. As a result, they have rarely been at home to help look after the house or family, and it has been the task of their wives to bring up their children in contemporary Japanese society. While men gauged their success, or lack of it, by promotion through the ranks of a company, women had to seek alternative criteria for public recognition. One means of doing this was by devoting themselves wholeheartedly to their children's education. Known as 'education mamas' (*kyōiku mama*), these housewives were primarily responsible for pushing their children through the examination hell, encouraging them to study all hours of the day and night, and insisting on attending crammer schools. Why? Because the success of a child in gaining admittance to a top-ranking university was ultimately seen as a mother's success. In other words, the social status of women in Japan, at one stage, depended upon the education system.

The situation was made more acute by the fact that, like many women elsewhere in the world, Japanese women were not expected to seem too intelligent. As a result, their own education was primarily seen in terms of the acquisition of such domestic arts as cooking, music etc. In other words, one result of the entrance exams system, and hence of the way in which mothers socialise their children, was that Japan's education system kept women firmly in their public place. With recent acceptance of gender equality, however, this situation has begun to change.

Of course, those whose husbands earn good salaries have tended to be more successful with their children's education than those who are less well off. After all, people need money to send their children to private schools and to give them extra tuition, and nowadays it is those who went to top universities and work in large corporations who can most easily afford to give their children the necessary education to get them into top universities and hence into good jobs. In other words, present-day Japan is rapidly becoming an education-class society.

WHAT YOU'LL HEAR

A TYPICAL DAY

CD ▶ 154

@ Listen to the interviews (1 to 3). Three different people were asked about what time they get up, start work, go to bed, etc. on a typical working day. As you listen, fill in the times in the spaces below:

1 Ms Ichikawa gets up at _____ : _____. She leaves for work at _____ : _____, finishes work at _____ : _____ and goes to bed at _____ : _____.

2 Ms Hayashi has breakfast at _____ : _____. She works from _____ : _____ to _____ : _____.

3 Mr Morita usually gets up at _____ : _____. He works from _____ : _____ to _____ : _____. When he goes drinking after work, he goes to bed around _____ : _____.

DAILY ROUTINE

CD ▶ 155

@ Listen to one person's self-introduction on the CD and fill in the form below with the appropriate details. Stop the CD when you hear the tone, and rewind and listen again as many times as necessary.

Name: _____

Address: _____

Telephone number: _____

Occupation: _____

Now listen to the continuation of the self-introduction (after the tone), and fill in the times when Masako does the things in these pictures:

A

:

B

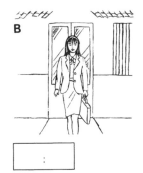

:

C

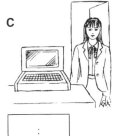

:

D

:	—	:

E

:

F

:	—	:

G

:

H

:	—	:

I

:	—	:

J

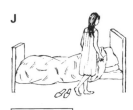

:

HISTORY QUIZ `CD ▸ 156`

@ Listen as two senior high school pupils struggle through a ten-question quiz on world history. In the task that they were given, they had to draw lines from ten dates on the left of the page to ten events mixed up on the right. In your task, the events are in the *correct* order of occurrence on the right, but there are no dates written. Write down the dates *in the order you hear them* – don't rely on the CD for which event each date goes next to (the students make lots of mistakes). Write the dates in the Japanese order (e.g. '1992/5/21' for 21 May 1992).

1 _____ Mozart was born

2 _____ The Battle of Waterloo

3 _____ The end of the American Civil War

4 _____ The Panama Canal was opened

5 _____ The arrest of Czar Nicholas in the Russian Revolution

6 _____ Hitler was arrested after the failure of the Munich Putsch

7 _____ Israel became an independent country

8 _____ Yuri Gagarin became the first man to go into space

9 _____ The Beatles had their first hit

10 _____ Martin Luther King was killed

Rewind the CD and listen again. Bearing in mind that the dates you've written on the left are the *correct* answers, work out how many questions the students get right.

WHAT YEAR? `CD ▸ 157`

@ The fact that school is the main focus of young people's lives in Japan is shown in the way a young person's age tends to be described not directly, but in terms of the year he or she has attained at school. Thus, a fourteen-year-old boy might be described by his mother as *chūgaku sannensei* (third-year pupil) and his nine-year-old sister as *shōgaku yonensei* (fourth-year pupil), with no reference being made to their age.

Listen to some young people describing both their age and what year they're in at school or university. In each case, write both pieces of information down (including the type of educational institution they attend).

	Educational institution	Year	Age
1	_____	____	____
2	_____	____	____
3	_____	____	____
4	_____	____	____
5	_____	____	____
6	_____	____	____
7	_____	____	____
8	_____	____	____
9	_____	____	____
10	_____	____	____

WRITTEN JAPANESE

school

学校

gak kō

student

学生

gaku sei

Two combinations of kanji intimately connected with the process of learning are 学校 (*gakkō:* 'school') and 学生 (*gakusei:* 'student'). 学, the kanji for 'study', may be seen to represent a child under an ornate roof, suggesting a place of learning. The tree on the left in 校 – known as a 'radical', since it occurs in many built-up kanji like this one – possibly relates to the fact that until recently schools were made of wood (whereas now, unfortunately, most are constructed of regulation concrete). 生, meaning 'life' or 'birth', is believed to represent a seedling or the sprouting shoot of a plant. *Gakusei*, then, literally means '(someone enjoying) a life of study'.

Practise writing the three kanji below, useful in their own right to represent the adjectives *ōkii, takai* and *chiisai*, as well as to indicate the various types of school in Japan:

These kanji (with the addition of 中) are used to represent the educational levels a young Japanese might hope to progress through:

university	university student
大 学 **dai gaku**	大 学 生 **dai gaku sei**
senior high school	senior high school pupil
高 校 **kō kō**	高 校 生 **kō kō sei**
junior high school	junior high school pupil
中 学 校 **chū gak kō**	中 学 生 **chū gaku sei**
elementary school	elementary school pupil
小 学 校 **shō gak kō**	小 学 生 **shō gaku sei**

 big	大	一 ナ 大	*'on'*: **dai** *'kun'*: **ō** (大きい: **ōkii**)
watchtower	高 high	亠 亠 古 古 古 古 高 高 高 高	*'on'*: **kō** *'kun'*: **taka** (高い : **takai**)
three small objects (or grains of rice)	小 small	亅 亅 小	*'on'*: **shō** *'kun'*: **chii/ko** (小さい: **chiisai**)

year

year 年 **nen**	ノ	┗	┢	仁	午	年
month 月 **gatsu**	┃	刀	月	月		
day 日 **nichi**	┃	刀	月	日		

Up until senior high school, it's rare to find students of very different ages in the same class. Since the year group remains stable in this way, it's possible (and extremely common) for young people to be referred to according to the year they've attained within the educational system, rather than by age. Armed with the knowledge that 'year' (*nen*) is represented by the kanji above, and remembering the number characters you came across in the previous @ unit, try reading aloud and translating the following:

1 中学二年生
2 小学五年生
3 高校三年生
4 小学六年生
5 大学四年生
6 中学一年生

Date of birth – crucial in determining both a child's entry into the Japanese education system and its every move within it – is *seinengappi* in Japanese, written 生年月日 (literally, 'birth year, month, (and) day'). Let's take a closer look at the last three kanji, which are used in the writing of dates in general:

Nowadays, the numerical parts of dates are usually written with Arabic numerals (rather than kanji), so that 25 June 1992, for example, would be 1992 年 6 月 25 日 (read as *sen kyūhyaku kyūjūninen rokugatsu nijūgonichi*). As you'll remember from p. 115, some dates don't end in *-nichi*, but they are nevertheless written using 日: 1日, for example, is pronounced as *tsuitachi*, 2日 as *futsuka*, 20日 as *hatsuka*, etc.

@   Read these dates aloud, and write them in English:

1 1995年 3月16日
2 1966年10月21日
3 2000年 1月 1日
4 1872年 7月 5日
5 1993年12月 9日

Finally, try writing down your date of birth in Japanese, along with the dates of birth of some of your family.

LANGUAGE SUMMARY

Days of the week
getsuyōbi
kayōbi
suiyōbi
mokuyōbi
kinyōbi
doyōbi
nichiyōbi

Dates
tsuitachi
futsuka
mikka
yokka
itsuka
muika
nanoka
yōka
kokonoka
tōka
hatsuka
(ni)jūyokka
• *Other days:* ...-nichi

Seasons
haru
natsu
aki
fuyu

Education
shōgakkō
chūgakkō
kōkō
tandai
daigaku
ichinensei
benkyō
jugyō
(aru)baito
juku

Classroom words
jisho
isu
tēburu
chizu
nōto
tsukue
mado

Means of transport
chikatetsu
basu
kuruma
densha
jitensha
baiku
aruite
e.g. Nan de ikimasu ka?
     Basu de ikimasu.
     Aruite ikimasu.

Telling the time
(hours) -ji
(minutes) -fun/ -pun
e.g. Nanji desu ka?
     Hachiji jūsanpun
     desu.

Saying when
gozen hachiji **ni**
gogo sanji **kara** sanji han
     made
asa/yoru no rokuji **goro**

Saying the date
(year) -nen *(month)* -gatsu
     (day) -nichi
e.g. sen kyūhyaku
     nanajūninen
     shigatsu nijūgonichi

Ages
issai, nisai, sansai, etc.
e.g. O-ikutsu desu ka?
     Nijūsansai desu.
     Nansai desu ka?
     Yonsai desu.

Language for learning
Mō ichido onegai
     shimasu.
Mō sukoshi yukkuri
     onegai shimasu.
'Teacher' wa nihongo
     de nan to iimasu ka?
'Chūgakkō' to iu no wa
     nan desu ka?

Actions
okimasu
tabemasu
kimasu
ikimasu
yomimasu
nomimasu
demasu
mimasu
shimasu
kaerimasu
nemasu
kikimasu
hajimarimasu
owarimasu

sōji
sentaku
kaimono } (+ o shimasu)
doraibu
tenisu
shigoto

Saying how long
Dono gurai kakarimasu ka?
Ichijikan (gurai)
     kakarimasu.

Main language structures

Present polite (used to
describe regular events)
Statement: **-masu**
Rokuji han ni okimasu.
Itsumo nanyōbi ni
     kaimono o shimasu ka?
Negative statement:
     -masen
Rokuji ni nemasu ka?
Iie, rokuji ni wa nemasen.
     Jūichiji ni nemasu.

Present continuous
(used to describe events
happening now)
Statement: -te/ -de *form*
     + imasu
Nanako-san wa nani
     o shite imasu ka?
Nete imasu.

To deepen your understanding of some of the
language presented in this unit, you may like to
look at the following parts of the Grammar section:
'Verbs' (5A), 'Sentence building' (8C, G–I) and 'Time
expressions' (11A).

6
ON THE
ROAD

Travelling by train
Japanese hotels
Town and country
Stock questions to foreigners
Describing people

About Japan

The Japanese love to travel, both at home and abroad. Whether luxuriating in the baths of a local hot spring *(onsen)*, swimming in the Andaman Sea, or wandering round the capital cities of Europe, they also love to take photographs. They peer at you through their video cameras out of passing coaches and trains; they pose at all the best-known sites of Europe, the Americas, the world, and have themselves photographed by camera-carrying companions who, with *Hai! Chiizu!* encourage them to smile in front of the Statue of Liberty, the Tower of London or the Sydney Opera House.

Still, the Japanese passion for travel is by no means new. During the Edo Period (1603–1868), a system of highways linked each domain's castle town throughout the land, and people walked all over the country in large numbers. Some of these travellers were traders; others were sent on government business. Indeed, the feudal lords (or *daimyō*) themselves were obliged to spend alternate years in the capital, and this meant that they had to travel back and forth between their castle towns and Edo (as Tōkyō was then called) with their retinues. Along the major highways, stage posts were soon established, and the fifty-three stages along the Tōkaidō ('Eastern Sea Highway') between Edo and Ōsaka have been depicted by Andō Hiroshige, whose woodblock prints are much admired in the West.

In Japan, the relationship between art and travel, is very close. Not only did a number of woodblock printers like Hiroshige and Hokusai depict famous views and sites, but a number of literary men – like the *haiku* poet Bashō – used to write accounts of their long travels around Japan. These accounts, which go back to the tenth century, are almost invariably a mixture of poetry and prose and are fine expressions of Japanese literature. Not surprisingly, they are much loved by Japanese today.

Nowadays, of course, most people travel by modern means of transport, and it is only the occasional brave – or possibly romantic – foreigner who decides to walk the length of Japan or follow in the steps of Bashō on one of his long trips to the north. There are frequent plane services between the major cities of Japan – Sapporo, Tōkyō, Ōsaka and Fukuoka – but often it is simpler for those living in Tōkyō to take a train to cities nearer at hand, like Nagoya or Sendai.

The 'bullet train' (*shinkansen* in Japanese) is possibly the most famous train in the world. There was a time, too, when it was the fastest, and at 240 kilometres an hour the journey is still often quicker than by plane. Completed just before the Tōkyō Olympics in 1964 (at the same time as the monorail between the city centre and Haneda airport), the original service began by running high-speed trains every twenty minutes between Tōkyō and Ōsaka. Now the network of lines has been extended so that it stretches from Kyūshū in the south to the northern part of the main island of Honshū, with an extension to Hokkaidō under construction, as well as across the country from Tōkyō to Niigata on the Japan Sea coast.

'Shōno', from the *Fifty-three Stages of the Tōkaidō Highway* sequence of woodblock prints by Andō Hiroshige (1797–1858)

ASKING ABOUT TRAINS; BOOKING TICKETS IN ADVANCE

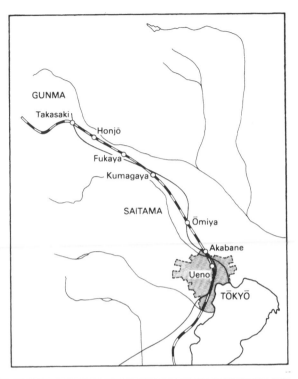

- To ask when a train arrives: **Nanji chaku desu ka?** E.g. 'What's the arrival time in Fukaya?': *Fukaya wa nanji chaku desu ka? (chaku or tōchaku = arrival)*

- To ask when a train departs: **Nanji hatsu desu ka?** E.g. 'What's the departure time from Takasaki?': *Takasaki wa nanji hatsu desu ka? (hatsu or shuppatsu = departure)*

SPOTCHECK 1

@ Answer the two example questions in the box above by looking at the times in the table below (to review times, see p. 106):

Takasaki	Honjō		Fukaya		Kumagaya		Ōmiya		Akabane		Ueno
hatsu	chaku	hatsu	chaku	hatsu	chaku	hatsu	chaku	hatsu	chaku	hatsu	chaku
8:13	8:36	**(1)**	8:45	**(2)**	**(3)**	**(4)**	**(5)**	**(6)**	**(7)**	10:00	10:09

LEAVING AND ARRIVING | CD ▶ 158 |

@ **A** Fill in the gaps in the table by asking the CD questions.

E.g. (1) *You:* **Honjō wa nanji hatsu desu ka?**
CD: **Hachiji sanjūhappun hatsu desu.**
→ You write '8:38' in the box marked '1'.

| CD ▶ 159 |

B Now the CD will ask the questions. Answer with times from the table.

E.g. *CD:* **Ōmiya wa nanji chaku desu ka?**
You: **Kuji yonjūsanpun chaku desu.**

BUILD-UP | CD ▶ 160 |

Apart from the famous *shinkansen* (bullet train), there are several types of train to choose from in Japan, all varying in speed – and price! Listen and say:

futsū densha	lit. 'ordinary train'
kaisoku	faster but no surcharge
kyūkō	express: surcharge payable
tokkyū	'limited express': bigger surcharge
shinkansen	'super express': very fast, very expensive

- With all this variety it's important to be able to say precisely which train you're interested in. Do so like this:

tsugi no ... (= the next)/ time hatsu ...	place yuki no ... (yuki = going to)	densha (= any type of train)/ futsū densha/ kaisoku/kyūkō/ tokkyū/ shinkansen

@ How would you say
  a the next bullet train to Ueno?
  b the 11:52 limited express to Morioka?

WHICH TRAIN?

CD ▶ 161

@ **A** Imagine you're at Takasaki station. You overhear five conversations in which trains from the timetable at the foot of this page are identified. Write down the letters (at the top of the timetable) which correspond to the trains mentioned.

E.g. (1) *CD:* **hachiji sanjuppun hatsu Ueno yuki no futsū densha** → Train G

CD ▶ 162

B Identify the following five trains to the CD, as fully as possible:

1 B **2** E **3** I **4** M **5** O

The CD will follow up with what you could have said; repeat this.

- If you're travelling around Japan as a tourist, you're likely to want to make advance enquiries about train times, and probably book tickets in advance, too. (The trains can get very crowded.) Now you know how to identify trains, the rest is relatively easy:

1 Identify the train E.g. 'It's about the 8:09 bullet train to Ueno …' **Hachiji kyūfun hatsu Ueno yuki no shinkansen desu ga …**

2 Enquire E.g. 'What time does it arrive in Ōmiya?': **Ōmiya wa nanji chaku desu ka?**

3 Book E.g.
'Two *singles* please': **Katamichi nimai kudasai.**
'One *return* please': **Ōfuku ichimai kudasai.**

	A	B	C	D	E	F	G	H	I	J	K	L	M	N	O
	FUTSŪ	TOKKYŪ	SHINKANSEN	TOKKYŪ	KAISOKU	SHINKANSEN	FUTSŪ	TOKKYŪ	FUTSŪ	KAISOKU	SHINKANSEN	TOKKYŪ	FUTSŪ	KAISOKU	SHINKANSEN
Type	普通	特急	新幹線	特急	快速	新幹線	普通	特急	普通	快速	新幹線	特急	普通	快速	新幹線
Takasaki (hatsu)	7.57	8.05	8.09	8.12	8.13	8.20	8.30	8.38	8.53	9.28	9.32	9.58	10.32	10.22	10.51
Honjō (chaku)	8.15	↓			4		8.55	↓	9.19	9.44			10.51	10.43	↓
Fukaya (chaku)	8.24	8.28			8.50		9.05	9.00	5	9.52			11.00	10.51	
Kumagaya (chaku)	1	8.36	↓	↓	9.01	↓	9.19	9.09	9.42	10.01	↓	↓	11.15	11.00	↓
Ōmiya (chaku)	9.24	9.04	8.36	9.08	9.45	8.47	9.57	9.35	10.21	10.31	10.00	10.44	12.01	11.31	11.16
Akabane (chaku)	9.38	2	↓	9.20	10.00	↓	10.16	9.49	10.40	10.45	↓	↓	12.16	11.46	↓
Ueno (chaku)	9.50	9.27	3	9.30	10.09	9.08	10.28	10.00	10.53	10.56	10.20	11.06	12.28	11.57	11.36

ENQUIRE

CD ▶ 163

A The CD will ask you for five departure or arrival times. Answer by referring to the timetable, then listen as the CD tells you what you should have said.

E.g. (1) *CD:* **Kuji gojūhappun hatsu Ueno yuki no tokkyū desu ga . . . Ueno wa nanji chaku desu ka?**
You: **Jūichiji roppun chaku desu.**

CD ▶ 164

@ **B** In the timetable you'll have noticed five empty boxes (numbered 1 to 5). Ask the CD for the time that goes in each box. Before giving you the answer, the CD tells you what you could have asked.

E.g. (1) *You:* **Shichiji gojūnanafun hatsu Ueno yuki no futsū densha desu ga . . . Kumagaya wa nanji chaku desu ka?**
Write the times you hear into the timetable.

BOOK

CD ▶ 165

@ **A** Listen to five people booking tickets at Takasaki station. Fill in the grid below with the train letter (from the timetable on the opposite page), whether they want singles (S) or returns (R) and the number of tickets required.

	1	2	3	4	5
Train letter					
S or R?					
No. of tickets					

CD ▶ 166

B Now it's your turn. Book your tickets on the basis of the information in boxes 6 to 10 below. Each time, first identify the train and ask what time it arrives in Ueno (the CD will reply), then ask for the tickets.

	6	7	8	9	10
Train letter	B	F	K	L	O
S or R?	S	R	R	S	R
No. of tickets	1	3	2	4	1

Rush hour on the Yamanote line, Tōkyō

BUYING TICKETS; ASKING PLATFORM NUMBERS

On this page we'll be looking at the different types of compartment you can travel in on Japanese trains, and what to say when you're buying tickets just before departure.

If you're travelling by *futsū densha* or *kaisoku*, tickets can be bought from a machine. The only problem is understanding the kanji map above the machine (which tells you the prices). However, if you can find a not too busy-looking bystander, you can always ask *Sumimasen, ... made ikura desu ka?*: 'How much is it to ...?' For example, *Ueno made ikura desu ka?*

If you're going by express, you'll need to buy a supplement ticket (in the booking office), and you may want to specify one of the following kinds of seat (listen and say):

BUILD-UP
CD ▸ 167

jiyūseki	unreserved seat
shiteiseki	reserved seat
kin'enseki	no smoking
guriinsha	first class (lit. 'green car')

- Give as much information as you can when asking for your ticket(s): e.g. **Ueno made tokkyū de katamichi ichimai kudasai** or **Kyōto made shinkansen de ōfuku nimai kudasai.**

- Any special requests can be slipped in afterwards: e.g. **Shiteiseki/Kin'enseki/Guriinsha onegai shimasu.**

- If you don't give all this information, you're likely to be asked for it: e.g. **Ōfuku desu ka, katamichi desu ka?**: 'Return or single?'

JAPANESE LIVE 1
CD ▸ 168

Yuka buys tickets for the shinkansen *to Ōsaka.*

Yuka	Ōsaka made <u>shinkansen</u> de <u>ōfuku nimai</u> kudasai.	A
Clerk	Hai. Shiteiseki desu ka, jiyūseki desu ka?	
Yuka	<u>Shiteiseki</u> kudasai. *(adding quickly)* Kin'enseki onegai shimasu.	B
Clerk	Hai. Rokuman gosen sanbyaku gojū-en desu.	
Yuka	*(handing over the money)* Hai. Ryōshūsho onegai shimasu. Ōsaka hōmen no <u>shinkansen</u> wa nanbansen desu ka?	C
Clerk	Jūyonbansen desu.	
Yuka	Arigatō gozaimasu.	
	Rewind and repeat!	

Ōsaka hōmen nanbansen?	in the direction of Ōsaka what platform? (lit. 'what number track?')

SPOTCHECK 3

@ Write down
  a the cost of the tickets
  b the platform number.

YOUR TURN
CD ▸ 169

@ Take Yuka's part in 'Japanese live 1' above. (The CD will take the part of the clerk.) Adapt what you say at points *A, B* and *C* above according to the seat/ticket requirements listed below, and note down the ticket prices and platform numbers.

1 to Sendai by *shinkansen*: one return (reserved, 1st class)

2 to Karuizawa by *tokkyū*: two singles (unreserved)

3 to Kyōto by *shinkansen*: three returns (reserved, non-smoking)

BUYING THINGS AT A STATION KIOSK

You're unlikely to go hungry if you're travelling by train in Japan; on the *shinkansen* and most *tokkyū* trains, trolleys ply the aisles carrying everything from **o-bentō** (lunch boxes containing rice and various tasty morsels) to **o-miyage** (souvenirs – often regional foodstuffs – to be taken back for friends, family or colleagues who couldn't make the trip). On the platform, too, you can get drinks, snacks, etc. either from the omni-present vending machines or from a 'kiosk' like the one in the photograph.

> • To ask what varieties of something are available:
> **... wa nani ga arimasu ka?**
> E.g. 'What kinds of snack (to accompany alcohol) have you got?': *O-tsumami wa nani ga arimasu ka?*

JAPANESE LIVE 2   CD ▸ 170

Overheard at a 'kiosk':

Passenger	Sumimasen, <u>o-tsumami</u> wa nani ga arimasu ka? *A*
Kiosk attendant	Saki'ika to piinattsu to poteto chippu ga arimasu.
Passenger	Jā, saki'ika o futatsu kudasai. *B*
Kiosk attendant	Hai, dōzo.
Passenger	Sore kara <u>sandoitchi</u> wa arimasu ka? *C*
Kiosk attendant	Hai, soko no chokorēto no mae ni arimasu.
Passenger	(*finding them*) Jā, kore mo kudasai.

Rewind and repeat!

saki'ika	dried squid
sore kara	and then/in addition
kore mo kudasai	I'll have this, too (note that **mo** replaces **o**)

SPOTCHECK 4

@ **a** What are *piinattsu, sandoitchi* and *chokorēto*?
b What does the customer buy?

TAKE NOTE

One of the most difficult aspects of Japanese is the very subtle difference between *wa* and *ga*. For the moment, just remember that *wa* or *ga* (not *o*) comes before *arimasu*, but that *wa* is never used after question words: so you say *Nani **ga** arimasu ka?* It may also help you to think of *wa* as a kind of spotlight, singling something out for special comment (try translating it as 'regarding .../'as for ...' in 'Japanese live 2'), whereas *ga* simply indicates the grammatical subject of a sentence.

WHAT'S AVAILABLE?   CD ▸ 171

Take the part of the customer in 'Japanese live 2' above. (The CD will take the part of the kiosk attendant.) Replace the underlined words (in the lines marked *A* and *C*) with:

1 *A*: sandoitchi   *C*: saki'ika
2 *A*: jūsu   *C*: bisuketto
3 *A*: biiru   *C*: o-bentō

At the place marked *B*, you decide what and how many of something you want, according to your preference.

About Japan

As we've seen, there are various kinds of train besides the bullet train, though their names can be slightly confusing to the uninitiated. Why, for example, is the 'limited express' (*tokkyū*) faster (and more expensive) than the normal 'express' (*kyūkō*)? It seems that it is limited not in its speed, but in the number of stops it makes en route to its destination. Although things may sometimes be confusing to the foreigner, they are not necessarily illogical. All that is happening is that a different kind of logic is being used.

Almost all kinds of transport in Japan are very crowded, and at certain times of the year – like the midsummer All Souls (*o-bon*) festival or the new year holiday (*shōgatsu*) – when many people travel back to their family homes, it can be very difficult to get tickets to go anywhere. During such trips, Japanese people often buy souvenirs (*o-miyage*) for relatives, neighbours and colleagues back home. A popular gift is one of the local specialities sold on long-distance trains or at airports. Food is not only something you consume for yourself, therefore, but something that you give to others (and hope to share with them). Just as we tend to take a bottle of wine for our hosts when invited out to dinner, the Japanese make sure that they buy something very special (and almost invariably beautifully wrapped), whether it be a box of expensive cakes, some special tea or perhaps in-season fruit. At some stations, you can find souvenirs from all over Japan, which means that it is possible to pretend to go somewhere and buy a gift to show that you have in fact been there, when all the time you were living it up in a nightclub or lying low in a love hotel!

Hotels in Japan vary, from large Western-style blocks to small wooden two-storeyed Japanese inns known as *ryokan*. Probably the cheapest is the 'capsule hotel' with space only to lie down. The most basic is the 'business hotel', which caters for businessmen on the road. Both Western-style hotels and Japanese inns can be quite reasonable, but they can also be extremely expensive. The latter very often have a communal bath in which all visitors soak themselves (washing outside the pool-like tub) soon after they check in and before dinner, which is usually served in their rooms. Here, and at 'bed and breakfasts', called *minshuku*, food will be traditionally Japanese, and that means learning how to drink green tea and eat a raw egg with rice, fish, pickles and seaweed for breakfast.

The most likely place for you to find Japanese inns is at one of the numerous hot springs (*onsen*) scattered around the country. The Japanese love to 'take the waters', and frequently go to onsen in large groups. This can make life a little noisy for the single traveller, since they will drink a lot in the evenings and start singing loudly before the men wander off to sample the local attractions – mainly somewhat run-down bars and strip joints. And when one of them gets too drunk to stand up, a bar hostess will be able to tell a local taxi-driver where to take him by the *yukata* (a kind of loose kimono) that he is wearing, since it bears the mark of the inn at which he is staying. Advertising certainly has its advantages at times!

A Japanese inn (*ryokan*)

HOTEL FACILITIES

Whereas in *minshuku* and *ryokan* the only rooms available are **washitsu** ('Japanese-style rooms', i.e. where you sleep on a futon on the tatami mat floor), small so-called 'business' hotels offer only **yōshitsu** ('Western-style rooms', i.e. with beds). Larger hotels often have some *washitsu* as well as *yōshitsu*.

BUILD-UP   CD ▶ 172

Say these words for facilities in hotels and hotel rooms (*hoteru no heya*), trying to guess the meanings of those words you haven't come across before (check in the glossary in the back of the book if you're not sure):

**resutoran   bā   daburu   tsuin
shinguru   terebi   denwa   eakon   shawā**

Write one word from the above list on each line in the chart on the right, next to the appropriate symbol or katakana word. (Check the katakana in the chart on the inside back cover of the book.)

READING

@ Now fill in the left-hand column of the chart by looking at this advertisement for the Orient Hotel. All you have to do is see whether the symbols or katakana in the chart appear in the advert. If a particular facility is listed, write a tick (and where appropriate a number), and if not, write a '?'.

		Orient Hotel	Hotel Sakura
和	washitsu		
洋	yōshitsu		
S			
D			
T			
(shower)			
(phone)			
TV			
A/C			
バー			
レストラン			

オリエントホテル   ☎095-76-0681

〒872   山口県中川市森田町2-16
交 通   JR 中川駅 🚗15分
料 金   11,800円〜   Ⓟ 20台
建 物   鉄筋 ▦15階建 200室 和40 洋160 全TV ☎ A/C
立地環境   市街 ▦
特 長   カードキーシステム
設 備   バー、フランスレストラン

LISTEN

CD ▶ 173

@ Listen to a travel agent ringing up to find out about the Hotel Sakura. In the phone conversation, information about six of the facilities in the chart is given. Write the information into the right-hand column of the chart.

YOUR TURN

CD ▶ 174

@ Now complete the chart by asking the receptionist of the Hotel Sakura about the remaining five facilities. Ask about them in the form *Hoteru/Heya ni wa ... wa arimasu ka?*

> E.g. (1) *CD:*   **washitsu**
> *You:* **Hoteru ni wa washitsu wa arimasu ka?**

Meal in a *ryokan*

BOOKING AND CHECKING INTO A HOTEL

Just as with trains, it's often advisable to book hotels in advance in Japan, especially during busy holiday periods such as 'Golden Week' (a series of public holidays at the beginning of May). If you have a booking, all you have to do when entering the hotel is say **yoyaku ga arimasu**: 'I have a reservation'. Otherwise:

- To say you want to make a reservation: **Yoyaku onegai shimasu/Yoyaku onegai shitai n' desu ga …** (lit. 'I want to ask the favour of a reservation.')

- To ask whether rooms are available: **Heya wa arimasu ka?/Heya wa aite imasu ka?** (lit. 'Are any rooms free?')

- To specify the number of nights: … **-haku/ … -paku.** E.g. 1 night: *ippaku*, 2 nights: *nihaku*, 3 nights: *sanpaku*.

Excursion to the Imperial Palace, Tōkyō

JAPANESE LIVE 3 `CD ▸ 175`

Two travellers reserve: Robert Hope well in advance, Alan Booth (seasoned travel writer) in person on the day.

Receptionist	(*answering the phone*) Oriento hoteru de gozaimasu.
Robert	Moshi moshi. Yoyaku onegai shitai n' desu ga ...
Receptionist	Hai.
Robert	Sangatsu mikka ni heya wa aite imasu ka?
Receptionist	Hai, gozaimasu. Shinguru deshō ka tsuin deshō ka?
Robert	Daburu wa arimasu ka?
Receptionist	Hai, gozaimasu. Nanpaku de gozaimasu ka?
Robert	Nihaku onegai shimasu. Ippaku ikura desu ka?
Receptionist	Niman-en de gozaimasu.
Robert	Dewa, onegai shimasu.
Alan	(*entering a 'ryokan'*) Gomen kudasai!
Proprietress	(*coming into sight*) Hai, irasshaimase!
Alan	Konban heya wa arimasu ka?
Proprietress	Hai, gozaimasu.
Alan	Jā, onegai shimasu.
Proprietress	Hai. Kochira ni o-namae to go-jūsho onegai shimasu ...
Alan	(*Writes his name and address.*)
Proprietress	(*showing the way to the room*) Kochira e dōzo.

Rewind and repeat!

...deshō ka?	a polite form of **desu ka?**
nanpaku?	how many nights?
konban	tonight

SPOTCHECK 5
@ Write down
  a the type of room Robert will stay in
  b the number of nights he will stay
  c the room rate.

BOOKINGS `CD ▸ 176`

@ **A** Listen to a prospective guest phoning the Hotel Sakura, and complete the form below with her details.

```
Name _____
Telephone _____     Type of room
Date of                  (single/twin)
arrival    _____
No. nights _____     Price _____
```

`CD ▸ 177`

@ **B** Complete the form below with your own name etc., and decide when and for how long you'd like to stay. Call the hotel and book the room, following the instructions on the CD. Write down the price you are given.

```
Name _____
Telephone _____     Type of room
Date of                  (single/twin)
arrival    _____
No. nights _____     Price _____
```

Alan Booth

STOCK QUESTIONS TO FOREIGNERS (1): FACTUAL QUESTIONS

If you're travelling in Japan, people you get talking to are likely to ask a series of predictable 'getting to know you' questions. The form the questions take will vary, but just expecting to be asked the questions and being able to pick out key words should enable you to understand.

@ Here are some of the most favoured topics, along with example forms for the questions you haven't encountered before (try to remember and write in the questions for topics **A**, **D**, **F** and **G**, looking back at pp. 36, 69 and 120 if necessary). On the right are key words likely to occur in other versions of the same question, and example replies.

Topic	Example question	Key words	Example reply
A Nationality	_____ _____	(o-)kuni, doko/dochira?, kara, . . . -jin	Igirisu(jin) desu.
B City/Town	Igirisu no dochira kara desu ka?	. . . no doko/dochira?	Rondon desu.
C Period of stay in Japan	(Mō)nihon ni dono gurai irasshaimasu ka? (*How long have you (already) been in Japan?*)	nihon, dono gurai?	Ninen desu/imasu. (*For two years*)
D Occupation	_____ _____	(o-)shigoto, (o-)tsutome	Kaishain desu./IBM ni tsutomete imasu.
E Marital status	Kekkon shite irasshaimasu ka? (*Are you married?*)	kekkon, oku-san, go-shujin	Hai, kekkon shite imasu./Iie, dokushin desu. (*I'm single*)
F Children	_____ _____	o-ko-san, kodomo	Hai, imasu./Iie, imasen.
G Age	_____ _____	ikutsu?, nansai?	Nijūissai desu.

LISTEN

CD ▶ 178

@ Listen to the variations on the questions opposite and, by consulting the key word column, decide which topic (A to G opposite) the question is referring to. Write the letter of that topic next to the question number below:

1 B   2 ___   3 ___   4 ___   5 ___   6 ___

7 ___   8 ___   9 ___   10 ___   11 ___

12 ___   13 ___   14 ___

TAKE NOTE

Whereas in English we say 'How long **have you been** (in a place)?', the Japanese question is literally 'Already how long **are** you in Japan?': *Mō dono gurai nihon ni imasu ka?* (or, more politely, *irasshaimasu ka?*). The reply might be literally 'Already I **am** here for two years': *Mō ninen imasu* (not *irasshaimasu*, since this is a respectful term used only about other people, never about yourself). To say, for example, 'I'll be here for another two years', just replace *mō* with *ato* ('from now'): *Ato ninen imasu*.

BUILD-UP

To talk about periods of time in Japanese (i.e. saying the equivalent of '**for** two weeks/three months', etc.), refer to this table and to part 11B of the Grammar section.

ippun(kan)/nifun(kan)	for 1/2 minute(s)
ichijikan/nijikan	for 1/2 hour(s)
ichinichi/futsuka(kan)	for 1/2 days(s)
isshūkan/nishūkan	for 1/2 week(s)
ikkagetsu(kan)/ nikagetsu(kan)	for 1/2 month(s)
ichinen(kan)/ninen(kan)	for 1/2 year(s)

SPOTCHECK 6

@ Write down the Japanese for:

a for five minutes   d for four weeks
b for ten hours   e for seven months
c for six days   f for nineteen years.

JAPANESE LIVE 4

CD ▶ 179

Robert Hope gets into conversation with a fellow passenger on the *shinkansen* to Morioka (in Tōhoku).

Robert	Sumimasen ga Morioka made dono gurai kakarimasu ka?
Japanese	Morioka made desu ka? Ato ichijikan gurai desu ne . . .
Robert	Ā, sō desu ka.
Japanese	Shitsurei desu ga, o-kuni wa dochira desu ka?
Robert	*Igirisu desu.
Japanese	Ā, sō desu ka. Nihon ni mō dono gurai irasshaimasu ka?
Robert	*Muikakan desu.
Japanese	O-shigoto wa?
Robert	*Konpyūta no sērusuman desu.
Japanese	Ā, sō desu ka. Kekkon shite irasshaimasu ka?
Robert	*Hai, kekkon shite imasu.
Japanese	O-ko-san wa?
Robert	*Musuko to musume ga imasu.
Japanese	Ā, sō desu ka. Shitsurei desu ga, o-ikutsu desu ka?
Robert	*Yonjūnisai desu.

Rewind and repeat!

sērusuman	salesman
shitsurei desu ga . . .	it is rude (of me) but . . .

SPOTCHECK 7

@ How long has Robert been in Japan?

YOUR TURN

CD ▶ 180

Now practise your own answers to stock questions by taking Robert's part in 'Japanese live 4' above. (The dialogue is recorded again with spaces left for your replies at the points marked with *.) Prepare your answers before beginning; if you're not in Japan now, imagine you arrived three weeks ago.

About Japan

One thing that you will notice about Japan is that it is extremely centralised. Not only are government offices all located in the capital, but so are the headquarters of almost all the largest corporations and financial institutions, the campuses of the most prestigious universities, the largest department stores and so on. Size seems to breed size, and most Japanese now think it is virtually impossible to conduct business efficiently without living in Tōkyō.

Whether this is true or not is hard to say. However, one thing is certain. Because all major political, bureaucratic, financial and business institutions are located in the capital, more and more people find themselves having to live in Tōkyō – or as near as they can get to it. This means that most of them have to spend at least three hours a day commuting to and from work in overcrowded trains, where students are employed to push passengers into the carriages during morning and evening rush hours.

But if more and more people are being obliged to flock into Tōkyō and other big cities, many of them still have their roots in rural Japan. It is from the country villages in places like Tōhoku, Hokkaidō, Shikoku and Kyūshū that many of today's suited salary men once came, and it is to these same villages that they like to return with their families once, or maybe twice, a year.

But there is a strange ambivalence felt by most Japanese about the countryside, or *inaka*. Rural areas are seen to be *sabishii* (lonely), in comparison to urban centres that are *modan* and *nigiyaka* (lively). To call someone an *inakamono* has the same insulting connotations as our own 'country bumpkin', and most migrants to Tōkyō will do their utmost to disguise the fact that they are from the country. Since each part of Japan is marked by its own distinctive dialect, however, this can sometimes prove difficult. But Japanese may well spend a lot of time trying to adapt to 'standard speech' (*hyōjungo*), in much the same way that aspiring Conservative politicians in England have been known to take speech lessons in 'BBC English'. The only difference is that whereas the British do this to hide their class, the Japanese do so to conceal their local geographical origins.

At the same time, the Japanese have a great feeling of nostalgia for the countryside, especially their *furusato*, or 'native home'. There are several reasons for this. One of them has to do with standards of living. Most country houses are far more spacious than the cramped apartments which most people in cities find themselves inhabiting. Both the air and the pace of life, too, are far more pleasant than in places like Tōkyō or Ōsaka.

Another reason for nostalgia has to do with Japan's rapid industrialisation and modernisation. Most Japanese are convinced that the countryside is a repository for values that no longer exist in the big cities. Country people are not 'selfish' or 'individualistic' in the way city people are. They live in 'communities', where people help one another out when in difficulty; not like city people, who do not even know who their neighbours are. In short, the country is seen to maintain the old and traditional values that served to make Japan what it is today.

That this is not just nostalgia for the past, but romanticisation, is fairly obvious to anyone who has tried to live in the Japanese countryside. But it is a romanticisation that is typical of all industrialised urban societies, and not just of present-day Japan. We are equally guilty of looking to the countryside for guidance as to 'the way we once were'.

Takachiho Gorge, Kyūshū

STOCK QUESTIONS TO FOREIGNERS (2): LIKES AND DISLIKES

Apart from the factual questions on p. 144, Japanese people like to ask foreigners what they think of Japanese food, people and places:

> * To ask someone's opinion of something:
>   ... **wa dō desu ka?** ('How do you like ...?')
>   ... **ga/wa suki desu ka?** ('Do you like ...?')
>   E.g. *Nihon wa dō desu ka?/ Nihon wa suki desu ka?*
>
>   CD ▸ 181
>
> * To answer (listen and repeat):
>
>   I like it very much. **Daisuki desu.**
>
>   I like it. **Suki desu.**
>
>   I don't mind it. **Kirai ja arimasen.**
>
>   I don't really like it. **Amari suki ja arimasen.**
>
>   I dislike it. **Kirai desu.**
>
>   I dislike it intensely. **Daikirai desu.**

LISTEN

CD ▸ 182

@ Listen as Alan is asked what he thinks of the things in the pictures below and right. Draw appropriate faces next to the pictures according to his replies.

1 o-sake

2 biiru

AND YOU?

CD ▸ 183

This time the CD will ask you your own opinion of the things in the pictures; answer with one of the expressions from the box.

TAKE NOTE

Another thing you should be prepared for is people exclaiming at your amazing mastery of chopsticks or of Japanese. However excessive, banal or condescending such comments may seem, they're intended simply as ice-breakers, and are most suitably responded to with a self-deprecating phrase like **lie, mada heta desu** ('No, I'm still no good') or **lie, mada mada desu** ('I've still got a long way to go').

JAPANESE LIVE 5

CD ▸ 184

Robert is in his hotel bar.

Fellow guest	O-hashi ga o-jōzu desu nē ...
Robert	lie, mada heta desu.
Fellow guest	Nihongo mo o-jōzu desu nē ...

Rewind and repeat!

... **ga o-jōzu desu**	(you're) skilful/good ...
mada	still
heta desu	(I'm) unskilful/not very good.

3 tabako

4 sushi

5 terebi

6 rokku

7  sumō

8 nihonjin

DESCRIBING APPEARANCE

If you venture off the beaten track in Japan, you're quite likely to meet people who've rarely seen, and certainly never talked to a foreigner before. Don't be surprised, then, if people stare, or if children follow you exclaiming *'gaijin!'*, *'harō'* (hello), 'this is a pen', *'ashi ga nagai desu ne'* (your legs are long!) or *'hana ga takai desu ne'* (your nose is high!). Apart from noses, here are some other ways of describing looks:

se ga takai	tall
kaminoke ga nagai	long-haired
sutairu ga ii	has a good figure
wakai	young(-looking)
sumāto (na)	slim
hansamu (na)	handsome

Suzuki

Miyahara

DESCRIPTIONS

CD ▶ 185

@ Write in the names of the people on the left below, according to these descriptions (listen and repeat):

Kamiyama-san wa . . . se ga takai desu . . . kaminoke ga nagai desu . . . totemo kirei desu.

Arai-san wa . . . se ga amari takaku arimasen . . . kaminoke ga mijikai desu . . . amari hansamu ja arimasen.

se ga amari takaku arimasen	(he/she) isn't very tall
amari hansamu ja arimasen	(he) isn't very handsome

TAKE NOTE

To form the 'negative' of an adjective, you first have to know whether or not it takes *na* before a noun. (Look back to p. 89 to remind yourself of this distinction.) This is how 'normal' and 'na' adjectives change:

'normal' adjectives:

*taka**i** desu* → *taka**ku** arimasen*
*yo**i**/i**i** desu* → *yo**ku** arimasen*

'na' adjectives:

hansamu desu → *hansamu **ja** arimasen*

SPOTCHECK 8

@ Write in Japanese:
  a He isn't young.
  b She isn't slim.
  c She isn't very pretty. (use *amari*)
  d He hasn't got very long legs.

YOUR TURN

Write descriptions of Ms Suzuki and Mr Miyahara, using those of Ms Kamiyama and Mr Arai above as models.

WHAT DO YOU THINK?

CD ▶ 186

The CD will ask you ten questions about the people in the picture. Answer according to what you yourself think.

  E.g. (1) *CD:* **Suzuki-san wa kawaii desu ka?**
      You: **Hai, (totemo) kawaii desu./ Iie, (amari) kawaiku arimasen.**

About Japan

One thing about those living in rural communities is that they tend to lead very secluded lives, and one hears stories of local families carrying on feuds for generation after generation, in much the same way as Sicilian families do in tales of the mafia. At the same time, people in the country frequently regard the outside world as beginning two hundred yards down the village road. Japan is no exception to this rule. A man can move from the hamlet next door because his house has burned down, live in his newly adopted community for twenty or thirty years, and still be referred to as 'that guy who moved in recently'!

Japanese society as a whole is marked by a strong sense of exclusiveness. We have already seen how people tend to identify with the company or university to which they belong(ed), and how this results in the formation of exclusive cliques in which one group of people is pitted in rivalry against another. At the same time, however, these groups can and will come together when threatened by an external force of some kind. This sense of 'groupness' becomes most apparent when the Japanese nation as a whole comes into contact with foreigners, and it is this 'closing of ranks' in political or trade matters which so annoyed Western businessmen and politicians in the 1980s.

A sense of 'exclusiveness' often results in protestations of the 'uniqueness' of Japanese culture, in arguments that Japan is somehow a special case when it comes to international trade agreements. Of course, it is possible for every nation to argue that it is a special case (witness the frequent position in recent years of Britain in European Community negotiations), but Japan does have a historical – though not necessarily valid – excuse for its occasional exclusive attitudes.

During the early years of the Edo Period (1603–1868), the shogunate decided that all foreigners should be barred from living in Japan – except for a small island off Nagasaki. Until the middle of the nineteenth century, Japan was thus a 'closed country' (*sakoku*), and it was only opened up when the American Commodore Perry sailed into Tōkyō Bay with his famous iron 'black ships' (*kurofune*) and threatened the shogunate unless it agreed to supply foreign (whaling) ships with food and water.

For some reason or other, the *sakoku* feeling has continued among the Japanese right up to the present day. At times, one wonders whether this *shimaguni* or 'island country' complex has not been deliberately fostered by a government determined to keep Japan 'different' from other industrialising and modernising nations in the West. Many Japanese suffer from a strange mixture of intense curiosity and hazy ignorance about what is going on abroad, together with out-of-date stereotypes about foreigners and the places where they live – 'foggy London' (*kiri no Rondon*) and 'a country of gentlemen' (*shinsu no kuni*) being two particularly prevalent stereotypes about England!

You may laugh. But now think about Western images of the Japanese as living in a land of samurai, geisha and cherry blossoms, and more recently of rabbit hutches, economic animals and sumō wrestlers. With luck, this book will have demonstrated that Japan and 'the Japanese' are much more interesting than these stereotypes might suggest.

Senior High School girls on a school trip

WHAT YOU'LL HEAR

MY KIND OF PLACE ・ CD ▶ 187

@ In these interviews (1 to 3), three different people staying at an onsen were asked how often they came there, why they liked it so much, whether they came in a group, how many nights they usually stayed, and which season they preferred for visiting the onsen.

   Listen to Yuka's interviews and fill in the answers below. For the first question ('Why do you like it here?'), choose from the following three reasons:

Good food	Beautiful scenery	Relaxing bathing

Remember that the counter for nights is -haku/-paku and that the names of the seasons are *haru* (spring), *natsu* (summer), *aki* (autumn) and *fuyu* (winter).

Why do you like it here?   **Did you come in a group?**

1 _____   Yes/No
2 _____   Yes/No
3 _____   Yes/No

How many nights do you usually stay?   **Best season?**

1 _____ nights   _____
2 _____ nights   _____
3 _____ nights   _____

CONNECTIONS ・ CD ▶ 188

@ Sitting on a train in Japan as you come into one of the larger stations, you'll hear the guard announce all the available connections: where they're going to, at what time and from which platform they leave. If you're planning to change trains at the station, this can be a great help. Practise making sense of one of these announcements: the guard on this recording talks about the trains shown below, in the order indicated. Your task is to listen out for the departure times and platform numbers; write these in the appropriate columns.

	Destination	Platform number	Departure time
1	Ueno	13	15:20
2	Niigata		
3	Ueno		
4	Ueno		
5	Yokokawa		
6	Nagano		
7	Kodama		
8	Shimonita		

BOOKING BY PHONE CD ▶ 189

@ Listen to the six phone conversations (1 to 6) in which people call to reserve the things on the left below. In each case listen out for what is being reserved, when it is being reserved for, how much it is going to cost, who is doing the reserving and what that person's telephone number is. The options are mixed up below; write the number of a conversation next to each one. Numbering for the first conversation has been done as an example.

Two tickets for a pop concert	10/8/91	¥19 000	Yamada	3763–4832
A return air ticket to New York	5/6/92	¥64 000	Saitō (*1*)	2845–8661
One night at the Hotel New Ōtani	3/4/91 (*1*)	¥11 700	Guriin	3924–1007
A table for four at a restaurant (*1*)	24/7/91	¥72 000	Kimura	3244–7533
Four seats to see a *kabuki* play	19/1/92	¥23 000 (*1*)	Sakurai	3921–8461
A hire car for three days	27/3/91	¥198 000	Ogawa	3743–9050 (*1*)

STOCK QUESTIONS CD ▶ 190

@ One of the things you learned in this unit was to expect and recognise some of the stock questions you're likely to be asked as a foreign visitor to Japan. For some more practice, listen to the conversation on the CD between a Japanese man and a foreign woman.

A Play the track once and try to pick out the gist of the questions. Following the order in which topics are discussed, write one of these question summaries in front of each question mark below:

Where from? Age? Period of stay? Married? Job? Children?

1 A: _____ ? 4 A: _____ ?
  B: _____   B: _____
2 A: _____ ? 5 A: _____ ?
  B: _____   B: _____
3 A: _____ ? 6 A: _____ ?
  B: _____   B: _____

B Now rewind the CD and (in English) note down the substance of B's answers.

C Listen one last time. A asks B whether she likes something. What? He also compliments her on something. What?

153

WRITTEN JAPANESE

If you're 'on the road' in Japan, these characters may prevent you from getting too lost. (Useful ways to remember the kanji are suggested on the left.)

someone travelling north, with back to the sun	north 北	'on' : **hoku** 'kun' : **kita**
sun rising behind a tree	east 東	'on' : **tō** 'kun' : **higashi**
plant in a building with southern aspect	south 南	'on' : **nan** 'kun' : **minami**
bird going to sleep as sun sets in the west	west 西	'on' : **sei/sai** 'kun' : **nishi**

While *kita*, *higashi*, *minami* and *nishi* are the words in common usage for the basic points of the compass, 'northeast', 'southeast', 'southwest' and 'northwest' are *hokutō*, *nantō*, *nansei* and *hokusei* respectively. 'On' readings also apply in the case of place names: for example, as you know, 東京 is read as *Tōkyō*.

Below are the names of Japan's four main islands (listed in order of size), followed by the names of another area you might like to visit – Tōhoku, the northeastern part of the main island, Honshū – and two areas you almost certainly will visit if you come to Japan: Kantō, the eastern plain on which Tōkyō is located, and Kansai, location of Kyōto and Ōsaka in the west. By identifying the Chinese characters you're already familiar with, try drawing lines from the place names on the left to what you think are the correct kanji on the right:

1	Honshū	A	四国
2	Hokkaidō	B	東北
3	Kyūshū	C	関東
4	Shikoku	D	関西
5	Tōhoku	E	本州
6	Kantō	F	九州
7	Kansai	G	北海道

The kanji you haven't come across before are as follows:

province	sea	road, way	barrier
州	海	道	関
shū	kai	dō	kan

The kanji for 'province' is related to a character you've already come across, 川, and is said to depict sandbanks in a river, or land bounded by rivers. Honshū is the 'original' or 'main' province, the main island of Japan, while Kyūshū and Shikoku were originally divided into nine and four provinces or 'countries' respectively, hence their names. Hokkaidō lies in the far north of Japan, and literally means 'northern sea road'. The same character for 'sea' appears in 日本海 (*nihonkai*: the 'Japan Sea' separating Japan from the Asian mainland), while 道 (*dō*) can have a spiritual connotation, for example when used to describe the 'ways' of *jūdō*, *kendō* (Japanese fencing) or *sadō* (tea ceremony).

Travel in Japan used to be severely monitored, and journeyers on the Tōkaidō (東海道 : 'eastern sea road') had to cross many checkpoints or 'barriers' on their way between Edo and Kyōto or Ōsaka in the west. The eastern plain around Edo therefore became known as Kantō ('east of the barrier(s)'), while the western plain was called Kansai ('west of the barrier(s)'). These regions retain quite separate identities even today, though you're unlikely to be asked for your passport when travelling between them!

Nowadays the journey between Kantō and Kansai is likely to be by train. In Kantō you may see a sign like this on the sides of carriages:

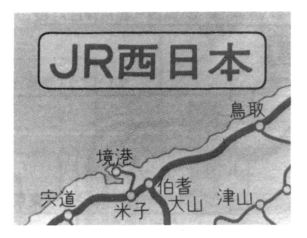

Here are some useful 'station' kanji to help you in the right direction:

enter 入 i(ri)	one river entering another *or* person stooping to enter	⁄ 入
leave 出 de	plant leaving the ground	↓ 屮 屮 出 出
mouth/ entrance 口 kuchi/ guchi	person's mouth *or* cave entrance	↓ 冂 口

In Kansai, you are likely to see signs like the one above. The two major railway companies in Japan are *JR higashi nihon* and *JR nishi nihon*, mainly serving the Kantō and Kansai regions respectively.

@ Finally, read aloud the signs in these photographs
(use 'kun' readings for the points of the compass):

1

3

2

4

Left Ticket barriers: entrance (*iriguchi*) and exit (*deguchi*).

LANGUAGE SUMMARY

Types of train
futsū densha
kaisoku
kyūkō
tokkyū
shinkansen

Types of compartment
jiyūseki
shiteiseki
kin'enseki
guriinsha

'Kiosk food'
o-bentō
saki'ika
chokorēto
piinattsu
o-miyage

Hotel facilities
washitsu
yōshitsu
resutoran
denwa
terebi
bā
eakon
shawā
daburu
tsuin
shinguru
e.g. Heya ni wa eakon
    wa arimasu ka?
    Hai, gozaimasu.

Number of nights
ippaku/nihaku/sanpaku
e.g. Nanpaku desu ka?
    Roppaku desu.

Length of time
ippun(kan)
ichijikan
isshūkan
ikkagetsu(kan)
ichinen(kan)
e.g. Dono gurai nihon ni
    imasu ka?
    Mō/Ato ninen(kan)
    desu.

Physical appearance
se ga takai
kaminoke ga nagai
sutairu ga ii
wakai
sumāto (na)
hansamu (na)

Arrival and departure
chaku
hatsu
e.g. Nanji chaku desu ka?

Identifying a train
(time) hatsu
(place) yuki/hōmen
no *(type of train)*
e.g. Sanji hatsu Ueno
    yuki no kyūkō

Single or return
katamichi
ōfuku
e.g. Katamichi ichimai
    kudasai.

Platform number
(number) -bansen
e.g. Ōsaka hōmen no
    shinkansen wa
    nanbansen desu ka?
    Jūyonbansen desu.

Booking a hotel room
Yoyaku onegai shitai
    n' desu ga …
Heya wa arimasu ka?/
    aite imasu ka?

Stock questions
Igirisu no dochira kara
    desu ka?
Kekkon shite
    irasshaimasu ka?
Hai, kekkon shite imasu.
Iie, dokushin desu.

Likes and dislikes
Daisuki desu.
Suki desu.
Kirai ja arimasen.
Amari suki ja arimasen.
Kirai desu.
Daikirai desu.
e.g. Nihɔn wa dō desu
    ka? Daisuki desu.

Compliments
O-hashi ga o-jōzu desu
    ne.
Iie, mada mada desu/
    mada heta desu.

Main language structure

Negative of adjectives
'-i' adjectives: -i desu
    → -ku arimasen
e.g. Arai-san wa wakai
    desu ka? Iie, wakaku
    arimasen.
'na' adjectives:
    (adjective) desu →
    (adjective) ja arimasen
e.g. Suzuki-san wa kirei
    desu ka? Iie, kirei ja
    arimasen.

To deepen your understanding of some of the language presented in this unit, look at these parts of the Grammar section: 'Time expressions' (11B), 'Adjectives' (12A, B), 'Verbs' (5D) and 'Sentence building' (A–C).

7 EATING, DRINKING AND ENTERTAINING

Restaurants and coffee shops
Business entertaining
Ordering food and drink
Talking about the past

About Japan

In many respects life in Japan is like a film. Although events seem to run together in a continuous flow, in fact they are made up of dozens of still frames, and Japanese adapt their behaviour according to the frame in which they find themselves. As we've seen, their language, too, changes accordingly. A man will use polite language to his managing director, but humble language when talking about him to someone from outside the group. In other words, nobody is ever absolutely superior or inferior in Japanese society. Everything depends on the social frame.

One of the features of a society which places great emphasis on contextual frames is that work and play tend to be set apart from each other. Visitors to Japan are often struck by the fact that there seem to be not one, but two cultures: one for the day and one for the night. During the daytime all good salary men are at their desks, or out and about doing their business. After dark, however, you will often find them in one of the area's various bars, restaurants or cabarets, eating, drinking and entertaining. In short, while the daytime is for work, the night-time is for play.

And variety is what the world of Japanese food and drink is all about. There can hardly be another country in the world with such a large number of restaurants and cooking styles on the one hand, coupled with such a wide range thereof on the other. Walk down one of the busier streets of any of Tōkyō's many entertainment areas, such as Shibuya or Shinjuku, and you will find – sandwiched between the *pachinko* parlours, *mahjong* clubs, 'stand' bars (where you can in fact sit), street vendors' carts (known as *yatai*) and the occasional 'authentic' English pub – Thai, Chinese, French and Indian restaurants, Korean *horumon* (hormone) grills, American fast-food chains and pizza parlours, not to forget the myriad types of food, from noodles (*soba, udon* or *rāmen*) to barbecued chicken (*yakitori*), served up by the Japanese themselves. It would seem, then, that not only is there nothing you cannot find to eat in a city like Tōkyō, but also that you do not have to go too far to find it.

Coffee shops (called *kissaten* or simply *kōhii shoppu*) are also very popular places for people to gather at any time of the day or night. You can sit there all day for the price of a drink of some sort or other, and around universities you will find places that specialise in playing certain kinds of music – classical or modern jazz, for example – for customers to listen to as they study or talk to friends.

Most people, however, use coffee shops for rendezvous or to snatch a quick (belated) breakfast or lunch. Like a large number of restaurants, they often provide a display case outside their entrance, showing plastic models of the food and drinks they serve. Some of them also have menus written in English and, since these tend to be translated directly back from Japanese versions of English, you come across the occasional culinary delight – like 'hot sand' ('sand' being an abbreviation of 'sandwich', eaten perhaps for 'desert'!), 'humbug steak' (for a hamburger), 'scalloped mariner' (marinated scallops) and 'green peace' (for the environmentally conscious vegetarian?). Given that you can also eat Queer-Aid chocolate and buy such drinks as Calpis (guess how foreigners pronounce that name) and Pocari Sweat, you can be sure, when it comes to food and drink in Japan, that life will never be dull.

ORDERING FOOD AND DRINK

If you enter a busy coffee shop or restaurant, you'll be asked how many people there are in your group before being shown to a table. In the very polite Japanese typical of waiters and waitresses, the question will probably be **Nanmei-sama deshō ka?** (in more 'everyday' Japanese, **Nannin desu ka?**: 'How many people?').

CD ▸ 191

- The 'counter' for people is **-nin** (though there are special words for one or two people). Listen and repeat:

  hitori   one person
  futari   two people
  sannin   three people
  yonin   four people
  gonin   five people
  nannin?   how many people?

LISTEN

CD ▸ 192

@ Listen to restaurant staff welcoming five sets of customers (1 to 5). Note down how many people there are in each group.

YOUR TURN

CD ▸ 193

Now you answer the waitress, consulting your notes from 'Listen' above.
     E.g. (1) *CD:* Number 4: **Nanmei-sama deshō ka?**
         You: **Gonin desu.**

WHAT'S ON THE MENU?

There are two or three ways of finding out what's on the menu. There might be a window containing plastic replicas like these to help . . .

1   kōhii
2   mōningu setto
3   orenji jūsu
4   remon tii
5   mikkusu sando
6   piza tōsuto
7   sarada
8   chiizu kēki
9   karē raisu
10   biiru

If not, you can always ask. For example, in a coffee shop: **Orenji jūsu wa arimasu ka?** ('Do you have orange juice?') or **Tabemono wa nani ga arimasu ka?** ('What kinds of food do you have?').

Imagine for the moment that your coffee shop does have a display window, and that you're ready to order. Waiters and waitresses are generally very attentive, and you can usually attract their attention through eye contact and a nod. Otherwise, call out **onegai shimasu!** or **sumimasen!**, just as you would in a shop. To order, too, you can use the language you used for shopping in Unit 4: *Remon tii (o)* **kudasai**, for example, or (slightly more politely) *Kōhii (o) futatsu* **onegai shimasu**.

食事		1	2	3
カレーライス	(_____) ¥650			
ピザトースト	(_____) ¥450			
ミックスサンド	(_____) ¥500			
サラダ	(_____) ¥300			
チーズケーキ	(_____) ¥350			
モーニングセット	(_____) ¥500			
(8.00 a.m.–11.00 a.m.)				
飲物				
コーヒー	(_____) ¥300			
レモンティー	(_____) ¥350			
オレンジジュース	(_____) ¥250			
ビール	(_____) ¥550			

EXCUSE ME

CD ▶ 194

Listen to the CD saying the names of the items in the pictures on the opposite page. Each time, practise ordering by first attracting the waiter or waitress's attention, then saying the name of the item plus *kudasai* or *onegai shimasu*.

   E.g. (1) *CD:* **kōhii**
         You: **Sumimasen! Kōhii kudasai.**

KATAKANA

@ The names of many of the items on offer in coffee shops and Western-style restaurants are foreign, and therefore written on menus in katakana (the script used for 'foreign' words). There's a chart containing all the katakana symbols on the inside back cover of the book: use it now to decipher the menu above,

and write the name of one item from the picture next to each katakana word on the menu.

ORDERING

CD ▶ 195

@ Listen to the orders of three groups (1 to 3) in the coffee shop. Write down how many of each thing they order, in the boxes to the right of the menu above.

JAPANESE LIVE 1   CD ▸ 196

@ This is the third of the conversations you've just listened to: Tomoko Sakai is ordering for her friends, Keiko and Mayumi. Try to remember (or work out) what words should go in the gaps. Then listen to check.

Tomoko	*Jā, nani ni shimasu ka?
Keiko	Watashi wa _____ ni shimasu.
Mayumi	Watashi mo piza tōsuto desu.
Tomoko	*_____!
Waitress	Hai. Nani ni nasaimasu ka?
Tomoko	*Piza tōsuto _____ to mikkusu sando hitotsu kudasai. (*to her friends*) Nomimono wa?
Mayumi	Hotto kōhii _____.
Keiko	Watashi wa remon tii ni shimasu.
Tomoko	*Jā, hotto hitotsu to remon tii o futatsu kudasai.

nani ni shimasu ka?	what will you have?
nani ni nasaimasu ka?	what will you have? (very polite)
nomimono	drink(s)
hotto (kōhii)	hot coffee (as opposed to iced: aisu kōhii)

YOUR TURN   CD ▸ 197

Take Tomoko's part in 'Japanese live 1', saying exactly what she says at the points marked *. The next three times, continue to speak at the points marked *, but order for different sets of friends. Each time, you'll have to listen out carefully for what your friends want. (It may help you to take notes.) This is what *you* want each time:

1 cheese cake and a coffee
2 curry rice and a beer
3 a morning set and an orange juice.

Tomoko Sakai in a coffee shop (*kissaten*)

Plastic food replicas in the display case outside a coffee shop

DURING AND AFTER THE MEAL

BUILD-UP

CD ▶ 198

You can expect to hear the following expressions pepper any meal eaten out in a restaurant and, apart from the bill of course, at home too (listen and say):

____ **itadakimasu** (like 'bon appétit', said at the beginning of a meal)

____ **gochisōsama deshita** (said at the end of a meal, by way of thanks)

____ **kanpai!** ('cheers!')

____ **oishi-sō!** ('it looks delicious!')

____ **oishikatta!** ('it was delicious!')

____ **(mō) kekkō desu** ('I've (already) had enough')

____ **okanjō onegai shimasu** ('the bill, please')

____ **biiru mō ippon kudasai** ('one more bottle of beer, please')

LISTEN

CD ▶ 199

@ You'll hear some excerpts from a conversation between friends during a meal out. Beforehand, try to predict the (rough) order in which the expressions in 'Build-up' might occur. (Write numbers next to the expressions above.) Then listen to check.

PEPPER THE MEAL!

CD ▶ 200

Now listen to the same excerpts, but with the 'Build-up' expressions left out. Practise interjecting the appropriate expressions in the right places. Then try again, this time without looking at 'Build-up'.

- To ask how something was: **Dō deshita ka?** (*deshita* = was)

- To say 'It was delicious/interesting, etc.': *Oishikatta/Omoshirokatta (desu)*. The final *i* of 'normal' adjectives is replaced with *katta* (optionally followed by *desu*). However, 'na' adjectives (e.g. *kantan*) have no special past form: 'It was easy', for example, is simply *Kantan* **deshita**.

BUILD-UP

@ Look up and note down the meanings of these adjectives, and match each one with one of the pictures opposite (by writing a letter in the box next to the appropriate picture). Then work out the past forms of the adjectives, and write them on the lines.

A oishii _____
B tanoshii _____
C kanashii _____
D tsumaranai _____
E kowai _____
F kantan (na) _____
G nigiyaka (na) _____

HOW WAS IT?

CD ▶ 201

Listen to the conversations (1 to 7), which correspond to the pictures 1 to 7 opposite. Then rewind and repeat.

YOUR TURN

CD ▶ 202

This time you answer the questions (*Dō deshita ka?*), as if you were the people in the pictures. The background sound effects will indicate which picture is being referred to.

    E.g. *CD:* (sound of yawning) **Dō deshita ka?**
       You: **Tsumaranakatta!**

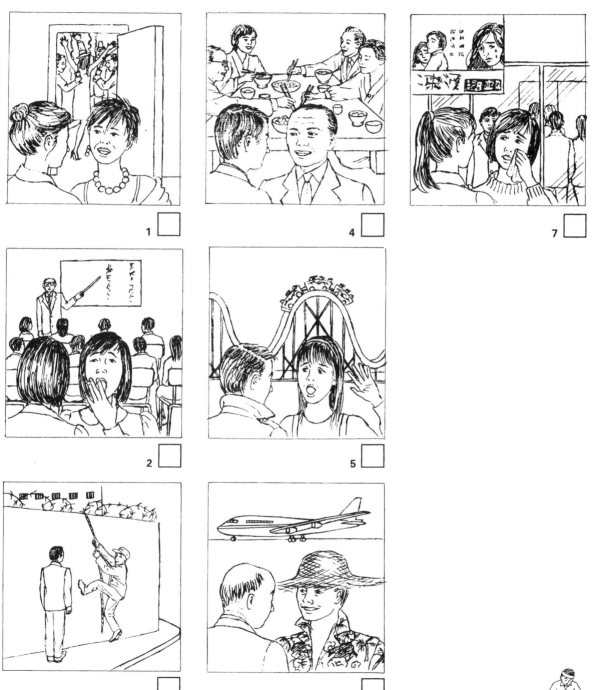

1 ☐

4 ☐

7 ☐

2 ☐

5 ☐

3 ☐

6 ☐

SAYING WHEN YOU DID SOMETHING

Jun Sakai is sorting out his business expenses for the past month or so. Here are the receipts for lunches he has eaten on business trips:

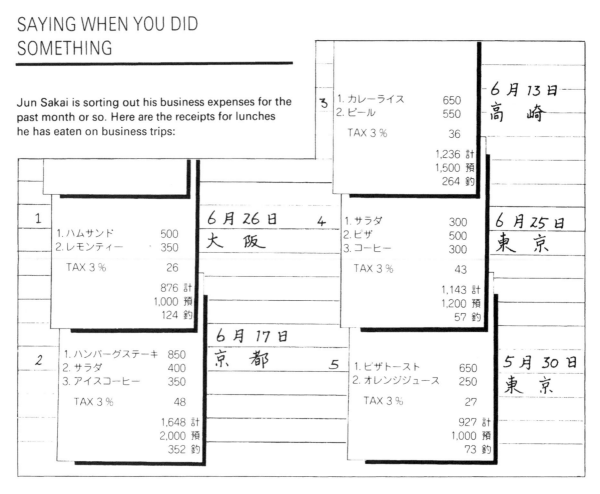

3
1. カレーライス	650
2. ビール	550
TAX 3 %	36
	1,236 計
	1,500 預
	264 釣

6 月 13 日
高 崎

1
1. ハムサンド	500
2. レモンティー	350
TAX 3 %	26
	876 計
	1,000 預
	124 釣

6 月 26 日
大 阪

4
1. サラダ	300
2. ピザ	500
3. コーヒー	300
TAX 3 %	43
	1,143 計
	1,200 預
	57 釣

6 月 25 日
東 京

2
1. ハンバーグステーキ	850
2. サラダ	400
3. アイスコーヒー	350
TAX 3 %	48
	1,648 計
	2,000 預
	352 釣

6 月 17 日
京 都

5
1. ピザトースト	650
2. オレンジジュース	250
TAX 3 %	27
	927 計
	1,000 預
	73 釣

5 月 30 日
東 京

SPOTCHECK 1

@ Which of the following has Jun *not* eaten? (Look back at the menu on p. 163 for help.)

a karē raisu   **c** mikkusu sando
b piza   **d** sarada

SPOTCHECK 2

@ Look at the date next to each receipt (月 = -*gatsu* (month), 日 = -*nichi* (day)). If today is Thursday 27 June, describe when Jun ate each meal by selecting one word per meal from 'Build-up' below.

BUILD-UP

CD ▶ 203

Say these time words:

kyō	today	**kinō**	yesterday	**ototoi**	the day before yesterday
konshū	this week	**senshū**	last week	**sensenshū**	the week before last
kongetsu	this month	**sengetsu**	last month	**sensengetsu**	the month before last
kotoshi	this year	**kyonen**	last year	**ototoshi**	the year before last

TAKE NOTE

You can combine the words in 'Build-up' with other time words by using *no*; e.g. 'yesterday morning': *kinō no asa*, 'last Thursday': *senshū no mokuyōbi*, 'April last year': *kyonen no shigatsu*. However, note that 'this morning' is *kesa*, as well as *kyō no asa*, and that the word *yūbe* is often used instead of *kinō no yoru* to mean 'yesterday evening'.

SPOTCHECK 3

@ Write the answers to these questions, using *deshita* ('was'):

a Kyō wa mokuyōbi desu. Kinō wa? Ototoi wa?

b Senshū no mokuyōbi wa rokugatsu hatsuka deshita. Sensenshū no mokuyōbi wa?

c Kotoshi wa 2006-nen desu. Kyonen wa?

ANSWER

CD ▸ 204

Answer the six similar questions on the CD.

E.g. (1) *CD:* **Kinō wa kinyōbi deshita. Ototoi wa?**

You: **Mokuyōbi deshita.**

READ AND WRITE

@ Read this description. Which of the receipts opposite is it a summary of?

Senshū no getsuyōbi Jun-san wa Kyōto no resutoran de shokuji o shimashita. Hanbāgu sutēki to sarada o tabemashita. Sore kara aisu kōhii o nomimashita.

shokuji o shimashita	ate/dined out
hanbāgu sutēki	hamburger steak
tabemashita	ate
nomimashita	drank

@ Now write three similar sentences about receipt number 4.

Businessmen relaxing after work

About Japan

We have noted that one of the features of a salary man's working life is that he often accompanies his colleagues or business associates out for a drink or two after work. Late every afternoon in districts like the Ginza, the throngs of shoppers are gradually replaced by well-kept women in subdued-hued kimonos or fashionable Western evening wear, who walk the narrow streets on their way to work. Even though it is approaching evening, they will bid one another a cheerful *ohayō gozaimasu* (literally, 'it is early'), the customary greeting used when arriving at work in the evening by people in the media and *mizushōbai*, or 'water trade', as the entertainment business is called.

The water trade is an enormous industry, although estimates vary considerably as to just how big it is because not all income comes to the notice of the tax authorities. Officially, business entertainment expenses (*settai-hi*) are 100 per cent taxable after a few million yen. In other words, if you spend ¥100 000 taking a customer out to dinner, you should be paying the same amount in tax. But most companies have ways of getting round some of the costs involved in wining and dining their (potential) clients.

That entertainment is expensive can be seen in the fact that just to step into a Ginza bar may well cost a couple of men ¥50 000. Since the Japanese rarely limit themselves to a single establishment, but move on to a second (known as the *nijikai*, or 'second stage meeting') and thereafter to even a third or fourth bar in what can become 'ladder' (*hashigo*) drinking, the host needs to prepare quite a lot of cash in advance. Perhaps that is why people prefer to drink on credit!

And what do men do in bars? They talk, of course, and laugh about this and that, allowing themselves to be pampered by the endlessly cheerful, made-up girls who pour their drinks and make their own living by being able to talk about nothing in particular as well as be petted by the most unlikely of paramours. Such amorous goings-on are kept from getting out of hand, so to speak, by the *mama-san* – the (usually older) woman who manages the establishment in question. And as the combination of scented hostesses, soft lights, music, and beer, sake or whisky (and frequently a mixture of all three) warms their innards, the men themselves begin to discuss matters closer to their hearts. These affairs are often connected with work, company and business, and it is said that most Japanese business deals are concluded in one or other of the country's water trade establishments.

This is, however, not entirely correct. It is true that business matters are broached during the course of an evening's drinking and that things are said in private which do not normally come to one's hearing during the normal daylight hours of work. But it is always necessary to make sure that what appears to have been agreed 'under the influence' has in fact been agreed. This process of ratification must be conducted during the day, for it is then that business deals are officially signed and sealed.

This distinction between daytime and night-time cultures is valid not only for the world of business, but for politics, too. And, as in Britain during the late eighteenth century, when most real government decision-making was done in the coffee shops of London, so do Japanese politicians come to their political arrangements in the expensive restaurants of the Akasaka district. Here we see the contrast between the public (*tatemae*) and private (*honne*) faces of Japan.

The Kabuki-chō entertainment district, Shinjuku, Tōkyō

TALKING ABOUT THE PAST (1)

> • To make the past form of a verb, change the *-masu* ending to **-mashita**. In the negative, say **-masen deshita**.
>
> E.g. Present:
> *Tenisu o shimasu.* (I play tennis.)
> *Tenisu o shimasen.* (I don't play tennis.)
>
> Past:
> *Tenisu o shimashita.* (I played tennis.)
> *Tenisu o shimasen deshita.* (I didn't play tennis.)

NANAKO'S YESTERDAY

@ Look back at p. 108, where you learned about the things Nanako does every school day (and when she does them). On the basis of that information, write about what Nanako did yesterday. (Start: *Shichiji ni okimashita. Shichiji nijuppun ni ...*, etc.) However, yesterday Nanako had a cold, so she didn't do gymnastics and she didn't go to *juku*: say so!

BUILD-UP

To make a sentence, you have to relate a verb to the words around it. In English we use words like 'from', 'with', 'to', etc. In Japanese similar words are used, but they come *after* the words they control:

to (issho ni)	with
e	to (a place)
kara	from (a person or a place)
ni	at (a time), to (a person)
de	by (a means of transport), in (a place)
o	(signals the object of an action)

DEAR DIARY 1 CD ▸ 205

@ Fill in the gaps in this diary entry with words from 'Build-up'. Listen to check your answers, then rewind and repeat.

Nichiyōbi: Kyō wa totemo tanoshikatta! Asa Honda-san _____ denwa o shimashita. Kare _____ doraibu o shimashita. Omoshirokatta! Sanji _____ densha _____ Tōkyō _____ ikimashita. Kaimono _____ shimashita. Yoru Tōkyō _____ kaerimashita. Bideo _____ mimashita. 'Porutagaisuto'. Kowakatta!

denwa o shimashita	telephoned
kare	he/him
'Porutagaisuto'	'Poltergeist'

BUILD-UP

Here are some new verbs:

... *to* **hanashimasu/ hanashi o shimasu**	speak to/with (somebody)
... *ni* **aimasu**	meet (somebody)
... *ni* **agemasu**	give to (somebody)
... *kara/ni* **moraimasu**	receive from (somebody)

DEAR DIARY 2 CD ▸ 206

@ Fill in the gaps in this diary entry. Listen to check your answers, then rewind and repeat.

Getsuyōbi: Kyō wa watashi no tanjōbi! Jūniji han _____ Ueda-san _____ aimashita. Kare _____ subarashii resutoran _____ shokuji _____ shimashita. Oishikatta! Ueda-san _____ suteki na nekkuresu o moraimashita. Yoru Takeuchi-san _____ aimashita. Kanojo _____ iroiro hanashi o shimashita. Totemo ii tomodachi desu!

tanjōbi	birthday
kanojo	she/her
iroiro	(about) various (things)
tomodachi	friend

> - To ask 'what?': **nan/nani?** 'where?': **doko?**
>   'who?': **dare?** 'when?': **itsu?**
>
> - Remember that *wa* never follows a question word.
>   E.g. 'What is there (on offer)?' *Nani ga arimasu ka?*
>   E.g. 'Who came?' *Dare ga kimashita ka?*

> - To say 'something': **nani ka**
>   'someone': **dare ka**
>   'somewhere': **doko ka**
>
> - After these words you don't need to use *wa, ga,*
>   or *o.*
>   E.g. 'Did someone come?'
>   *Dare ka kimashita ka?*
>   'Did you receive anything?'
>   *Nani ka moraimashita ka?*

QUESTIONS

To ask for information in Japanese just place a question word in the slot where the information would go in a reply and add *ka?* to form a question.

@ Write a question word into each space below:

1 _____ o nomimashita ka? Biiru o nomimashita.
2 _____ ikimashita ka? Senshū ikimashita.
3 _____ to hanashi o shimashita ka? Tomodachi to hanashi o shimashita.
4 _____ de kimashita ka? Basu de kimashita.
5 _____ e ikimashita ka? Tōkyō e ikimashita.
6 _____ ga imashita ka? Suzuki-san ga imashita.

A BUSY SCHEDULE CD ▶ 207

It's Saturday evening, and Mr Sakai is relaxing at home after a hard week. Ask him what he did over the last few days using the cue words supplied below.

E.g. (1) *You:* **Suiyōbi no asa nani o shimashita ka?**

Unfortunately, part of his reply will be obliterated by the sound of a vacuum cleaner, so in each case you'll have to ask a follow-up question.

E.g. (1) *Mr Sakai:* _____ **to hanashi o shimashita.**
You: **Sumimasen, dare to hanashi o shimashita ka?**

@ Note down what Mr Sakai did each day.

Wed.	a.m.	**1**	Suiyōbi no asa ...?
	eve.	**2**	Suiyōbi no yoru ...?
Thurs.	a.m.	**3**	Ototoi no asa ...?
	eve.	**4**	Ototoi no yoru ...?
Fri.	a.m.	**5**	Kinō no asa ...?
	eve.	**6**	Yūbe ...?
Sat.	a.m.	**7**	Kesa ...?

AKIKO'S SUNDAY CD ▶ 208

@ Listen to the four sets of sound effects indicating what Jun Sakai's friend, Akiko, did last Sunday, and draw a line from the first half of each sentence on the left to its corresponding second half on the right:

1 Dare ka to issho ni	**A** yomimashita.
2 Doko ka e	**B** denwa o shimashita.
3 Dare ka ni	**C** jitensha de ikimashita.
4 Nani ka	**D** shokuji o shimashita.

JUN'S SUNDAY CD ▶ 209

@ Now listen to sound effects of what Jun did. This time write the sentences yourself. Begin with these words:

1 Dare ka ... **2** Doko ka ... **3** Doko ka ...
4 Dare ka ...

THAT'S WRONG! CD ▶ 210

The CD will make five false statements about what Akiko or Jun did last Sunday; correct the CD each time, saying who really did the activity mentioned.

E.g. (1) *CD:* **Akiko wa dare ka to issho ni tenisu o shimashita.**
You: **Chigaimasu. Akiko wa tenisu o shimasen deshita; Jun ga shimashita.**

173

TALKING ABOUT THE PAST (2)

On the left below are the past forms of some verbs you've already come across, while on the right are a few unfamiliar ones:

kaerimashita	akemashita (*opened*)
nemashita	iimashita (*said*)
shimashita	motte imashita (*was holding/had*)
okimashita	nakunatte imashita (*was missing*)
mimashita	
moraimashita	

Read this detective story, using the Index to help with unfamiliar words. Fill in each space with one verb from the above list.

ONE DRINK TOO MANY

Detective Yamamoto has a mystery to solve: last night Mr Nakamura – president of Nakamura Arumi Securities – entertained an important client, who entrusted him with a valuable necklace. Mr Nakamura took it home for safe-keeping, but, on hearing a noise during the night, surprised his son, Takeshi, with the necklace in his hands – and one diamond was missing! Now Takeshi is in custody, and a distraught Mr Nakamura is in Detective Yamamoto's office.

Y (entering the room) Nakamura-san desu ka?
N (standing up) Hai.

Y Yamamoto to mōshimasu. Dōzo, okake kudasai. Dewa, Nakamura-san wa Nakamura Arumi no shachō desu ne?
N Hai, sō desu.
Y Go-kazoku wa irasshaimasu ka?
N Kinō made wa musuko to otōto no musume to issho ni sunde imashita ga . . .
Y Takeshi-san to Eriko-san desu ne?
N Hai, sō desu. Shikashi, kesa kara wa watashi hitori desu. Takeshi mo . . . Eriko mo . . . imasen.
Y Jā, kesa nani ga okorimashita ka?

shikashi	but
okorimashita	happened

N Yūbe wa taisetsu na o-kyaku-sama to issho ni shokuji o (*A*) _____. Uchi no Sakurai-buchō mo issho ni ikimashita.
　Sono o-kyaku-sama kara totemo takai daiya no nekkuresu o (*B*) _____.

taisetsu na	important
o-kyaku-sama	client
daiya	diamond

Y Sore kara uchi e kaerimashita ne?
N Hai.
Y Nekkuresu wa?
N Uchi e motte kaerimashita....
De, boku wa jūniji goro ni (*D*) _____....

Shikashi asa no ichiji goro ni hen na oto ga
shimashita. Soshite boku wa (*E*) _____.
Y Nekkuresu wa tonari no heya ni arimashita ne?
N Hai, sō desu. Sore de, boku wa sono heya no doa
o sugu (*F*) _____.

sore kara	and then
motte kaerimashita	took (it) back
de	and then/so
hen na oto ga shimashita	there was a strange sound
soshite	and
sore de	and so/then

Y Nakamura-san wa sugu uchi e kaerimashita ka?
N Iie, Sakurai wa (*C*) _____ ga watashi to
sono o-kyaku-sama wa jūichiji made uisukii o
nonde imashita.

| sugu | straight away |
| nonde imashita | were drinking |

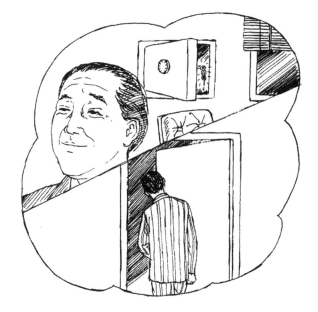

N Takeshi ga nekkuresu o te ni
(*G*) _____.

Y Sore kara nani o shimashita ka?
N Boku wa sugu nekkuresu o (*H*) _____.
Daiya ga hitotsu (*I*) _____.

te ni in (his) hand(s)

175

Y Takeshi-san ni nani ka (♪) _____ ka?
N Ē, shikashi Takeshi wa damatte imashita. . . .
N De, boku wa keisatsu ni denwa o shimashita. . . .

damatte imashita	was/remained silent
keisatsu	police (station)

N Takeshi wa mada keisatsu ni imasu . . . Shikashi kare wa hontō ni warui deshō ka?

mada	still
hontō ni	really
warui	bad

CD ▸ 211

@ Now listen to the story on the CD to check you filled in the words correctly.

SPOTCHECK 4

@ **A** Write answers to these questions:

 a Nakamura-san to Sakurai-buchō wa dare to issho ni shokuji o shimashita ka?

 b Nakamura-san wa o-kyaku-sama kara nani o moraimashita ka?

 c Doko e nekkuresu o motte ikimashita ka?

 d Hen na oto wa nanji ni shimashita ka?

 e Dare ga nekkuresu o te ni motte imashita ka?

 f Daiya wa ikutsu nakunatte imashita ka?

 g Takeshi-san wa ima doko ni imasu ka?

CD ▶ 212

B Having checked your answers, listen to the same questions on the CD, but in a different order. Answer aloud, without looking at what you've just written.

TAKE NOTE

In the story there were several useful new words for linking sentences and parts of sentences:

soshite . . .	and . . .
(sore) de . . .	and so/and then . . .
sore kara . . .	and then . . .
shikashi . . .	but . . .

Kantan desu!

Iie, muzukashii desu yo.

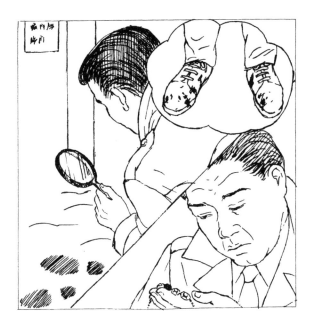

γ Takeshi-san no shiroi kutsu wa makkuro deshita – kare wa soto e ikimashita . . . sore kara mō ichido heya ni kaerimashita. Hnn . . .

Nekkuresu ni wa daiya ga muttsu arimashita. Shikashi hitotsu dake nakunatte imasu. Kantan ja arimasen ne!

makkuro	completely black
heya ni	into the room
hitotsu dake	only one

SPOTCHECK 5

@ **a** What two things are troubling Detective Yamamoto?

 b Make a list of all the characters named in the story so far; who do you think might have stolen the diamond?

To be continued . . .

OPEN AND SHUT?

CD ▶ 213

The police are convinced they have their man, but Detective Yamamoto is troubled by two things. Listen:

About Japan

Foreigners often talk about the public 'mask' of the Japanese. What they are referring to, of course, is *tatemae*. *Tatemae* (public, outer, closed) and *honne* (private, inner, open) are found in almost all societies in one form or another. The thing about the Japanese is that they openly talk about the distinction between the two, and can usually tell when somebody is saying one thing but means something different. Any bureaucrat, for example, who informs you that he is 'positively considering the matter' (*maemuki ni kentō shite imasu*) really means that he has put your petition at the bottom of the pile on his desk, or even thrown it in the nearest rubbish bin!

What is part of the linguistic confusion that faces the foreigner when he or she first tries to understand spoken Japanese can be no less confusing for a Japanese. For example, when a Tōkyō businessman says 'I understand' (*wakarimashita*), it means that he has accepted your proposal and will work on it. However, when an Ōsaka businessman says that he has understood a matter and is 'thinking' (*kangaete imasu*) about it, it means precisely the opposite.

Drinking together provides Japanese with a good opportunity to overcome the difficulties of tatemae and enter into heart-to-heart communication, which allows their honne to come out into the open. There are one or two basic rules which should be observed during the process: always fill your partner's glass or cup, and never pour your own drinks; and always be prepared to stand up and sing along to the melodious orchestration of the *karaoke* (literally, 'empty orchestra') machine.

Although eating and drinking may provide opportunities for frivolous games and karaoke songs, they are also serious occasions during which participants have to keep their wits about them. This is particularly the case in rural community drinking parties, where usually one man from each house in a village will gather on festive occasions to share some sake. Instead of drinking the alcohol from their own cups, however, the way city people do, they often exchange sake cups (*sakazuki*) during the course of conversation.

Exchanging sake cups is an important ritual in such communities. The man offering his sakazuki will call out his friend's name and, once the latter has accepted it, pour him some sake. Ideally this should be downed in a gulp or two, before the recipient returns the cup to its original owner and fills it for him. Once again the contents are quickly downed and the cup is passed over to the same or another person. When there are two dozen or so people passing sakazuki around in this manner, it does not take very long for some of them to get rather the worse for wear.

However, these sake cup exchanges are used by politically active men to approach their colleagues and embark on serious discussions affecting community life. This means that those who do not drink in the country tend not to have access to important information about village affairs. At the same time, what is said under the influence of drink is very definitely not forgotten, but is used during everyday affairs. The same can be said of businessmen's *settai*. In this way, we can see how the public face of tatemae is actively influenced by the private bargaining of honne. In Japan, although you have to drink if you wish to be successful, you drink at your peril!

TALKING ABOUT THE PAST (3)

ONE DRINK TOO MANY
(continued)

INVESTIGATIONS

A Did Takeshi really try to steal the diamond
necklace? Detective Yamamoto has a theory, but to
find out what it is you'll have to ask him some
questions about Takeshi's cousin, Eriko. The words
for the questions are written below, but in the wrong
order. Write out each question properly:

@ **1** shimashita Eriko-san denwa ni ga ka Dare o ?
Dare ga _____ ?

2 ikimashita Eriko-san doko asa ka wa jūniji han no
e ni ?
Eriko-san _____ ?

3 ka motte nani ikimashita kara o Heya ?
Heya _____ ?

4 motte Doko made nekkuresu ikimashita o ka ?
Doko made _____ ?

5 ka ni Dare nekkuresu agemashita o ?
Dare _____ ?

CD ▸ 214

@ **B** Check your questions are written correctly, then
start the CD and put them to Detective Yamamoto.
Note down his answers.

ALL IS REVEALED

@ Here is Detective Yamamoto's explanation of the
crime. Fill in the spaces by referring to the notes
you've just taken.

'(*A*) _____ wa jūji ni resutoran o
demashita. Shikashi kare wa uchi e kaerimasen
deshita. Resutoran no chikaku no kōshū denwa
kara Eriko ni denwa o shimashita. 'Nekkuresu o
mitsukete kudasai' to iimashita.
Sore de, asa no jūniji han ni Eriko wa
(*B*) _____ o (*C*) _____

made motte ikimashita. Soko ni wa
(*D*) _____ ga matte imashita.
Soshite Eriko-san wa kare ni nekkuresu o
watashimashita.'

mitsukete kudasai	please find
matte imashita	was waiting
watashimashita	passed

SPOTCHECK 6
@ **a** Who stole the necklace?
b Who was it given to?
c What time was the crime arranged?
d What time was the crime committed?

Detective Yamamoto thinks the whole necklace was
handed over, not just one diamond – but what
happened then?

SUMMING-UP

CD ▶ 215

Detective Yamamoto has got to the root of the problem, as usual. Here he sums up (listen):

'(*1*) Takeshi wa jūniji han ni okimashita. Sono toki Sakurai to Eriko wa genkan ni imashita. Takeshi wa nekkuresu o mimashita. (*2*) Soshite Sakurai to kenka o hajimemashita. (*3*) Takeshi wa Sakurai no te kara nekkuresu o torimashita, demo daiya ga hitotsu nakunatte imashita. Sakurai wa nigemashita. (*4*) Soshite Takeshi wa nekkuresu o heya ni motte kaerimashita. (*5*) Chōdo sono toki Nakamura-san ga okimashita. Takeshi wa Eriko ga daisuki deshita kara, o-tō-san no mae de wa damatte imashita. (*6*) Eriko wa kesa Sakurai to issho ni nigemashita. Yappari kanojo wa Sakurai no aijin deshita.'

(chōdo) sono toki	(just) then/at that time
... to kenka o hajimemashita	started to fight with ...
torimashita	took away
demo	but
nigemashita	escaped
Eriko ga daisuki deshita kara	because he was in love with Eriko
yappari	as I thought
aijin	lover

SPOTCHECK 7

@ Put these pictures in the right order by writing numbers from 1 to 6 in the boxes (to correspond with the numbers in Detective Yamamoto's summing-up above).

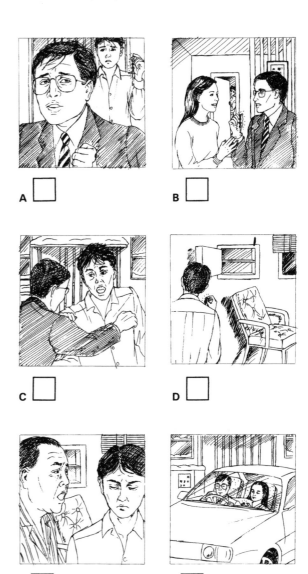

A ☐   B ☐

C ☐   D ☐

E ☐   F ☐

181

About Japan

One reason for the Japanese often getting rather drunk and incoherent during 'ladder' drinking sessions is that they tend not to eat much while they imbibe. Although almost all bars serve snacks, and many of them specialise in a particular kind of dish, most customers leave much of what is served on the dishes before them.

There is a reason for this. 'Food' in Japanese is practically synonymous with 'rice': as we have seen, *asagohan* (breakfast) is literally 'morning rice', *hirugohan* (lunch) 'noon rice', and *bangohan* (dinner) 'evening rice'. Anything served without rice in the Japanese cuisine does not really count as 'proper' food, and every self-respecting man refuses to eat his *gohan* (food) until he has had his fill of drink. He may partake of 'snacks' (*tsumami*), but since many of the dishes served in bars or *kaiseki* Japanese restaurants are arranged for aesthetic, rather than bodily, satisfaction, a drinker can take in far too much alcohol during the course of a 'meal'.

Rice, of course, is the staple ingredient of sake, which is rice wine and is also known as 'Japanese alcohol' (*nihonshu*). Because of its traditional importance in agriculture, rice is used in one form or another on ritual occasions. Rice cakes (*mochi*), for example, are made during new year celebrations, while sake will be placed at the mouth of a potter's kiln to purify the fire. Another purificatory ingredient is salt, which is thrown in large handfuls by sumō wrestlers about to enter the ring and fight.

Other staple ingredients of Japanese cuisine are tea, red beans, seaweed and fish. Indeed, in the past, it could be said that the Japanese diet was extremely healthy – except that people insisted on polishing their rice, thereby not only taking all the nutrients out, but encouraging an extremely high incidence of stomach cancer in the process. Even in the country, where farmers eat their own rice, it is usually only the health-conscious foreigner who asks for unhusked brown rice (*genmai*).

Nowadays, however, the old diet of rice and fish is fast giving way to one of bread and meat. Few young Japanese eat rice, pickles, dried seaweed and a raw egg, washed down with green tea, for breakfast; instead they prefer coffee, toast and jam. The proliferation of American fast-food chains and family restaurants shows how much the Japanese diet is changing. With it, people's physiques are also changing: not only are young Japanese people becoming taller; they are heavier and more likely to suffer in their old age from the kinds of (heart) disease that have hitherto been confined to people in Europe and the United States. Westernisation may have brought many material advantages to the average Japanese person, but it has also introduced its fair share of disadvantages.

WHAT YOU'LL HEAR

I KNOW A LOVELY LITTLE PLACE ...

CD ▸ 216

@ Look back at the map of part of Shinjuku-ku on
p. 54. With the famous Waseda University close by,
this is a lively area with many restaurants and bars
catering for student tastes and finances.

Listen to the people on the CD recommending
places to eat in Shinjuku-ku. Write the area in which
the restaurant is to be found next to the type of food
to be eaten there (e.g. Japanese food (*nihonryōri*) –
Ōkubo).

Italian	_____
Chinese (*chūkaryōri*)	_____
Japanese	_____
Thai	_____
French	_____

FAST FOOD

CD ▸ 217

@ One thing which is sure to impress you in Japan is
the extremely high quality of service, and nowhere
will this strike you more than when it comes to the
little things: transactions which are so routine that
you probably wouldn't expect those involved to take
the time to be formal. Ordering a hamburger at a
fast-food outlet is just one such occasion: you'll be
offered choices in such polite Japanese that, unless
you're expecting it, you probably won't understand
a word. Listen out for these set phrases:

1 Honjitsu wa kochira de o-meshiagari deshō ka?
Soretomo o-mochikaeri deshō ka?
Eat in or take away?

2 Sore dewa, o-kaikei no hō onegai shimasu/
yoroshii deshō ka?
Can I take your money now?

3 Shōshō o-jikan ga kakarimasu node, dekimashitara
o-todoke ni agarimasu node, o-seki de o-machi
kudasaimase.
*It will take a moment to prepare ... I'll bring it to
you when it's ready, so would you please wait at
your table?*

4 Saizu ga esu to emu to eru to gozaimasu keredo,
dochira ni nasaimasu ka?
Do you want small, medium or large?

5 Irasshaimase!
Welcome!

6 Go-chūmon o-kimari ni narimashitara, dōzo.
Can I take your order?

7 Go-yukkuri dōzo/o-meshiagari kudasaimase.
Enjoy your meal.

a Listen to two different customers (1 and 2) ordering
at the counter of a fast-food restaurant. First, write
down the order in which the set phrases above
occur. (They may not all occur.)
1 _____ 2 _____

b Now rewind and note down what each customer
orders, and how much they have to pay.

KARE TO KANOJO: HIM AND HER

CD ▶ 218

ⓐ You'll hear three short dialogues in which men and women meet under different circumstances.

a Listen to dialogues 1 and 2. Then read the eight sentences below. Decide which four sentences describe the first encounter, and which four go with the second. (Write 1 or 2 to the left of each sentence.)

A ____ Kare wa nijūhassai deshita ga kanojo wa mada nijūissai deshita.

B ____ Kanojo wa atarashii denkiseihin no puran o shashin ni torimashita.

C ____ Kare wa sono firumu o kanojo kara kaimashita.

D ____ Kare wa ototoshi kara kanojo no tomodachi deshita.

E ____ Soshite sensengetsu kanojo ni puropōzu o shimashita.

F ____ Futari wa hābā no soba de aimashita.

G ____ Shikashi keisatsu wa sore o mimashita.

H ____ Kanojo wa kare to kekkon shimasen deshita.

puran	plan
...o shashin ni torimashita	took a photograph of ...
kaimashita	bought
puropōzu o shimashita	proposed (marriage)
hābā	harbour

b Now listen to dialogue 3. After listening, try to fill in the gaps in this letter, which Akiyama-san wrote to a friend later the same evening:

Kyō no (*time*) _____ ni _____-san kara denwa o moraimashita. Kare to _____-san to issho ni (*time*) _____ ni (*place*) _____ no suteki na resutoran de aimashita. Futari wa totemo ii tomodachi de sugoku tanoshikatta.

MUKASHI MUKASHI ... : ONCE UPON A TIME ...

CD ▶ 219

@ Listen to this adaptation of a famous Japanese folk tale. The pictures below illustrate the story, but are in the wrong order. Put the pictures in the correct order by writing a number from 1 to 5 in the box next to each one.

o-jii-san	grandfather/(as here) old man
o-bā-san	grandmother/(as here) old woman
take	bamboo
akachan	baby
o-kane	money
tsuki	moon

A

B

C

D

E

WRITTEN JAPANESE

	'kun'	'on'				
rice 米	kome	bei/ mai				米
fish 魚	sakana/ uo	gyo				魚
tea 茶		cha/sa				茶
sake 酒	sake/ saka-	shu				酒
meat 肉		niku				肉

The ingredients of Japanese eating and drinking most familiar to Westerners are perhaps rice, fish, (green) tea and sake. Above are the kanji for these staples of food and drink, together with the character for 'meat', a no less important element in the modern Japanese diet.

Shops specialising in the sale of these commodities are known by the following names: *komeya* (rice merchant's), *sakanaya* (fishmonger's), *o-chaya* (tea merchant's), *sakaya* (liquor store) and *nikuya* (butcher's). The final *ya* in all these words (meaning 'house' or 'store') is represented by the kanji 屋.

@ Try writing one shop name under each of the shops below:

米国 日米
bei koku nichi-bei

お酒
o- sake

日本酒
ni hon shu

ビール
bii ru

お茶 茶道
o- cha sa dō

牛肉 豚肉
gyū niku buta niku

とり肉
to ri niku

While the names of Western countries are nowadays usually written in katakana, you may also hear some of them called by kanji names, which used to be in more common use. The USA – assigned the name 米国 (*beikoku*, or 'rice country') – is a case in point. Although it is nowadays usually referred to as アメリカ ('amerika'), you can still hear the element *bei* whenever Japan–US relations – *nichi-bei* (日米) *kankei* – are under discussion.

Japan has also been Westernised where the consumption of alcohol is concerned. Sake, known in Japan as *o-sake* (お酒) or *nihonshu* (日本酒) remains a popular drink, especially heated up in the cold winter months, but in summer the Japanese are more likely to quench their thirst with *biiru*. Recently, 生ビール (*nama biiru*: so called 'live beer') has made large inroads into the bladders of the Japanese drinking public.

Business throughout Japan – during the daylight hours, at least – is lubricated with endless cups of green tea (in Japanese, simply *o-cha*), placed before visiting clients by cohorts of uniformed, self-effacing 'office ladies'. During their leisure hours, some of the same young women may attend lessons in the traditional pursuit of *sadō* ('tea ceremony', literally the 'way of tea').

The kinds of meat most commonly available in Japanese restaurants are beef (*gyūniku*), pork (*butaniku*) and chicken (*toriniku*). 牛 and 豚 came about as follows:

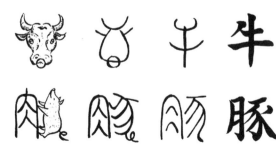

187

魚
sakana

そば
so ba

うどん
u do n

ラーメン
rā me n

すし
su shi

The most famous (and, you may find, delicious) forms in which fish is eaten in Japan are as *sashimi* (sliced raw fish) or *sushi* (slices of raw fish on bite-sized portions of rice). If you're not quite ready to face fish in the raw, you could try asking for やき魚 (*yakizakana*: 'grilled fish').

Identifying which restaurants and bars are suited to your palate (and wallet) can be something of a problem in Japan: what's on offer within restaurants *isn't* always displayed in plastic form outside, and you should learn to recognise the words on the left (often written on the *noren*, a kind of 'curtain' you have to duck through to enter many small family-run restaurants).

Soba, udon and *rāmen* are different kinds of noodle. (*Rāmen* are Chinese-style noodles, and this word is written in katakana.) The hiragana for *sushi* are often written in rather artistic fashion, as in the photograph on the right. For relatively cheap drinking places where you can also order food (*izakaya* or *akachōchin*), look out for red lanterns (*akachōchin* literally means 'red lantern'). In a so-called 'snack' (in katakana, スナック, you won't find a great selection of food, but you can expect to be attended to by a *mama-san* or hostess. Be warned that 'snacks' can be expensive (though cheaper ones also exist).

@ Now try matching the places listed on the left below with the photographs:

A sushiya
B akachōchin
C sobaya
D rāmenya
E udonya
F sunakku
G kōhii shoppu

1

2

3

4

5

6

7

LANGUAGE SUMMARY

Food and drink
mikkusu sando
piza (tōsuto)
karē raisu
sarada
chiizu kēki
mōningu setto
hanbāgu sutēki
orenji jūsu
remon tii

Time words
kyō
konshū
kongetsu
kotoshi
kinō
senshū
sengetsu
kyonen
ototoi
sensenshū
sensengetsu
ototoshi

Actions
shokuji o shimasu
denwa o shimasu
hanashimasu
aimasu
agemasu
akemasu
iimasu
motte imasu
motte ikimasu
moraimasu

Adjectives
tanoshii
kanashii
tsumaranai
kowai
warui
nigiyaka (na)

Linkwords
Sore de uchi e kaerimashita.
Soshite ichiji goro ni okimashita.
Sore kara nekkuresu o mimashita.
Shikashi Takeshi wa damatte imashita.

Ordering food
Sumimasen! Kōhii (o) kudasai.
Watashi wa piza tōsuto ni shimasu.

Waitress/Waiter language
Nanmei-sama deshō ka?
Nani ni nasaimasu ka?

While eating
Kanpai!
Itadakimasu!
Biiru mō ippon kudasai.
Oishi-sō!
Mō kekkō desu.
Oishikatta!
Gochisōsama deshita.
Okanjō onegai shimasu.

Question words
Nani o nomimashita ka?
Nan de ikimashita ka?
Itsu ikimashita ka?
Dare to hanashimashita ka?
Doko e ikimashita ka?

Putting actions into context
Tōkyō **e** ikimashita.
Mori-san **to (issho ni)** ikimashita.
Tomodachi **kara** daiya o moraimashita.
Sakai-san **ni** nekkuresu o agemashita.
Densha **de** ikimashita.
Uisukii **o** nomimashita.

Main language structures

The past of adjectives
'-i' adjectives: oishii desu → oishikatta desu
'na' adjectives: kantan desu → kantan deshita

The past of verbs
-masu → mashita
e.g. Tenisu o shimasu.
→ Tenisu o shimashita.
Negative: -masen → -masen deshita
e.g. Tenisu o shimasen. → Tenisu o shimasen deshita.

To deepen your understanding of some of the language presented in this unit, you might like to look at the following parts of the Grammar section: 'Verbs' (5B), 'Sentence building' (8), and 'Adjectives' (12A, B).

8 TIME OUT

Sports and leisure activities
Saying how often
Saying what you like
Talking about the future
Making invitations
Saying what you can and can't do

About Japan

Although the Japanese work hard, they play hard, too. Whether singing vociferously to *karaoke* as they sip sake under the cherry blossoms on a spring evening, sitting apparently mesmerised by the whirl of tiny silver balls in a *pachinko* (pinball) parlour or uttering blood-curdling cries as they attack their opponents in one of the martial arts, the Japanese participate in their leisure activities with the same intensity that they devote to work. From the loud hubbub of a local festival (*matsuri*), baseball 'nighter' or sumō championship to the more sedate atmosphere of a tea ceremony, golf driving range or *ikebana* flower-arrangement lesson, it is clear that when it comes to leisure the Japanese are as capable as anyone else of having a good time.

For most people, however, the problem with leisure activities is finding both the time and the space to make them possible. Because there is such a shortage of land in and around the big cities – a shortage which makes its price absurdly high – people find themselves travelling great distances to play a game of tennis or soccer. They are also obliged to practise their baseball pitching in the streets and their golf swings (with rolled-up magazines or newspapers substituted for clubs) on station platforms or – at best – in minute (occasionally two-tiered) driving ranges.

Of course, there are fixed seasons for leisure activities. In the winter months, a lot of people go skiing, either in the north in Hokkaidō or in the Japan Alps that form the backbone of the main island of Honshū. The moment the baseball season starts in April, however, attention shifts to the fortunes of teams like the Yomiuri Giants, Hanshin Tigers, Seibu Lions and Softbank Hawks. Once every six weeks, avid viewers immerse themselves in the fifteen-day-long sumō competitions and watch the grand champions (*yokozuna*), who these days often include foreigners, battle it out.

There are two so-called leisure activities – golf and mahjong – which are not easily divorced from the sphere of work. Many businessmen in the evenings repair from their company to a nearby mahjong 'club', where they while away the hours in intense sessions of this Chinese imported game, and thus build up a rapport with clients. Similarly, at weekends – or even during the week – senior salary men will entertain customers at golf clubs where, during a leisurely round or two, they will try to make the kind of 'heart-to-heart' contact that is vital to Japanese business.

As in most advanced industrialised countries these days, sporting events are heavily sponsored by large corporations, and we find motor corporations financing car racing teams, securities firms contributing to tennis tournaments, and airline companies giving donations towards marathon races. Similarly, anyone who has watched sumō will not have failed to notice the banners carried round the ring (*dohyō*) prior to every bout. These carry the names of those who have presented sums of money (wrapped in ceremonial envelopes) to be given to the winner.

So the pursuit of leisure is a serious business. Not only are some games played in the hope that they will bring in company business, but also most mahjong and golf players bet on the outcome of their games, and serious mahjong players can make a fair living from their earnings. Some businessmen, however, are known to lose on purpose, in the hope that their associates will then agree to sign a new business deal! Leisure is not just a serious business; it can be good business, too.

Tōkyō golf driving range

SAYING HOW OFTEN YOU DO SOMETHING

In the Japanese leisure business, fashions come and go with bewildering rapidity: one year it may be 'in' to play table tennis, the next to go bowling, one year to play pool, the next to practise golf. One of the more recent 'booms' has been the frequenting of sports centres, sometimes to be found on the top floors of department stores. Here is what people do at one such club, the Tōbu sports centre near Tōkyō:

tenisu o shimasu	play tennis
badominton o shimasu	play badminton
earobikkusu o shimasu	do aerobics
pūru de oyogimasu	swim in the pool
sauna ni ikimasu	use ('go into') the sauna
sorariumu ni ikimasu	use the solarium

CD ▸ 220

- To ask *'Do you often ...?'*: **Yoku ...-masu ka?** E.g. 'Do you often play tennis?': *Yoku tenisu o shimasu ka?*

- To say how often you do something (listen and repeat):

  oo often *yoku* **badominton o shi***masu*

  o sometimes *tokidoki* **earobikkusu o shi***masu*

  x not very often *amari* **pūru de oyogi***masen*

  xx hardly ever *hotondo* **sauna ni iki***masen*

  xxx never *zenzen* **sorariumu ni iki***masen*

In the exercises on this and the opposite page you'll be hearing, in turn, from four members of the Tōbu sports centre. As they say how often they use the various facilities, your task is to complete the chart below:

	Suzuki	Saitō	Aoki	Watanabe
tenisu		× ×		
badominton				× × ×
earobikkusu			4/wk	
pūru	×			
sauna		o	ev. wk	
sorariumu	oo			2/mth

LISTEN **CD ▸ 221**

@ First, Hideki Suzuki will tell you how often he uses each of the facilities available at the club. Write appropriate symbols (oo, o, ×, etc.) under his name in the chart above.

ASK **CD ▸ 222**

@ Junko Saitō is another club member. Ask her how often she uses each of the facilities. (Start with tennis and work down.) Write symbols in the chart according to her answers.

E.g. (1) *You:* **Yoku tenisu o shimasu ka?**

ANSWER **CD ▸ 223**

The CD will ask you eight questions about Hideki Suzuki and Junko Saitō. Answer by consulting the chart.

E.g. (1) *CD:* **Suzuki-san wa yoku oyogimasu ka?**
You: **Iie, amari oyogimasen.**

CD ▶ 224

- To say more precisely how often you do something (listen and repeat):

(per day)	**ichinichi ni**	**ikkai**	(once)
(per week)	**shū ni**	**nikai**	(twice)
(per month)	**tsuki ni**	**sankai**	(three times)
(per year)	**nen ni**	**yonkai**	(four times)

E.g. 'I do it four times a week': *Shū ni yonkai shimasu.*

every day	**mainichi**
every week	**maishū**
every month	**maitsuki**
every year	**mainen** (or **maitoshi**)

E.g. 'I do it every month': *Maitsuki shimasu.*

TAKE NOTE

The counter for 'times' (*-kai*) sounds the same as the counter for floor numbers you've already come across, so look back at p. 94 to find out how to say 'five times', 'six times', etc. As with other counters, you can ask questions using *nan* ...?

 E.g. '(About) how many times per week do you play tennis?':

  Shū ni nankai (gurai) tenisu o shimasu ka?

SPOTCHECK 1

@ Translate into Japanese:

 a Roughly how many times per month do you do aerobics?

 b I do it about six times per month.

LISTEN

CD ▶ 225

@ Listen to the interview with another club member, Miwa Aoki. Note down in the table precisely how often she uses each of the club facilities.

 E.g. **shū ni yonkai** → Write '4/wk'

  maishū → Write 'ev. wk'

ASK

CD ▶ 226

@ Using the names of facilities or sports mentioned on the tape, ask the final club member, Kenji Watanabe, questions beginning with *Yoku* ...

 E.g. (1) *CD:* **pūru**

   You: **Yoku pūru de oyogimasu ka?**

Note down precisely how often he uses each of the facilities.

TAKE NOTE

In English, when we hesitate before giving a reply, we say things like 'erm ...' or 'let me see ...'. You heard some of the Japanese equivalents in the replies of the four sports club members: *anō* ... and *ēto* ... (meaning 'erm ...') and *sō desu nē* ... (meaning, in this context, 'let me see ...', and *not* 'that's right').

AND YOU?

CD ▶ 227

Answer the CD's questions about how often you yourself do the things you've been asking about up to now. Hesitate, if necessary, by saying *anō ...*, *ēto ...* or *sō desu nē ...*, and then give your reply.

 E.g. (1) *CD:* **Yoku tenisu o shimasu ka?**

   You: **Sō desu nē ...** etc.

Say, both roughly and then more precisely, how often you take part in each activity.

YOUR LEISURE PURSUITS; THE KINDS OF THING YOU LIKE

Hima na toki ni nani o shimasu ka?: 'What do you do in your spare time?'

BUILD-UP

CD ▶ 228

To say you do any of these things, just add ... **o shimasu**. Say the words, adding *o shimasu* each time:

gorufu	golf	**haikingu**	hiking
jogingu	jogging	**sanpo**	going for walks
sukasshu	squash	**ryōri**	cooking
sukii	skiing	**niwaijiri**	gardening
dansu	dancing	**dokusho**	reading for pleasure

LISTEN 1

CD ▶ 229

Listen to this short dialogue:

A Yoku jogingu **o** shimasu ka?
B Iie, hotondo shimasen.
A Haikingu wa?
B Haikingu **wa** tokidoki shimasu.

Rewind and repeat!

haikingu wa?   how about hiking?

TAKE NOTE

Note how *o* becomes *wa* because a new topic (*haikingu*) is 'spotlit' in contrast with the previous one (*jogingu*).

HOW OFTEN?

CD ▶ 230

The CD will ask you the same questions; answer according to how often you yourself go jogging or hiking. The CD will then continue asking about new topics (e.g. *CD:* **Dokusho wa?**), so continue to answer using *wa* rather than *o*.

BUILD-UP

CD ▶ 231

Say these words for different kinds of music, film and TV programmes:

ongaku	*music*
rokku	rock
poppusu	pop
jazu	jazz
kurashikku	classical
enka	Japanese ballads
eiga	*films*
komedii	comedy
sasupensu	suspense
horā	horror
rabusutōrii	love story
SF	science fiction
terebi bangumi	*TV programmes*
eiga	films
supōtsu	sports
dokyumentarii	documentaries
nyūsu	news
hōmu dorama	soap operas

- To ask *'What kind(s) of* music do you like?': *Donna* **ongaku ga suki desu ka?**

- To say 'Rock, jazz, *and so on* ...': **Rokku** *toka* **jazu** *toka* ... (or, more formally, **Rokku** *ya* **jazu** *nado* ...)

LISTEN 2

CD ▶ 232

@ We asked Mr Sakai what kinds of music, film and TV programme he likes. Tick the things he likes in 'Build-up' above, and mark the things he dislikes with crosses.

AND YOU?

CD ▶ 233

The CD will ask you what kinds of music, film, TV programme, sport, food and drink you like. Answer with ... *toka* ... *toka ga suki desu*.

E.g. (1) *CD:* **Donna ongaku ga suki desu ka?**

Left Archery (*kyūdō*)

- To ask 'why?': **naze?/dōshite?**

- To say 'because ...': ... **kara**
  E.g. 'because it's old': *furui kara desu*

BECAUSE ...

CD ▸ 234

Two people are discussing the homes in the pictures below.

A Donna uchi ga suki desu ka?
B (*pointing to one of the pictures*) Konna uchi ga suki desu.
A Naze desu ka?
B Ōkikute subarashii kara desu.

Rewind and repeat!

konna	this kind of (that kind of = **sonna/anna**)
ōkikute subarashii	large and splendid

SPOTCHECK 2
@ Which kind of home does B like?

kuruma

a

b

c

yasumi

a

b

c

uchi

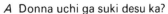

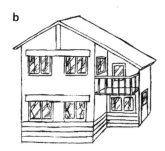
b

a

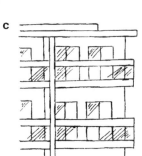
c

ii	
atsui	iya (na)
subarashii	kirei (na)
omoshiroi	benri (na)
sugoi	fuben (na)
tanoshii	suteki (na)
tsumaranai	kantan (na)
kowai	nigiyaka (na)
kawaii	
ōkii	hayai (*fast/early*)
chiisai	osoi (*slow/late*)
takai	kitanai (*dirty*)
yasui	kirei (na) (*clean*)
atarashii	urusai (*noisy*)
furui	shizuka (na) (*quiet*)

SPOTCHECK 3

@ Some adjectives you've already come across are listed in the box on the left, together with a few useful new ones. Practise describing the pictures opposite by linking some of these words. For example, how would you say: **a** expensive and boring, **b** inconvenient and slow, **c** enjoyable and cheap?

IDENTIFY `CD ▸ 235`

@ Listen to two friends, Mr Kuwata and Mr Suzuki, talking about the pictures opposite. Identify which home, car and holiday each of them likes best.

AND YOU? `CD ▸ 236`

Take B's part in the dialogue in 'Because' opposite. The CD will ask you what kinf of home, car and holiday you like best. Point to the picture as you say *Konna ... ga suki desu.* Then give your reasons when the CD asks *Naze desu ka?*

TAKE NOTE

How to link two adjectives (e.g. to say 'old *and* pretty' or 'convenient *and* new') depends on whether the first word is a 'normal' or a 'na' adjective:

'normal' adjective first: **furu*i* → furu*kute* kawaii**
but note: **ii → yo*kute* yasui**
'na' adjective first: **benri (na) → benri *de* atarashii**

Sumō practice in the grounds of a shrine

About Japan

The Japanese take part in all kinds of sports and games. Some of these – like skiing, golf or American football – have been imported from the West; others – like mahjong – have been borrowed from China (and frequently adapted in the process); yet others – such as sumō or jūdō – are native to Japan. The distinction between 'traditional' (native) and 'modern' (non-native) is also found in other areas of leisure: an aspiring bride, for example, might learn the tea ceremony (*sadō*) or flower arrangement (*ikebana*) on the one hand, and Cordon Bleu cookery or classical guitar on the other.

However, a modern, non-native sport is not necessarily practised in Japan in the same way as in its country of origin. Take baseball, for example. For a start, the ground is much smaller in Japan than in the United States, but more fundamentally, the whole psychology of the game takes on a different aspect. Sports in all countries, of course, have philosophies of one sort or another attached to them. The British pride themselves on a sense of 'fair play', Americans on 'individualism'. When the Japanese play baseball, therefore, they not surprisingly imbue it with particularly Japanese values.

The midsummer high school baseball competition provides a good example of these values. Every high school in Japan competes in a knock-out baseball contest and the winners from each prefecture gather at Ōsaka's Kōshien Stadium in early August for the final session of the competition, which is played before the television cameras for all the nation to watch.

And watch the games the nation does. Whether in restaurants or bars, company offices or even taxis, people are glued to their television screens as they follow the fortunes of their local team. For two weeks in the middle of the hot and humid summer, it seems as if Japan is about to grind to a standstill.

And how are these games reported by the media? For a start, the focus is squarely on the individual struggle between pitcher and batter. It is around their psychological battle that the whole game seems to revolve, as the commentators discuss the players' *shinbō* (perseverance), *gaman* (endurance), *gattsu* (guts) and *seishin* (spirit). Baseball is no longer a mere game; it is the very epitome of what it means to be Japanese – in much the same way as the Super Bowl becomes the annual reminder to those living in the United States (and much of the rest of the world these days) of what it means to be American.

One of the interesting things about contemporary Japan is that there is a permanent tension between traditional concepts of 'groupness' and Western-inspired notions of 'self'. It is intriguing, therefore, that while a country like England which prides itself on its individualism has developed many team games, the Japanese – with their emphasis on 'groupism' – not only view a team game like baseball in essentially individualistic terms, but have also developed largely individual-centred sports like sumō, karate and *kendō* (Japanese fencing).

Still, we should realise that the true Japanese sportsman ideally submerges his individualism in a kind of philosophical selflessness. As those who have read anything about the martial arts will know, one is supposed to lose one's self and act in a Zen-like state of 'no mind'. Since the concept of the individual is denied in this manner, participation in apparently individualistic sports may in fact tend to reinforce rather than subvert the predominant group-oriented social ideology. And that this is an ideology which needs continual reinforcement can be seen in the way the media extol the particularly 'Japanese' virtues of the nation's successful sportsmen and women.

Elementary school baseball

BASEBALL; TALKING ABOUT THE FUTURE

As you've been reading, baseball – along, perhaps, with sumō – is the most popular spectator sport in Japan. There are two professional leagues: the Central League (*seriigu*) and the Pacific League (*pariigu*), with six teams in each. Most of the teams are named after the major Japanese companies which sponsor them, usually with the addition of a nickname (often the English-derived name of an animal).

TEAM NAMES

@ Try to work out the nicknames of the teams in the *seriigu*. Draw lines from the names to the pictures of the team mascots:

doragonzu

hoēruzu

kāpu

suwarōzu

taigāsu

jaiantsu

JAPANESE LIVE 1   `CD ▸ 237`

Listen to the recording of a day's baseball results from Japanese television, and work out which company (or, in the case of Hiroshima, city) is associated with which team. Write one of the following names on each line:

Chūnichi Hiroshima Yomiuri Taiyō Hanshin Yakuruto

_____ kāpu	(:)	_____ hoēruzu
_____ taigāsu	(:)	_____ jaiantsu
_____ doragonzu	(:)	_____ suwarōzu

@ Rewind, listen again and write the scores in the brackets. To do this, you'll need to understand two new words: **kachimashita** ('won'), and **tai** ('to', as in *go tai ichi de kachimashita*: 'they won by five to one').

BUILD-UP   `CD ▸ 238`

You can use these words when talking about future events (listen and repeat):

ashita	tomorrow
asatte	the day after tomorrow
raishū	next week
saraishū	the week after next
raigetsu	next month
saraigetsu	the month after next
rainen	next year
sarainen	the year after next

There are no special verb forms for talking about the future in Japanese; just use ... *-masu* (for example, 'I'm going to go to Tōkyō next week': *Raishū Tōkyō e ikimasu*).

FUTURE DATES   `CD ▸ 239`

Answer the questions on the CD about future dates.

    E.g. (1) *CD:* **Kyō wa jūgonichi desu; asatte wa nannichi desu ka?**
           You: **Jūshichinichi desu.**

- To say 'two weeks *from now*': **nishūkan *go* (ni)**
  'one month *from then*': ***sono* ikkagetsu *go* (ni)**

- To say 'three days *ago*': **mikka *mae* (ni)**
  'two years *before then*': ***sono* ninen *mae* (ni)**

- Review how to talk about periods of time on p.145.

Tōkyō dōmu	Tōkyō Dome (home ground of the Giants)
nishiai	two games (**-shiai** is the counter for games)
mata	again
Chūnichi to no gēmu	a game with Chūnichi

SPOTCHECK 4

@ Translate into Japanese:
  a I came to Japan three years ago.
  b Five years before then I went to China.
  c I'm going to go back to England three months from now.
  d I'll go to France three weeks after that.

JAPANESE LIVE 2   CD ▶ 240

@ Listen to a TV presenter explaining the Giants' schedule over the next few weeks. Using the pause button, fill in the gaps below with the time words he mentions:

Presenter   Konshū, jaiantsu wa
_____ to
_____ ni Tōkyō
dōmu de Chūnichi doragonzu to nishiai
ga arimasu. Mata _____ kara
_____ _____ ni mo Tōkyō dōmu
de Chūnichi to no gēmu ga arimasu.
Soshite _____ no _____ to
_____ (_____
_____ , _____) ni wa
kāpu to no nishiai ga arimasu. _____
_____ _____ ni wa Ōsaka de
Hanshin to no nishiai ga hajimarimasu.
_____ no
_____ kara
_____ no
_____ made wa shiai ga
arimasen.

SPOTCHECK 5

@ Fill out this schedule with **a** the initials of the teams the Giants will be playing, and **b** the dates. Finally, **c**, what is the date today (the day of the TV report)?

This week

S.	M.	T.	W.	T.	F.	S.

Next week

S.	M.	T.	W.	T.	F.	S.	S.

IN OTHER WORDS . . .

@ Find where the expressions on the left below occur in 'Japanese live 2'. On the basis of your knowledge of when the presenter was speaking, draw lines from the expressions on the left to the phrases on the right (two in each case) which the presenter could have used instead to convey the same meaning:

1 getsuyōbi to kayōbi
2 sono futsuka go
3 kongetsu no sanjūnichi

A ashita to asatte
B konshū no suiyōbi
C raishū no mokuyōbi
D kongetsu no nijūhachinichi, nijūkunichi
E (kyō kara) mikka go
F raigetsu no nanoka

INVITING

- To say 'let's ...': change *-masu* to *-mashō*.
  E.g. 'let's go': *ikimashō*

- To say 'shall we ...?': ... **-mashō ka?**
  E.g. 'shall we go?': *ikimashō ka?*

- To invite someone to do something: use **-mashō ka?** or less directly **-masen ka?** ('won't you ...?').
  E.g. 'Won't you (i.e. Would you like to) go to the movies (with me)?': *(Issho ni) eiga ni ikimasen ka?*

JAPANESE LIVE 3   `CD ▸ 241`

Tomoko Sakai invites a friend to go and see a film. Before you listen, try filling in the gaps with the words below. Then check your answers by listening.

Yoshida, eiga, ashita, makaroni uesutan (*spaghetti western*), Bunkamura (*'culture village'* – a leisure complex in the Shibuya district of Tōkyō), Bunkamura, sanji, sanji, Sakai

Yoshida	(*picking up the phone*) Moshi moshi, _____ desu.
Tomoko	Moshi moshi, _____ desu ga ... Genki desu ka?
Yoshida	Hai, okagesama de.
Tomoko	Anō, _____ eiga ni ikimasu ga, issho ni ikimasen ka?
Yoshida	Donna _____ desu ka?
Tomoko	_____ _____ desu.
Yoshida	Ii desu ne. Nanji ni shimashō ka?
Tomoko	_____ wa dō desu ka?
Yoshida	Daijōbu desu. Doko de aimashō ka?
Tomoko	_____ wa dō desu ka?
Yoshida	Hai, kekkō desu.
Tomoko	Jā, _____ ni _____ de aimashō.
Yoshida	Hai.
Tomoko	Ja, mata.
Yoshida	Jā ...

Rewind and repeat!

daijōbu	all right/OK
aimasu	meet
kekkō	all right/fine
ja, mata/jā ...	well, 'bye (informal)

TAKE NOTE

To accept an invitation, just say *ii desu ne* ('that's good'). However, saying 'no' in Japanese is a more delicate affair, and the Japanese themselves go to great pains to avoid giving a blunt refusal. Don't be misled, then, into thinking that a long drawn-out *sō desu nē* ... (often accompanied by a sucking sound through the teeth) signals agreement; in fact it usually means exactly the opposite: 'I'm giving the matter my fullest consideration, but actually it's not possible'. Just saying *sō desu nē* ... or *chotto* ... (more fully, *chotto tsugō ga warui n' desu ga* ...: 'conditions are a little bad ...') should be enough for anyone inviting you to get the message you can't make it; the Japanese are expert at picking up signals in this way. To soften the blow, you could blame the day chosen (*doyōbi wa chotto* ...), say it's a pity (*zannen desu ga* ...) or suggest vaguely 'some other time': *mata kondo* ...

BUILD-UP

As you know, 'go to (a place)' in Japanese is: ... *e ikimasu* (e.g. *ashita Tōkyō e ikimasu*). However, when you want to say 'go to (an activity)', you should @ replace *e* with **ni** (e.g. *eiga ni ikimasu*). Try to match the phrases on the left and right below by drawing lines:

go			ni ikimasu
	1 to a film	**A** doraibu	
	2 to a concert	**B** sukii	
	3 skiing	**C** kaimono	
	4 shopping	**D** shokuji	
	5 out for a drink	**E** ohiru o tabe	
	6 out for lunch	**F** eiga	
	7 out for a meal	**G** nomi	
	8 for a drive	**H** konsāto	

WARM-UP   [CD ▸ 242]

Rehearse inviting someone, using the words the CD provides (first a time, then an activity). From 1 to 4 use this pattern: (*time*) *ni* (*activity*) *ni* ... *-masen ka?* From 5 to 8 be more positive, and ask ... *-mashō ka?*

E.g. (1) *CD:* **raishū no doyōbi – doraibu ni ikimasu**

You: **Raishū no doyōbi ni doraibu ni ikimasen ka?**

FOR REAL   [CD ▸ 243]

@ Now you've plucked up courage, invite the person on the CD to do the following things with you. (If you're rejected make a cross, if accepted a tick.)

E.g. (1) *You:* **Konshū no nichiyōbi ni (issho ni) tenisu o shimasen ka?**

1 Sunday this week – play tennis
2 The 11th of this month – go to a concert
3 Wednesday next week – go shopping
4 The 3rd of next month – go out for a meal
5 April next year – go to France

LISTEN   [CD ▸ 244]

@ Suzuki-san invites five people to do different things, but only three of them accept. In the schedule below, note down their names and the arrangements she makes with them:

nichiyōbi	
getsuyōbi	
kayōbi	
suiyōbi	
mokuyōbi	
kinyōbi	
doyōbi	

YOUR TURN   [CD ▸ 245]

Take Tomoko's part in 'Japanese live 3' on the opposite page, and invite Mr Tanaka to see different films. Rewind the CD each time. You choose the kinds of film you want to see. (Look back at p. 197.) Otherwise the arrangements you suggest are as follows:

1 Saturday next week – 7:00 – in front of the station (*eki no mae de*)
2 The day after tomorrow – 4:00 – in McDonald's (*Makudonarudo de*)
3 Wednesday the week after next – 9:00 – inside the cinema (*eigakan no naka de*)

About Japan

Historically, Zen Buddhism played an important part in the development not only of sports such as jūdō or kendō, but also of such varied arts as the tea ceremony and the classical Nō theatre. Ideals about the 'nature of self', the importance of selflessness and so on are therefore found not just in sports, but in traditional Japanese arts, too.

What is of particular interest in the contemporary context is who participates in what (traditional or modern) leisure activities, and so who imbibes what ideals. Thus, while most schoolchildren are put through their paces in the kendō hall (dōjō) or the karate or jūdō ring, when they go to university or join a company they may find themselves more interested in 'modern' sports like tennis. With time, they may switch to golf, and end their lives trotting round a local park or school ground playing a mean game of 'gate ball' (the Japanese version of croquet) with their elderly companions.

The more 'refined' arts are generally the province of women. It is they who tend to participate most actively in *ikebana* (flower arrangement) and the tea ceremony, they who give apparently inordinate attention to the trimming of a twig or flower stem to aesthetic perfection, or to stirring, with a bamboo whisk, bitter green tea (*matcha*) into just the right state of foaming pea soup. Alternatively, they may spend hours kneeling on their haunches learning the art of the three-stringed *shamisen* (Japanese lute). At the same time, of course, they imbibe the ideals surrounding these arts – ideals of selflessness and harmony with one's surroundings – and so find themselves immersed in the 'spirit' of what it means to be Japanese.

Although almost all those learning ikebana and the tea ceremony in Japan today are women, the schools to which they belong are run by men. Given the way in which men in many other societies tend to take over women's lives in the public domain, this is perhaps to be expected. Nevertheless, the schools of traditional arts are organised in a particularly Japanese manner. Every teacher (*sensei*) will have his or her pupils (*deshi*), and will himself or herself be the *deshi* of another teacher. This teacher, too, will have learned the art in question from another teacher, so that we find an extremely hierarchical set of one-to-one teacher–pupil relations established between the headquarters of, say, a *shodō* (calligraphy) school and its several hundred thousand students.

These relations are upheld and strengthened by a complicated system of tuition fees and examinations, whereby a teacher will pass on a small percentage of his or her students' fees to the head of the school. Diligent pupils can take examinations and so graduate to different levels of difficulty in the art concerned, and their patience is finally

Calligraphy (*shodō*) school

rewarded when, after paying a lot of money for the privilege, they are issued with certificates licensing them to take on their own students. This family-like organisation in its extreme form is known as the *iemoto* (or 'headmaster') system and is a typical example of the hierarchical one-to-one relations that have traditionally characterised Japanese society.

That the Japanese like to create family-like relations between teachers and pupils in their sports and arts can also be seen in the organisation of the world of sumō. Each group of wrestlers is organised into a 'stable' (literally, 'room': *heya*), consisting of 'brothers' (*kyōdai*) overseen by a 'father' (*oyakata*). Nor is this kind of fictive kinship organisation limited to sport and the arts; it is also practised by – among others – Japan's gangsters, the *yakuza*.

SAYING YOU CAN OR CAN'T DO SOMETHING

In Japanese, there are one or two ways of saying you can or can't do something. Start with the easiest, and work towards the harder:

- In cases where the verb *shimasu* is used to describe an activity, replace this with **(ga) dekimasu.**
  E.g. *tenisu o shimasu → tenisu dekimasu*
  ('I can play tennis')
  ryōri o shimasen → ryōri dekimasen
  ('I can't cook').
  Dekimasu is also used to describe ability in foreign languages: 'I have no ability in Japanese', for example, is *Nihongo dekimasen.*

  | CD ▸ 246 |

- To describe different degrees of ability (listen and say):

can ... well	**yoku dekimasu/jōzu desu**
can ... a little	**sukoshi dekimasu**
can't really ...	**amari dekimasen/ amari jōzu ja arimasen**
can hardly ...	**hotondo dekimasen**
can't ... at all	**zenzen dekimasen/ totemo heta desu**

BUILD-UP

| CD ▸ 247 |

Here are some more names of leisure pursuits which can be followed by *shimasu*, and therefore by *dekimasu*. Repeat the words after the CD, adding *dekimasu* or *dekimasen* each time:

pachinko	form of upright pinball
mājan	mahjong
chesu	chess
shōgi	'Chinese chess'

LISTEN

| CD ▸ 248 |

Listen to this short dialogue.

A Furansugo dekimasu ka?
B Hai, sukoshi dekimasu.
A Supeingo wa?
B Supeingo wa amari jōzu ja arimasen.
Rewind and repeat!

SPOTCHECK 6
@ Is the person answering better at French or Spanish?

YOUR TURN

| CD ▸ 249 |

The CD will ask you the same questions (about your abilities in French and Spanish) and will then continue with some more questions.

A *minyō* singer accompanied on the shamisen

BUILD-UP

In cases where verbs other than *shimasu* are normally used to describe an activity, the verb endings change when you want to say you can or can't do that activity. Look at these examples (above are three leisure pursuits which take *shimasu*; below are three which don't):

shōgi o shimasu	→ shōgi (ga) dekimasu
gorufu o shimasu	→ gorufu (ga) dekimasu
pachinko o shimasu	→ pachinko (ga) dekimasu
piano o hikimasu *(play the piano)*	→ piano (ga) hikemasu *(can play the piano)*
aburae o kakimasu *(paint oil paintings)*	→ aburae (ga) kakemasu *(can paint oil paintings)*
minyō o utaimasu *(sing folk songs)*	→ minyō (ga) utaemasu *(can sing folk songs)*

We asked four women to tell us how well they do the things below. The women's names were Mrs Yamaguchi (Y), Mrs Tanaka (T), Mrs Mizuhara (M) and Mrs Kubota (K).

	Y	T	M	K
shōgi				
gorufu				
pachinko				
piano				
aburae				
minyō				

JAPANESE LIVE 4 [CD ▸ 250]

@ Listen to the interview with Mrs Yamaguchi and Mrs Tanaka. Since they were interviewed at the same time, listen very carefully for their names and make ticks or crosses in the chart, according to whether they can or can't do the things listed.

TAKE NOTE

Even when Japanese people are very good at something, their sense of modesty will usually prevent them from saying so outright; instead, as you heard in 'Japanese live 4', they may say how much they *like* something – interpret this as meaning they're probably pretty good.

INTERVIEW [CD ▸ 251]

@ Unfortunately we've lost the interview with the other two women; would you mind repeating it for us? Ask about the skills in order from top to bottom, always asking Mrs Mizuhara first.

E.g. (1) *You:* **Mizuhara-san wa shōgi dekimasu ka?**

After she replies, ask: **Kubota-san wa?**

Put ticks or crosses in the chart on the left according to their replies.

ANSWER [CD ▸ 252]

The CD will ask you eight questions about some of the women's abilities. Answer by looking at the box on the left above.

E.g. (1) *CD:* **Yamaguchi-san wa pachinko ga dekimasu ka?**
You: **lie, dekimasen.**

209

About Japan

The *yakuza* are Japan's answer to the mafia. Heavily involved in betting, drug trafficking, prostitution and all those other illegal activities that make the life of gangsters everywhere so profitable, the yakuza are self-styled *samurai*, the last remaining representatives of a way of life that depends on those essentially 'Japanese' virtues of social obligation (*giri*) and human spontaneity (*ninjō*). Like members of the mafia, they have created an elaborate code of honour. Unlike the mafia, however, they espouse precisely those ideals of Japaneseness put forward by politicians, business leaders, teachers and others responsible for the 'education' of the people of Japan.

The exact part played by yakuza in the demi-monde of Japan's nightlife is not clear. Nor is it precisely apparent what role they act out in Japan's political world, although that they have an important role is not in dispute. Provided that they do not cause open trouble in the streets, however, the yakuza are generally left alone by the police. They are the tolerated outsiders of Japanese society.

Other outsiders exist in the demi-monde of leisure and entertainment. Many of the thriving pachinko parlours, for example, are run by Koreans, while quite a few of the mama-sans and hostesses who pander to salary men in bars are unmarried mothers or divorcees. In a society which until recently has frowned on divorce on the one hand, and rarely offered career opportunities to women on the other, these women on the fringes of family life have sometimes had little choice but to enter the entertainment world in order to make their living.

Not all women in this kind of employment are outsiders, of course. Many students, for example, seek extra pocket money as members of 'companion clubs', whose glossy stickers can be found in telephone booths in entertainment areas, offering sexual services for greater or lesser sums of money. Other women get visiting men properly 'lathered up' in Japan's so-called 'Turkish baths', although these at one point had to be renamed – for diplomatic reasons. After much thought, the Japanese came up with the entirely appropriate word 'soapland'!

When men and women wish to get together in private, they often repair to a love hotel. Over the years, these have been called by a number of different names, from *abekku* ('avec') to 'city' or 'fashion' hotel, but the principle on which they operate has remained the same. Customers pay for rooms two hours at a time, although special cheap rates apply after eleven at night and during the early part of the day. Indeed, one of the nicer

A love hotel in Kyūshū

examples of Japanese English can be found at love hotel entrances, which occasionally boast of a 'no time service' between early morning and mid-afternoon!

Quite a number of married couples go to love hotels, too, if only to get some peace and quiet away from the cramped conditions of the average family home. Other people need to be more circumspect in their amorous undertakings, and so drive out along those highways which boast a number of love hotels at every major exit. As with pachinko parlours, there are some splendid examples of architecture among these hotels – from medieval castles to an imitation of the QE II. And the rooms themselves can be splendidly equipped, with everything from vibrating beds to the latest audio-visual technology.

Whether in bouts of sex then, or of sumō, the Japanese take full advantage of their leisure time!

WHAT YOU'LL HEAR

PACHINKO
CD ▸ 253

@ Listen to three 'hardened' players talking about pachinko, a form of upright pinball. They were asked how often they play, how much they spend and how much they win. (Note that some pachinko players take their winnings in the form of goods, not cash.)

Fill out the chart below with notes on the information they provide:

	How often do you come?	How much do you spend?	How much (or what) do you win?
1			
2			
3			

AT THE MOVIES
CD ▸ 254

@ Before starting, turn back to p. 197 to review the names for different genres of film in Japanese.

Listen to the five interviews with people (or in some cases couples) waiting in a cinema queue. Note down the kinds of film you hear them say they like and dislike. One enthusiastic punter dislikes nothing at all; another feels the same as long as the film in question has her favourite star in it.

	Likes	Dislikes
1		
2		X
3		
4		X
5		

WHEN I'VE GOT A MOMENT ...
CD ▸ 255

@ Four interviews (1 to 4) about what people do in their spare time are recorded on the CD. Which of the activities below are mentioned in each interview? Write the number of the interview next to the activities mentioned.

Before beginning, check you remember the meaning of each word.

Sports		*Leisure activities*	
yakyū	_____	disuko	_____
gorufu	_____	kaimono	_____
sumō	_____	sadō	_____
tenisu	_____	eiga	_____
sukii	_____	shokuji	_____
sukasshu	_____		

One of the activities was mentioned twice. Which one?

Right A *Kendō* class

WHAT IS IT?

CD ▸ 256

@ We showed pictures of all sorts of different objects to some Japanese children and teenagers. We told them that they mustn't say the name of the thing, but that they should try to describe it and say how they felt about it. Listen to the ten sets of recordings (1 to 10), and in each case write the number of the recording next to the object you think is being described.

maru | circle
shikaku | square

A

B

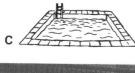

C

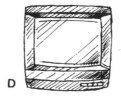

D

E

F

G

H

I

J

WRITTEN JAPANESE

As we've seen, the Japanese are far from short of ideas when it comes to what to do with their leisure time. The problem is that work takes precedence: hours on the job are long, and, although the government has tried to encourage adoption of a five-day week, many people still work straight through from Monday to Saturday. The kanji below, then, are among the most beloved of pleasure-seekers throughout Japan.

休 日
kyū jitsu

休みの日
yasu mi no hi

祭 日
sai jitsu

The element on the left in 休 is the character for 'person' (人), which you've already come across, rotated to the left. The kanji as a whole, then, represents somebody resting under a tree, and in combination with 日 has the meaning 'rest day' (*yasumi no hi* – using 'kun' readings – for days 'taken' off, and *kyūjitsu* – using 'on' readings – for official rest days, e.g. Sundays). *Saijitsu* refers to national holidays, the number of which the government has gradually increased. *Sai* ('on' reading) literally means 'festival'.

@ Here are the dates of some of the national holidays in Japan; read the dates aloud, and write them down in English:

1月15日	成人の日	**Seijin no hi** (Coming of age day)
12月23日	天皇誕生日	**Tennō tanjōbi** (The Emperor's birthday)
5月5日	子どもの日	**Kodomo no hi** (Children's day)
10月10日	体育の日	**Taiiku no hi** (Sports day)
11月3日	文化の日	**Bunka no hi** (Culture day)
4月29日	みどりの日	**Midori no hi** (Green day)

Although many characters have several readings, most don't have as many as 日. Since you may be feeling a little confused as to how to read this kanji, here are examples of the main readings (all of which you've come across before):

'on'		'kun'	
日本	*ni*hon	休みの日	yasumi no *hi*
15日	jūgo*nichi*	生年月日	seinenga*pi*
休日	kyū*jitsu*	誕生日	tanjō*bi*
		2日	futsu*ka*

When it comes to writing the days of the week, 日 works overtime – especially in the writing of 'Sunday': *nichiyōbi*.

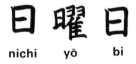

日 曜 日
nichi yō bi

Yō – 'day of the week' – has the sun as a 'radical' on the left. The other elements combine to make it mean the sun winging like a bird, and thus 'day'. Usually, when you see the day of the week written (as in diaries or on wall calendars), the characters for *yōbi* are omitted. All you're left with are these kanji:

sun (Sun.) 日 nichi	☼ ◉ ⊖	⥼ ⎠ ⎠ 日
moon (Mon.) 月 getsu	🌙 🌙 🌒	⥼ 月 月 月
fire (Tues.) 火 ka	🔥 火 火	` ` ⎠ 火
water (Weds.) 水 sui	水 水	⼗ ⼪ 水
wood (Thurs.) 木 moku	🌳 木 本	⼀ ⼗ 才 木
gold/metal(Fri.) 金 kin	金 金 金	⼃ 八 今 今 全 全 金 金
earth (Sat.) 土 do	△ ◇ 土	⼀ ⼗ 土

Interestingly, Sunday is literally 'sun-day' and Monday 'moon-day', just as in English and other Western languages. Kanji for the five remaining days represent the five major elements as perceived by the ancient Chinese philosophers and alchemists. The 'kun' readings of these characters represent useful vocabulary items in their own right: *hi* ('fire'), *mizu* ('water'), *ki* ('tree' or 'wood'), *kane* ('money') and *tsuchi* ('earth' or 'ground'). Add -*sei* (meaning 'star') to the 'on' readings above and you get the names of five planets: *kasei* ('Mars'), *suisei* ('Mercury'), *mokusei* ('Jupiter'), *kinsei* ('Venus') and *dosei* ('Saturn'). In languages like French and Italian, the names for the same days of the week are connected with precisely the same planets – mysterious, perhaps . . . ?

@ Finally, look at this excerpt from a pocket diary showing some of the holidays which constitute 'Golden Week' at the beginning of May. Read and answer aloud the questions written below.

5 MAY		
1	水	メーデー
2	木	八十八夜
3	金	憲法記念日
4	土	休　日
5	日	こどもの日
6	月	立　夏　振替休日
7	火	
8	水	
9	木	

1　5月1日は木曜日ですか。
2　5月4日は水曜日ですか。
3　5月6日は火曜日ですか。
4　子どもの日は月曜日ですか。

LANGUAGE SUMMARY

Sports

earobikkusu	sukii
tenisu	badominton
sukasshu	gorufu
yakyū	jogingu
haikingu	

Other pursuits

dansu	minyō o utaimasu
sanpo	dokusho
niwaijiri	ryōri
shōgi	konsāto
chesu	mājan
oyogimasu	pachinko
piano o hikimasu	
aburae o kakimasu	

Music/Films/TV

ongaku	eiga	terebi bangumi
rokku	komedii	supōtsu
poppusu	sasupensu	dokyumentarii
jazu	horā	hōmu dorama
kurashikku	rabusutōrii	nyūsu
enka	SF	

Time words

ashita	asatte
raishū	saraishū
raigetsu	saraigetsu
rainen	sarainen
nishūkan go	
mikka mae	

Asking how often

Yoku tenisu o shimasu ka?

Saying how often (approximately)

Hai, **yoku** shimasu.
Hai, **tokidoki** shimasu.
Iie, **amari** shimasen.
Iie, **hotondo** shimasen.
Iie, **zenzen** shimasen.

Saying how often (precisely)

ichinichi		ikkai
shū	ni	nikai
tsuki		sankai
nen		yonkai

mainichi/maishū/maitsuki/maitoshi

Asking about ability

(Tenisu) wa dekimasu ka?
(Piano) wa o-jōzu desu ka?

Describing ability

Hai, **yoku** dekimasu (jōzu desu).
Hai, **sukoshi** dekimasu.
Iie, **amari** dekimasen (amari jōzu ja arimasen).
Iie, **hotondo** dekimasen.
Iie, **zenzen** dekimasen (totemo heta desu).

Inviting and responding

Tōkyō e ikimashō ka/ ikimasen ka?
Ii desu ne.
Sō desu nē …
Chotto (tsugō ga warui n' desu ga …)
Zannen desu ga …
Mata kondo …

Main language structures

O → Wa

e.g. Yoku jogingu o shimasu ka?
     Iie, hotondo shimasen.
     Gorufu wa? Gorufu wa tokidoki shimasu.

Combining adjectives

'normal' adjectives: -i → -kute
e.g. ōkikute subarashii
'na' adjectives: na → de
e.g. kirei de omoshiroi

Let's … / Shall we …?

-masu → -mashō
e.g. Issho ni ikimashō. Tōkyō e ikimashō ka?

To deepen your understanding of some of the language presented in this unit, you may like to look at the following parts of the Grammar section: 'Verbs' (5C), 'Time expressions' (11C), and 'Adjectives' (12B).

9

GIVE AND TAKE

Giving and receiving presents
Visiting someone's home
Making requests
Plain verb forms
Talking about possibilities
Saying what must be done

About Japan

All people in all societies like to give and receive presents of one sort or another, and they usually institute special occasions on which to exchange gifts. In Christian countries, of course, people celebrate Christmas and, to a lesser extent, Easter in this way. In Japan, there are two major times for gift-giving – mid-year, *o-chūgen*, and year-end, *o-seibo* – and a number of other occasions when gifts of some sort are exchanged.

Indeed, it can be said that giving and receiving are fundamental to the Japanese way of life. We see this in the exchange of namecards between businessmen, in religious (Buddhist and Shintō) rituals, in company entertainment involving businessmen, in the exchange of sake cups in rural communities, and in the giving and receiving of presents at wedding receptions. Whoever you are, wherever you are, it is virtually impossible to escape the apparently endless cycle of give and take in Japanese society.

Registration of a gift of money at a wedding reception

The Japanese give presents to friends on their birthdays, to employees who have completed a certain number of years of devoted service to their companies, to colleagues who are going away on a trip and to neighbours who have been hospitalised or treated by a doctor. They also give presents twice a year to those to whom they have in one way or another been indebted over the past months or years. In the midsummer *o-chūgen* season, for example, a rural household may present a crate of beer or a couple of bottles of sake to its nextdoor neighbour, while a young salary man might visit the home of his superior to present a carefully wrapped box of expensive exotic fruits to the man who acted as go-between at the time of his marriage some years previously.

So in Japan gifts are exchanged not just between individuals, as in most Western countries, but between households or families as well. In other words, traditionally a debt incurred between one person and another has often been seen as a debt between their households (which even record gift transactions in books), so that the giving and receiving of presents can be handed down from one generation to the next.

This traditional custom, however, is giving way to a more contemporary attitude which regards indebtedness as being between individuals rather than between their families. One thing that has remained constant, however, is that in Japan a gift is always reciprocated in some way. So, a young woman who receives a present of money (*senbetsu-kin*) from an aunt just before she sets out on her first trip abroad will make sure to buy that same aunt a suitably expensive souvenir (*o-miyage*) to give her on her return. Similarly, the mother of a boy who has been in hospital and received presents of money (*o-mimaikin*) from all households in the neighbourhood or community must later ensure that everyone who has contributed is repaid.

It can be seen, then, that a lot of gift-giving is done out of a sense of obligation (*giri*) rather than of spontaneity (*ninjō*). A good example of this is the way St Valentine's Day – in the West, the most spontaneous of gift-giving occasions – has been cleverly adapted to traditional notions of 'give and take' by the Japanese chocolate industry. On St Valentine's Day girls are under strong media pressure to distribute small boxes or packets of chocolate, not only to their boyfriends but also to male classmates, colleagues etc., who are themselves encouraged to return the favour one month later on 'White Day', 14 March, with white chocolates (the invention of this latter custom being a clever ploy on the part of the chocolate industry to ensure that chocolates received from one girl are not returned unopened to another on White Day). This annual exchange of *giri choko* (obligation chocolates), as they are often called, shows not only the continuing importance of relations of obligation, but also the way commercial interests encourage and stand to profit from the give and take of contemporary Japan.

BUYING PRESENTS

- To say 'bigg*er*': ***motto*** ōkii (*motto* = more)
  '*more* beautiful': ***motto*** kirei (na)

- To say 'a big *one*', 'beautiful *ones*' etc., use **no**.
  'normal' adjectives   **ōkii sētā** → **ōkii no**
  'na' adjectives   **kirei *na* sētā**
                    → **kirei *na no***
  words followed by 'no' **pinku *no* sētā** → **pinku *no***

JAPANESE LIVE 1   CD ▶ 257

Tomoko Sakai is buying *giri choko* ('obligation' (Valentine) chocolates) for her male colleagues.

Tomoko	Sumimasen! Chokorēto wa doko ni arimasu ka?
Shop assistant	Kochira ni gozaimasu.
Tomoko	Motto yasui no wa arimasen ka?

Shop assistant	Hoka no wa chotto gozaimasen ga ...
Tomoko	Ā, sō desu ka. Jā, dōmo. (*Shrugs shoulders and leaves.*)
Shop assistant	(*in another shop*) Irasshaimase!
Tomoko	Chokorēto wa arimasu ka?
Shop assistant	Hai, kochira ni gozaimasu. (*showing her one box*) Kore wa ikaga de gozaimasu ka?
Tomoko	Sō desu nē ... Ano kirei na no misete kudasai.
Shop assistant	Kore de gozaimasu ka?
Tomoko	Hai, sō desu. Ā, ii desu ne. Kore kudasai.
Shop assistant	Hai, kashikomarimashita.
Tomoko	Purezento desu ga ...

Rewind and repeat!

... wa arimasen ka?	don't you have ...?
hoka (no)	other
kashikomarimashita	(a very polite equivalent of **wakarimashita**)
purezento desu ga ...	it's a present (a good way to ask for something to be wrapped nicely)

Yuka shopping

SPOTCHECK 1

@ Why didn't Tomoko like the first box of chocolates?

SPOTCHECK 2

@ How would you ask the following?
   a Haven't you got a more handy one?
   (handy = *benri* (*na*))
   b Could you show me that red one?
   c Haven't you got any others?

LISTEN

CD ▶ 258

@ Listen to the five conversations. In each case circle
the object (from the two choices) which the
customer decides to buy.

YOUR TURN

CD ▶ 259

Go shopping for these presents, following the
instructions on the CD. (Looking at 'Japanese live
1' opposite will help you, but gradually try to speak
without looking.)

1 a watch (*tokei*) **3** a dress (*wanpiisu*)
2 a hat (*bōshi*)   **4** a fan (*sensu*)

1

a   b

2

a 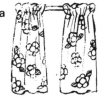   b

4

a   b

3

a   b

5

a    b

MAKING REQUESTS

You've already come across several phrases for politely asking someone to do something: *chotto matte kudasai* (p. 60), *massugu itte kudasai/migi e magatte kudasai/tomete kudasai* (all on p. 62) and *sētā o misete kudasai* (p. 91). Just by comparing these phrases, you can probably guess how to make requests in Japanese:

> • To ask someone to do something: use the **-te** (sometimes **-de**) form of a verb (see p.111) plus **kudasai**.
>   E.g. *mimasu → Kore o mite kudasai.* (Look at this!)
>   *akemasu → Doa o akete kudasai.* (Open the door, please.)

SPOTCHECK 3

@ Look at the verb list (part 6 in the Grammar section) to find and write down the *-masu* forms of the verbs in the phrases above (*chotto matte kudasai → machimasu* etc.).

BUILD-UP 1   CD ▶ 260

> @ Here are some more things you might want to ask people to do. Use the verb list again to write down the request forms of these sentences. Then listen to the CD to check your answers, and repeat:
>
> | 1 *write in rōmaji* | rōmaji de kakimasu |
> | 2 *draw you a map* | chizu o kakimasu |
> | 3 *speak slowly* | yukkuri hanashimasu |
> | 4 *lend you a pen* | pen o kashimasu |
> | 5 *tell you an address* | jūsho o oshiemasu |
>
> E.g. (1) **Rōmaji de kaite kudasai.**

WHAT WOULD YOU SAY?   CD ▶ 261

Make requests according to the situations the CD tells you about.

> E.g. (1) *CD:* It's hot – ask someone to open the window.
>   *You:* **Sumimasen, mado o akete kudasai.**

The tape will follow up each time with what you should have said.

> • To ask if it's all right for *you* to do something: use the **-te** form of the verb, plus **mo ii desu ka?**
>   E.g. May I open the window?: *Mado o akete mo ii desu ka?*

BUILD-UP 2   CD ▶ 262

> @ Write down how you'd ask permission to do the following things (then listen to the CD to check, and repeat):
>
> | 1 *close the door* | doa o shimemasu |
> | 2 *switch on the radio* | rajio o tsukemasu |
> | 3 *switch off the TV* | terebi o keshimasu |
> | 4 *smoke a cigarette* | tabako o suimasu |
> | 5 *sit here* | koko ni suwarimasu |
> | 6 *give someone a kiss* | kisu o shimasu |
>
> E.g. (1) **Doa o shimete mo ii desu ka?**

LISTEN

CD ▸ 263

@ Listen to eight people requesting permission to do various things. Match their requests (1 to 8) with the pictures below:

RECREATE

CD ▸ 264

The CD will say the letter of one of the pictures below; request permission to do what's shown in the picture.

E.g. *CD:* C

You: **Rajio o keshite mo ii desu ka?**

A

B

C

D

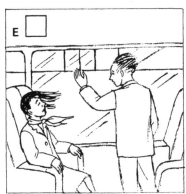

E

F

G

H

GIVING A PRESENT;
LEAVING SOMEONE'S HOME

As you'll remember from Unit 7, guests are usually entertained in restaurants, hotels or bars rather than in the home, but if you *are* invited to someone's house, don't forget to take a present. As a foreigner, a souvenir from your country will probably be most appreciated. (Stock up on small souvenirs before you go to Japan – they'll always come in handy.) However expensive your present, hand it over modestly, saying **Dōzo, tsumaranai mono desu ga ...** ('This is just a trifling thing'). Visiting someone's home is highly ritualised, in particular when you arrive and depart. Look back at p. 40 to review the language useful on arrival.

Display of presents in a department store

JAPANESE LIVE 2 | CD ▶ 265 |

Predict Michael Follin's words as he arrives at and is shown into his colleague's house (where he's been invited for dinner): write your predictions in the spaces below.

Michael	(*sliding open the front door*)
	_____ _____!
Mr Honda	Ā, Fōrin-san, konban wa. (*motioning Michael in*) Dōzo!
Michael	_____ _____.
	(*giving his present*) _____,
	_____ ga ...
Mr Honda	A, dōmo sumimasen. Dōzo, suwatte kudasai.
Michael	_____ _____.

@ Now listen and check your answers.
                                    Rewind and repeat!

REVIEW

Write down the mini-conversations you imagine will occur in the following situations. (Review the pages indicated if you're in need of help.)

1 Mr Honda introduces his wife, Hanako, to Michael. They exchange greetings (p. 68).
2 Mr Honda offers Michael some beer. Michael accepts (p. 41).
3 Mrs Honda asks whether it's all right to open the present (p. 223). Michael tells her to go ahead (p. 40). Mrs Honda says it's beautiful, and thanks him.
4 Mrs Honda says she's prepared *sushi* (*o-sushi o yōi shimashita ga . . .*) and asks Michael whether he likes it (he does!) (p. 148). Michael says it looks delicious (*oishi-sō desu ne*).
5 Mr Honda urges Michael to eat. Michael goes ahead (p. 37).

| CD ▸ 266 |

@ Now listen to the continuation of the conversation in 'Japanese live 2' opposite, and see how much of it you were able to predict. When there are variations from your version (as there no doubt will be), ask yourself (and check on the pages indicated) whether what you wrote could have replaced what was actually said.

TAKE NOTE

To introduce members of your family, you can use the pattern '(family word) *no* (name) *desu*', as Mr Honda did when he introduced his wife: *Kanai no Hanako desu* ('This is my wife, Hanako'). However, note that Japanese people often omit the names of family members in introductions: Mr Honda, for example, might equally well have said simply *Kanai desu*.

When it's time to leave, the formalities begin again in earnest. A convenient way of bringing things to a head is to say (with a glance at the clock) **Jā, soro soro (shitsurei shimasu)** (lit. 'Well, soon/gradually (I'll excuse myself)'). This may be met with conventional protests such as **Mada ii ja arimasen ka?** ('Isn't it still all right (for you to stay)?') – but if you did decide to stay your host would probably be surprised. Instead, continue your slow progress towards the door with **Iie, osoku made ojama shimashita** ('No, I've stayed (lit. interrupted you) until late'). But there's still lots more to say before you make your getaway! . . .

JAPANESE LIVE 3 | CD ▸ 267 |

It's time for Michael to leave.

Michael	Jā, soro soro shitsurei shimasu.
Mr Honda	Ā, sō desu ka. Mada ii ja arimasen ka?
Michael	Iie, osoku made ojama shimashita. Gochisōsama deshita.
Mrs Honda	Iie, dō itashimashite.
Mr Honda	Mata kite kudasai.
Michael	Dōmo arigatō gozaimasu. (*in the 'genkan'*) Ojama shimashita. Kyō wa dōmo arigatō gozaimashita.
Mr Honda	Iie, kochira koso.
Michael	Sore dewa, shitsurei shimasu.
Mr Honda	Oyasuminasai.
Michael	Oyasuminasai.
Mrs Honda	(*as Michael finally disappears*) Ki o tsukete.
Michael	Hai, arigatō gozaimasu.

Rewind and repeat!

mata kite kudasai	please come again
kochira koso	thank *you* (lit. 'from my side, too')
ki o tsukete (kudasai)	take care! (said to departing travellers)

TAKE NOTE

The thanking never seems to end! The next time Michael meets Mr or Mrs Honda, he'll have to remember to thank them once more, for example with *kono aida wa* ('regarding the other day') ... (*dōmo*) *arigatō gozaimashita*. The same applies to *sumimasen*; if someone did you a favour or you did something wrong yesterday, apologise for it again today: *kinō wa* (*dōmo*) *sumimasen deshita*. Note the past forms of these words, used to refer to incidents which are over (similarly, *ojama shimashita* – used when you've finished 'disturbing' someone by being in their house – and *shitsurei shimashita* when you're over with 'being rude' by, for example, entering someone's office or leaving someone temporarily to answer a phone call).

FORMALITIES

@ Try to work out what is going on in the pairs of pictures below, and think of an appropriate polite phrase for the first speech bubble of each pair. Put the same phrase into the past for the second picture of the pair.

Can you spot the deliberate mistake relating to Japanese etiquette in one of the pictures?

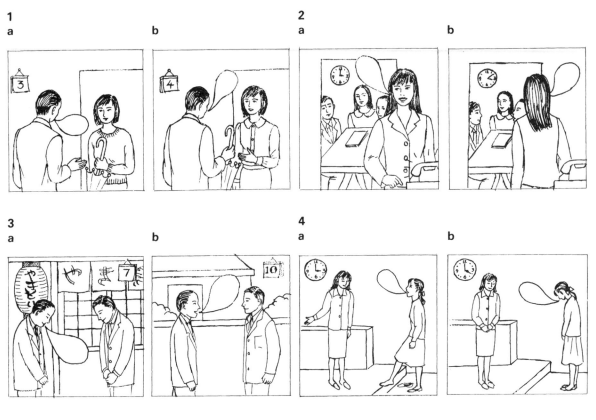

1 a   b

2 a   b

3 a   b

4 a   b

Prayers at a Buddhist temple in Tōkyō

About Japan

If the giving and receiving of presents in Japan depends primarily on notions of *giri* and the proper way in which social relations should be conducted, an emphasis on form is also apparent in the way in which gifts are actually handed over. There are certain rules of etiquette to be followed if one is to avoid causing embarrassment – both to oneself and to others.

Formal kneeling (*seiza*) and bowing

In the first place, gifts should never be handed over 'naked' (*hadaka*), but should be wrapped tastefully. In second place, it is not necessary to accompany the present with a card, for gifts are usually handed over in an atmosphere of modesty and 'holding back' (*enryo*) rather than of Western-style effusiveness. Third, although more and more people nowadays are tending to open presents in front of others, the more usual custom is to set aside the present once it has been accepted and not to open it until your visitor has left.

Wrapping is an important element in the presentation of commodities in all consumer societies, but in Japan it is given even more importance than in other countries. Not only do department stores provide stylish carrier bags free of charge, but their salesgirls are taught how to wrap articles sold there with a sense of aesthetic perfection and care that is lacking elsewhere in the world.

Of course, wrapping is sometimes used to disguise the poverty of the contents. We see this in our own advertising, where a beer manufacturer, for example, will focus on its new style of can in order to make it seem as if the beer itself has been renewed in some way or other. In Japan, then, the meticulous attention to detail in wrapping may also serve to hide the fact that the gift itself is really just one more cog in the mechanism of social obligation.

Nevertheless, it is important to remember that presents must be covered and that it offends most Japanese to be given things that are 'naked'. In particular, money – whether given to small children on New Year's Day or handed to a *shamisen* teacher in payment for monthly lessons – should always be wrapped. There are special envelopes for these money gifts – red, silver and gold for congratulatory occasions such as weddings, or black and silver for funerals – and the giver usually writes his or her name (in best calligraphy!) at the bottom of the envelope. Sometimes sheets of paper similar in style to the envelopes are affixed to particularly large gifts that cannot easily be wrapped – like crates of beer.

The formality of many gift-giving occasions can be seen not simply in the style of wrapping, but also in the way in which gifts are handed over and received. Sumō wrestlers, for example, will wave the palm of their hand in a stylised manner over the envelopes of money presented to them by the referee at the end of a bout. Similarly, people involved in an exchange of gifts will often kneel formally (*seiza suru*) on the tatami floor of a room and bow, while the giver utters a phrase such as *tsumaranai mono desu ga* ... (this is just a trifling thing ...), intended to belittle the present. As with etiquette anywhere, however, such behaviour tends to disguise what is really going on between people ...

THINGS YOU CAN DO WITH VERBS

TURNING POINT

In Unit 10 you'll be revising the language you've come across up to this point in the book; this is a 'turning point' in the sense that you're already in a position to carry out a basic conversation in Japanese, and in the remaining pages of this unit we'll be showing you some 'things you can do with verbs' which will take you beyond a beginning level. You might therefore find these pages difficult, but keep returning to them and you'll discover that they act as a kind of springboard into the world of learning beyond *Japanese – Language and People*!

VERBS

You can do a lot of things with verbs in Japanese, just by changing their endings. You've already seen how *-masu* can change to *-masen*, *-mashita* or *-mashō*, and you've also used *-te* (or 'participle') forms to make requests and talk about continuous actions. In the book so far, we've emphasised polite present (*-masu*) forms and their derivatives as being most appropriate for you to use in the beginning stages of learning Japanese. However, as you can see from the chart on page 232, the basic verb form in Japanese (i.e. that from which all other verb endings can be derived) is not the *-masu* form but the 'plain present' form, otherwise known as the 'dictionary' form (since this is the form verbs are listed under in dictionaries).

FORMATIONS

Verbs behave differently according to whether they drop *-ru* (like *taberu*) or *-u* (like *nomu*) from their dictionary form to make other forms. By using the chart on page 232, you can work out the various forms of any verb, *as long as* you know its dictionary form and whether it is a *-ru* or *-u* verb. From now on, try to get into the habit of remembering these two pieces of information whenever you come across a new verb. For all the verbs in this book, you can find these things out by looking at the verb list in the Grammar section (part 6).

SPOTCHECK 4

@ By looking them up in part 6 of the Grammar section, write down the plain present ('dictionary') forms of these verbs, separating them into three groups according to whether they are **1** *-ru* verbs, **2** *-u* verbs or **3** irregular:

a agemasu (*give*)   **e** yomimasu (*read*)
b kikimasu (*listen*)   **f** shimemasu (*close*)
c shimasu (*do*)   **g** hanashimasu (*speak*)
d kaerimasu (*return*) **h** nemasu (*sleep*)

Opposite **Schoolgirls visiting a Shintō shrine**

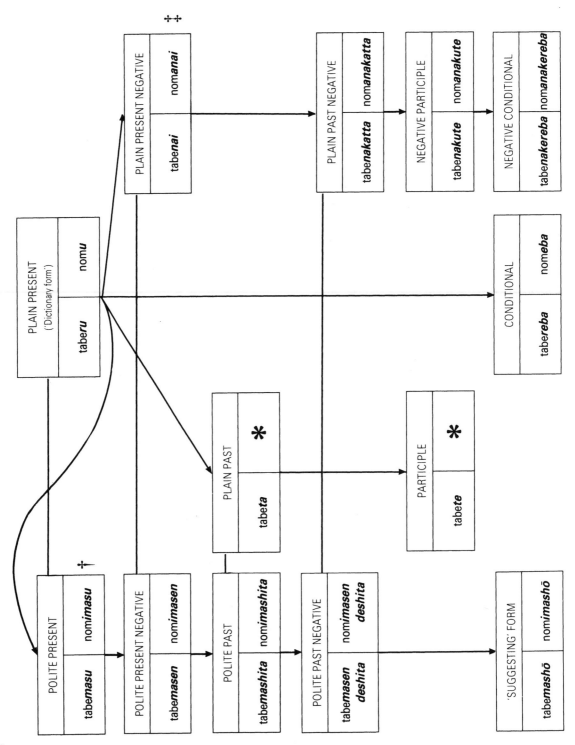

PLAIN PRESENT ('Dictionary form')

taber***u*** | nom***u***

PLAIN PRESENT NEGATIVE ‡

tabe***nai*** | nom***anai***

PLAIN PAST NEGATIVE

tabe***nakatta*** | nom***anakatta***

NEGATIVE PARTICIPLE

tabe***nakute*** | nom***anakute***

NEGATIVE CONDITIONAL

tabe***nakereba*** | nom***anakereba***

CONDITIONAL

tabe***reba*** | nom***eba***

PLAIN PAST

tabe***ta*** | ✱

PARTICIPLE

tabe***te*** | ✱

POLITE PRESENT †

tabe***masu*** | nom***imasu***

POLITE PRESENT NEGATIVE

tabe***masen*** | nom***imasen***

POLITE PAST

tabe***mashita*** | nom***imashita***

POLITE PAST NEGATIVE

tabe***masen deshita*** | nom***imasen deshita***

'SUGGESTING' FORM

tabe***mashō*** | nom***imashō***

TAKE NOTE

There are only two irregular verbs in Japanese: *kuru/kimasu* (come) and *suru/shimasu* (do). *Da/desu* (be) also behaves rather strangely, as you can see from part 6 of the Grammar section. In some areas there are exceptions to the normal patterns (these are indicated at the bottom of the page), but in general verbs behave very regularly in Japanese as compared with in other languages such as English or French.

BUILD-UP 1

@ By using the chart on the opposite page, write on the lines below **1** the polite present (*-masu*) forms, and **2** the plain present negative forms of these new verbs:

a ire*ru* (*include/put in*) _____ _____
b tsutsum*u* (*wrap*) _____ _____
c ki*ru* (*cut*) _____ _____
d ki*ru* (*wear*) _____ _____

TAKE NOTE

The only rather complicated rules are those applying to formation of the plain past and participle of *-u* verbs: in these cases, account needs to be taken of the sound preceding the final *-u* in the verb's dictionary form, so that, for example, a verb ending in *-su* like *hanasu* (speak) becomes *hanashita/**shite***, whereas a verb ending in *-mu* like *nomu* (drink) will become *no**nda**/**nde***. As you can see, knowing either the plain past or the participle form of a verb is sufficient, since they only differ in the final *-a* or *-e*.

BUILD-UP 2

Write down **1** the plain past and **2** the participle forms of all the verbs in 'Spotcheck 4' on p. 231 and 'Build-up 1' (apart from *shimasu/suru*) by following the rules in the chart opposite and the notes below. Then check your answers by looking up the participle forms in the verb list in part 6 of the Grammar section (for the plain past forms, simply change *-e* to *-a*). While looking at the Grammar section, take this opportunity to learn the different (irregular) forms of *suru*, *kuru* and *da* off by heart.

✳ The form of the PLAIN PAST depends on the final letters of the PLAIN PRESENT:

-mu -nu -bu	→ -nda	e.g. no*mu* → no*nda*
-ku	→ -ita	e.g. ki*ku* → ki*ita*
		BUT i*ku* → i*tta*
-gu	→ -ida	e.g. oyo*gu* → oyo*ida*
-tsu -ru	→ -tta	e.g. a*u* → a*tta*
-vowel + u		
-su	→ shita	e.g. hana*su* → han*shita*

Change the final 'a' of the PLAIN PAST to 'e' to make the PARTICIPLE.

† Certain verbs may change in a way which looks strange but is in fact regular in terms of the Japanese sound system:

hana<u>su</u> → hana<u>sh</u>i*masu*
ma<u>tsu</u> → ma<u>ch</u>i*masu*

As you can see from the sound chart on page 325, *-su* is in fact related to *-shi(masu)* and *-tsu* to *-chi(masu)* in pronunciation terms.

‡ Verbs whose PLAIN PRESENT has a vowel before the final 'u' add a 'w' in the NEGATIVE for easier pronunciation:

a<u>u</u> > a**w**a*nai*

PLAIN FORMS

Up to now, verbs have been presented in this book in their so-called 'polite' forms (ending in -*masu* or -*masen* in the present and -*mashita* or -*masen deshita* in the past). These forms are the most appropriate for you to use in the early stages of learning Japanese, since you won't risk offending anyone by being over-familiar; however, you should be aware that just as there are 'super-polite' forms of some verbs (e.g. *irasshaimasu* instead of *imasu*, or *gozaimasu* instead of *arimasu*), so-called 'plain' forms exist for all verbs and are commonly used at a familiar level of speech (for example, among friends or family members).

SPOTCHECK 5

@ By looking at the chart on p. 232 and following the horizontal lines across from the polite forms on the left write down the plain form equivalents of:

a tabemasu   _____**taberu**_____

b tabemasen   _____

c tabemashita   _____

d tabemasen deshita   _____

e nomimasu   _____

f nomimasen   _____

g nomimashita   _____

h nomimasen deshita   _____

TELEPHONING   CD ▶ 268

@ Jun telephones three different people, and although he says much the same things each time, he varies his language to suit the formality (or informality) of the situation. Listen once, and decide which conversation (1, 2 or 3) is the most and which is the least formal. Then listen again, and write down the 'super-polite' and 'plain' forms you hear of these verbs:

a imasu   b desu   c shimasu.

SPIES   CD ▶ 269

@ Just as you would in real life, you've actually heard a lot of plain forms being used already, in the 'What you'll hear' conversations from Units 1 to 8. One such conversation was the one between the industrial spies Mayumi and Kenji on p. 185. Listen once more, and this time write into the spaces in the dialogue below the plain present forms you hear of these verbs:

agemasu   desu   imasu   nomimasu
kaerimasu   shimasu   arimasu

Kenji	Mayumi?
Mayumi	Kenji?
Kenji	Firumu motte _____ ka?
Mayumi	Ē . . . O-kane wa?
Kenji	Ima _____ . Kuruma wa doko?
Mayumi	Asoko ni _____ . Dō _____ ?
Kenji	Jā, boku Mayumi to _____ . Ima chōdo jūji da.
Mayumi	Ā, samui. Kore _____ ?
Kenji	Ā, kōhii ka? (*sound of police sirens*)
Mayumi	A, keisatsu _____ !

TALKING ABOUT POSSIBILITIES

CD ▶ 270

A knowledge of plain forms is useful not only when it comes to understanding familiar speech, but also in the formation of several important constructions at a 'polite' level of speech. For example, to say someone 'probably will/won't do' or 'probably has/hasn't done' something, **deshō** is added after plain forms (listen and say):

'I'll probably go'	**iku deshō**
'I probably won't go'	**ikanai deshō**
'he probably went'	**itta deshō**
'he probably didn't go'	**ikanakatta deshō**

HE PROBABLY ...

@ **A** You can read this man's mind! Write four sentences about what he probably did yesterday (the table next to him says it all!) and four more sentences about what he's wishfully thinking of doing today. Look up (in the Grammar section (part

6)) and use the plain past or present forms of these verbs, adding *deshō* each time:

okiru	suru	suu	neru
miru	oyogu	taberu	nomu

E.g. **Shichiji ni okiru deshō.**

@ **B** According to the evidence in the picture, now write eight sentences about what the man probably won't or didn't do, using the plain present or past NEGATIVE forms of the verbs above plus *deshō*. Using the verbs in order from left to right above, start your sentences with the following words (note that *wa* is used for contrast with what the man actually did or didn't do):

1 Jūji ni wa ...
2 Gorufu wa ...
3 Paipu wa ...
4 Jūichiji ni wa ...
5 Bideo wa ...
6 Umi de wa ... (umi = *sea*)
7 Sarada wa ...
8 Orenji jūsu wa ...

E.g. (1) **Jūji ni wa okinai deshō.**

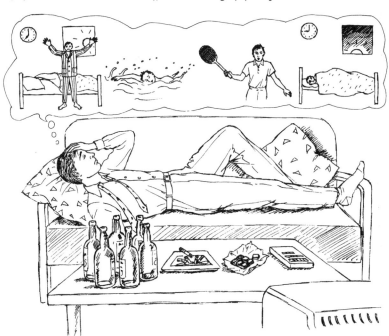

235

TALKING ABOUT OBLIGATION

As you've already read, the Japanese are bound together by a sense of mutual obligation, a feeling that certain things 'must' be done to maintain the fabric of their relations with others. As a foreigner, knowing where (or whether) *you* fit into the cycle of 'give and take' can be quite a headache, and you'll be wanting to ask questions about what's expected or not expected of you in a whole variety of unfamiliar situations.

> • To say you 'have to' do something: change the negative *-nai* (plain form) ending of a verb to **-nakereba narimasen**.
>   E.g. 'you have to give a present': *purezento o agenakereba narimasen* (lit. 'if you don't give ..., it will not do')
>
> • To say you 'don't have to' do something: change the *-nai* ending of a verb to **-nakute mo ii desu**.
>   E.g. 'you don't have to give a present': *purezento o agenakute mo ii desu* (lit. 'not giving ... is all right')

LISTEN `CD ▸ 271`

@ Michael is asking Hiromi for some advice on giving gifts. Write numbers in the boxes in the chart at the bottom of this page according to the order in which Michael receives the advice, and check that what Hiromi says Michael must do tallies with the columns you ticked from memory.

BEING SURPRISED `CD ▸ 271`

@ Michael was surprised and interested by all the advice Hiromi gave, and he showed this by repeating what she said (with the addition of *ka*) and using 'aizuchi' such as *ā, sō desu ka* and *hē* ... Rewind, and write down the verbs exactly as Michael repeats them, next to their 'dictionary' forms below:

a (ageru) _____ ka
b (ireru) _____ ka
c (tsutsumu) _____ ka
d (akeru) _____ ka
e (seiza suru) _____ ka

YOUR TURN `CD ▸ 272`

Now listen to a recording of the same conversation with Michael's (surprised and interested) replies left out. You supply them: start with an 'aizuchi', then say what you've just written down above.

> E.g. (1) *Tape:* **O-kane o agenakereba narimasen.**
> *You:* **Ā, sō desu ka. Agenakereba narimasen ka.**

BUILD-UP

In the 'About Japan' section on pp. 228 and 229, you received some advice on gift-giving; trying to remember that advice, tick the columns to the left or right depending on whether you have to or don't have to do these things:

HAVE TO DO			DON'T HAVE TO DO
	open (*akeru*) the present immediately	☐	
	kneel formally (*seiza suru*)	☐	
	wrap (*tsutsumu*) a present	☐	
	wrap money	☐	
	give money at a wedding (*kekkonshiki*)	☐	
	include (*ireru*) a card	☐	

To say 'you'd better' do something: use the **-ta** (past plain form) ending of a verb, and add **hō ga ii desu**.

E.g. 'you'd better give a present': *purezento o ageta hō ga ii desu*

JAPANESE LIVE 4

CD ▸ 273

Michael is asking Hiromi about what to take (*motte iku*) on holiday to Hokkaidō in August.

Michael	Sētā wa?
Hiromi	Motte ikanakereba narimasen.
Michael	Sandaru wa dō desu ka?
Hiromi	Motte ikanakute mo ii desu yo.
Michael	Kōto wa?
Hiromi	Sō desu nē ... Motte itta hō ga ii desu.

Rewind and repeat!

SPOTCHECK 6

@ What does Hiromi say Michael
 a has to take?
 b had better take?
 c doesn't have to take?

LISTEN

CD ▸ 274

Listen to two more conversations (1 and 2) in which people going on holiday ask what to take. In columns 1 and 2, tick the things they're told they have to or should take, and put crosses beside the things they don't have to take:

	1	2	3
sandaru			
sankuriimu			
kōto			
mafurā			
sētā			
mizugi (*swimsuit*)			
bōshi			

@ Where do you think the people in 1 and 2 are going on holiday? Choose from **a** *hawai*, **b** *fuyu no kanada* and **c** *nyūjiirando*.

YOUR TURN

CD ▸ 275

Now someone will ask *you* for advice on what to take on holiday to Australia in December. First put ticks and crosses under **3** in the table according to what you think they have to or don't have to take. Then play the CD and answer the questions (with *motte ikanakereba narimasen, motte itta hō ga ii desu* or *motte ikanakute mo ii desu*).

Shintō wedding ceremony

About Japan

As we have seen, the Japanese spend a lot of time exchanging gifts of one sort or another, and we should ask why this might be so. Is there some kind of religious or social philosophy that encourages gift exchange in Japan? To answer this question, we need to take a look at Japanese religions. There are two important religions, Shintō and Buddhism, which exist fairly happily side by side without impinging much on each other. The rituals of both involve much give and take.

Shintō – or the 'Way of the Gods' – is the indigenous religion of Japan. Unlike most of the world's major religions, Shintō has no written creed. It is this, perhaps, that leads some people to suggest that the Japanese are not religious. But this does not mean that they do not believe in anything. According to Shintō animistic beliefs, the gods and spirits inhabit all aspects of nature: rocks, trees, mountains, rivers, seas. In some respects, this makes the Japanese very conscious of a two-way relationship between the environment and their lives. It also partly explains their so-called 'love' of nature.

These days, belief in Shintō is largely concerned with obtaining the blessing of the gods for major events in people's lives: blessing new-born babies, for example, or children of certain ages (at *shichi-go-san*); asking for success in school entrance exams or at the start of a new enterprise; ensuring that the ground on which a new building is to be erected is purified; or sanctifying a wedding.

If Shintō is concerned with marking the main events in a person's life, the rituals of Buddhism, which came to Japan via China in the sixth century, have more to do with death and the honouring of the ancestors. A Japanese funeral, therefore, is usually a Buddhist ceremony, and other ceremonies are held over the months and years following a person's death to ensure that his or her soul reposes in peace.

These ceremonies are important because many households in Japan honour their ancestors. These usually consist of relatives, but they may include anyone who has lived and died in a particular house. The ancestors are enshrined in a box-like altar, known as the *butsudan*, where memorial tablets, each carrying the name of a deceased person, are placed. Every day, usually in the morning at breakfast, a member of the household will serve a cup of tea (and sometimes a bowl of rice) to the ancestors, and many people pray daily to ask for their protection.

The main festival connected with the ancestors is called *o-bon*, or All Souls, and is held in mid-August. At this time the dead are believed to return to their homes, and elaborate preparations are made to welcome them. The house is cleaned and tidied, the *butsudan* decorated with lanterns, and special foods prepared. It is during this period that many people now living in cities will return to their family homes for a few days' summer holiday.

Prayers are said by Buddhist priests for the souls not just of the ancestors, but of dead animals, too, since animals as well as humans are believed to be endowed with souls. Humans can become indebted to animals, as well as to fellow human beings, ancestors and deities: in this way, the give and take of life extends to death as well ...

Prayers at a Buddhist temple

SAYING 'IF ...'

In a country where the gods and spirits are everywhere – in a river, a tree or an old stone – it's hardly surprising, perhaps, if the Japanese tend to be rather superstitious. While many superstitions are remarkably similar to those in the West, below are pictures of some with which you'll probably be unfamiliar ...

1 Asa kumo o _____,

. . . .

2 O-cha no happa ga yunomi no naka de

_____,

. . . .

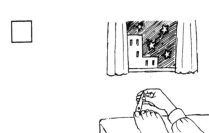

3 Yoru ni tsume o _____,

. . . .

4 Reikyūsha o _____,

. . . .

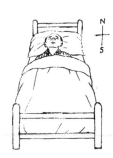

5 Kitamuki ni _____,

. . . .

6 Hashi kara hashi e tabemono o

_____,

. . . .

7 Nuketa ha (*a tooth that has fallen out*) o

_____,

. . . .

8 Gohan ni o-hashi o _____,

. . . .

SPOTCHECK 7

@ By looking at the pictures and the incomplete sentences, guess (or remember) the Japanese words for the following:

chopsticks _____

towards the north _____

rice _____

spider _____

tea cup _____

(toe)nails _____

food _____

leaves _____

hearse _____

- One of the (various) ways of saying 'if ...' in Japanese is simply to add *to* after the plain form of a verb.
  E.g. *'If you see* a black cat, good things will happen': *Kuroi neko o **miru to** ii koto ga aru deshō.*

FILL IN

@ Write one of these verbs plus *to* on each solid line under the pictures to describe the superstitions shown there. (You'll need to use *miru* twice.)
  E.g. (1) **Asa kumo o *miru to*, . . .**

miru	see
nageru	throw
neru	sleep
kiru	cut
tateru	stand (something) up
tatsu	stand up (of one's own accord)
watasu	pass

GOOD OR BAD?

Now guess whether each phenomenon brings good or bad luck, and write a + (for good luck) or a − (for bad luck) in each box.

LISTEN `CD ▸ 276`

@ Michael asked his colleague Mr Honda about the various superstitions in the pictures. Listen to find out whether your guesses were correct, and change your answers if necessary. Finally, complete the sentences by writing on the dotted lines either *ii koto ga aru deshō* ('good things will probably happen') or *warui koto ga aru deshō* ('bad things ...'), as appropriate.

RECREATE `CD ▸ 277`

Try to remember which things are good and which are bad luck. Michael will mention a superstition; without looking at the opposite page, say either *ii koto ga aru deshō* or *warui koto ga aru deshō*.
  E.g. (1) *CD:* **Kitamuki ni neru to . . .**
  You: **warui koto ga aru deshō.**

241

YOUR TURN

@ **A** Prepare to tell your Japanese friend about some Western superstitions (the ones pictured below). Write one of these verbs on each line, adding *to* to make 'if' sentences:

kowasu (break) **sawaru** (touch) **aruku** (walk)
miru (see) **au** (meet) **utau** (sing)

1 Kuroi neko o _____

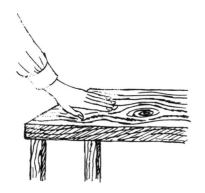

2 Ki o _____

3 Kagami o _____

4 Hashigo no shita o _____

5 Asagohan no mae de _____

6 Kekkonshiki no ato de buta ni _____

kagami	mirror	...no shita	under
ki	wood	...no mae	before
hashigo	ladder	...no ato	after

CD ▶ 278

@ **B** Check in the key that you know the significance
of each of the phenomena shown in the pictures.
Then respond to the prompts on the CD by
describing the superstition and saying whether it's
good or bad luck. Try not to look at what you've
written.

E.g. (1) *CD:* **Kuroi neko ...**
You: **Kuroi neko o miru to ii koto ga
aru deshō.**

Girls reading their horo-
scopes (*omikuji*) at a Shintō
shrine

About Japan

If Shintō and Buddhism involve notions of reciprocity between human beings and their environment on the one hand, and between the living and the dead on the other, we should also recognise the importance of another philosophy, Confucianism, to the normal give and take of everyday life.

Confucianism was first imported from China well over a thousand years ago, but was really given importance by the feudal shogunate of Japan in the seventeenth and eighteenth centuries. Then, the ideals of the four human virtues and five fundamental relationships were expounded by the elite samurai class. According to these Confucian ideals, a servant should be loyal to his lord, who should in turn treat him with benevolence; a son should behave in a filial manner towards his father, a younger brother be respectful to his elder brother, a woman be obedient to her husband, and friends treat one another with love.

These ideals have been handed down through the centuries and still permeate certain social relations in Japan today. We have seen, for example, how the family retains its central importance in contemporary Japan and how women have traditionally been expected to look after their fathers, husbands and sons. The modes of behaviour that accompany such expectations – based on concepts of social obligation (*giri*) and human spontaneity (*ninjō*) – are also found between members of yakuza gangs on the one hand, and between teachers and pupils on the other. At the same time, we can see that Confucian-style relations are for the most part authoritarian in structure, and this partly explains the comparatively hierarchical nature of Japanese society.

Not that all relations are hierarchical. Indeed, one of the more noticeable features of Japanese society is the way in which it is divided into discrete groups. For a Japanese, the world consists of groups to which he or she does or does not belong – groups which are continuously being collapsed into larger, or prised apart into smaller, entities depending on the context in which one finds oneself. Thus a civil servant may voice the interests of his department vis-à-vis those of another at one moment, and those of his educational clique (*gakubatsu*) versus another's in the same ministry the next. But then, when it seems as if the budget allocation for his ministry may not be very favourable when compared with that of a rival ministry, he will close ranks with all his rivals to fight the newly perceived threat.

Of course, the exchange of gifts between people to some extent reinforces such forms of group identification. A man presents a bottle of whisky to his superior and so asserts the fact that they are members of the same department at work. But by so doing he also reinforces the paternalistic relation between them, and intimates that he expects that type of behaviour to continue in the future. In other words, gift-giving at midsummer and year-end seasons is not only a thanks for past favours. It is a kind of insurance against the future.

This can lead the Japanese into immense difficulty, for it is sometimes difficult to distinguish when a gift is given as mere thanks for the past, and when as a kind of 'bribe' for the future. This difficulty has been brought to light in the past with the Lockheed and Recruit affairs. As long as notions of *giri* and *ninjō* continue to be important, however, it is unlikely that what we in the West might call 'bribery' will be very distant from everyday relations of give and take in Japanese society.

Schoolchildren's prayers for success in entrance examinations

WHAT YOU'LL HEAR

LUCKY CHARMS

At Japanese shrines you can find *o-mamori* (lucky charms) for just about any eventuality, from pendants that guarantee children to childless couples to trinkets that get you into the university of your choice. Somehow, though, the charms don't always seem to work, and so, not surprisingly, even the people who buy them tend to have rather an ambiguous attitude towards them.

CD ▸ 279

Listen to the five interviews (1 to 5) with people buying *o-mamori* at a shrine.

A The first time you listen, decide why each of the people interviewed has bought his or her charm and write the number of the interview to the left of the appropriate reason below:

_____	**A** for good health	_____
_____	**B** for safe driving	_____
_____	**C** to have children	_____
_____	**D** to enter university	_____
_____	**E** for success in business	_____

@ **B** Now listen again, and – depending on whether or not the speaker believes in the power of the charm – put a tick or a cross to the right of each reason.

... **o shinjiru**	believe in ...
(shinjimasu)	

HAVEN'T YOU GOT ANYTHING CHEAPER?

CD ▸ 280

@ Listen to five conversations (1 to 5) in the jewellery department of a large department store as customers admire the rings, necklaces and earrings shown below. They didn't all decide to buy something, but, when they did, write the number of the conversation next to the object(s) purchased.

tori	bird
yubiwa	ring
hoshi	star

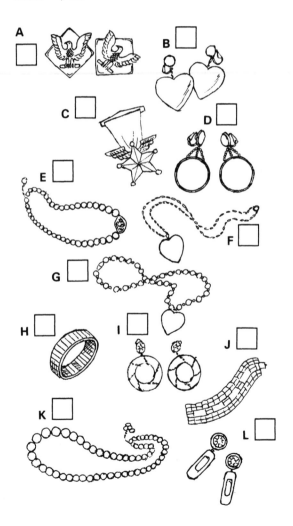

MODEL-MAKING

You're going to be given instructions to make some simple animal models. You'll need three sheets of paper, some scissors and a pencil. You'll also need to understand these words:

maru ◯   sankaku △   shikaku ▢

sen o hik*u*	(*draw a line*)	_____ kudasai
nur*u*	(*colour*)	_____ kudasai
kir*u*	(*cut*)	_____ kudasai
sute*ru*	(*throw away*)	_____ kudasai

Before beginning, work out (or look up in Grammar section 6) and write down the -*te* forms of the verbs on the lines above.

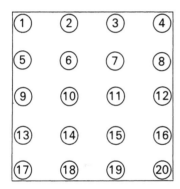

Now read and follow the instructions below and make the first model. If you're told, for example, to cut from number three to number eight, imagine that the numbers are written as above on your sheet of paper (You don't need to write the numbers on your paper.)

San kara hachi made kitte kudasai. San kara nana made sen o hiite kudasai. San to nana to hachi no sankaku o kuro ni nutte kudasai. Ni kara roku made, roku kara jūichi made, jūichi kara jū made, jū kara kyū made kitte sutete kudasai. Jūichi kara jūroku made sen o hiite kudasai. Jūsan kara jūhachi made kitte sutete kudasai. Hachi kara nana made, nana kara jūni made kitte sutete kudasai.

@ Now make two more models by following the instructions on the CD.

IF WE DON'T GET HOME QUICKLY ...

As you already know, one way of saying 'if ...' is to use the plain form of a verb plus *to*. Another way is to use the special so-called 'conditional' form (easy to pick out since it always ends in -*eba*, or -*nakereba* in the negative). You'll often (though not always) hear the word *moshi* at the beginning of 'if ...' sentences.

E.g. (*Moshi*) *kaeranakereba* ...: 'If we don't go home ...'

@ Listen to five conversations (1 to 5) in which people talk about things that may or may not happen, and possible events or outcomes. In each case, draw a line from the possibility on the left to the picture representing what might or might not be the outcome on the right.

dorobō	robber
ame	rain

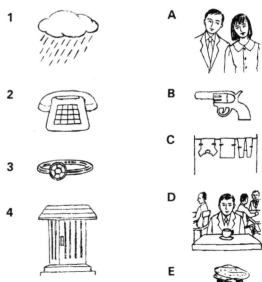

WRITTEN JAPANESE

Religious life for most people in Japan revolves around (Shintō) shrines and (Buddhist) temples. A shrine (*jinja*) can easily be recognised by the *torii* gateway at the entrance. Temples ((*o-*)*tera*) sometimes have fearsome-looking guardians at their gates.

jin　ja　　shin　tō

神社

お寺

The Shintō gods and spirits are known as *kami*, and this is the 'kun' reading of the character 神 (read in an 'on' way as *shin/jin*). This kanji, which started life as a picture of an altar combined with three thunderbolts, originally meant 'god of lightning', but is now used to refer indiscriminately to any of the gods, whether of sky, sea or earth. Similarly, 社 ('on' reading: *sha/ja*) appears originally to have meant '(altar of the) earth god', but is now used in combination with 神 to refer to a place where any of the Shintō gods is worshipped (神社: *jinja*). 神道 (*shintō*) literally means 'way of the gods'; you've come across this 'spiritual' use of the character 道 before, in 茶道 (*sadō*: 'tea ceremony'). More prosaically, 道 can also mean a normal road (*michi* in everyday Japanese).

zen

tera

Sadō, along with other traditional Japanese 'ways' such as kadō (ikebana), shodō, jūdō and kendō are infused with the spirit not of Shintō but of Zen

Buddhism, first introduced from China around the eighth century and refined into its particularly Japanese form from the late twelfth century onwards. The character for *zen* – 禅 – contains the familiar representation of an altar, in combination with what some say was originally a picture of a weapon split down the middle; this is held to symbolise the 'sameness' of attack and defence and of all oppositions, the overcoming of which zen meditation (*zazen*) has as its ultimate goal. The kanji for 'Buddhist temple' (zen or otherwise) – 寺 – appears originally to have meant a government office, a place of hustle and bustle where people moved their hands and feet around. Government officials were often priests, being those who knew best how to read and write, and this may be why 寺 gained its present meaning. *Tera* (*-dera*) is the 'kun' reading of this kanji, but the names of some of the temples you visit may end with the 'on' reading *ji*; e.g. 東大寺 (*Tōdaiji*, the largest and most famous temple in Nara).

時　分　間

The character on the left above is one you'll often see; it means 'time', 'hour' or 'o'clock' and has the readings *toki* ('kun') and *ji* ('on'). This kanji is used to write times, in combination with 分 (*fun/pun*: 'minutes'). 3時15分, for example, means *sanji jūgofun*: 'three fifteen'. Periods of time are written with the addition of 間 (*kan*), so that 'for one hour', for example, is 一時間: *ichijikan*. As for the derivations and 'literal' meanings of these characters, 時 seems to be a combination of the radical for 'sun' on the left and the character for 'temple' on the right. One possible explanation is that, in ancient times, sundials were usually to be found on temple premises. The sun also appears – shining through a gate – in 間, which means 'space' or 'interval' and is read in a 'kun' way as *aida*. In Japanese the word for 'time' in general is *jikan* ('time space'), written – as you might expect – as 時間. 分 means 'division'/'part' (or 'minute' – 'division of an hour') and represents an object cut into pieces by a sword, the kanji for which is 刀.

午　前　　午　後
go　zen　　go　go

Some more kanji you'll often see in connection with times are those above: 午前 (*gozen*: 'a.m.') and 午後 (*gogo*: 'p.m.'). Individually, these characters mean 'noon' (午), 'before/in front' (前 – 'kun' reading: *mae*) and 'after/behind' (後 – 'kun' reading: *ushiro*). *Gozen* is therefore literally 'before noon' and *gogo* 'after noon' (including evening!).

@ Practise reading some times written in Japanese, and reviewing the kanji for the days of the week which you came across in the last unit. What are the opening times and days shown on these signboards?

1

2

3

5

4

LANGUAGE SUMMARY

Verbs

hanas*u*	kir*u*
kak*u*	kir*u*
kas*u*	nage*ru*
oshie*ru*	tats*u*
shime*ru*	watas*u*
tsuke*ru*	kowas*u*
kes*u*	sawar*u*
su*u*	aruk*u*
suwar*u*	sute*ru*
ire*ru*	shinji*ru*
tsutsum*u*	

Superstitions

reikyūsha	nuketa ha
kumo	hashigo
happa	ki
tsume	kagami
kitamuki	neko
kekkonshiki	buta

Before and after

... no mae
... no ato

Comparing

motto (+ *adjective*)
e.g. motto ōkii

Shopping

Motto yasui no wa arimasu ka?
Hoka no wa arimasen ka?
Purezento desu ga ...

To deepen your understanding of the various verb forms presented in this unit, look at 'Verbs' (5) and the verb list (6) in the Grammar section.

Giving a present

Dōzo, tsumaranai mono desu ga ...

Leaving someone's home

Jā, soro soro (shitsurei shimasu)
Mada ii ja arimasen ka?
Osoku made ojama shimashita.
Sore dewa, shitsurei shimasu.
Mada ii ja arimasen ka?
Mata kite kudasai.
Ki o tsukete kudasai.
(Kono aida wa) dōmo arigatō gozaimashita.

Main language structures

A _____ one
'i' adjectives: yasui → yasui no
'na' adjectives: kirei → kirei na no
words followed by 'no': hoka → hoka no

Using '-te' forms (participles) of verbs
Requesting: -te *form* + kudasai
e.g. Pen o kashite kudasai.
Asking permission: -te *form* + mo ii desu ka?
e.g. Kisu o shite mo ii desu ka?

Using plain forms
Talking about probabilities: *plain form* + deshō
e.g. Iku deshō/Ikanai deshō.
　 Itta deshō/Ikanakatta deshō.
Saying 'if ...': *plain present form* + to
e.g. Asa kumo o miru to, ii koto ga aru deshō.

Degrees of obligation
Saying you have to do something:
-nakereba narimasen
e.g. Sētā o motte ikanakereba narimasen.
Saying you don't have to do something:
-nakute mo ii desu
e.g. Sandaru o motte ikanakute mo ii desu.
Saying you'd better do something:
plain past form + hō ga ii desu
e.g. Kōto o motte itta hō ga ii desu.

JAPAN TOMORROW

Language review
Saying what you want
How to continue

About Japan

For a small island nation which was almost totally cut off from the rest of the world for more than two centuries until the Meiji Restoration in 1868, Japan has come a very long way. During the decades following the end of the Pacific War, in particular, the Japanese astonished all by their ability to learn, adapt and innovate. Their economic success was often referred to, indeed, as a miracle.

But what is the nature of this so-called miracle? What does it really mean to be a member of a population of 123 million Japanese who in concert have raised their country's GNP until it is second only to that of the United States? Are the Japanese really so well off? And what does the future hold for them, both at home and in their relations with the rest of the world?

That there is a lot of money around in Japan can hardly be in doubt. The number of expensive imported Mercedes Benz and BMW cars being driven round the nation's cities should be enough to persuade the visitor that there are nowadays quite a few very wealthy Japanese. Even those who do not visit Japan will know from the way in which tourists flock to do their shopping at the most expensive stores in European and American cities that the Japanese are comparitively well off. They will have noted the preponderance of designer labels and accessories that adorn the bodies of the Japanese men and women they pass in the streets. Indeed, not only are the Japanese among the most expensively dressed people in the world, Tōkyō is now the fashion capital of Asia, regularly visited by enthusiastic shoppers from Korea, Taiwan and Hong Kong.

Japan's explosive economic growth after the Pacific War was not without its social costs. In the 1980s, Tōkyō was regularly ranked as the most expensive city in the world. In a country whose urban population density was not very different from that of Hong Kong or Singapore, people found themselves living cheek by jowl in conditions that, by Western standards at least, were far from ideal. Homes were often cramped and badly built (in the sense that their construction did not allow for much privacy). Public spaces, in the form of parks, were desperately lacking so that children were obliged to play in streets without pavements or in cramped neighbourhood playgrounds that were often found under overhead expressways. Old people, too, had nowhere to go.

The kind of social environment that existed during Japan's high growth period, however, has improved immensely in recent years. Excellent facilities now exist for the old and handicapped. New developments regularly provide public promenades and rest areas in addition to the mandatory restaurants and cafés. The bay areas in which many of Japan's largest cities are located have been redeveloped to include spacious residential apartments, hotels, shopping centres and amusement parks. As a result, contemporary Japanese now live in surroundings that are among the best in East and South East Asia.

Playground in Tōkyō

LANGUAGE REVIEW

Over the next few pages we'll be following a day in the life of William Horsley, for seven years BBC correspondent in Tōkyō, and reviewing some of the language you've learned in this book. Look in the boxes for reminders of the language you've learned, and to review it more thoroughly look back at the pages mentioned.

Greetings page 16

- Ohayō gozaimasu.
- Konnichi wa.
- Konban wa.

Saying how something is/was page 166

- Dō desu/deshita ka?
- Atsui desu/Atsukatta desu.
- Ii desu/Yokatta desu.

Giving a present page 224

- Dōzo, tsumaranai mono desu ga ...
- (Dōmo) arigatō (gozaimasu).

GREETINGS

CD ▶ 283

@ Arriving at the office in the morning after a weekend's filming in Kyūshū, William greets his colleagues. They enquire how Kyūshū was (it was good) and how the weather was (it was hot and humid). Then he presents them with some cakes from Kagoshima, the southernmost city in Kyūshū. His colleagues thank him, taste the cakes and exclaim how delicious they are.

Write down the conversation you imagine they might have. Then listen to find out how close you came to what was actually said.

Time words pages 114, 115, 202

- ashita
- asatte
- jūrokunichi (ni)
- suiyōbi (ni)
- raishū no kayōbi (ni)

Saying what you do/will do pages 111, 204

- Nani o shimasu ka?
- Tenisu o shimasu.
- Tōkyō e ikimasu.
- Nomi ni ikimasu.

THE DAYS AHEAD ...

William's first task of the day is to go over his schedule with his assistant and plan out the next few weeks. Today is Monday 14 August, and here is his partially completed schedule:

Mon 14	12 a.m.	Ishihara Shintarō interview
	7 p.m.	Go to NHK Hall (for TV panel discussion)
Tue 15		
Wed 16		
Thu 17		Go to Ōsaka
Fri 18		
Sat 19		Golf with Mr Yoshida
Sun 20		
Mon 21		Go for a drink with Mr Ida
Tue 22		

CD ▶ 284

A Take the part of William's assistant, and answer his questions about what plans (*yotei*) have been made for certain days.

E.g. (1) *CD:* **Doyōbi no yotei wa?**
You: **Yoshida-san to issho ni gorufu o shimasu.**

CD ▶ 285

@ **B** Now take William's part, and ask your assistant what you'll be doing on the unfilled days. Ask in order from top to bottom, and fill in the schedule according to the replies.

E.g. (1) *You:* **Ashita no yotei wa?**

> *Greetings*   *page 16*
>
> • Shibaraku desu ne.
> • O-genki desu ka?
> • Ē, okagesama de.
>
> *Using the telephone*   *page 52*
>
> • Moshi moshi
> • Sakai desu ga ...
> • Ueda-san onegai shimasu.
> • Yoroshiku onegai shimasu.
> • Shitsurei shimasu.
>
> *Inviting*   *page 204*
>
> • Suiyōbi ni ohiru o tabe ni ikimasen ka/
>   ikimashō ka?
> • Ii desu ne.
> • Doko de aimashō ka?
> • Eki no mae wa dō desu ka?

AN INVITATION

CD ▶ 286

William phones a journalist friend, Mr Suzuki of the *Yomiuri Shinbun*, to suggest a lunchtime meeting. He hasn't talked to Mr Suzuki for some time. Before listening, fill in what you think William's words will be in the following conversation:

Suzuki	(*answering the phone*) Yomiuri Shinbun de gozaimasu.
William	BBC no Uiriamu Hōzurii _____
	_____
Suzuki	Watashi desu ga ...
William	Ohayō gozaimasu. _____
Suzuki	Sō desu ne. O-genki desu ka?
William	_____
	_____ -san wa?
Suzuki	Genki desu.

William	(*inviting him out for lunch on Thursday*) Anō ... _____
	_____ ?
Suzuki	Ii desu ne. Doko de aimashō ka?
William	(*suggests in front of the Mitsukoshi lion in the Ginza*) _____
	_____ ?
Suzuki	Hai, kekkō desu. Nanji ni shimashō ka?
William	(*suggests 12.30*) _____
	_____ ?
Suzuki	Daijōbu desu. *Jā ... mokuyōbi no jūniji han ni Mitsukoshi no raion no mae de aimashō.
William	Hai, _____ .
Suzuki	Kochira koso yoroshiku.
William	Dewa, _____ .
Suzuki	Shitsurei shimasu.

@ Now listen to the actual conversation to check your answers. You might have produced something a bit different, but don't worry as long as you got the essential messages across.

YOUR TURN

CD ▶ 287

A You're a member of a TV company of your choice; speaking where William does in the above conversation, invite Mr Suzuki to lunch on Friday. Suggest that you meet at 1:00 p.m. in the lobby (*robii*) of the Hotel New Ōtani.

CD ▶ 288

@ **B** Now pretend that you're Mr Suzuki, and allow yourself to be invited. As you converse, note down:
a who is doing the inviting
b where and when you are to meet.
Say exactly what Mr Suzuki says in the above dialogue, except at the point marked*; here, use your notes to reply.

> *Taking a taxi*   page 62
>
> - Ueno eki made onegai shimasu.
> - Tsugi no kado de hidari e magatte kudasai.
> - Futatsume no shingō de migi e onegai shimasu.
> - Eki no saki de tomete kudasai.
> - Massugu itte kudasai.
> - Ryōshūsho onegai shimasu.
> - Koko de ii desu/kekkō desu.

TAKING A TAXI   `CD ▸ 289`

Now it's late morning, and William Horsley is on his way to interview a well known politician, Ishihara Shintarō, co-author of *The Japan that can say 'no'*. Listen to the instructions William gives the taxi driver, and trace the route on the map:

RECREATE   `CD ▸ 290`

Now recreate the journey by giving the taxi driver (on the tape) instructions at each of the points you've numbered on the map. Give the next instruction whenever you hear a tone.

> E.g. *CD:* Give the first instruction (tone).
> *You:* **Hitotsume no kado de hidari e onegai shimasu.**

FIRST MEETINGS   `CD ▸ 291`

@ Having arrived, William is introduced to Mr Ishihara by Mr Ishihara's secretary. Write down exactly what you hear. Who uses the more formal expressions, William or Mr Ishihara?

In the evening, William has been invited to appear on a Japanese TV panel discussion about how the world sees Japan. But first he has to find his way to the NHK Hall (*NHK Hōru*).

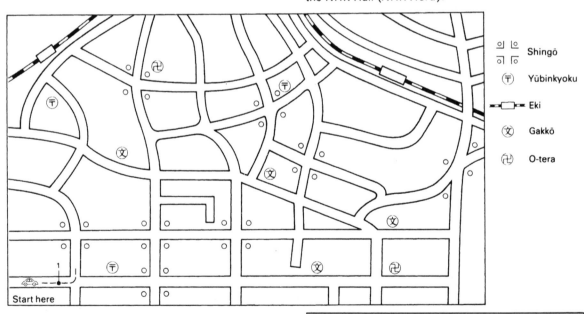

@ Listen again, and on the map write numbers according to (roughly) where the taxi is at the time each instruction is given. The first instruction (1) is *Hitotsume no kado de hidari e onegai shimasu*. This number has been written for you. Altogether there are another six numbers (2 to 7) for you to write in.

> *Finding the way*   page 62
>
> - Sumimasen ga, NHK Hōru wa doko/dochira desu ka?
> - Massugu itte, migigawa ni arimasu.
> - Yūbinkyoku no temae ni arimasu.

DIRECTIONS

CD ▶ 292

@ Mark where the NHK Hall is on the map by listening to the conversations William has on the way. (He asks for directions for the first time at the point marked 'Start'.)

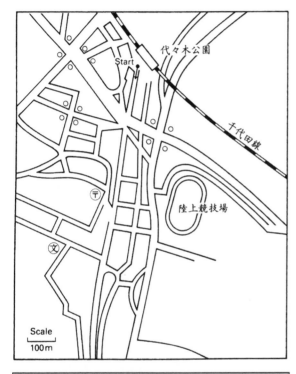

Self-introductions
First meetings   **pages 12 and 144**

- Uiriamu Hōzurii to iimasu/to mōshimasu.
- Dōzo yoroshiku.
- Yoroshiku onegai shimasu.
- Dōzo yoroshiku onegai (ita)shimasu.

Sociable questions   **pages 69 and 144**

- O-namae wa nan to iimasu ka?
- O-kuni wa dochira desu ka?
- O-shigoto wa nan desu ka?
- O-tsutome wa dochira desu ka?
- Nihon ni mō dono gurai irasshaimasu ka?
- O-ikutsu desu ka?

SELF-INTRODUCTIONS

CD ▶ 293

@ **A** Having finally arrived, William is ushered in, and the panelists are introduced on air (or rather, they introduce themselves). Listen to what they say and fill in the columns in rows 1 to 4 only. (The final row won't be letting you off so lightly!)

	Name	Organisation	Job
1			
2			
3			
4			
5			

	Nationality	Time in Japan	Age
1			
2			
3			
4			
5			

@ Listen again. Note down all the different expressions the participants use to:
a say their name
b say the name of their organisation
c say where they're from.
Check in the key and try to remember the variations you hadn't learned before.

    Practise introducing yourself aloud, using some of the expressions you've just looked up.

CD ▶ 294

@ **B** Work out the questions you would have to ask participant number 5 in order to fill in his or her details on the chart above. Ask the questions (in order from 'Name' to 'Age') and note down the answers in the chart.

About Japan

One major problem that the Japanese have always said they face is shortage of land. And a shortage of anything, as we know, means that more has to be paid for it. Land is no exception to this rule of the market. Tōkyō is not only one of the most crowded cities in the world; when it comes to land it is also among the most expensive. At the height of the 'bubble' in the late 1980s, you could place a ¥10 000 note on the ground at your feet in

Senri, near Ōsaka

certain parts of the capital and not be able to purchase the area of land covered by it. For the total price of Tōkyō's real estate, it was said, you could buy the whole of the United States. Even though land prices have eased in the 'post-bubble' era, the shortage of land remains. And yet, in remoter parts of the country beyond the highly urbanized eastern seaboard linking Tōkyō and Fukuoka, there are vast tracts of uninhabited land. Land seems to be in short supply partly because the Japanese like to centralise everything.

The high price and shortage of land has had a number of social effects. In the first place, over the years the average Japanese salary man found it harder and harder to afford a plot of land, and when he did so, it was a very small plot. This contributed to the crowded conditions of urban life. Because of the exorbitant cost of land in the cities, many aspiring homeowners searched further afield for an affordable and more spacious place to live. This meant they had to make longer and longer commuter trips to and from work. Not surprisingly, perhaps, the Japanese did not, and still do not, see themselves as being 'well off' when they compare their living conditions with those of Europeans and Americans.

So the social cost of rapid economic development was not simply environmental. Most Japanese people felt that they led lives that were in no way commensurate with those of their counterparts in other parts of the industrialised world. Yet they were prepared to work hard, to stick things out (*gaman suru*), and put aside personal self-interest on behalf of their country's economic development. Such self-sacrifice more or less worked so long as Japan's economy itself continued to grow, providing them with a long series of consumer aspirations – from the 'three treasures' (*sanshu no jingi*) of refrigerator, TV set and washing machine in the 1950s, to quality brand goods in the 1980s, by way of the 'three Cs' of car, cooler (air conditioner) and colour television in the 1960s and 70s.

Once the economy stopped growing, however, and once the slow-growth period revealed serious problems in the organization and management of Japan's industrial structure, which had failed to meet the demands of a 'post-industrial' society, people began to put self-interest first. Few young people today join a company with the intention of staying there until death or retirement forces them apart. A new generation of teenagers hasn't experienced the kind of arrogance bred by economic success that was apparent in Japan during the 1980s. Young people today seem to hardly care about 'traditional' Japanese culture. With dyed hair, flamboyant clothes, deeply tanned skin, and trendy mobile phones on which they endlessly communicate with friends and acquaintances, they know instinctively that all work and no play make Tarō a dull boy. In short, young Japanese today are busy creating their own new living culture.

LANGUAGE REVIEW

TŌHOKU ADVENTURE (1)

One of the themes running through this book has been that of variety, that there is not one Japan but many. Nowhere is this more important to remember than when it comes to quality of life. Many foreign visitors hardly get beyond the outer reaches of Tōkyō, and Japan to them may seem like one huge city. So we're going to take you off . . . to an area of Japan that still has large open spaces and a relaxed pace of life: Tōhoku, the northern part of the main Japanese island, Honshū. As you would if you really were going, you're going to be planning, booking and then, we hope, enjoying a few days away from the bustle of city life.

Below are descriptions from a brochure of seven of the most famous and, in some cases, most beautiful tourist attractions in northeastern Tōhoku. The names of the places described are boxed on the map on the

@ opposite page; by reading the descriptions and consulting the map, write in the names of the places on the lines below:

1 _____
One of the most beautiful and thoroughly 'Japanese' places in Japan. Boatmen will transport you up a deep, fast-flowing river between stupendous cliffs, serenading you with traditional Japanese songs.

2 _____
Arrive here early from a night at Tamagawa Onsen, then spend the day walking through the breathtaking natural beauty of the woods and reed flats around this lake. Move on again in the afternoon.

3 _____
An hour and forty minutes east of Matsushima, this is how things must have seemed hundreds of years ago. The only accommodation is on the shrine precincts. At night the island is hushed in a haunting, melancholy silence.

4 _____
Visit this traditional hot spring (*onsen*). Book into an old wooden inn and then relax in its hot outdoor pool of minerally rich water. In winter, expect to share your bath with monkeys which come out of the woods to bathe.

5 _____
One of the traditional 'big three' tourist venues in Japan: Japanese will say you have not seen Tōhoku if you haven't been here. Come to this coastal town 35 minutes east of Sendai, if only to relish the souvenir shops and swan-shaped cruisers.

6 _____
Twenty minutes by bus west of Ichinoseki, this city is the home of the Chūson Temple. Set amongst immense cedar trees, the temple houses a priceless Japanese treasure, the *Konjikidō*, or Golden Hall.

7 _____
After a day spent travelling north along the awe-inspiring Rikuchū coastline, arrive at this bustling fishing town east of Morioka for a sunset boat trip around the rocky coastal inlets.

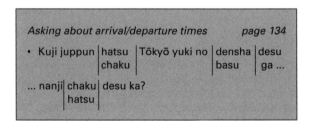

Asking about arrival/departure times   page 134

• Kuji juppun | hatsu chaku | Tōkyō yuki no | densha basu | desu ga . . .

. . . nanji | chaku hatsu | desu ka?

TIMES   CD ▶ 295

@ On the map you'll notice ten empty boxes (numbered 1 to 10). To fill them in (with bus or train times), ask the tape.

E.g. (1) *You:* **Kuji gojūgofun hatsu Matsushima yuki no densha desu ga . . . nanji chaku desu ka?**

Listen to the replies and write down the times in the boxes.

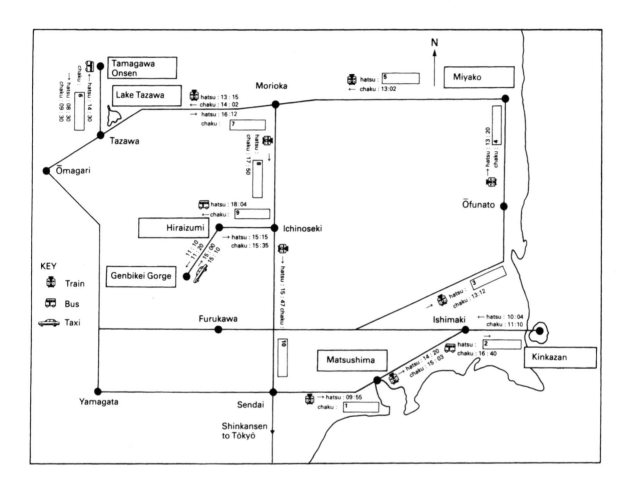

ITINERARY

@ Imagine you're visiting Tōhoku and have time to spend four nights away from Sendai. Using only the trains and buses whose departure and arrival times are indicated on the map, plan an itinerary whereby you visit all the places described on the opposite page. What four places will you spend the night in? Circle them on the map, and write them into the itinerary on the right:

Sendai →

Night 1
_____
(17 Aug.)

→

Night 2
_____
(18 Aug.)

→

Night 3
_____
(19 Aug.)

→

Night 4
_____
(20 Aug.)

→ Sendai

How will you go? *page 116*

- Gakkō kara eki made nan de ikimasu ka?
- Jitensha de ikimasu.

How long will it take? *page 116*

- Takasaki kara Tōkyō made dono gurai kakarimasu ka?
- Ichijikan nijuppun kakarimasu.

GETTING THERE

CD ▸ 296

The CD will ask you ten questions about your itinerary. Answer by looking at the map on p. 261.

E.g. (1) *CD:* **Sendai kara Matsushima made nan de ikimasu ka?**
You: **Densha de ikimasu.**

Below Mountain scene in Tōhoku

WHERE TO STAY

@ Read these excerpts from a brochure describing accommodation in the four places you're planning to stay at during your trip around Tōhoku. By comparing the excerpts with the descriptions and map on pp. 260 and 261, write the names of the places on the lines below:

1 _____

This small wooden *minshuku* set halfway up the valley offers its own outdoor hot spring pool (*rotenburo*).

8 和
TV

2 _____

One of the few shrines in Japan incorporating a Youth Hostel. Very secluded. Guests welcome to Shintō rituals.

15 和 レストラン

3 _____

This modern hotel, 20 minutes by bus from the *shinkansen* line to Tōkyō, offers the very highest standards to tourists.

250 洋 A/C バー
レストラン TV

4 _____

Fresh fish and stupendous views make this *ryokan* the ideal place for a weekend to restore your spirits.

19 和 ☏ TV

Reserving a hotel room   *page 142*

- Yoyaku onegai shitai n' desu ga ...
- Sangatsu mikka ni heya wa arimasu ka?/aite imasu ka?
- Dewa, onegai shimasu.

Number of nights   *page 142*

- ippaku/nihaku/sanpaku ...
- Ippaku ikura desu ka?

BOOKING

Fill in this form for yourself, to book a room in Hiraizumi. (Consult your itinerary for the date, and don't fill in the price yet.)

Name _____
Telephone _____
Date of arrival _____
No. of nights _____
Type of room you want

_____
Price per night _____

CD ▶ 297

@ Now ring the hotel to book the room, following the instructions given on the tape. Fill in the price of the room.

Iwakisan Shrine, Hirosaki, Tōhoku

One thing you'll probably want to do during your trip is buy some souvenirs. If you're planning to visit Japanese friends in another part of the country later on, you may like to take them some of the food specialities of the place you visit. For example, perhaps you'll be tempted by the ubiquitous (o-)*manjū* (a doughy dumpling filled with sweet bean paste).

Prices   *page 85*

• Ikura desu ka?
• Gohyaku-en desu.

Position   *pages 56 and 137*

• ko../so../a..
• *W no mae ni arimasu. X no tonari ...*

WHAT'S ON OFFER?   CD ▸ 298

@ Listen to a shopkeeper describing his wares and how much they cost. Look at the picture below and identify the *manjū* boxes (*hako*) he describes. Write the prices of the boxes on the appropriate labels.

| **Y no ue** | above Y |
| **Z no shita** | below Z |

Shopping   *pages 91 and 220*

• O-manjū wa nani ga arimasu ka?
• Sumimasen, ano manjū (o) misete kudasai.
• Kore (o) kudasai.
• Chotto chiisai desu ne...
• Motto ōkii no wa arimasen ka?

SHOPPING

A customer goes into the shop to buy some souvenirs. At first she isn't satisfied with the *manjū* the shopkeeper offers, so twice she asks for something different.

CD ▸ 299

@ **A** Listening to the conversation, identify in the picture on the left the different boxes the customer is shown (by writing 1, 2, 3 and 4 on the picture) and circle the kind of box she finally decides to buy.

CD ▸ 300

B The conversation is recorded again, this time without the customer's words. You play the customer, using the plan below to help you.

| You enter and ask for *manjū* | → | Shopkeeper offers 1st kind | → | You ask for a bigger box |

| Shopkeeper offers 3rd and 4th kinds | ← | You ask for a cheaper box | ← | Shopkeeper offers 2nd kind |

| You ask how much they are | → | Shopkeeper replies | → | You decide; pay and leave |

About Japan

To ask what Japan's future holds is the kind of question Westerners like to put to themselves – if only to convince themselves that this strange nation of upstart capitalists from East Asia will not be able to continue in the way that it has done hitherto. It is unlikely, however, that they will get any clear answer to their question. The Japanese have in the past consistently upset all predictions about their future, and there would seem to be little point in offering conclusions of any sort here. A few ideas, however, are perhaps in order about where Japan seems to be headed, both at home and abroad.

First, let us return to the problem of land. Hemmed in by sea and mountains, by commuter lines, by highways that pass overhead, by an expanding urban and suburban megalopolis that now extends almost the entire length of the eastern seaboard from Tōkyō to Fukuoka, Japanese have nowhere to turn. No wonder, then, that some of them have quite happily taken up former Prime Minister Nakasone's suggestion that they retire abroad – to places like the Australian Gold Coast, where the sun shines brightly, the air is unpolluted, the cost of living is comparatively cheap … and where the Japanese government will no longer have to worry so much about how to care for them.

And this brings us to a second problem. The Japanese population is getting older and older. The average lifespan of both men and women is the highest in the world, into the eighties. Within a few years, there will be fewer people employed than unemployed in Japan, and that of course means that the tax burden on the salary men of the future is going to be considerable.

Just how an increasingly elderly population is going to affect social organisation is hard to say. If the former reliance upon essentially 'traditional' and 'Japanese' morals is fading away rapidly, will children continue to shoulder the responsibilty of looking after their elderly parents, as they have done for the most part until now? Or will they insist that the state intervenes to care for the old? And what effect will that have on Japanese family structure?

All the evidence suggests that in many respects Japan is following in the footsteps of advanced industrial societies in the West. Nowadays, fewer and fewer people are prepared to stick with a single company for the whole of their working lives, and young employees are prepared to change jobs the moment they notice that something better is on offer elsewhere. Higher pay, shorter hours, longer vacations – these are the criteria by which they now decide how to lead their lives. In short, their attitudes are becoming increasingly 'Western'.

Westernisation is also affecting the traditional organisation of Japanese business. The opening up of Japan's domestic market to foreign competition has led to a radical rethinking of business methods as corporations struggle to survive in this new 'global' world of business. Westerners, and many Japanese themselves, call for the typically 'wet' (emotional) personal business relationships practised by older Japanese to yield to the 'dry' (rational) methods of business practised, they say, in most of Europe and the United States. The potential cronyism inherent in Japanese corporate relations may need to be stamped out. Japan's 'welfare capitalism', whereby the employee is looked after by the company and corporations by the state, may have to give way to the functional fairness of the 'free market' economy. If these calls for radical change are heeded, it will mean rethinking the basic premises upon which Japanese society and culture have been founded.

LANGUAGE REVIEW

TŌHOKU ADVENTURE (2)

WHEN I WAS THERE ...

	CD ▸ 301

@ Admittedly, it was a while back, but William Horsley also once spent a memorable week travelling around the area you've been visiting. Listen as he flicks through the diary he kept at the time and talks with a Japanese friend. Mark the course of his journey with arrows on the map below. Circle the places he stayed, and write in the dates he arrived there, and the number of nights he spent in each place. One new verb you'll hear is *tomaru* (spend the night). E.g. 'I spent the night in Hiraizumi': *Hiraizumi ni tomarimashita*.

Saying the date   pages 114–15

• (*year*) -nen   (*month*) -gatsu   (*day*) -nichi
E.g. sen kyūhyaku nanajūninen shigatsu nijūgonichi

DATES

	CD ▸ 302

The CD will ask you when William visited some of the places.

     E.g. (1)   *CD:*   **Itsu Sendai e ikimashita ka?**
             You: **Hachigatsu yokka ni ikimashita.**

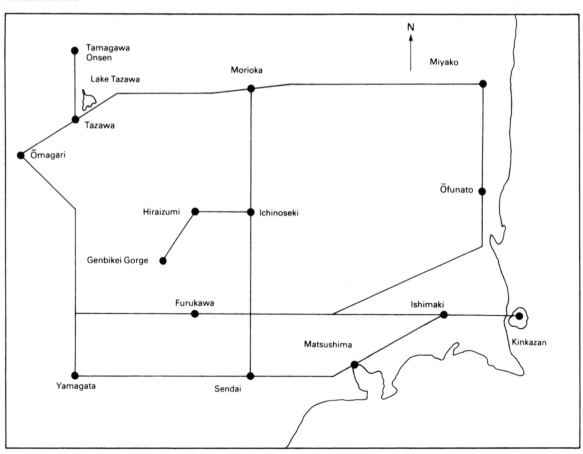

ASKING FOR INFORMATION

@ Below are a few of the answers William gave his friend (in some cases more fully expressed than was the case in the actual conversation). From your notes on the map on the opposite page, and from memory (or by replaying the CD) try to write in the questions William's friend asked, on the lines.

1 _____ ?
Hachigatsu yokka ni ikimashita.

2 _____ ?
Asa no rokuji deshita.

3 _____ ?
Tsuma to issho ni ikimashita.

4 _____ ?
Nijikan kakarimashita.

5 _____ ?
Hiraizumi ni tomarimashita.

6 _____ ?
Takushii de ikimashita.

REMINISCE | CD ▸ 303

The CD will ask *you* the same questions, about your trip to Tōhoku. To answer, you'll need to look back at the map and your itinerary on p. 261. Use your imagination to reply to the third question.

MEMORIES: THEN AND NOW | CD ▸ 304

You'll hear an interview with one elderly resident of Tōhoku. We asked him to tell us what Tōhoku was like sixty years ago as compared with now.

A Before listening, try to predict what words in the chart on the right above he used to describe 'then', and what words he used to describe 'now'. In pencil, write ticks in the columns marked 'Then' and 'Now' in the chart according to what you think.

shinpuru (na)	simple
shiawase (na)	happy
kitanai	dirty

	THEN	NOW
ii _____		
warui _____		
yasui _____		
takai _____		
shinpuru _____		
muzukashii _____		
tanoshii _____		
tsumaranai _____		
shiawase _____		
kanashii _____		
kitanai _____		
kirei _____		

@ **B** Now listen, and check whether you were right about the ticks you made.

Past of adjectives   *page 166*

- Dō deshita ka?
- *'-i' adjectives:* oishii desu → oishikatta (desu)
- *'na' adjectives:* kirei desu → kirei deshita
- *exclaiming:* Tanoshikatta (desu) ne!

SPOTCHECK 1

@ **A** Write out the past forms of all the adjectives in the chart above, on the lines.

B How would you exclaim that something was **a** hot **b** new **c** beautiful **d** lively **e** delicious?

YOUR TURN | CD ▸ 305

The CD will ask you what you thought of the places you stayed at during your trip to Tōhoku. Answer (using your imagination) with an exclamation which matches the character of each place you stayed at. (Look at the tourist guide again on p. 260.) The CD will also ask you about the food ... it's almost certain to have been delicious!

269

About Japan

In this book, we have tried to explain some of the important principles – in particular, family, company and education – that have sustained Japan's post-war economic growth and rise to superpower status. At the same time, we have shown that the country is in the process of undergoing significant changes and that a new generation of Japanese is emerging with little or no experience of the 'good old days' of economic prosperity and the energetic spirit of their parents and grandparents whose hard work, tenacity and long suffering created that prosperity.

These days, indeed, that energy and desire for economic growth have shifted to the Asian continent and it is in cities like Shanghai and Hong Kong that Japan's former entrepreneurial energy is now most obvious. This does not mean that Japanese no longer know how to do business. They merely do it in a different way. Whereas in the 1960s and 70s, they focused their energies on manufacturing and mass production, now their role is more in financial investment and the development of high-end technology. Production is carried out in large part in other countries around East and South East Asia.

Why the change? Much can be attributed to the so-called Plaza Accord of 1986, when leaders of the world's largest economies gathered in New York and agreed that the US dollar's exchange rate should not be fixed but allowed to float on the financial markets. The immediate result of this policy initiated by the US Government, which had been seeking somehow to curb Japanese exports throughout the 1980s, was a sharp rise in the value of the yen, by as much as 40 per cent. This itself had an immediate negative effect on Japan's export trade.

The American plan worked, but only in the short term. After initial panic, Japan's corporate managers began to work out a way to overcome the disadvantage of the high-valued yen. Their solution was to shift their manufacturing facilities abroad to the Asian continent. In Thailand, Indonesia and mainland China, for example, Japanese companies could make use of a cheap workforce whose energy and desire to get ahead were exactly the qualities that were fading in Japan itself. By stamping their colour television sets, video recorders and so on with 'Made in Thailand' or 'Made in China' labels, moreover, Japanese industry was able to evade the American demands for a curb on Japanese exports. In the longer term, therefore, Japan's balance of payments continued to flourish.

There have been two important side-effects of the Plaza Accord. The first has to do with Japanese industrial structure. As we noted earlier in this book, large Japanese corporations prefer not to concentrate their production activities in a single firm, but to

subcontract them to dozens – sometimes hundreds – of smaller firms with which they have entered into long-term technology, product development, finance and personnel partnerships. These corporations have now established similar patterns of relationships in those Asian countries to which they have shifted their manufacturing processes. In other words, a 'Japanese style' of industrial organisation, which worked so well during Japan's own economic development, has been transplanted to Asian countries that are themselves in the process of rapid economic development.

The second side-effect is more broad-sweeping. By shifting its previously 'inner directed' economic attention abroad, and by both directly and indirectly contributing to the economic development of East and South East Asian countries, Japan itself has in part formed the kind of 'parent-child' (*oya-ko*) relationship with those countries that Japanese parent companies form with their subcontractors. This may work well enough while those Asian countries need Japanese financial investment and expertise, but in the longer term it is politically problematic. How it will be resolved remains to be seen. It is clear, though, that Japan's role in Asia ultimately has an important bearing on the future of the world.

WRITTEN JAPANESE

As you approach the end of this first stage in your studies of *nihongo*, it's about time, perhaps, that you learned to read and write the kanji both for this and the English language – *eigo*:

日 本 語
ni hon go

英 語
ei go

英

語

		say
		言

As you can see, the kanji for 'say' – a representation of words flowing from a mouth – appears as a radical on the left in the character for 'language': 語. There's also another mouth on the right (after all, it takes two to talk!), together with the kanji for 'five', included simply for its pronunciation value (this reminds us that the 'on' reading of the character is *go*). What at first sight might have seemed quite a daunting kanji isn't so after all – nor, perhaps, is it very difficult to write, since you've already learned the stroke orders of the individual elements 口 and 五.

In general, the more kanji you know, the easier it becomes to understand and remember new characters and combinations, since you'll often find you already know some of the elements – just as you do in the case of 語. Employ your detective powers to the full in the following exercises, designed to show how much further you can go, even with the relatively few kanji you've come across in this book. (Consult the kanji list on p. 302 when necessary.)

1 As in the case of 語, many kanji are built up from other elements. Understanding these elements, especially so-called 'radicals' (like 言) which occur in a lot of words, will make many unfamiliar characters more accessible. Here are three more of the radicals you've come across before, together with the characters you've seen them in. Hazard a guess at what the new kanji on the right *might* mean before looking at the explanations below:

a イ (person)   休   信 , 体
b 日 (sun)   曜時   明
c 宀 (roof)   安   字 , 家

a 信 means 'trust', and literally represents a man 'standing by his word', while 体 means 'body' (*karada*), the 'basis' of a person; b 明 means 'bright' (the sun and moon together making things very bright!); c 字 means 'character' (as in 'Chinese character') and may be seen to represent a child diligently studying his kanji at home, while 家 means 'house' or 'home' (*ie/uchi*) – ancient Chinese homes having been shared with the pigs at night.

2 Knowing the meanings and readings of individual kanji also unlocks the door to whole words you've never come across before. Here are some new combinations using the kanji you can see in 英語 on the left above. Try reading them aloud and guessing their meanings before reading the explanations below (remember, 'on' readings usually apply in the case of 'compound' words):

a 米語 b 英国 c 国語 d 外国語

a This word – *beigo* – means 'American English';
b This word – *eikoku* – is sometimes used instead of イギリス (*igirisu*) to refer to Britain;
c It may be reassuring for you to know that Japanese schoolchildren (and many adults) have problems writing kanji too; lessons concerning their mother tongue are known as *kokugo*, 'national language';
d The foreign language (*gaikokugo*) the vast majority of schoolchildren study is 英語 – most of them for six years, from the time they enter 中学校. However, they don't necessarily end up speaking fluent English, so your hard efforts to learn 日本語 certainly won't go unappreciated.

@ **3** Here are some Japanese family names you haven't come across in the book before. However, the kanji have all appeared previously; remembering that surnames are usually read in a 'kun' way, try saying the names aloud and guessing their 'meanings':

a 山口　**b** 内田　**c** 高木　**d** 西山　**e** 小林

Now check your answers in the key. You're also in a position – almost – to read the names of the two families featured in the *Japanese – Language and People* television programmes.

神　　川　　酒　井
Kami　**kawa**　**Saka**　**i**

Kamikawa, the name of the family living in 九州, literally means 'river of god'; the Sakais, who live in 東京, have an equally auspicious name: 井 means 'well', so the name as a whole means 'sake well'.

@ **4** Finally, you don't have to understand everything to 'get by' with kanji. You'll find yourself able to recognise words just by being familiar with one of the kanji and remembering the rest as a kind of 'block'. Imagine, for example, that you want to go to the stations in Tōkyō written on the right above in rōmaji. Find them on the map simply by picking out the characters you know (pronounced in the ways underlined) and ignoring the other kanji. Write numbers next to the rōmaji names, then check your answers.

a <u>Tōkyō</u>　———————
b <u>Gotanda</u>　———————
c <u>Nishi</u>-<u>Nippori</u>　———————
d <u>Yotsuya</u>　———————
e <u>Takadanobaba</u>　———————
f <u>Yoyogi</u>　———————
g <u>Ō</u>saki　———————
h <u>Ochanomizu</u>　———————
i <u>Suidōbashi</u>　———————
j Shina<u>gawa</u>　———————

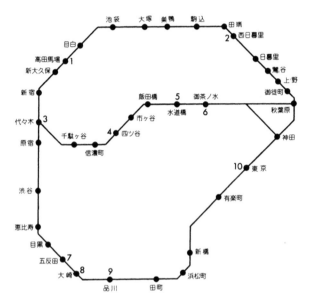

Incidentally, this map shows the same stations as those on the rōmaji map on page 72. You may like to compare the maps to find out how to read some more Tōkyō place names.

273

SAYING WHAT YOU WANT

One of the major concerns older Japanese feel about the future regards the 'moral fibre' of the younger generation, much less willing than they were – the complaint goes – to try hard (*ganbaru*), to be patient (*gaman suru*) or to sacrifice individual desires to the good of the group. However, are their attitudes really as untraditional as all that? Yuka asked some young people about their hopes and desires for the future...

- To say what you want to do: . . . **-tai desu.**
  (Drop the *-masu* ending from any verb, and replace with *-tai desu.*)
  E.g. 'I want to go abroad': *Gaikoku e ikitai desu.*
  'I want to get married': *Kekkon shitai desu.*

- To say what you *don't* want to do: . . . **-taku arimasen.**
  (Change *-tai desu* to *-taku arimasen.*)
  E.g. 'I don't want to go abroad': *Gaikoku e ikitaku arimasen.*
  'I don't want to become a company employee': *Kaishain ni naritaku arimasen.*

- To say 'I want (to have) something': . . . **ga hoshii desu.**
  E.g. 'I want a car': *Kuruma ga hoshii desu.*

HOPES AND DESIRES CD ▸ 306

@ Listen to Yuka's interviews with five young people (1 to 5), and fill in the grid:

	Name	Age	Occupation	Main desires
1				
2				
3				
4				
5				

ANATA WA? CD ▸ 307

How about you? Now you're coming to the end of the book, it's time to start thinking of life without *Japanese – Language and People*. Have any of your ideas changed about Japan? Do you want to go to Japan? Where do you want to go? What do you want to do there? Try to write answers to the following questions, then answer them as the CD puts them to you:

1 Nihon e ikitai desu ka?
2 Itsu ikitai desu ka?
3 Nihon no doko e ikitai desu ka?
4 Tōhoku e ikitai desu ka?
5 Nihon de nani o shitai desu ka?
6 Sadō o shitai desu ka?
7 Nani o tabetai desu ka?
8 Sashimi o tabetai desu ka?
9 Nani o kaitai desu ka?
10 Kimono o kaitai desu ka? (Takai desu yo!)
11 Nihongo o motto benkyō shitai desu ka?
12 Dōyatte (*in what way*) benkyō shitai desu ka?

If your answer to question 11 was 'yes', the next page may give you some ideas for an answer to 12!

HOW TO CONTINUE

Otsukaresama deshita! Now you've come to the end of this book, you may be wondering where to go from here. In approximate order of importance, we suggest you do the following:

1 GO TO JAPAN

Learning a language without using it to meet people, buy things or go places is like saving up for an expensive sports car and then keeping it in the garage. Why not take your Japanese for a spin on the open road? You know enough now to be able to travel freely, to chat to those you meet on your travels, and thereby to deepen further your understanding of Japan and the Japanese.

2 KEEP TALKING

If you're far away from a country, it's difficult to find opportunities to maintain contact with it. Finding chances to *speak* Japanese may be your biggest problem, but it's a problem you have to solve if you're not to lose everything you've learned. Most importantly, find other like-minded learners. Isolation is the greatest enemy of progress:

a Find out from the Japan Foundation about evening classes in Japanese.
b Failing this, you may have a Japanese company near you. You could try getting in touch with the company and finding out whether any of the dependents of Japanese employees would be interested in meeting you (and any like-minded friends) over a cup of coffee.

3 GET EVEN BETTER AT JAPANESE

Learn to read and write Japanese. You've had a bit of practice in this course – enough, we hope, for reading and writing not to seem too daunting. Proceed like this:

a Systematically learn hiragana. If you're in or near a place with a large Japanese expatriate community, there's sure to be at least one bookshop which stocks Japanese children's books. These are written almost exclusively in hiragana. (Japanese children have problems with kanji too!) Read as much as you can.
b Buy a dictionary which lists words in hiragana (*not* rōmaji). Just using it will improve your hiragana.
c Begin a penfriend relationship with someone living in Japan. When you write, each time write two letters: one in Japanese and one in English. Ask your friend to reply in a similar way. In the beginning, ask your penfriend to write completely in hiragana; then, as your kanji improve, he or she can gradually add these in.
d Set yourself kanji learning targets, e.g. two or three new kanji a day. There are some good kanji reference books on the market (see the recommended reading list on the next page).
e Remember this simple revision rule: To truly learn something you should revise it (i) an hour later, (ii) a day later, (iii) a week later, (iv) a month later, (v) a year later. Build revision into your learning.

RECOMMENDED READING

ABOUT JAPAN

Alan Booth, *The Roads to Sata*, Penguin, 1987

Rodney Clark, *The Japanese Company*,
Yale University Press, 1979

Ronald Dore, *Stock Market Capitalism: Welfare Capitalism*,
Oxford University Press, 2000

Michael Gerlach, *Alliance Capitalism*, University
of California Press, 1992

Joy Hendry, *Understanding Japanese Society*,
Routledge, 2003

William Horsley and Roger Buckley, *Nippon,
New Superpower*, BBC Books, 1990

Koichi Iwabuchi, *Recentering Globalization*,
Duke University Press, 2002

Brian Moeran, *A Far Valley*, Kodansha International, 1998

Haruki Murakami, *Underground: The Tokyo Gas Attack and
the Japanese Psyche*, Vintage, 2003

Chie Nakane, *Japanese Society*, Penguin, 1973

Oliver Statler, *A Japanese Pilgrimage*, Pan, 1984

Karel van Wolferen, *The Enigma of Japanese Power*,
Macmillan, 1989

FOR FURTHER LANGUAGE STUDY

Spoken Japanese

Helen Ballhatchet and Stefan Kaiser, *Teach Yourself
Japanese*, Hodder & Stoughton, 1989

Osamu Mizutani and Nobuko Mizutani, *Nihongo Notes*
(1–4), The Japan Times Ltd, 1977–81

Grammar

Everett Bleiler, *Basic Japanese Grammar*, Charles E. Tuttle,
1963

John Breen, *Japanese in Three Months*, Hugo's Language
Books, 1997

Hiragana and Katakana

P.G. O'Neill, *Japanese Kana Workbook*, Weatherhill,
1995

Kanji

Wolfgang Hadamitzky and Mark Spahn, *Kanji and Kana*,
Charles E. Tuttle, 1981

Kenneth Henshall, *A Guide to Remembering Japanese
Characters*, Charles E. Tuttle, 1988

Tae Moriyama, *The Practical Guide to Japanese Signs*,
Kodansha International Ltd, 1987

ANSWER KEY

UNIT 1

p. 4 *Spotcheck 1*:
Robert **Hope**, Elizabeth **Green**
p. 5 *Spotcheck 2*:
The fact that they're both reporters
p. 6 *Soundcheck (long vowels)*:
1 sofa **2** Christmas card **3** beef stew **4** taxi
5 computer **6** (swimming) pool **7** cake **8** curry and rice **9** coffee **10** chocolate
p. 7 *Soundcheck (disappearing vowels)*:
1 Adam Smith **2** Karl Marx **3** Winston Churchill
4 Ronald Reagan **5** Paul Newman **6** Meryl Streep
7 Carl Lewis **8** Ringo Starr **9** Yves St Laurent
10 Barbra Streisand
p. 10 *Spotcheck 3*:
He's British, from London.
p. 11 *Answer*:
1 Steffi Graf **2** Sanjit Gandhi **3** Elizabeth Taylor
4 Pele **5** Alain Delon **6** Greg Norman **7** Ben Johnson **8** Tina Turner
p. 13 *Introduce yourself*:
Hajimemashite . . .
1 Kāru Gurafu desu. Doitsujin desu. Kōmuin desu.
2 Bābara Guriin desu. Airurandojin desu. Enjinia desu.
3 Meriru Jonson desu. Kanadajin desu. Moderu desu.
4 Ibu Doron desu. Furansujin desu. Kaishain desu.
5 Erizabesu Nōman desu. Ōsutorariajin desu. Gakusei desu.
. . . Dōzo yoroshiku/Yoroshiku onegai shimasu.
p. 13 *Guess who*:
A Greg Norman (Australian golfer) **B** Robert Hope
p. 16 *Spotcheck 4*:
Ms Yamada
p. 17 *Listen*:
A4, B1, C5, D3, E7, F2, G8, H6
p. 20 *Where's home?*:
A Don Cooper **B** Michael Williams **C** Sophie Colbert
D Anna Manzoni **E** Pedro Garcia **F** John Lee **G** Larry Bridges **H** salesman **I** computer company employee
J restaurant employee **K** 'OL' ('office lady') **L** civil servant **M** company employee **N** bank employee

p. 21 *Unaccustomed as I am . . .*:
Your completed chart should look like this:

	Name	Nationality	Job
1	Ronald Green	New Zealand	Bank employee
2	Franz Bauer	Germany	Student
3	Li Fen	China	Housewife
4	Paul Robert	France	Engineer
5	John Baker	Canada	Company employee

The final speech goes as follows: *Hajimemashite. Jon Bēkā desu. Kanadajin desu. Kaishain desu. Dōzo yoroshiku.*
p. 21 *A lovely day for it . . .*:
A4, B2, C5, D3, E1
p. 23 *Written Japanese*:
In rōmaji, the questions are as follows:
1 Nihonjin desu ka? **2** Amerikajin desu ka? **3** Tōkyō kara desu ka? **4** Kyōto kara desu ka?

UNIT 2

p. 28 *Spotcheck 1*:
a She likes it (it's a good smell). **b** She thinks it's rather small. **c** She likes it a lot.
p. 29 *What is it?*:
1 Kore . . . **2** Kore . . . **3** Are . . . **4** Sore . . .
5 Sore . . . **6** Are . . . **7** Kore . . . **8** Are . . . wa nan desu ka?
p. 29 *Test yourself*:
Next to the words in 'Build-up' you should have written the following numbers:
3 suteki **5** kirei
1 subarashii **4** kawaii
8 sugoi **2** oishii
6 benri **7** omoshiroi
p. 30 *Spotcheck 2*:
Mrs Kamikawa's house is big.
p. 30 *Spotcheck 3*:
a Watashi no yunomi wa dore desu ka? Kore desu.

b Honda-san no ie/uchi wa dono ie/uchi desu ka? Sono ie/uchi desu.

c Watashi no hashi wa doko desu ka? Asoko desu.

p. 31 *Listen*:

You should have written a 'T' next to the rice bowl and plate near to Mrs Ueno, the glass and hand towel near to Mrs Tanaka, and the chopsticks and tea cup away from both of them.

p. 31 *Possessions*:

1S, 2T, 3S, 4T, 5S, 6T

p. 34 *Spotcheck 4*:

Yuka says Mrs Kamikawa's son's textbook is difficult.

p. 35 *Family matters*:

The following things are not true:

2 Her father's not a teacher, he's an engineer.

5 Her son isn't a senior high school student, he's a bank employee.

7 Her younger sister isn't an 'office lady', she's a fashion designer.

p. 36 *Where are they all?*:

Mr Tanaka's family members are in these places: **2** wife – sūpā, **3** father – byōin, **4** older sister – ginkō, **5** younger brother – kaisha, **6** son – gakkō

p. 37 *Spotcheck 5*:

He has fish, miso soup and two bowls of rice.

p. 40 *Spotcheck 6*:

Robbie offers Mrs Kaneko coffee and biscuits.

p. 40 *Soundcheck*:

1b, 2a, 3b, 4a, 5b, 6a

p. 41 *Stimulus–response*:

1c, 2a, 3d, 4f, 5b, 6e

p. 44 *Family excursions*:

A4, B3, C1, D5, E2

p. 44 *This and that*:

First picture: Robbie and Mrs Kaneko are standing between the curtains (*kāten*) and the boat (*bōto*), a little distance away from the stereo (*sutereo*).

Second picture: Robbie and Mrs Kaneko are both sitting at the 'kotatsu'. They talk about the bench (*benchi*) in the kitchen (*kitchin*).

Third picture: Robbie and Mrs Kaneko are standing in the foreground in front of the table.

p. 45 *Happy families*:

A2, B3, C1

p. 47 *Written Japanese*:

In rōmaji, the sentences read as follows: **1** Ano otoko no hito wa nihonjin desu. **2** Ano hito wa gaijin desu. **3** Ano onna no ko no o-kā-san wa amerikajin desu. **4** Haha wa Tōkyō kara desu. **5** O-tō-san no o-kā-san wa amerikajin desu ka?

The translations are as follows: **1** That man is Japanese. **2** That person is a foreigner. **3** That girl's mother is American. **4** My mother is from Tōkyō. **5** Is your father's mother American?

UNIT 3

p. 52 *Spotcheck 1*:

Mr Yamada works in sales.

p. 52 *Listen*:

1 Ms Nakamura of Hitachi calls Mr Yamada in general affairs. **2** Mr Sakurai of Nikon calls Ms Yamada in accounts. **3** Ms Ogino of Kirin beer (*biiru*) calls Mr Yamada in public relations. **4** Mr Takahashi of NHK calls Mr Yamada in marketing. **5** Ms Nakajima of Honda calls Mr Yamada in the international division.

p. 53 *Spotcheck 2*:

The number is 1240–9781.

p. 53 *Numbers*:

1 1258–4470 **2** 2573–6939 **3** 3319–8902 **4** 4983–2684 **5** 5302–9827 **6** 6205–2940 **7** 7274–1983 **8** 8208–3841 **9** 9398–2945 **10** 1294–3957

p. 55 *Spotcheck 3*:

a station **b** police box **c** hospital **d** temple

p. 55 *Japanese live 3*:

You should have written '*JR no Yamaguchi*'.

p. 55 *Spotcheck 4*:

Yamamoto: Takadanobaba 2–5; Satō: Takadanobaba 1–33; Suzuki: Toyama-chō 3–8; Kuwata: Ōkubo 2–30

p. 55 *Addresses*:

A Satō (NHK) **B** Tanaka (Hitachi) **C** Fukuda (Honda) **D** Yamada (Toyota) **E** Nishida (Daihatsu)

p. 56 *Describing where*:

A2, B5, C1, D4, E3, F6

p. 60 *Japanese live 4*:

You should have filled in the gaps as follows: A: **Tōykō Gasu** no **Sakai** desu ga **kokusaibu** no **Uchida**-san wa irasshaimasu ka? . . . B: Moshi moshi, **Uchida** desu ga **Sakai**-san desu ka? . . . B: Chotto matte kudasai. **Shinjuku-ku, Toyama-chō 1–3** desu. **Byōin** no **chikaku** ni arimasu. . . . B: **1345–9872** desu.

p. 60 *Put it all together*:

1 Minato-ku, Shinbashi 1–9 . . . 2357–9804

2 Nakano-ku, Honchō 3–6 . . . 3256–4534

3 Shinjuku-ku, Kagurazaka 1–2 . . . 4235–8011

You may also have heard that the restaurant was **1** next to a shrine, **2** opposite a school, **3** near a post office.

p. 60 *Take note*:

The *aizuchi* you heard (in order) were: '*Ē, sō desu*', '*Ē*', '*Hai*', '*Hai*', '*Ā, sō desu ka*', '*Hai*', '*Ē*', '*Hai*', '*Ā, sō desu ka*', '*Sō desu ne*'.

p. 63 *Spotcheck 5*:
a Massugu itte kudasai.   **b** Migi e magatte kudasai.
c Tsugi no shingō de hidari e magatte kudasai.
d Hitotsume no kado no saki de tomete kudasai.

p. 64 *Spotcheck 6*:
On the way they passed a petrol station, a post office and a temple. (They stopped just past the temple.)

p. 64 *Listen*:
The places they went to were: **1** point B,   **2** the post office,   **3** point B.

p. 65 *Replies* and *Ask*:
When you have completed these two exercises, the directions on the left should be linked to the symbols on the right (through the pictures in the middle) in the following way:
A to 2, B to 1, C to 5, D to 3, E to 4.

p. 65 *Listen*:
1 A kara **o-tera** made   **2** B kara **jinja** made   **3** C kara **gakkō** made   **4** D kara **yūbinkyoku** made

p. 65 *Taxi!*:
Here are suggested directions:
1 Hitotsume no shingō de hidari e magatte kudasai. Tsugi no shingō de migi e magatte, gasorin sutando no temae de tomete kudasai.
2 Massugu itte, mittsume no shingō de hidari e magatte kudasai. Eki no hantaigawa de tomete kudasai.
3 Hitotsume no shingō de hidari e magatte, kōban no hantaigawa de migi e magatte kudasai. Futatsume no kado de migi e magatte, yūbinkyoku no hantaigawa de tomete kudasai.
4 Tsugi no shingō de migi e magatte, futatsume no kado de hidari e magatte kudasai. O-tera no hantaigawa de tomete kudasai.

p. 68 *Spotcheck 7*:
Ms Asano works for TDK, Robert for 'London Computers' and Mr Ueda for Fujitsū (the same company as Mr Nakajima).

p. 68 *Listen*:
2 Yamaguchi (Nissan) Sakata (shachō)
3 Watanabe (Sony)   Kitamura (kachō)
4 Ogura (Mitsubishi)   Tajima (buchō)

p. 69 *Spotcheck 8*:
'Are you a teacher?': **a** Sensei desu ka?   **b** Ino-san wa sensei desu ka?
'Where's your school?': **a** Gakkō wa doko ni arimasu ka?
b Ino-san no gakkō wa doko ni arimasu ka?

p. 72 *Where do you work?*:
The places and jobs mentioned are: Shinbashi – salesman; Iidabashi – works for a computer company; Shibuya – (senior high school) teacher; Ueno – bank employee; Yotsuya – civil servant; Ochanomizu – student; Shinjuku – housewife

p. 72 *Aizuchi*:
1D, 2B, 3A, 4C

p. 73 *Moshi moshi*:
The people on the left and right should be linked as follows:
Sakamoto Eriko – son; Aizawa Junji – mother; Arai Masako – stranger; Ogawa Shin'ichi – lover; Saitō Yuri – friend; Suzuki Takeshi – boss.

p. 73 *Getting there . . .*:
The route and the position of the office are marked on the map below.

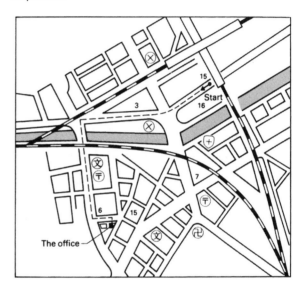

The office

p. 75 *Written Japanese*:
The names in rōmaji are: **1** Yamakawa   **2** Yamada
3 Nakagawa   **4** Nakayama   **5** Tayama   **6** Yamanaka
7 Kawamoto   **8** Yamamoto   **9** Nakabayashi
10 Uchiyama   **11** Kikawa   **12** Honda
The sentences read as follows in rōmaji: **1** *Kochira wa Honda no Tanaka-san desu.* (This is Mr/Ms Tanaka of Honda.)
2 *Uchi no Yamakawa desu.* (This is Mr/Ms Yamakawa of my company.)   **3** *Ano onna no hito wa Tanaka-san desu ka?* (Is that woman Ms Tanaka?)   **4** *Kawata-san no o-kā-san wa chūgokujin desu ka?* (Is Mr/Ms Kawata's mother Chinese?)

UNIT 4

p. 80 *Sums*:
3 9−4=5   **4** 1+7=8   **5** 6−3=3   **6** 4+2=6
7 8−3=5   **8** 6−6=0   **9** 1+8=9   **10** 9−3=6

p. 80 *Spotcheck 1*:

a jūsan **b** gojūroku **c** rokujūnana **d** hachijūyon
e kyūjūkyū **f** nihyaku **g** sanbyaku gojū **h** kyūhyaku kyūjūkyū

p. 80 *Write*:

1 1458 **2** 72 **3** 15 000 **4** 10 401 **5** 68 704
6 2170 **7** 750 000 **8** 3 500 000

p. 80 *Listen*:

1 635 **2** 186 **3** 8615 **4** 794 **5** 3347 **6** 41 162
7 458 **8** 930 000 **9** 863 **10** 23 000 000

p. 80 *More sums*:

1 450 − 230 = 220 **2** 1350 + 2460 = 3810
3 4250 − 240 = 4010 **4** 2459 + 41 = 2500
5 9782 − 473 = 9309 **6** 10 000 + 5450 = 15 450
7 20 000 − 550 = 19 450 **8** 55 000 + 4650 = 59 650
9 175 000 + 246 000 = 421 000
10 975 500 − 47 400 = 928 100

p. 81 *Japanese live 1*:

The items on special offer are: bacon, lettuce, canned tuna, pizzas, tomatoes, cabbages, bananas, jam, pineapples, tomato sauce, butter, yoghurt.

The prices are: bēkon ¥200; sarada ¥148; tsunakan ¥150; piza ¥158; tomato ¥150; kyabetsu ¥100; banana ¥120; jamu ¥178; painappuru ¥398; tomatosōsu ¥158; batā ¥168; yōguruto ¥198.

p. 81 *Shopping lists*:

1 Sarada 200g. Painappuru niko. Tomato yonko. Piza nimai. Total cost: ¥1550. **2** Tsunakan sanko. Yōguruto yonko. Banana yonhon. Tomatosōsu sanbon. Total cost: ¥1242.
3 Bēkon 400g. Jamu niko. Batā ikko. Kyabetsu niko. Total cost: ¥1524.

p. 84 *Colouring in*:

Miyahara-san: hat = red, dress = blue, belt = red, stockings = pink, bag = green, shoes = blue. Ueda-san: blouse = black, sweater = yellow, trousers = purple, sneakers = white, socks = orange. Watanabe-san: suit = black, shirt = pink, braces = brown, tie = red, belt = brown, shoes = black, socks = grey, raincoat = green.

p. 85 *Spotcheck 2*:

a kuroi sūtsu **b** burū no sētā **c** chairoi kutsu **d** shiroi bōshi **e** guriin no baggu **f** orenji no zubon

p. 85 *How much?*:

The prices are: **A** ¥20 000 **B** ¥45 000 **C** ¥33 000
D ¥50 000 **E** ¥19 000 **F** ¥35 500 **G** ¥89 000
H ¥74 000 **I** ¥4 900

p. 88 *Spotcheck 3*:

a They're in a clothes shop. **b** Belts are not in stock.

p. 88 *Spotcheck 4*:

shanpū = shampoo, *rinsu* = conditioner, *sutairingu rōshon* = (hair) styling lotion, *tisshu* = paper tissues, *handokuriimu* = handcream, *rippukuriimu* = lipsalve, *hea burashi* = hairbrush, *firumu* = film (for a camera)

p. 88 *What's in stock?*:

The items in stock are: *shanpū, sutairingu rōshon, handokuriimu, firumu*. Items not in stock are: *rinsu, tisshu, rippukuriimu, hea burashi*.

p. 89 *Spotcheck 5*:

They're too big.

p. 89 *Spotcheck 6*:

a atarashii ie **b** benri na baggu **c** muzukashii tekisuto **d** oishii kēki **e** suteki na wanpiisu **f** gurē no sukāto

p. 89 *Get what you want!*:

What you should have inserted at points A and B in each case: **1** yasui rajio → takai **2** benri na kamera → fuben **3** nagai kutsushita → mijikai **4** karui terebi → omoi **5** kantan na hon → muzukashii

p. 90 *Spotcheck 7*:

a Hea burashi (o) futatsu kudasai **b** Shanpū (o) yottsu kudasai **c** Tisshu (o) mittsu kudasai **d** Kore (o) nanatsu kudasai

p. 90 *Japanese live 4*:

The customers ask for: **1** three oranges, four (packs of) onions and two cabbages **2** one (pack of) mandarin oranges, six apples and nine lettuces **3** two water melons, three (packs of) carrots and five cucumbers.

p. 90 *Your turn*:

The prices you should have written are: apple ¥200; orange ¥98; melon ¥398; water melon ¥598; (pack of) mandarin oranges ¥398; lettuce ¥248; cucumbers ¥150; (pack of) onions ¥240; cabbage ¥198; (pack of) carrots ¥158.

p. 91 *Japanese live 5*:

The words you should have filled in are: **Ano shanpū** o misete kudasai … **Yonhyaku gojū-en** de gozaimasu … Jā, **futatsu** kudasai … Hai, **kyūhyaku-en** de gozaimasu.

p. 91 *Spotcheck 8*:

The shop is a *kusuriya* (chemist's).

p. 91 *Listen*:

Your charts should look something like this:

1

Item	Quantity	Price
bracelet	1	¥2880
earrings	1	¥1290
TOTAL		¥4170

2

Item	Quantity	Price
belt	1	¥2500
braces	1	¥3600
TOTAL		¥6100

3

Item	Quantity	Price
computer	1	¥198 000
floppy disk	5	¥ 380
TOTAL		¥199 900

p. 91 *Go shopping*:
The prices for one of each item are as follows:
1 blouse ¥7800, sweater ¥9300, underpants ¥620
2 lipsalve ¥390, film ¥1100, shampoo ¥780
3 apple ¥120, orange ¥150, lettuce ¥70
p. 94 *Departments*:
denkiseihin = electrical goods; *shokuryōhin* = foodstuffs;
shinshiyōhin = men's goods; *fujinyōhin* = women's goods;
keshōhin = make-up; *akusesarii* = fashion accessories;
supōtsuyōhin = sports goods
p. 95 *Reading*:
Your pictorial guide should look something like this:

4F	
3F	
2F	
1F	
B1	

p. 95 *Your turn*:
The items/departments are situated as follows:
1 foodstuffs: B1   **2** cameras: 6F   **3** women's clothes:
2F   **4** bags: 4F   **5** make-up: 1F   **6** earrings: 3F
7 sports goods: 8F   **8** kimonos: 5F   **9** public telephones:
B2, 1F, 3F, 6F, 8F.
p. 98 *What's it like?*:
1 (gold) ring   **2** (purple) carpet   **3** (grey) raincoat
4 (black) car   **5** (pink, orange and green) swimsuit.
The washing-up liquid is not described.
p. 98 *And it does 190!*:

	1	**2**	**3**
Top speed	250 km/h	140 km/h	160 km/h
No. of doors	2	2	4
Fuel consumption	5 km/l	17 km/l	10 km/l
c.c.	5000	550	3000
Price	¥15 000 000	¥1 000 000	¥5 100 000

You should have matched the cars with the pictures as
follows: A3, B1, C2.
p. 98 *Desirable residence*:
The prospective tenant in the first conversation is told about
numbers 6, 8 and 9 (in that order) and asks to be shown
number 6. In the second conversation, numbers 4, 3 and 7
are discussed and the prospective tenant asks to be shown
around 7.
p. 99 *Going up . . .*:
denkiseihin: 4F; shokuryōhin: 1F; shinshiyōhin: 3F;
fujinyōhin: 2F; keshōhin: 1F; akusesarii: 2F; supōtsuyōhin: 3F
p. 100 *Written Japanese*:
The telephone numbers are as follows: **1** (03) 3946–7231,
2 (06) 239–9962,   **3** (0273) 22–2688,   **4** (0245) 49–
6165,   **5** (0886) 45–3379.
p. 101 *Written Japanese*:
The prices are as follows: **1** ¥2000 (*nisen-en*)   **2** ¥8500
(*hassen gohyaku-en*)   **3** ¥19 700 (*ichiman kyūsen
nanahyaku-en*)   **4** ¥857 000 (*hachijūgoman nanasen-
en*)   **5** ¥64 320 (*rokuman yonsen sanbyaku nijū-en*)
p. 101 *Written Japanese*:
The prices in the photographs are as follows:
1 ¥600   **2** ¥500   **3** ¥8000   **4** ¥320   **5** ¥250.

UNIT 5

p. 106 *Soundcheck*:
The times are as follows: **1** 9:00   **2** 5:20   **3** 4:00
4 8:41   **5** 3:15   **6** 2:56   **7** 1:53   **8** 7:30
p. 106 *Japanese live 1*:
The times are as follows: **1** 5:00   **2** 4:45   **3** 8:32
4 9:36   **5** 3:47   **6** 1:26   **7** 5:10   **8** 3:30   **9** 6:03
10 4:04
p. 109 *Spotcheck 1*:
asagohan = breakfast (lit. 'morning rice'); *hirugohan* = lunch
(lit. 'noon rice'); *bangohan* = dinner (lit. 'evening rice')
p. 109 *Japanese live 2*:
The times Nanako does the various things are:
1 7:00   **2** 7:20   **3** 8:00   **4** 8:30–3:40   **5** 12:20
6 4:00–5:30   **7** 5:45   **8** 6:00   **9** 6:30   **10** 11:30
p. 109 *Spotcheck 2*:
a Itsumo nanji goro (ni) asagohan o tabemasu ka?
b Itsumo nanji goro kara nanji goro made nemasu ka?
p. 110 *Interview*:
The times Mr Mori does the various things are:
A 6:30–7:00   **B** 7:00–7:10   **C** 8:30–6:20   **D** 6:30
E 6:45–9:00   **F** 10:00–11:00
p. 111 *Interview*:
At the times indicated, Naoki does the following things:
1 okimasu   **2** hirugohan o tabemasu   **3** uchi o demasu
4 benkyō o shimasu   **5** uchi e kaerimasu   **6** bangohan o
tabemasu   **7** baito o shimasu   **8** nemasu

p. 111 *Spotcheck 3*:

The '-te' forms are as follows: **a** tabete **b** mite **c** nete **d** itte **e** nonde **f** yonde **g** shite **h** kiite

p. 114 *Interview*:

Naoki does the activities on the following days: **1** *sōji*: Sunday **2** *sentaku*: Saturday **3** *kaimono*: Monday, Wednesday and Friday **4** *doraibu*: Saturday and Sunday **5** *tenisu*: Tuesday and Thursday

p. 115 *Spotcheck 4*:

a sen kyūhyaku kyūjūnen gogatsu nijūsannichi

b sen happyaku jūninen jūnigatsu jūgonichi

c sen kyūhyaku hachijūsannen shichigatsu yokka

d sen kyūhyaku kyūjūhachinen jūichigatsu itsuka

e senkyūhyaku kyūjūgonen shigatsu tsuitachi

p. 115 *What date?*:

The dates you should have written down are as follows:

1 1987/6/25 **2** 1996/9/12 **3** 1876/2/3 **4** 1961/6/15 **5** 1958/10/8 **6** 1936/3/6 **7** 1789/7/14 **8** 1999/12/31

p. 116 *Build-up*:

chikatetsu = underground; *basu* = bus; *kuruma* = car; *jitensha* = bicycle; *baiku* = motorbike; *aruite* = on foot

p. 116 *Japanese live 3*:

1 by bicycle (about twenty minutes) **2** by train (about one hour) **3** on foot (about fifteen minutes) **4** by bus (about one and a half hours) **5** by (elder sister's) car (about twenty-five minutes)

p. 117 *Spotcheck 5*:

'Tekisuto' wa eigo de nan to iimasu ka? 'Textbook' to iimasu.

p. 117 *Classroom words*:

1e, 2d, 3a, 4c, 5b, 6g, 7f

p. 120 *How old?*:

The ages you should have written under the names are: Ogawa: 35, Hara: 32, Shimada: 24, Yoshida: 23, Kobayashi: 20, Yamamoto: 30, Uchiyama: 28, Watanabe: 21

p. 121 *Spotcheck 6*:

a (Tōkyō no) Shinjuku-ku desu/ni sunde imasu. **b** Rokuji han ni (asagohan o) tabemasu. **c** (Gogo) rokuji kara jūji made desu. **d** Iie, ichiji ni wa (hirugohan o) tabemasen. Jūniji ni tabemasu.

p. 121 *Questions*:

You could have written these questions:

2 O-ikutsu desu ka? **3** O-sumai wa dochira desu ka? **4** Itsumo nanji ni okimasu ka? **5** Itsumo nanji ni asagohan o tabemasu ka? **6** Shigotoba made nan de ikimasu ka? **7** O-tsutome wa dochira desu ka? **8** O-shigoto wa nanji kara nanji made desu ka?/Nanji kara nanji made shigoto o shimasu ka? **9** Itsumo nanji ni hirugohan o tabemasu ka? **10** Itsumo nanji ni uchi e kaerimasu ka? **11** Gakkō wa nanji kara nanji made desu ka?/Nanji kara nanji made benkyō o shimasu ka? **12** Itsumo nanji ni nemasu ka?

p. 121 *Interview*:

1 Shimada Yumiko **2** 24 **3** Shinagawa-ku **4** 7:00 a.m. **5** × (she doesn't eat breakfast) **6** chikatetsu de **7** resutoran (she's a waitress) **8** 8:00 a.m.–4:00 p.m. **9** 11:30 a.m. **10** 4:30 p.m. **11** 6 p.m.–10 p.m. **12** 11:15 p.m.

p. 121 *Writing*:

You might have written something like this:

Shimada Yumiko-san wa nijūyonsai desu. Tōkyō no Shinagawa-ku ni sunde imasu. Shichiji ni okimasu. Shimada-san wa asagohan o tabemasen! Shigotoba made chikatetsu de ikimasu. Resutoran ni tsutomete imasu. Shigoto wa hachiji ni hajimarimasu – hachiji kara yoji made desu. Hirugohan wa jūichiji han desu. Yoji han ni uchi e kaerimasu. Jugyō wa rokuji ni hajimarimasu. Jūji ni owarimasu. Shimada-san wa uchi e kaerimasu. Jūichiji jūgofun ni nemasu. Taihen desu ne!

p. 124 *A typical day*:

1 Ms Ichikawa gets up at **6:00 a.m.** She leaves for work at **7:30 a.m.**, finishes work at **8:00 p.m.** and goes to bed at **12:00**. **2** Ms Hayashi has breakfast at **7:00 a.m.** She works from **9:00 a.m.** to **5:00 p.m.** **3** Mr Morita usually gets up at **9:00 a.m.** He works from **12:00 (midday)** to **10:00 p.m.** When he goes drinking after work, he goes to bed around **5:00 a.m.**

p. 124 *Daily routine*:

Name: Sugimoto Masako; Address: Suginami-ku, Kugayama; Telephone number: 8354–2073; Occupation: 'office lady'. Masako's daily routine is as follows: Gets up: 7:00; Leaves home: 8:00; Starts work: 9:00; Lunch break: 12:00–1:00; Finishes work: 5:00; Swims (on Mondays and Thursdays): 6:00–7:00; Dinner: 8:00; Watches TV: 9:00–10:00; Listens to the radio: 10:00–11:00; Goes to bed: 12:00.

p. 125 *History quiz*:

The dates you should have written down, in the order you heard them, are as follows: **1** 1756/1/27 **2** 1815/6/18 **3** 1865/4/26 **4** 1914/8/15 **5** 1917/3/15 **6** 1923/11/17 **7** 1948/5/14 **8** 1961/4/12 **9** 1962/10/5 **10** 1968/4/4

The students got four questions right: the date Mozart was born, the date the Panama Canal was opened, the date of Yuri Gagarin's space flight and the date of the Beatles' first hit.

p. 125 *What year?*:

The ages and 'years' of the young people interviewed are as follows: **1** 7 – elementary school 1st year **2** 14 – junior high school 2nd year **3** 10 – elementary school 4th year **4** 19 – university 1st year **5** 16 – senior high school 1st year **6** 11 – elementary school 5th year **7** 8 – (elementary school) 3rd year **8** 20 – junior college 1st year **9** 18 – senior high school 3rd year **10** 23 – university 4th year

p.127 *Written Japanese*:
The readings and translations are as follows: **1** *chūgaku ninensei* (junior high school second-year pupil)
2 *shōgaku gonensei* (elementary school fifth-year pupil)
3 *kōkō sannensei* (senior high school third-year pupil)
4 *shōgaku rokunensei* (elementary school sixth-year pupil) **5** *daigaku yonensei* (university fourth-year student) **6** *chūgaku ichinensei* (junior high school first-year pupil)
The dates are read and translated as follows: **1** *sen kyūhyaku kyūjūgonen sangatsu jūrokunichi* (16 March 1995) **2** *sen kyūhyaku rokujūrokunen jūgatsu nijūichinichi* (21 October 1966) **3** *nisennen ichigatsu tsuitachi* (1 January 2000) **4** *sen happyaku nanajūninen shichigatsu itsuka* (5 July 1872) **5** *sen kyūhyaku kyūjūsannen jūnigatsu kokonoka* (9 December 1993)

UNIT 6

p.132 *Spotcheck 1*:
a 8:45 (hachiji yonjūgofun chaku desu)
b 8:13 (hachiji jūsanpun hatsu desu)

p.132 *Leaving and arriving A*:
The times you should have written in the numbered boxes are: **1** 8:38 **2** 8:50 **3** 9:00 **4** 9:01 **5** 9:43
6 9:45 **7** 9:57

p.133 *Spotcheck 2*:
a Tsugi no Ueno yuki no shinkansen.
b Jūichiji gojūnifun hatsu Morioka yuki no tokkyū.

p.134 *Which train? A*:
1G, 2C, 3J, 4D, 5A

p.135 *Enquire B*:
1 8:41 **2** 9:17 **3** 8:56 **4** 8:36 **5** 9:28

p.135 *Book A*:
The completed grid should look like this:

	1	2	3	4	5
Train letter	G	N	C	D	E
'S' or 'R'?	R	S	S	R	R
No. of tickets	2	1	3	4	2

p.136 *Spotcheck 3*:
a ¥65350 **b** Platform 14

p.136 *Your turn*:
The total ticket prices, and the platform numbers, are as follows: **1** ¥28580, platform 18 **2** ¥5320, platform 6
3 ¥74950, platform 19

p.137 *Spotcheck 4*:
a *piinattsu* = peanuts, *sandoitchi* = sandwich(es), *chokorēto* = chocolate **b** The customer buys two packets of dried squid and some sandwiches.

p.140 *Build-up* and *Reading*:
The completed chart for the Orient Hotel should look like this:

Orient Hotel

washitsu	√ (40)
yōshitsu	√ (160)
shinguru	?
daburu	?
tsuin	?
shawā	?
denwa	√
terebi	√
eakon	√
bā	√
resutoran	√

p.141 *Listen*:
The caller is informed that there **are** 30 Western-style rooms, single and twin rooms, a shower in every room and a restaurant. There **aren't** any double rooms.

p.141 *Your turn*:
The answers you received were that there **are** television sets in the rooms but that there **aren't** any Japanese-style rooms, telephones or air-conditioning in the rooms, and there **isn't** a bar.

p.143 *Spotcheck 5*:
a a double **b** two nights **c** ¥20000 (per night)

p.143 *Bookings A*:
The completed form should look like this:
Name   *Watanabe Yumiko*
Telephone *0489–43–8762*
Date of   Type of
arrival   *9 June*   room *Single*
No. nights *3*   Price *¥14800* (per night)

p.143 *Bookings B*:
The room rate is ¥12800.

p.144 *Questions*:
You should have written questions like these in the spaces:
A O-kuni wa dochira desu ka? **D** O-shigoto wa nan desu ka?/O-tsutome wa dochira desu ka? **F** O-ko-san wa imasu ka?/irasshaimasu ka? **G** O-ikutsu desu ka? Nansai desu ka?

p.145 *Listen*:
The topic letters are: 2G, 3C, 4E, 5F, 6A, 7B, 8F, 9A, 10D, 11D, 12G, 13E, 14C

p.145 *Spotcheck 6*:
a gofun(kan) **b** jūjikan **c** muika(kan)
d yonshūkan **e** nanakagetsu(kan) **f** jūkyūnen(kan)

p.145 *Spotcheck 7*:
Robert has been in Japan for six days.

p.148 *Listen*:
The degrees to which Alan likes the things in the pictures are as follows: **1** daisuki desu **2** daisuki desu **3** daikirai desu **4** suki desu **5** amari suki ja arimasen **6** kirai desu **7** kirai ja arimasen **8** suki desu

283

p. 149 *Descriptions*:
Kamiyama-san is the woman, Arai-san is the man.

p. 149 *Spotcheck 8*:
a wakaku arimasen   **b** sumāto ja arimasen   **c** amari kirei ja arimasen   **d** ashi ga amari nagaku arimasen

p. 152 *My kind of place*:
The answers are as follows:

1 Good food	Yes	2/3 nights	Winter
2 Relaxing bathing	No	1 night	Summer
3 Beautiful scenery	No	4 nights	Autumn

p. 152 *Connections*:
The platform numbers and times of the trains are as follows:
2 12, 15:25   **3** 2, 15:33   **4** 4, 15:16   **5** 6, 15:20   **6** 1, 15:10   **7** 3, 15:10   **8** 0, 15:20

p. 153 *Booking by phone*:
2 kabuki, 19/1/92, ¥64 000, Sakurai, 3763–4832   **3** pop concert, 5/6/92, ¥11 700, Ogawa, 3244–7533   **4** hotel, 27/3/91, ¥19 000, Yamada, 2845–8661   **5** air ticket, 24/7/91, ¥198 000, Guriin, 3921–8461   **6** car hire, 10/8/91, ¥72 000, Kimura, 3924–1007

p. 153 *Stock questions*:
A The questioner asked about the topics in this order:
1 Where from?   **2** Period of stay?   **3** Job?
4 Married?   **5** Children?   **6** Age?
B The answers were as follows: **1** from Britain (London)
2 been in Japan one week, leaving in two weeks   **3** IBM employee   **4** married with children   **5** children's ages are 13 and 8   **6** own age is 34
C She was asked whether she likes Japan. (She replied she likes it very much.) She was complimented on her Japanese.

p. 155 *Written Japanese*:
The kanji for the place names are as follows: 1E, 2G, 3F, 4A, 5B, 6C, 7D

p. 157 *Written Japanese*:
The readings of the direction indicators are as follows:
1 higashiguchi   **2** minamiguchi   **3** nishiguchi
4 kitaguchi

UNIT 7

p. 162 *Listen*:
The numbers of people in each group are as follows:
1 3   **2** 4   **3** 1   **4** 5   **5** 2

p. 163 *Katakana*:
You should have written in the names of items as follows (in order from top to bottom): karē raisu, piza tōsuto, mikkusu sando, sarada, chiizu kēki, mōningu setto, kōhii, remon tii, orenji jūsu, biiru.

p. 163 *Ordering*:
The orders of the three groups are as follows: **1st group:** assorted sandwiches × 1, salad × 1, pizza toast × 1, lemon

tea × 1, beer × 1; **2nd group:** curry rice × 2, assorted sandwiches × 1, coffee × 2, orange juice × 1; **3rd group:** pizza toast × 2, assorted sandwiches × 1, coffee × 1, lemon tea × 2.

p. 164 *Japanese live 1*:
The words you could have filled in are:
Watashi wa **piza tōsuto** ni shimasu; **Sumimasen!**; Piza tōsuto **(o) futatsu** to mikkusu sando . . .; Hotto kōhii **(o) kudasai/onegai shimasu**.

p. 166 *Listen*:
The order was: **1** Kanpai!   **2** Oishi-sō!   **3** Itadakimasu.
4 Biiru mō ippon kudasai.   **5** Mō kekkō desu.
6 Oishikatta!   **7** Okanjō onegai shimasu.
8 Gochisōsama deshita.

p. 166 *Build-up*:
A4 delicious – oishikatta (desu)   **B6** enjoyable – tanoshikatta (desu)   **C7** sad – kanashikatta (desu)
D2 boring – tsumaranakatta (desu)   **E5** frightening – kowakatta (desu)   **F3** easy – kantan deshita   **G1** lively – nigiyaka deshita

p. 168 *Spotcheck 1*:
Jun has **not** eaten c (*mikkusu sando*).

p. 168 *Spotcheck 2*:
1 kinō   **2** senshū   **3** sensenshū   **4** ototoi   **5** sengetsu

p. 169 *Spotcheck 3*:
a (Kinō wa) suiyōbi deshita. (Ototoi wa) kayōbi deshita.
b (Sensenshu no mokuyōbi wa) rokugatsu jūsannichi deshita.   **c** (Kyonen wa) 2005 -nen (nisengonen deshita.

p. 169 *Read . . .*:
This is a summary of receipt 2.
. . . and write: You might have written this:
Ototoi Jun-san wa Tōkyō no resutoran de shokuji o shimashita. Sarada to piza o tabemashita. Sore kara kōhii o nomimashita.

p. 172 *Nanako's yesterday*:
Shichiji ni okimashita. Shichiji nijuppun ni asagohan o tabemashita. Hachiji ni gakkō e ikimashita. Hachiji han kara sanji yonjuppun made benkyō o shimashita. Jūniji nijuppun ni hirugohan o tabemashita. Taisō o shimasen deshita. Goji yonjūgofun ni uchi e kaerimashita. Rokuji ni bangohan o tabemashita. Juku e ikimasen deshita. Jūichiji han ni nemashita.

p. 172 *Dear Diary 1*:
You should have filled in the gaps as follows:
Asa Honda-san **ni** denwa o shimashita. Kare **to (issho ni)** doraibu o shimashita . . . Sanji **ni** densha **de** Tōkyō **e** ikimashita. Kaimono **o** shimashita. Yoru Tōkyō **kara** kaerimashita. Bideo **o** mimashita . . .

p. 172 *Dear Diary 2*:
You should have filled in the gaps as follows:

Jūniji han **ni** Ueda-san **ni** aimashita. Kare **to (issho ni)** subarashii resutoran **de** shokuji o shimashita. ... Ueda-san **kara/ni** suteki na nekkuresu o moraimashita. Yoru Takeuchi-san **ni** aimashita. Kanojo **to** iroiro hanashi o shimashita.

p. 173 *Questions*:

1 Nani o nomimashita ka? **2 Itsu** ikimashita ka?
3 Dare to hanashi o shimashita ka? **4 Nan** de kimashita ka? **5 Doko** e ikimashita ka? **6 Dare** ga imashita ka?

p. 173 *A busy schedule*:

The things Mr Sakai did were as follows: **1** he spoke with the president of his company, **2** he went out for dinner with a client (*o-kyaku-sama*), **3** he went to Ōsaka, **4** he came back from Ōsaka by bullet train, **5** he met Sano-san, **6** he watched TV, **7** he went to his company.

p. 173 *Akiko's Sunday*:

The half sentences should be matched as follows: 1D, 2C, 3B, 4A

p. 173 *Jun's Sunday*:

You might have written sentences like these: **1** Dare ka to issho ni tenisu o shimashita. **2** Doko ka e baiku de ikimashita. **3** Doko ka de kōhii o nomimashita. **4** Dare ka ni chokorēto/purezento (*present*) o agemashita.

p. 176 *One drink too many*:

You should have written the verbs in the spaces as follows:
A shimashita **B** moraimashita **C** kaerimashita **D** nemashita **E** okimashita **F** akemashita **G** motte imashita **H** mimashita **I** nakunatte imashita **J** iimashita

p. 177 *Spotcheck 4*:

a (Taisetsu na) o-kyaku-sama to issho ni shokuji o shimashita. **b** (Totemo takai daiya no) nekkuresu o moraimashita. **c** Uchi e (nekkuresu o) motte ikimashita/kaerimashita. **d** (Hen na oto wa) ichiji goro ni shimashita. **e** Takeshi-san ga (nekkuresu o) te ni motte imashita. **f** (Daiya wa) hitotsu nakunatte imashita. **g** (Takeshi-san wa) ima keisatsu ni imasu.

p. 177 *Spotcheck 5*:

a First, the fact that Takeshi's white shoes were black (with mud): Takeshi went outside, but then came back in. Second, the fact that only one diamond is missing from the necklace. **b** Now you've made a list of who the protagonists are in the story, try to come up with a theory about who stole the diamond.

p. 180 *Investigations A*:

The correct questions are: **1** Dare ga Eriko-san ni denwa o shimashita ka? **2** Eriko-san wa asa no jūniji han ni doko e ikimashita ka? **3** Heya kara nani o motte ikimashita ka? **4** Doko made nekkuresu o motte ikimashita ka? **5** Dare ni nekkuresu o agemashita ka?

p. 180 *Investigations B*:

Answers to the questions were as follows: **1** Sakurai

telephoned Eriko, **2** Eriko went into the room where the necklace was being kept, **3** she took the necklace ... **4** ... to the entrance hall (*genkan*) ... **5** ... and gave it to Sakurai.

p. 180 *All is revealed*:

The words you should have filled in are: **A** Sakurai(-san) **B** nekkuresu **C** genkan **D** Sakurai(-san)

p. 180 *Spotcheck 6*:

a Eriko **b** Sakurai **c** 10:00 p.m. **d** 12:30 a.m.

p. 181 *Spotcheck 7*:

A3, B1, C2, D4, E5, F6

p. 184 *I know a lovely little place* ...

The recommended restaurants are to be found in: Italian – Toyama-chō, Chinese – Nishi-Waseda, Japanese – Ōkubo, Thai – Ōkubo, French – Takadanobaba

p. 184 *Fast food*:

a The phrases occur in this sequence: **1** 5 → 6 → 4 → 1 → 2 → 7 **2** 5 → 1 → 2 → 3 → 7
b The customers order: **1** one double burger, one french fries ('S' – i.e. 'small' – size), one cola ('M' – i.e. 'medium' – size). Total cost: ¥680 **2** one cheeseburger, one apple pie, one (chocolate) milk shake. Total cost: ¥560

p. 185 *Kare to kanojo*:

a The sentences which go with dialogue **1** are: A, D, E and H. With dialogue **2**: B, C, F and G. **b** The words (or numbers) you should have filled in are, in order: goji yonjūgofun/5:45; Suzuki; Ueda; 6:00/rokuji; Roppongi (6-chome).

p. 185 *Mukashi mukashi*:

A1, B2, C4, D5, E3

p. 186 *Written Japanese*:

The types of shops are (from left to right): komeya, sakaya, o-chaya, nikuya, sakanaya.

p. 188 *Written Japanese*:

The names of types of restaurant/bar are matched with the photographs as follows: A6, B1, C7, D5, E4, F3, G2

UNIT 8

p. 194 *Listen*:

The answers not already filled in are as follows: *tenisu* × ×, *badominton* oo, *earobikkusu* × × ×, *sauna* o

p. 194 *Ask*:

The answers not already filled in are as follows: *badominton* ×, *earobikkusu* oo, *pūru* o, *sorariumu* × × ×

p. 195 *Spotcheck 1*:

a Tsuki ni nankai gurai earobikkusu o shimasu ka? **b** Tsuki ni rokkai gurai shimasu.

p. 195 *Listen*:

The answers not already filled in are as follows: *tenisu* 10/yr, *badominton* × × ×, *pūru* 2/mth, *sorariumu* 6/yr

p. 195 *Ask*:
The answers not already filled in are as follows: *tenisu* ev.
day, *earobikkusu* 1/mth, *pūru* 3/wk, *sauna* 5/yr

p. 197 *Listen 2*:
Mr Sakai likes jazz, classical music and *enka*, comedies and
suspense films, documentaries, sports and news
programmes. He dislikes pop and rock music, horror and
science fiction films, and soap operas. He's indifferent to
(*kirai ja arimasen*) romantic films and films on TV.

p. 198 *Spotcheck 2*:
B likes home **b**.

p. 199 *Spotcheck 3*:
a takakute tsumaranai   **b** fuben de osoi   **c** tanoshikute
yasui

p. 199 *Identify*:
Mr Kuwata likes home **c**, car **c** and holiday **c**.
Mr Suzuki likes home **a**, car **a** and holiday **a**.

p. 202 *Team names*:
In English, the team names (in the order the mascots are
presented on the right) are: Carp (*kāpu*), Tigers (*taigāsu*),
Giants (*jaiantsu*), Swallows (*suwarōzu*), Whales (*hoēruzu*),
Dragons (*doragonzu*).

p. 202 *Japanese live 1*:
The full team names and scores are: Hiroshima kāpu (5:4)
Taiyō hoēruzu, Hanshin taigāsu (3:7) Yomiuri jaiantsu,
Chūnichi doragonzu (2:1) Yakuruto suwarōzu

p. 203 *Spotcheck 4*:
a Sannen mae ni nihon e kimashita   **b** Sono gonen mae
ni chūgoku e ikimashita   **c** Sankagetsu go ni igirisu e
kaerimasu   **d** Sono sanshūkan go ni furansu e ikimashita

p. 203 *Japanese live 2*:
The completed transcript should read as follows:
Konshū, jaiantsu wa **getsuyōbi** to **kayōbi** ni Tōkyō dōmu
de Chūnichi doragonzu to nishiai ga arimasu. Mata **kyō** kara
nishūkan go ni mo Tōkyō dōmu de Chūnichi to no gēmu
ga arimasu. Soshite **raishū** no **getsuyōbi** to **kayōbi**
(**rokugatsu yokka, itsuka**) ni wa kāpu to no nishiai ga
arimasu. **Sono futsuka go** ni wa Ōsaka de Hanshin to no
nishiai ga hajimarimasu. **Kongetsu** no **sanjūnichi** kara
raigetsu no **mikka** made wa shiai ga arimasen.

p. 203 *Spotcheck 5*:
Your completed schedule should look something like this
(CD = Chūnichi Dragons, HC = Hiroshima Carp,
HT = Hanshin Tigers):

This week

S.	M.	T.	W.	T.	F.	S.
5/27	5/28	5/29	5/30	5/31	6/1	6/2
	CD	CD ◄			OFF	

Next week

S.	M.	T.	W.	T.	F.	S.	S.
6/3	6/4	6/5	6/6	6/7	6/8	6/9	6/10
──► HC	HC		HT	HT			CD

Today (the day of the report) is Sunday, 27 May.

p. 203 *In other words ...*:
The expressions on the left and right are matched as follows:
1 A and D,   2 C and F,   3 B and E

p. 205 *Build-up*:
1F, 2H, 3B, 4C, 5G, 6E, 7D, 8A

p. 205 *For real*:
1 √   **2** ×   **3** √   **4** √   **5** ×

p. 205 *Listen*:
Suzuki-san successfully makes arrangements for the
following days: **1** Kayōbi: Ueno-san, go out for lunch (meet
at 12:30 in front of Ueno-san's company)   **2** Kinyōbi:
Okada-san, go to a film ('Ghostbusters') (meet at 6:15 inside
the cinema)   **4** Doyōbi: Watanuki-san, go for a drive (meet
at 1:00 in front of the station)

p. 208 *Spotcheck 6*:
The person answering is better at French than Spanish.

p. 209 *Japanese live 4*:
Yamaguchi: shōgi (√), gorufu (√), pachinko (×), piano (×),
abura e (×), minyō (×)
Tanaka: shōgi (√), gorufu (√), pachinko (√)
piano (√), abura e (×), minyō (×)

p. 209 *Interview*:
Mizuhara: shōgi (×), gorufu (√), pachinko (×),
piano (×), abura e (×), minyō (×)
Kubota: shōgi (√), gorufu (√), pachinko (√), piano (√),
abura e (√), minyō (×)

p. 212 *Pachinko*:
Player **1** comes 2/3 times a week, usually spends between
¥1000 and ¥10 000 and makes a profit of ¥10 000 to
¥20 000 **when** he wins. Player **2** comes almost every day
(*hotondo mainichi*), spends from ¥1000 to ¥5000 and takes
her winnings in the form of cigarettes (*tabako*). Player **3**
comes 4/5 times a week, only spends about ¥1000 and
sometimes wins a box of tissues or some orange juice.

p. 212 *At the movies*:
Likes: **1** comedies, love stories   **2** science fiction
3 suspense   **4** anything with Tom Cruise in it
5 adventure
Dislikes: **1** horror   **2** none   **3** love stories   **4** none
5 love stories

p. 212 *When I've got a moment*:
You should have written these numbers next to the activities:
yakyū 2, 4; *gorufu* 3; *sumō* 4; *tenisu* 1; *sukii* 2; *sukasshu* 3;
disuko 2; *kaimono* 2; *sadō* 1; *eiga* 2; *shokuji* 2. The activity
mentioned twice was *yakyū* (baseball).

p. 213 *What is it?*:

The pictures are matched with the recordings as follows: A2, B7, C3, D10, E1, F9, G4, H8, I5, J6

p. 214 *Written Japanese*:

The dates would be read as follows (with English translations): *ichigatsu jūgonichi* (15 January), *jūnigatsu nijūsannichi* (23 December), *gogatsu itsuka* (5 May), *jūgatsu tōka* (10 October), *jūichigatsu mikka* (3 November), *shigatsu nijūkunichi* (29 April).

p. 215 *Written Japanese*:

1 Gogatsu tsuitachi wa mokuyōbi desu ka? Iie, suiyōbi desu. **2** Gogatsu yokka wa suiyōbi desu ka? Iie, doyōbi desu. **3** Gogatsu muika wa kayōbi desu ka? Iie, getsuyōbi desu. **4** Kodomo no hi wa getsuyōbi desu ka? Iie, nichiyōbi desu.

UNIT 9

p. 221 *Spotcheck 1*:

It was too expensive.

p. 221 *Spotcheck 2*:

a Motto benri na no wa arimasen ka? **b** Ano akai no (o) misete kudasai? **c** Hoka no wa arimasen ka?

p. 221 *Listen*:

1a, 2b, 3b, 4b, 5a

p. 222 *Spotcheck 3*:

The '-masu' forms of these verbs are: machimasu (matte), ikimasu (itte), magarimasu (magatte), tomemasu (tomete), misemasu (misete)

p. 222 *Build-up 1*:

2 Chizu o kaite kudasai. **3** Yukkuri hanashite kudasai. **4** Pen o kashite kudasai. **5** Jūsho o oshiete kudasai.

p. 222 *Build-up 2*:

2 Rajio o tsukete mo ii desu ka? **3** Terebi o keshite mo ii desu ka? **4** Tabako o sutte mo ii desu ka? **5** Koko ni suwatte mo ii desu ka? **6** Kisu o shite mo ii desu ka?

p. 223 *Listen*:

A5, B3, C7, D4, E6, F8, G1, H2

p. 224 *Japanese live 2*:

The words you should have filled in are as follows:
Gomen kudasai! ... **Ojama shimasu.** ... **Dōzo, tsumaranai mono desu** ga ... **Shitsurei shimasu.**

p. 225 *Review*:

The actual conversations went as follows:

Honda	Kanai no Hanako desu.
Michael	Hajimemashite. Fōrin desu.
Hanako	Hajimemashite. Yoroshiku onegai itashimasu.
Michael	Dōzo yoroshiku.
Honda	Fōrin-san, biiru wa dō desu ka?
Michael	Ā, ii desu ne ... onegai shimasu. Atsui kara biiru ga oishii desu ne.
All three	Kanpai!

Hanako	Fōrin-san, shitsurei desu ga, o-miyage o akete mo ii desu ka?
Michael	Hai, dōzo.
Hanako	*(opening the present)* Ā, kirei desu ne. Dōmo arigatō gozaimasu.
Michael	Iie. Dō itashimashite.
Hanako	O-sushi o yōi shimashita ga ... Fōrin-san wa ikaga deshō ka?
Michael	Daisuki desu! Oishi-sō desu ne ...
Honda	Dōzo.
Michael	Itadakimasu.

p. 226 *Formalities*:

1a Dōmo arigatō (gozaimasu)/Dōmo sumimasen. **b** Dōmo arigatō (gozaimashita)/Dōmo sumimasen deshita. **2a** Shitsurei shimasu. **b** Shitsurei shimashita. **3a** Dōmo arigatō (gozaimasu)/Dōmo sumimasen. **b** Kono aida wa dōmo arigatō (gozaimashita)/dōmo sumimasen deshita. **4a** Ojama shimasu. **b** Ojama shimashita.

The 'mistake' is in picture **3a**: the men are bowing in a feminine way – men bow with their hands at their sides (see p. 8).

p. 231 *Spotcheck 4*:

In group **1** go **a** age*ru*, **f** shime*ru* and **h** ne*ru*. In group **2** go **b** kik*u*, **d** kae*ru*, **e** yom*u* and **g** hanas*u*. In group **3** goes only **c** sur*u*.

p. 233 *Build-up 1*:

a iremasu, irenai **b** tsutsumimasu, tsutsumanai **c** kirimasu, kiranai **d** kimasu, kinai

p. 234 *Spotcheck 5*:

b tabenai **c** tabeta **d** tabenakatta **e** nomu **f** nomanai **g** nonda **h** nomanakatta

p. 234 *Telephoning*:

The most formal conversation was **3**; the least formal was **2**. The alternative 'super-polite' and plain forms were (respectively) as follows: **a** (imasu) – irasshaimasu – iru **b** (desu) – de gozaimasu – da **c** (shimasu) – sashiagemasu – suru.

p. 234 *Spies*:

In the dialogue, the verbs should be inserted in the following order: iru – ageru – aru – suru – kaeru – nomu – da.

p. 235 *He probably ....*

A You could have written the following sentences: Shichiji ni okiru deshō; Pūru de oyogu deshō; Tenisu o suru deshō; Kuji ni neru deshō; Biiru o nonda deshō; Tabako o sutta deshō; Chokorēto o tabeta deshō; Terebi o mita deshō.

B You could have written the following sentences:
1 Jūji ni wa okinai deshō. **2** Gorufu wa shinai deshō. **3** Paipu wa suwanakatta deshō. **4** Jūichiji ni wa nenai deshō. **5** Bideo wa minakatta deshō. **6** Umi de wa oyogana deshō. **7** Sarada wa tabenakatta deshō. **8** Orenji jūsu wa nomanakatta deshō.

p. 236 *Listen*:

The numbers you should have written in the boxes (from top to bottom) are as follows, together with whether or not you have to do the thing mentioned: 5 (don't have to), 6 (don't have to), 4 (have to), 3 (have to), 1 (have to), 2 (don't have to).

p. 236 *Being surprised*:

a agenakereba narimasen ka   **b** irenakute mo ii desu ka   **c** tsutsumanakereba narimasen ka   **d** akenakute mo ii desu ka   **e** seiza shinakute mo ii desu ka

p. 237 *Spotcheck 6*:

a a sweater   **b** a coat   **c** sandals

p. 237 *Listen*:

Conversation **1**: Have to/should take: sandals, suncream, swimsuit. Don't have to take: the other things. Going to: **a** Hawaii.

Conversation **2**: Have to/should take: coat, scarf, sweater, hat. Don't have to take: the other things. Going to: **b** Canada in winter.

p. 241 *Spotcheck 7*:

chopsticks = (*o-*) *hashi*, towards the north = *kitakumi*, rice = *gohan*, spider = *kumo*, tea cup = *yunomi*, (toe) nails = *tsume*, food = *tabemono*, leaves = *happa*, hearse = *reikyūsha*

p. 241 *Fill in*:

1 miru to   **2** tatsu to   **3** kiru to   **4** miru to   **5** neru to   **6** watasu to   **7** nageru to   **8** tateru to

p. 241 *Listen*:

You should have written *ii koto ga aru deshō* under pictures 1, 2, 4 and 7, and *warui koto ga aru deshō* under pictures 3, 5, 6 and 8.

p. 242 *Your turn A*:

1 miru to   **2** sawaru to   **3** kowasu to   **4** aruku to   **5** utau to   **6** au to

p. 243 *Your turn B*:

Western superstitions: only 1 and 2 are good luck; 3, 4, 5 and 6 are bad luck.

p. 246 *Lucky charms*:

A5 ×   B2 ✓   C3 ✓   D1 ×   E4 ✓

p. 246 *Haven't you got anything cheaper?*:

1B, 2H and E, 3 nothing, 4 nothing, 5K

p. 247 *Model-making*:

The models should resemble: **1** a swan   **2** a fish   **3** an elephant

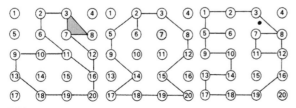

p. 247 *If we don't get home quickly* . . .:

If it turns out they didn't lock the front door, they might be robbed (4E). If she doesn't ring the restaurant, Junji will be left sitting alone, waiting (2D). If he doesn't pay for the damage, the gangster might shoot him (5B). If it rains (and they don't go home), the washing will get wet (1C). If he doesn't buy the ring, she won't marry him (3A).

p. 249 *Written Japanese*:

The opening times are as follows: **1** 9 a.m.–6 p.m.
2 Normally: 9.00–13.00 and 15.00–19.00. Saturdays: 9.00–15.00. Closed on Sundays and national holidays.
3 Normally: 11.00 a.m.–11.30 p.m. Closed on national holidays.   **4** 9.30 a.m.–12.30 p.m. and 3.00–9.00 p.m. Saturdays: 9.30 a.m. to 2.00 p.m. Closed on Sundays and national holidays.   **5** Normally: 11.00 a.m.–9.30 p.m. Saturdays: 11.00 a.m. to 4.00 p.m. Closed on Sundays and national holidays.

UNIT 10

p. 254 *Greetings*:

This is what you heard:

William	Ohayō gozaimasu.
Several voices	Ohayō gozaimasu.
Colleague A	Kyūshū wa dō deshita ka?
William	Ā, yokatta desu.
Colleague B	O-tenki wa dō deshita ka?
William	Mushiatsukatta desu yo.
Colleague B	Ā, sō desu ka. Iya desu ne.
William	O-miyage o dōzo. Tsumaranai mono desu ga . . .
Colleague A	O-miyage desu ka? Mā . . . Dōmo arigatō gozaimasu.
Colleague B	Arigatō gozaimasu.
Colleague A	Ima akete mo ii desu ka?
William	Dōzo, dōzo.
Colleague A	Itadakimasu. Oishii desu ne . . .

p. 255 *The days ahead B*:

On the unfilled days, William will: (Tue 15) go out for lunch with Honda-san, (Wed 16) interview Kurosawa Akira (at 2:30 p.m.), (Fri 18) interview Doi Takako (at 4 p.m.), (Sun 20) have the day off, (Tue 22) go to Britain (departure time: 10:20 a.m.)

p. 255 *An invitation*:

One set of possible solutions is given below:

Suzuki	Yomiuri Shinbun de gozaimasu.
William	Bii bii shii no Uiriamu Hōzurii **desu ga Suzuki-san onegai shimasu**.
Suzuki	Watashi desu ga . . .

William Ohayō gozaimasu. **Shibaraku desu ne . . .**

Suzuki Sō desu ne. O-genki desu ka?

William **E, okagesama de. Suzuki**-san wa?

Suzuki Genki desu.

William Anō . . . **mokuyōbi ni ohiru o tabe ni ikimasen ka?**

Suzuki Ii desu ne. Doko de aimashō ka?

William **Ginza no Mitsukoshi no raion no mae wa dō desu ka?**

Suzuki Hai, kekkō desu. Nanji ni shimashō ka?

William **Jūniji han wa dō desu ka?**

Suzuki Daijōbu desu. Jā . . . mokuyōbi no jūniji han ni Mitsukoshi no raion no mae de aimashō.

William Hai, **yoroshiku onegai shimasu.**

Suzuki Kochira koso yoroshiku.

William Dewa, **shitsurei shimasu.**

Suzuki Shitsurei shimasu.

p. 255 *Your turn B*:

a Ms Yamada of NHK   **b** Meet next week on Monday at 12:00 at the *Yomiuri Shinbun* (offices)

p. 256 *Taking a taxi*:

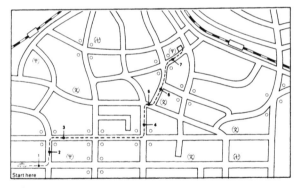

p. 256 *First meetings*:

This is how the conversation went:

Secretary Go-shōkai shimasu. Kochira wa bii bii shii no Hōzurii-san desu.

William Hajimemashite. Hōzurii de gozaimasu.

Ishihara Ishihara desu. Yoroshiku onegai shimasu.

William Dōzo yoroshiku onegai itashimasu.

William used more formal expressions (i.e. *de gozaimasu* as compared with Mr Ishihara's *desu*, and *dōzo yoroshiku onegai itashimasu* as opposed to Mr Ishihara's *yoroshiku onegai shimasu*).

p. 257 *Directions*:

NHK Hall is shown on the map. (William's route is also marked.)

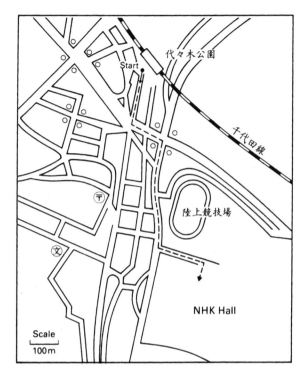

代々木公園

Start

千代田橋

陸上競技場

NHK Hall

Scale
100m

p. 257 *Self-introductions A*:

The details you should have filled in are as follows:

1 Susan Walker, IBM, system engineer, Canadian, 4 years, 34

2 Kim Tae Woo, Hyundai, sales department, South Korean, 10 years, 45

3 Anne Delon, Hitachi, international department, French, 5 years, 28

4 Javed Khan, Bank of India, bank employee, Indian, 8 years, 58

The different expressions you heard were: **a** *name* desu/to iimasu/to mōshimasu/de gozaimasu   **b** *organisation* ni tsutomete imasu/no shain desu   **c** . . . -jin desu, *country* kara kimashita (lit. *I came from . . .*)

p. 257 *Self-introductions B*:

The details you should have filled in are:

John Hughes, NBC, reporter, American, 3 years, 46.

p. 260 *Tōhoku adventure*:

1 Genbikei Gorge   **2** Lake Tazawa   **3** Kinkazan
4 Tamagawa Onsen   **5** Matsushima   **6** Hiraizumi
7 Miyako

p. 260 *Times*:
1 10:30 **2** 15:37 **3** 11:21 **4** 15:34 **5** 10:41
6 15:30 **7** 17:00 **8** 17:05 **9** 18:23 **10** 16:20

p. 261 *Itinerary*:
Night 1: Kinkazan, Night 2: Miyako, Night 3: Tamagawa
Onsen, Night 4: Hiraizumi

p. 263 *Where to stay*:
The place names you should have written are: **1** Tamagawa
Onsen **2** Kinkazan **3** Hiraizumi **4** Miyako

p. 263 *Booking*:
The price per night is ¥14 500.

p. 264 *What's on offer?*:
The prices of the boxes are as follows: in front of the
shopkeeper ¥2000, on the table in the foreground ¥600, on
the shelf next to the rice crackers ¥1500, on the bottom shelf
(under the rice crackers) ¥1800.

p. 264 *Shopping A*:
The customer is offered (1) the boxes labelled ¥600 (on the
table), (2) the ones labelled ¥2000 (in front of the
shopkeeper), (3&4) the ones labelled ¥1800 and ¥1500 (on
the shelves behind the customer). She decides to buy one
of the ¥1500 boxes (4).

p. 268 *When I was there . . .*:
Here is William's route, with the places he stayed at
boxed

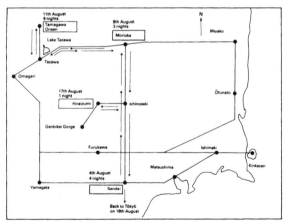

p. 269 *Asking for information*:
1 Itsu Sendai e ikimashita ka? **2** Sendai kara nanji hatsu
deshita ka? **3** Dare to issho ni ikimashita ka? **4** Morioka
kara Tamagawa Onsen made dono gurai kakarimashita ka?
5 Jūshichinichi ni doko ni tomarimashita ka? **6** Ichinoseki
kara Hiraizumi made nan de ikimashita ka?

p. 269 *Memories: then and now B*:
'Then': ii, yasui, shinpuru, tsumaranai, kanashii, kirei
'Now': warui, takai, muzukashii, tanoshii, shiawase, kitanai

p. 269 *Spotcheck 1*:
A yokatta, warukatta, yasukatta, takakatta, shinpuru deshita,
muzukashikatta, tanoshikatta, tsumaranakatta, shiawase
deshita, kanashikatta, kitanakatta, kirei deshita
B a atsukatta desu ne **b** atarashikatta desu ne **c** kirei
deshita ne **d** nigiyaka deshita ne **e** oishikatta desu ne

p. 273 *Written Japanese 3*:
The readings of the names are as follows: **a** Yamaguchi
b Uchida **c** Takagi **d** Nishiyama **e** Kobayashi

p. 273 *Written Japanese 4*:
You should have matched the station names with the
numbers on the map as follows: a10, b7, c2, d4, e1, f3, g8,
h6, i5, j9

p. 274 *Hopes and desires*:
You should have filled in the chart as follows:

	Name	Age	Occupation	Main desires
1	Oishi Ritsuko	25	'office lady'	To get married, have children
2	Takezawa Shunji	22	university student	To get a job in a 'good' company
3	Imai Kimiko	21	junior college student	To go abroad to study English
4	Hoshino Akira	21	works in a supermarket	To get a better job (a 'white collar' job). To find a girlfriend and have a car
5	Yokoyama Michiyo	17	high school student	To get into Tōkyō university

GRAMMAR SECTION

Contents

1 Some differences between English and Japanese

Starting with a few of the easier things about Japanese, here are some of the main differences between Japanese and English:

Articles (words like 'a' or 'the')
There are no articles in Japanese, so *tēburu*, for example, can mean 'a', 'the' or 'some table(s)', depending on the context. There are no 'genders' to learn as in French or German.

Nouns
In English we say 'a house' but 'two houses', 'a mouse' but 'three mice'. Japanese words don't have plural forms, so that *ie*, for example, can mean 'house' or 'houses', depending on the context.

Pronouns (words like 'he', 'she', 'it', etc., which take the place of nouns)
Such words do exist, but – as in Spanish or Italian – they're not usually used when it's clear who or what you're talking about.
  E.g. 'I'm American': *Amerikajin desu*.

Verbs (words describing actions)
In English we say, for example, 'I go' but 'she go**es**'. In Japanese, whether you're talking about 'I', 'you', 'he', 'she', 'it', 'we' or 'they', the verb stays the same: *ikimasu*. Although verbs do change their form to express past, present or other shades of meaning, these changes are quite regular. For more on verbs, see part 5 of this Grammar section.

Adjectives (descriptive words like 'small' or 'pretty')
As in English, adjectives come before the noun they describe (e.g. 'a small house': *chiisai ie*, 'pretty pictures': *kirei na e*).

There are two main groups of adjectives: so-called '-i' (or normal) and 'na' adjectives, which behave in different ways (but quite regularly). See part 12.

Sentence building
In English the usual order in a sentence is Subject–Verb–Object (e.g. 'The dog (subject) bit (verb) John (object)'). Unlike in English, the Japanese verb almost always goes at the end.

  In English, the order of nouns in a sentence is very important – there's a world of difference between, for example, 'the dog bit John' and 'John bit the dog', even though the words used are exactly the same. In Japanese, word order is more flexible, and to indicate things like who does what to whom, so-called *particles* are used. These are little words (like *wa*, *ga* and *o*) which are placed after the words they control, acting as signposts to their function in a sentence (see part 8).

2 Saying who

Words like 'I', 'you', 'she' and so on are usually omitted when it's clear from the context who you're talking about.

E.g. I'm British.
  Igirisujin desu.
  Are you American?
  Amerikajin desu ka?
  Is she Japanese?
  Nihonjin desu ka?

When it's necessary to be precise or to emphasise, the following words can be used (however, see the notes below):

291

I	*watashi*	we	*watashitachi*
you	*anata*	you	*anatatachi* (plural)
she	*kanojo*	they	*kanojotachi* (women)
he	*kare*	they	*karera* (men, or many women and just one man)

'I'

Slightly more formal than *watashi* is *watakushi*. Women sometimes say *atashi*, while men may be heard to say (familiarly) *boku* or *ore*.

'You'

Perhaps out of a concern not to be too direct, the Japanese go to great lengths to avoid using equivalents of 'you', except with intimates or complete strangers. (In such cases, *anata* may be heard, or between close friends *kimi*.) The most common alternative is to use the other person's (sur)name with *-san* attached (or the more respectful *-sensei* if the person is a teacher, doctor, or even politician). In addition, a whole variety of 'titles' may be used in the place of 'you' – for example, *shachō-san* (to a company president), just *sensei* on its own (to a teacher, etc.), *oku-san* (to somebody's wife), *mama* or *masutā* (to bar proprietors, female and male respectively).

'He' and 'she'

Like *anata*, the words *kare* and *kanojo* tend to imply a degree either of intimacy or of distance which is in many cases inappropriate to the relationship between the speaker and the person in question. Again, the use of someone's name is preferred (with *-san* if the person is an 'outsider', without it if he or she is a member of one's own (work) group). Also commonly heard are *ano hito* and *sono hito* (or, more politely, *kata*), which literally mean 'that person'.

'Who?'

To ask 'who?', use *dare?* or, more formally, *donata?* You may also hear the very polite *dochira-sama?*, for example when you're asked for your name on the telephone: *Dochira-sama deshō ka?*

3 Saying whose

Like 'I', 'you', 'he', etc., words for 'my', 'your', 'his', etc. are usually omitted when it's otherwise clear whose is the thing you're talking about.

E.g.	My office is in Tokyo.	Where's your school?
	Kaisha wa Tōkyō ni arimasu.	*Gakkō wa doko ni arimasu ka?*

Sometimes the existence of so-called 'honorific' and 'non-honorific' forms of the same noun makes the use of words like 'my' or 'your' even less necessary, since 'honorific' forms – usually marked by *o-*, *go-* or *-san* – are in general **only** used to refer to other people, rather than to oneself or one's own (family or work) group members.

E.g.	My name is Brown.	What's your name?
	Namae wa Buraun desu.	*O-namae wa?*
	In my family there are five people.	How about your family?
	Kazoku wa gonin desu.	*Go-kazoku wa?*

However, sometimes it is necessary to clarify or emphasise whose is the thing you're talking about, and in such cases the pattern '(possessor) *no* (possession)' is used:

E.g.	My house is pink.	Is this your car?
	Watashi no ie wa pinku desu.	*Suzuki-san no kuruma desu ka?*

This pattern is also used to express other meanings:

E.g. Ms Yamaguchi of Hitachi
Hitachi no Yamaguchi-san
French cheese
Furansu no chiizu
'Guernica' by Picasso
Pikaso no 'Gerunika'

'Whose . . .?' in Japanese is *dare no . . .?* (or, more formally, *donata no . . .?*), while to say, for example, 'it's mine', just omit the noun: *watashi no desu.*

E.g. Whose (book) is it?
Dare no (hon) desu ka?
It's my son's.
Musuko no desu.
It's Mr Satō's.
Satō-san no desu.

4 Saying which or where

Japanese nouns don't normally have plural forms, and they aren't preceded by articles (like 'the' or 'a'). For example, *tēburu* can mean 'a table', 'the table', 'tables (in general)', 'some tables', etc., depending on the context. When you need to indicate precisely which of something you're talking about, you can use one of these words for 'this', 'that', 'these' or 'those':

kore	*sore*	*are*
this (one)/these (ones)	that (one)/those (ones)	that (one)/those (ones)
kono + noun	*sono* + noun	*ano* + noun
this/those ____	that/those ____	that/those ____

Sore and *sono* ____ are used for things near the listener, or between the speaker and listener, whereas *are* and *ano* ____ refer to things 'over there', away from both speaker and listener.

E.g. My book is this one./My books are these (ones).
Watashi no hon wa kore desu.
What's that?/What are those? (near the listener)
Sore wa nan desu ka?
That house (over there) is Mrs Honda's./Those houses (over there) are Mrs Honda's.
Ano ie wa Honda-san no desu.

To ask 'which one(s)?' use *dore?* To ask 'which ____?' use *dono* ____?

E.g. Which car is Mr Tanaka's?
Tanaka-san no kuruma wa dore desu ka?/
Tanaka-san no kuruma wa dono kuruma desu ka?

To ask or say 'where' something is, use these words:

	Where?	Here
Place	*doko?* (where?)	*koko* (here)
Direction	*dochira?* (which way?)	*kochira* (this way)

	There	Over there
Place	*soko* (there)	*asoko* (there)
Direction	*sochira* (that way)	*achira* (that way)

Note that *dochira?* is often used as a more polite (vague) form of *doko?*, to mean simply 'where?'. Similarly, *kochira*, *sochira* and *achira* are sometimes used, for example by shop assistants, to mean 'here' and 'there'.

E.g. Where are you from?
O-kuni wa dochira desu ka?
It's here.
Kochira de gozaimasu. (very polite)

Kochira is also used to mean 'this' when performing introductions:

E.g. This is Ms Webber.
Kochira wa Uebā-san desu.

5 Verbs

Two of the easier things about using Japanese verbs have already been mentioned: (i) the same form is used regardless of the subject of a sentence, and (ii) changes in Japanese verb forms are generally quite regular. In fact, there are only two irregular verbs: *suru* (*shimasu*) and *kuru* (*kimasu*). (*Desu*, which is also irregular, is not usually considered to be a 'true verb'.) Here are brief explanations of the most useful verb forms and uses covered in this book. You can find a diagram showing how to construct these forms at the end of this section.

A The -*masu* (present polite) form
This is used to convey the same meanings as the 'simple present' in English, e.g. 'I go to school by car': *Gakkō e kuruma de ikimasu*, 'The school is in Tokyo': *Gakkō wa Tōkyō ni arimasu*. To form the **present polite negative** of a verb, simply change -*masu* to -*masen*, e.g. 'I don't go by train': *Densha de ikimasen*, 'It isn't in Ōsaka': *Ōsaka ni arimasen*. One easy thing about Japanese is that there's no new form to learn for talking about the future – just use -*masu* or -*masen*. The context (or the use of words like *ashita*: 'tomorrow') makes it clear you're not referring to the present. E.g. 'I'll go/I'm going (to go) to Nagoya tomorrow': *Ashita Nagoya e ikimasu*.

B The -*mashita* (past polite) form
To talk about the past, simply change -*masu* to -*mashita* (and, in the **past polite negative**, -*masen* to -*masen deshita*). E.g. 'He went to America': *Amerika e ikimashita*, 'She didn't go to school': *Gakkō e ikimasen deshita*.

C The *mashō* ('suggesting') form
To suggest a course of action, simply change -*masu* to -*mashō*, e.g. 'let's go': *ikimashō*. To be more tentative, add *ka?*, e.g. 'shall we go?': *ikimashō ka?*

D The -*tai* ('want to') form
To say you 'want to' do something, replace -*masu* with -*tai desu* (or, less formally, simply -*tai*). E.g. 'I want to go': *ikitai* (*desu*). You'll also hear the more formal -*tai no desu*, often shortened to -*tai n' desu*. To say you 'don't want to' do something, change -*tai* (*desu*) to -*taku arimasen* (or, in more familiar speech, -*taku nai*).

E The -*u* or -*ru* (present plain) form
This is used to convey exactly the same (present and future) meanings as the -*masu* form (see above), but at a more 'familiar' level of speech (for example, within the family and between close friends or colleagues). E.g. 'I go/I'll go to school by bicycle': *Gakkō e jitensha de iku*. One of the more

difficult things about Japanese is this use of different verb forms to convey different degrees of politeness (there are also 'super-polite' forms of some verbs). In this book the *-masu* forms are emphasised as being the most appropriate (least dangerous!) for you to use in the beginning stages of learning Japanese. However, it's as well to be aware of plain forms, since

(i) you'll often hear them used;
(ii) verbs are listed in dictionaries under their plain form (also known, for this reason, as the 'dictionary' form);
(iii) plain forms are used in some constructions even at a 'polite' level of speech – however, the only examples of these patterns presented in this book are '*-u/-ru* form plus *to*' to mean 'if ...', and '*-u/-ru* form plus *deshō*' to mean '(I'll) probably ...';
(iv) the distinction between so-called *-u* and *-ru* verbs is important to know about when it comes to forming other verb endings, as you can see from the diagram at the end of this section. For this reason, *-u* and *-ru* verbs are listed separately in section 6, where you can find important forms of all the verbs presented in this book;
(v) the **present plain negative** form also depends on the distinction between *-u* and *-ru* verbs, since *-u* is replaced by *-anai* but *-ru* simply by *-nai*. E.g. *taberu → tabenai* ('I don't/won't eat'), but *nomu → nomanai* ('I don't/won't drink'). You can find the negative plain forms of all verbs in this book in the verb list (section 6).

F The *-ta* (past plain) form

Using *-mashita* and *-masen deshita* to talk about the past is appropriate in most situations, and replacing them with past plain forms is best put off until you've learned when to use them 'safely'. Past plain forms are quite easy to recognise (they always end in *-ta* or *-da*), e.g. 'I went to the company': *Kaisha e itta*. However, the rules for forming past plain forms of *-u* verbs are rather complicated; you can either follow these rules, as presented in the diagram at the end of this section, or simply learn past plain forms off by heart (by looking at the verb list in section 6 and changing the *-te/ -de* forms presented there to *-ta/-da*). To form the **past plain negative** of a verb, simply change the present plain negative *-(a)nai* ending to *-(a)nakatta*. E.g. 'I didn't go to a love hotel': *Moteru e ikanakatta*.

Note that, to say 'had better', the past plain form of a verb is used before *hō ga ii desu*, e.g. 'You'd better study': *Benkyō o shita hō ga ii desu*.

G The *-te* (participle) form

The *-te* (sometimes *-de*) form is extremely useful in Japanese:

(i) to talk about 'continuous' actions in the present or past, by adding *imasu, imasen, imashita* or *imasen deshita*. E.g. 'He is sleeping': *Nete imasu*, 'I wasn't eating': *Tabete imasen deshita*;
(ii) to ask someone politely to do something, by adding *kudasai*. E.g. 'Turn to the right, please': *Migi e magatte kudasai*, 'Wait a moment, please': *Chotto matte kudasai*;
(iii) to ask permission to do something, by adding *mo ii desu ka?* E.g. 'May I go home?': *Uchi e kaette mo ii desu ka?*

You can find the *-te/-de* forms of all verbs presented in this book in the list in section 6.

H The *-nakute* (negative participle) form

This is useful for asking whether you have to do something (i.e. whether not doing something is all right). E.g. 'Is it all right not to read this?': *Kore o yomanakute mo ii desu ka?* Negative participle *-nakute* forms are derived by changing the *-(a)nai* present plain negative ending to *-(a)nakute*. E.g. *taberu → tabenai → tabenakute, nomu → nomanai → nomanakute*.

I The *-nakereba* (negative conditional) form

This form, followed by *narimasen*, is used for saying 'must', e.g. 'I have to go': *Ikanakereba narimasen* (literally, 'If I don't go, it will not do'). To form the negative conditional of a verb, change the *-(a)nai* present plain negative ending to *-(a)nakereba*. E.g. *taberu → tabenai → tabenakereba, nomu → nomanai → nomanakereba*.

J The *-eba* (conditional) form

One way of saying 'if I go', etc. in Japanese is (*moshi*) *ikeba*. Whereas in English we say 'if' followed by the present form of a verb, in Japanese saying 'if' (*moshi*) is optional, but the verb form changes. To form the conditional, there's no distinction between *-u* and *-ru* verbs: in both cases the final *-u* is replaced with *-eba* (e.g. *taberu → tabereba, nomu → nomeba*). To say 'if I don't ...', you can use the negative conditional *-nakereba* form (see paragraph I above).

The diagram opposite summarises the construction of the verb forms discussed above. You can use it to work out the different forms of any new verb you come across, as long as you know whether it's a *-ru* verb (like *taberu*) or a *-u* verb (like *nomu*).

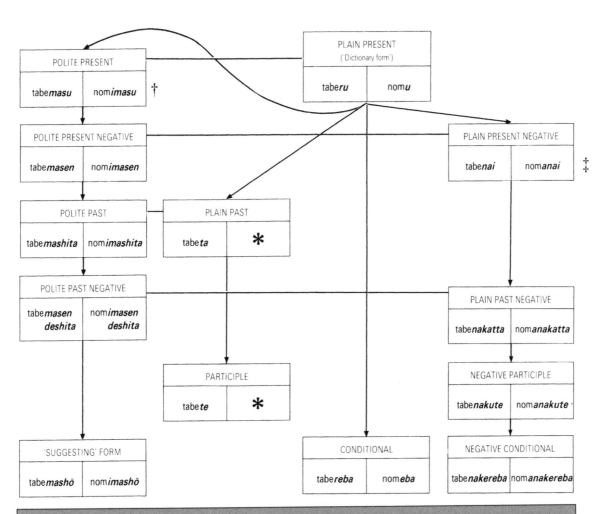

POLITE PRESENT		
tabe**masu**	nom**imasu**	†

PLAIN PRESENT	
('Dictionary form')	
tabe**ru**	nom**u**

POLITE PRESENT NEGATIVE	
tabe**masen**	nom**imasen**

PLAIN PRESENT NEGATIVE		
tabe**nai**	nom**anai**	‡

POLITE PAST	
tabe**mashita**	nom**imashita**

PLAIN PAST	
tabe**ta**	✳

POLITE PAST NEGATIVE	
tabe**masen** **deshita**	nom**imasen** **deshita**

PLAIN PAST NEGATIVE	
tabe**nakatta**	nom**anakatta**

PARTICIPLE	
tabe**te**	✳

NEGATIVE PARTICIPLE	
tabe**nakute**	nom**anakute**

'SUGGESTING' FORM	
tabe**mashō**	nom**imashō**

CONDITIONAL	
tabe**reba**	nom**eba**

NEGATIVE CONDITIONAL	
tabe**nakereba**	nom**anakereba**

✳ The form of the PLAIN PAST depends on the final letters of the PLAIN PRESENT:

-mu -nu -bu	→ -nda	e.g. no**mu** → no**nda**
-ku	→ -ita	e.g. ki**ku** → ki**ita**
		BUT i**ku** → i**tta**
-gu	→ -ida	e.g. oyo**gu** → oyo**ida**
-tsu -ru	→ -tta	e.g. a**u** → a**tta**
-vowel + u		
-su	→ shita	e.g. hana**su** → han**shita**

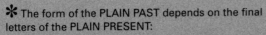

Change the final 'a' of the PLAIN PAST to 'e' to make the PARTICIPLE.

† Certain verbs may change in a way which looks strange but is in fact regular in terms of the Japanese sound system:

hana**su** → hanash**imasu**
mat**su** → mach**imasu**

As you can see from the sound chart on page 325, *-su* is in fact related to *-shi(masu)* and *-tsu* to *-chi(masu)* in pronunciation terms.

‡ Verbs whose PLAIN PRESENT has a vowel before the final 'u' add a 'w' in the NEGATIVE for easier pronunciation:

au > a**w**anai

295

6 Verb list

This chart includes all verbs presented in the book.

-RU VERBS

-masu	-te	-ru	-nai	Meaning
agemasu	agete	**ageru**	agenai	*give*
akemasu	akete	**akeru**	akenai	*open*
dekimasu	dekite	**dekiru**	dekinai	*be able to*
demasu	dete	**deru**	denai	*leave*
imasu	ite	**iru**	inai	*be*
iremasu	irete	**ireru**	irenai	*add, insert*
kangaemasu	kangaete	**kangaeru**	kangaenai	*think*
kimasu	kite	**kiru**	kinai	*wear*
mimasu	mite	**miru**	minai	*see, watch*
misemasu	misete	**miseru**	misenai	*show*
nagemasu	nagete	**nageru**	nagenai	*throw*
nemasu	nete	**neru**	nenai	*sleep*
nigemasu	nigete	**nigeru**	nigenai	*escape*
okimasu	okite	**okiru**	okinai	*get up*
oshiemasu	oshiete	**oshieru**	oshienai	*teach, tell*
shimemasu	shimete	**shimeru**	shimenai	*shut*
shinjimasu	shinjite	**shinjiru**	shinjinai	*believe*
sutemasu	sutete	**suteru**	sutenai	*throw away*
tabemasu	tabete	**taberu**	tabenai	*eat*
tatemasu	tatete	**tateru**	tatenai	*stand up*
tomemasu	tomete	**tomeru**	tomenai	*stop*
tsukemasu	tsukete	**tsukeru**	tsukenai	*switch on*
tsutomemasu	tsutomete	**tsutomeru**	tsutomenai	*work for*
yamemasu	yamete	**yameru**	yamenai	*stop*

IRREGULAR FORMS

-masu	-te	-ru	-nai	Meaning
kimasu	kite	**kuru**	konai	*come*
shimasu	shite	**suru**	shinai	*make, do*
desu	datte/de	**da**	ja nai	*be*

-U VERBS

-imasu	-te/-de	-u	-anai	Meaning
agarimasu	agatte	**agaru**	agaranai	*step up*
aimasu	atte	**au**	awanai	*meet*
arimasu	atte	**aru**	nai	*have, be*
arukimasu	aruite	**aruku**	arukanai	*walk*
chigaimasu	chigatte	**chigau**	chigawanai	*differ*
damarimasu	damatte	**damaru**	damaranai	*remain silent*
ganbarimasu	ganbatte	**ganbaru**	ganbaranai	*try hard*
hairimasu	haitte	**hairu**	hairanai	*enter*
hajimarimasu	hajimatte	**hajimaru**	hajimaranai	*begin*
hanashimasu	hanashite	**hanasu**	hanasanai	*speak*
hikimasu	hiite	**hiku**	hikanai	*draw (a line)*
hikimasu	hiite	**hiku**	hikanai	*play (stringed instrument)*
iimasu	itte	**iu**	iwanai	*say*
ikimasu	itte	**iku**	ikanai	*go*
kachimasu	katte	**katsu**	katanai	*win*
kaerimasu	kaette	**kaeru**	kaeranai	*return*
kaimasu	katte	**kau**	kawanai	*buy*
kakarimasu	kakatte	**kakaru**	kakaranai	*take (time)*
kakimasu	kaite	**kaku**	kakanai	*write, draw*
kashimasu	kashite	**kasu**	kasanai	*lend*
keshimasu	keshite	**kesu**	kesanai	*put out*
kikimasu	kiite	**kiku**	kikanai	*listen*
kirimasu	kitte	**kiru**	kiranai	*cut*
kowashimasu	kowashite	**kowasu**	kowasanai	*break*
machimasu	matte	**matsu**	matanai	*wait*
magarimasu	magatte	**magaru**	magaranai	*turn*
mochimasu	motte	**motsu**	motanai	*have*
moraimasu	moratte	**morau**	morawanai	*receive*
nakunarimasu	nakunatte	**nakunaru**	nakunaranai	*be lost*
narimasu	natte	**naru**	naranai	*become*
nomimasu	nonde	**nomu**	nomanai	*drink*
nurimasu	nutte	**nuru**	nuranai	*colour in*
owarimasu	owatte	**owaru**	owaranai	*finish*
oyogimasu	oyoide	**oyogu**	oyoganai	*swim*
sawarimasu	sawatte	**sawaru**	sawaranai	*touch*
suimasu	sutte	**suu**	suwanai	*smoke, inhale*
sumimasu	sunde	**sumu**	sumanai	*live*
suwarimasu	suwatte	**suwaru**	suwaranai	*sit*
tachimasu	tatte	**tatsu**	tatanai	*stand*
tomarimasu	tomatte	**tomaru**	tomaranai	*stay*
torimasu	totte	**toru**	toranai	*take away*
tsutsumimasu	tsutsunde	**tsutsumu**	tsutsumanai	*wrap*
utaimasu	utatte	**utau**	utawanai	*sing*
wakarimasu	wakatte	**wakaru**	wakaranai	*understand*
watashimasu	watashite	**watasu**	watasanai	*pass*
yomimasu	yonde	**yomu**	yomanai	*read*

7 Being and having

In English the verb 'to be' carries several meanings: 'to exist', 'to equal', 'to have the quality of', etc. In Japanese, there are some important distinctions to master.

First, whereas human or animal existence is expressed by the verb *iru* (*imasu*), the 'inanimate' existence of objects is described using *aru* (*arimasu*).

E.g. Mr Suzuki is in Tōkyō.
Suzuki-san wa Tōkyō ni imasu.
The NHK Hall is in Tōkyō.

NHK Hōru wa Tōkyō ni arimasu.
There's a cat in the room.
Heya ni wa neko ga imasu.
There's a 'kotatsu' in the room.
Heya ni wa kotatsu ga arimasu.

Iru and *aru* are also used in situations where we'd normally use the verb 'have':

E.g. Do you have any children?
O-ko-san wa imasu ka?
Do you have any shampoo (in stock)?
Shanpū wa arimasu ka?

If you 'have' something, Japanese sees it as 'existing in your possession'.

E.g. I have wonderful friends.
Subarashii tomodachi ga imasu.
I don't have any free time.
Hima ga arimasen.

The idea of possessing something can also be conveyed using *motte imasu* (literally 'be holding'), as long as what you have or don't have is a real thing (like a can of coke), and not something like 'free time' or 'the blues'). E.g. 'I have a car': *Kuruma ga arimasu* or *Kuruma o motte imasu*.

Getting away from 'having' and back to 'being', another important word is *desu*. This is used to describe not so much the existence of people or things as their 'attributes'.

E.g. I'm Japanese.   My house is pink.
Nihonjin desu.   *Watashi no ie wa pinku desu.*

and other states of 'being':

E.g. It's seven o'clock.   It's hot, isn't it?
Shichiji desu.   *Atsui desu ne.*

As verbs, *imasu* and *arimasu* behave predictably enough, except that the negative plain forms of *arimasu* are *nai* and *nakatta* (present and past respectively). *Desu* is somewhat exceptional:

Plain present:	*da*
Negative:	*ja nai*
Plain past:	*datta*
Negative:	*ja nakatta*
Polite present:	*desu*
Negative:	*dewa/ja arimasen*
Polite past:	*deshita*
Negative:	*dewa/ja arimasen deshita*

Finally, learn to recognise these **very** polite forms:
de gozaimasu (= *desu*)
gozaimasu   (= *arimasu*)
irasshaimasu (= *imasu*)

8 Sentence building

In studying particles it's a good idea to look at them in two groups.

The first group consists of those particles which have **no equivalent** in English. These are *wa*, *ga* and *o*. Whereas in English sentences you can tell the subject (the 'doer' of an action) and the object (the thing or person to which something is done) by recognising the word order, in Japanese, where the word order is more flexible, you listen out for *wa* or *ga* to recognise the subject and for *o* to identify the object.

A Wa indicates that the word before it is the word with which the whole sentence is concerned. It is like a spotlight. In English you might translate it by saying 'as for . . .' or 'regarding . . .'. It singles out the preceding word for special comment. *Wa* is not used after question words (*nani*, *dare*, etc.).

B Ga has a much 'softer' function. It simply marks the preceding word as the grammatical subject of the sentence. Use *ga* after question words.

C O indicates the direct object of a sentence.

The second group consists of those words which have an **equivalent** in English.

D Ka always comes at the end of a sentence and indicates a question. (In fact, adding it is all you have to do to make a question; there is no change in word order.)

E No can be used to bring two nouns together. It is very useful and powerful. In English we use ''s' (as in 'John's car') to do this but only in certain limited cases. *No* can be used in expressions like *asa no sanji* (lit. 'morning's three o'clock'): 'three o'clock in the morning', or *ki no uchi* (lit. 'wood's house'): 'a wooden house'.

F Kara means 'from' the place or time which comes before it in a sentence. You often hear it used with *made*, meaning 'until/as far as'.

G Ni can mean all sorts of things within the range of the English words 'in', 'to', 'at' or 'on'. You'll particularly notice it in the following situations:

(i) Time: With expressions of time, meaning 'at' (a time), 'on' (a day) or 'in' (a year), e.g. *sanji ni*: 'at three o'clock'.

(ii) Position: *Ni* is used with *aru* and *iru* to indicate where something or someone is, e.g. *Uchi ni imasu*: 'She's at home'.

It can also be used as an alternative to *e* (see below) to indicate motion towards a place, and to mean 'to (a person)', e.g. *Sakai-san ni nekkuresu o agemashita*: 'I gave a necklace to Ms Sakai.'

H De has the following two principal uses:

(i) Position: It is used when *ni* is not, i.e. in all situations other than with a verb indicating a state of being (e.g. *Eigakan de aimashō*: 'Let's meet at the cinema').

(ii) Means: It indicates that the preceding word is an instrument towards some end (such as a means of transport, e.g. *jitensha de ikimasu*: 'I go by bicycle').

I E implies motion towards a place: 'to', 'towards'.

J Mo has the meaning 'also' or 'too'.

K To (issho ni) means 'with'.

9 Numbers

For the numbers from one to ten, Japanese has two number systems, one Chinese in origin (except for *yon* and *nana*), the other indigenous to Japan:

	'Chinese'	'Japanese'
1	ichi	hitotsu
2	ni	futatsu
3	san	mittsu
4	shi (yon)	yottsu
5	go	itsutsu
6	roku	muttsu
7	shichi (nana)	nanatsu
8	hachi	yattsu
9	ku/kyū	kokonotsu
10	jū	tō

The 'Chinese' numbers are used to count on one's fingers, for example (the illustration shows how this is done in Japan), while the 'native Japanese' numbers presented above are used for counting objects. For quantities over ten, only 'Chinese' numbers are used, and these are formed in a quite regular way:

11, 12 . . . jū + (ichi, ni . . .) → jūichi, jūni . . .
20, 30 . . . (ni, san . . .) + jū → nijū, sanjū . . .
21, 32 . . . (nijū, sanjū . . .) + (ichi, ni . . .) → nijūichi, sanjūni . . .

Numbers continue to be built up in this way, using the following words for multiples of ten:

100	**hyaku**	(321 = sanbyaku nijūichi)
1000	**(is) sen**	(4321) = yonsen sanbyaku nijūichi
10,000	**ichiman**	(54,321 = goman yonsen sanbyaku nijūichi)
100,000	**jūman**	(654,300 = rokujūgoman yonsen sanbyaku)
1,000,000	**hyakuman**	(7,654,300 = nanahyaku rokujūgoman yonsen sanbyaku)
10,000,000	**(is) senman**	(87,650,000 = hassen nanahyaku rokujūgoman)
100,000,000	**(ichi) oku**	(987,650,000 = kyūoku hassen nanahyaku rokujūgoman)

- Note that the indigenous Japanese words *yon* and *nana* are usually used instead of *shi* and *shichi* (since another meaning of *shi* is 'death'). *Kyū* is usually used rather than *ku*.
- Irregular combinations are: (+*hyaku*) *sanbyaku* (300), *roppyaku* (600), *happyaku* (800), (+*sen*) *issen* (1000), *sanzen* (3000), *hassen* (8000).
- In order to say larger numbers, try covering up the final four (or eight) digits and saying the number you see, then saying *man* (or *oku*), then saying the number that remains. To understand larger numbers, remember that after you hear *man*, four digits remain to be filled (after *oku*, eight digits).

10 Counters

In English there are some (so-called 'uncountable') words which can't be counted using 'two', 'three', etc. + word + 's'. For example, we have to say 'two **packets/grains of** rice' intead of 'two rices'. Japanese takes this principle much further, so that **every** kind of object needs to be associated with a particular 'counter' (like 'packet', 'grain', etc.). Different sets of objects have different counters. For example, long thin things like bananas or pencils are associated with the counter -hon (e.g. 'two bananas': banana nihon), while flat things are counted using -mai (e.g. 'one record': rekōdo ichimai).

The wide variety of counters makes life very difficult for the beginner in Japanese; you'll usually be understood, though, if you simply use hitotsu, futatsu, mittsu, etc. to count objects of any size or shape. Here's a table of some of the more common counters. (Not all of them appear in this book, but if they do, a page reference is given in brackets.)

A TABLE OF COUNTERS

Unless otherwise indicated below, yon, nana and kyū are used instead of shi, shichi and ku to mean '4', '7' and '9' respectively. The only other words listed on the right below are cases where you can't simply add ichi, ni, san, etc. to the counter shown on the far left.

Counter	Meaning	Irregular forms
-ban (53)	number	
-en (81)	yen	yo-en
-guramu (81)	gram (g)	
-ko (81)	item, used generally	ikko, rokko, hakko/hachiko
-mai (81)	flat thin object	
-hon (81)	long thin object	ippon, sanbon, roppon, hachihon/happon
-kai (94)	floor (e.g. in a shop)	ikkai, rokkai, jukkai
-sai (120)	year of age	issai, hassai, jussai, hatachi (20)
-bansen (136)	track number	
-haku (142)	night	ippaku, sanpaku, roppaku, happaku, juppaku
-nin (152)	person	hitori (1), futari (2), yonin
-kai (195)	times (i.e. once, etc.)	ikkai, rokkai, jukkai
-shiai (203)	game	isshiai, hasshiai
-dai	vehicle	
-hiki	animal	ippiki, sanbiki, roppiki, happiki, hachihiki, juppiki
-hai	glass, cupful	ippai, sanbai, roppai, happai, juppai
-satsu	volume (of a book, etc.)	issatsu, hassatsu, jussatsu

B 'HOW MUCH?' AND 'HOW MANY?'

To ask 'how many?' or 'how much?' of something, add the appropriate counter after nan. (If an irregular form exists for san, then use that form after nan rather than the form listed on the left above.) E.g. 'how many grams?': nanguramu?, 'how many bottles?': nanbon?

Two more question words, which can be used more generally to mean 'how many?' and 'how much?', are ikutsu? and ikura? The question O-ikutsu desu ka? ('how many (years) are you?') is also a polite way of asking someone's age, while ikura desu ka? is used to mean 'how much?' when shopping.

11 Time expressions

A TIMES AND DATES

The words for telling the time and saying the date are also 'counters' of a sort, and are presented below in the same format as for the counters in part 10A:

'Counter'	Meaning	Irregular forms
-ji (106)	o'clock	yoji, shichiji, kuji
-fun (106)	minute	ippun, sanpun, yonpun, roppun, hachifun/happun, juppun
-nen (114)	year	yonen
-gatsu (114)	month	shigatsu, shichigatsu, kugatsu
-nichi (114)	day	tsuitachi (1), futsuka (2), mikka (3), yokka (4), itsuka (5), muika (6), nanoka (7), yōka (8), kokonoka (9), tōka (10), jūyokka (14), jūshichinichi (17), jūkunichi (19), hatsuka (20), nijūyokka (24), nijūshichinichi (27), nijūkunichi (29)

To ask the time say nanji desu ka?, to ask the date nannichi desu ka?

To say a time, use the pattern ...-ji ...-fun, e.g. 8:15: hachiji jūgofun, 9:10: kuji juppun.

To say a date, use the pattern ...-nen ...-gatsu ...-nichi, e.g. '15 January 1987': sen kyūhyaku hachijūnananen ichigatsu jūgonichi, '1 April 1994': sen kyūhyaku kyūjūyonen shigatsu tsuitachi.

B PERIODS OF TIME

To talk about periods of time ('for' fifteen days, two weeks, etc.), use the following words. (Irregular forms for *-jikan*, *-fun(kan)*, *-nichi(kan)* and *-nen(kan)* are the same as those in 'Times and dates' above, except that 'for one day' is *ichinichi*.)

'Counter'	Meaning	Irregular forms
-jikan (116)	*for ... hours*	(see 'Times and dates' above)
-fun(kan) (116)	*for ... minutes*	(see 'Times and dates')
-nichi(kan) (145)	*for ... days*	ichinichi (1) (see 'Times and dates')
-shūkan (145)	*for ... weeks*	isshūkan, hasshūkan, jusshūkan
-kagetsu(kan) (145)	*for ... months*	ikkagetsu, rokkagetsu, hakkagetsu, jukkagetsu
-nen(kan) (145)	*for ... years*	(see 'Times and dates')

C OTHER TIME EXPRESSIONS

	Every	Before last	Last
Day	mainichi	ototoi	kinō
Week	maishū	sensenshū	senshū
Month	maitsuki	sensengetsu	sengetsu
Year	maitoshi	ototoshi	kyonen

	This	Next	After next
Day	kyō	ashita	asatte
Week	konshū	raishū	saraishū
Month	kongetsu	raigetsu	saraigetsu
Year	kotoshi	rainen	sarainen

'once a day/week/month/year'	*ichinichi/shū/tsuki/nen ni ikkai*
'two hours/three weeks ago'	*nijikan/sanshūkan mae*
'four months/five days from now'	*yonkagetsu/itsuka go*

12 Adjectives

Japanese adjectives – descriptive words – can be divided into two major groups: (A) so-called '-i' or 'true' adjectives (referred to in this book as 'normal' adjectives), and (B) so-called 'na' (or 'pseudo') adjectives. Whenever you come across a new adjective, try to remember it as an '-i' or 'na' adjective, since – as you're about to read – they behave in quite different ways.

A '-I' OR 'TRUE' ADJECTIVES

By far the majority of Japanese adjectives fall into this group. All the group members end in *-ai* (e.g. *semai*: 'narrow'), *-ii* (e.g. *tanoshii*: 'enjoyable', *-oi* (e.g. *sugoi*: 'great') or *-ui* (e.g. *atsui*: 'hot'). In several ways these words behave rather like verbs, having special negative and past forms. These forms are derived by dropping the *-i* from the present ('dictionary') form and adding endings in the following ways:

Present	*-i (desu)*	*tanoshii (desu)* (it's enjoyable)
Present negative	*-ku arimasen*	*tanoshiku arimasen* (it isn't enjoyable)
Past	*-katta (desu)*	*tanoshikatta (desu)* (it was enjoyable)
Past negative	*-ku arimasen deshita*	*tanoshiku arimasen deshita* (it wasn't enjoyable)

B 'NA' OR 'PSEUDO' ADJECTIVES

The adjectives falling into this group are usually Chinese- or Western-derived words like *kirei* (originally from Chinese) or *hansamu* (from English). This group's members behave more like nouns than verbs; for example, whereas '-i' adjectives can be placed unchanged in front of nouns (e.g. 'an enjoyable party' is simply *tanoshii pātii*), the linking word *na* must be inserted in the case of 'pseudo' adjectives (e.g. 'a pretty picture': *kirei na e*, 'the handsome man': *hansamu na otoko no hito*). 'Pseudo' adjectives also behave like nouns in the sense that their forms do **not** change in the negative or past – what does change is the form of *desu*:

Present	(adj.) *desu*	*kirei desu* (it's pretty)
Present negative	(adj.) *ja arimasen*	*kirei ja arimasen* (it isn't pretty)
Past	(adj.) *deshita*	*kirei deshita* (it was pretty)
Past negative	(adj.) *ja arimasen deshita*	*kirei ja arimasen deshita* (it wasn't pretty)

C ADJECTIVES IN COMBINATION

'True' and 'pseudo' adjectives also differ in the way they combine together. 'True' adjectives have a special so-called 'suspending' form for this purpose, made by replacing the final *-i* with *-kute*. Thus, 'It's enjoyable and cheap' would be *Tanoshikute yasui desu*. 'Pseudo' adjectives, on the other hand, do not change their form, but are followed by *de*: 'She's pretty and kind', for example, is *Kirei de shinsetsu desu*.

D 'IT LOOKS ...'

Finally, to say something 'looks' or 'seems' delicious, convenient, etc., *-sō* is added after the adjective. 'True' adjectives drop the final *-i*, while 'pseudo' adjectives remain unchanged.

E.g. It looks delicious.   It seems convenient.
Oishi-sō desu.   *Benri-sō desu.*

KANJI PRESENTED IN THE BOOK

The following are the readings of kanji presented in the 'Written Japanese' sections.

Notes:

- 'On' (Chinese-derived) readings are in capitals and 'kun' (native Japanese) readings in lower-case letters.
- Letters in brackets after 'kun' readings represent parts of a word written in hiragana.
- Only 'basic' readings are given; sometimes the first letter may change to make a word easier to say (e.g. 中国 = chūgoku).

Unit 1 *pp. 22–3*

人	JIN, NIN, hito
木	MOKU, BOKU, ki
本	HON, moto
日	NICHI, JITSU, hi, -ka
林	RIN, hayashi
森	SHIN, mori
東	TŌ, higashi
都	TO, TSU, miyako
京	KYŌ, KEI

Unit 2 *pp. 46–7*

内	NAI, DAI, uchi
外	GAI, GE, soto, hoka, hazu(su)
女	JO, NYO, onna, me-
子	SHI, SU, ko, -shi
田	DEN, ta
力	RYOKU, RIKI, chikara
男	DAN, NAN, otoko
好	KŌ, kono(mu), su(ku)
安	AN, yasu(i)
母	BO, haha
父	FU, chichi

Unit 3 *pp. 74–5*

中	CHŪ, naka, -jū
国	KOKU, kuni
山	SAN, yama
川	SEN, kawa

Unit 4 *pp. 98–101*

一	ICHI, ITSU, hito(tsu), hito-
二	NI, futa(tsu), futa-
三	SAN, mit(tsu), mi(ttsu), mitsu-, mi-
四	SHI, yot(tsu), yo(ttsu), yo-, yon-, yon
五	GO, itsu(tsu), itsu-
六	ROKU, mut(tsu), mu(ttsu)
七	SHICHI, nana(tsu), nana-, nana
八	HACHI, HATSU, yat(tsu), ya(ttsu), ya-
九	KYŪ, KU, kokono(tsu), kokono-
十	JŪ, tō
百	HYAKU
千	SEN, chi
万	MAN, BAN
円	EN, maru(i)

Unit 5 *pp. 126–7*

学	GAKU, mana(bu)
校	KŌ
生	SEI, SHŌ, u(mu), i(kiru), ha(yasu), o(u), nama, ki
大	DAI, TAI, ō(kii)
高	KŌ, taka(i)
小	SHŌ, chii(sai), ko-, o-
年	NEN, toshi
月	GETSU, GATSU, tsuki

Unit 6 *pp. 154–7*

北	HOKU, kita
南	NAN, NA, minami
西	SEI, SAI, nishi
州	SHŪ
海	KAI, umi
道	DŌ, TŌ, michi
関	KAN, seki
入	NYŪ, i(ri)-, iri-, i(reru), hai(ru)
出	SHUTSU, SUI, de-, de(ru), da(su)
口	KŌ, KU, kuchi

Unit 7 *pp. 186–9*

米	BEI, MAI, kome
魚	GYO, sakana, uo
茶	CHA, SA
酒	SHU, sake
肉	NIKU
牛	GYŪ, ushi
豚	TON, buta

Unit 8 *pp. 214–15*

休	KYŪ, yasu(mi)
祭	SAI, matsu(ri)
曜	YŌ
火	KA, hi
水	SUI, mizu
金	KIN, KON, kane
土	DO, TO, tsuchi

Unit 9 *pp. 248–9*

神	SHIN, JIN, kami
社	SHA, yashiro
禅	ZEN
寺	JI, tera
時	JI, toki
分	BUN, BU, FUN, wa(keru), wa(karu)
午	GO
前	ZEN, mae
後	GO, KŌ, ushi(ro), ato, oku(reru)

Unit 10 *pp. 272–3*

英	EI
語	GO, kata(ru)
言	GEN, GON, koto-, i(u), yu(u)
信	SHIN, shin(jiru)
体	TAI, TEI, karada
明	MEI, MYŌ, aka(rui), aki(raka), a(keru)
字	JI, aza
家	KA, KE, ie, uchi, ya
井	SEI, SHŌ, i

GLOSSARY: JAPANESE–ENGLISH

- The number in brackets after a word refers to the page on which that word first occurs in the book.
- When it's important to see how a word combines with others in order to understand its meaning, a typical phrase is presented in brackets, and the translation given is the translation of the phrase, not of the word alone.
- Japanese personal and place names are not included in the list, although foreign names are.
- Apart from 1–10, numbers are not included either; look them up in part 9 of the Grammar section.
- Verbs are listed under their polite -*masu* forms.

ā (10) (ā, sō desu ka) *oh, really*
abura (209) (abura e) *oil painting*
achira (65) *in that direction over there, that/there (polite)*
Adamu (7) *Adam*
agarimasu, agaru (184) *step up*
agemashita (180) *gave (see agemasu)*
agemasu, ageru (172) *give*
aida (226) (kono aida wa) *regarding the other day*
aijin (181) *lover(s)*
aimashita (172) *met (see aimasu)*
aimashō (204) *let's meet (see aimasu)*
aimasu, au (172) *meet*
airurando (11) *Ireland*
aite (142) (heya wa aite imasu ka?) *are there any rooms free?*
aizuchi (8) *'sign of enthusiastic listening'*
aka (83), akai (84) *red*
akachan (185) *baby*
akachōchin (188) *cheap drinking place (lit. 'red lantern')*
akemashita (174) *opened (see akemasu)*
akemasu, akeru (174) *open*
akete (222) (doa o akete) *open the door! (see akemasu)*
aki (115) *autumn*
akusesarii (94) *fashion accessory*
amari (148) (amari suki ja arimasen) *I don't really like it*
ame (247) *rain*
amerika (11) *America*
amerikajin (4) *American (person)*
anata (69) *you*
ane (35) *(my) older sister*
ani (35) *(my) older brother*
ano (30) *that . . . over there*
anō . . . (195) *erm . . .*
ao (83), aoi (84) *blue/green*
apāto (99) *apartment, flat*
Aran (11) *Alan*
are (28) *that (one)/those (ones) over there*
arigatō (gozaimasu) (28) *thank you*
arimasen (12) *there isn't/aren't (see arimasu)* (ja arimasen) *isn't/aren't (see desu)*
arimashita (175) *there was/were (see arimasu)*
arimasu, aru (55) *there is/are, have*
arubaito (111) *part-time job (from German: 'Arbeit')*
aruite (116) *on foot, walking (see arukimasu)*
arukimasu, aruku (242) *walk*
asa (106) *morning*
asagohan (108) *breakfast (lit. 'morning rice')*
asatte (202) *the day after tomorrow*
ashi (149) *leg*
ashita (202) *tomorrow*
asoko (30) *over there*
atarashii (28) *new*
atatakai (17) *warm*

atchi (65) *in that direction (over there) (short form of achira)*
ato (145) (ato nishūkan) *two more weeks* (kekkonshiki no ato) *after a wedding*
atsui (16) *hot*
atsukatta (254) *it was hot*
bā (140) *bar*
Bābara (7) *Barbara*
badominton (194) *badminton*
baggu (82) *bag*
baiku (116) *motorbike*
baito (111) *part-time job (short form of arubaito)*
banchi (55) *subdivision of a* chōme *(used in addresses)*
bangohan (108) *dinner (lit. 'evening rice')*
bangō (53) *number*
bangumi (197) *(TV) programme*
-bansen (136) *platform number*
basu (116) *bus*
batā (40) *butter*
battā (40) *baseball batter*
beigo (272) *American English*
beikoku (187) *USA*
bēkon (81) *bacon*
benkyō (108) (benkyō o shimasu) *study (lit. 'do study')*
benri (na) (29) *convenient, handy*
(o-)bentō (137) *lunch box*
beruto (82) *belt*
bideo (94) *video*
biifu (6) (biifu shichū) *beef stew*
biiru (41) *beer*
bijinesuman (4) *businessman*
bisuketto (40) *biscuit*
boku (5) *I (men's Japanese: informal)*
bōshi (82) *hat*
-bu (52) *division (of a company)*
buchō (66) *division chief*
bunka (58) *culture*
bura(jā) (82) *bra*
burajiru (11) *Brazil*
burashi (88) *brush*
burausu (82) *blouse*
buresuretto (94) *bracelet*
burū (no) (83) *blue*
buta (187) *pig*
butaniku (187) *pork*
butikku (87) *boutique*
butsudan (29) *(Buddhist) household shrine*
byōin (36) *hospital*
Chāchiru (7) *Churchill*
chairo (83), chairoi (84) *brown*
chaku (132) *arrival*
-chan (16) *suffix added to names of girls and small children*
chawan (30) *rice bowl, tea cup*

chesu (208) *chess*
chichi (35) *(my) father*
chigaimasu, chigau (12) *be different/incorrect* (iie, chigaimasu) *no, I'm not/it isn't, etc.*
chiisai (28) *small*
chiizu (162) *cheese*
chika (94) *basement*
chikaku (56) *near*
chikagai (87) *underground shopping street*
chikatetsu (116) *underground, subway*
chippu(su) (41) (poteto chippu(su)) *potato crisps*
chizu (117) *map*
choko (219) *chocolate(s) (short form of* chokorēto*)*
chokorēto (6) *chocolate(s)*
chotto (60) *a little* (chotto matte kudasai) *wait a moment, please*
chōdo (89) (chōdo ii) *just right*
-chōme (55) *urban subdivision (used in addresses)*
chūgakkō (112) *junior high school (age 12–15)*
chūgaku (119) (chūgaku ninensei) *second-year junior high school pupil*
chūgakusei (108) *junior high school pupil*
(o-)chūgen (218) *mid-year gift/gift-giving occasion*
chūgoku (11) *China*
chūgokujin (11) *Chinese person*
chūka (184) (chūkaryōri) *Chinese food*
(go-)chūmon (184) *order, e.g. given to a waiter*

daburu (140) *double room*
daigaku (112) *university*
daigakusei (111) *university student*
daijōbu (204) *all right, OK*
daikirai (148) (daigaku ga daikirai desu) *I hate university*
daimyō (130) *Japanese feudal lord*
daisuki (148) (daiya ga daisuki desu) *I like diamonds very much*
daiya (174) *diamond(s)*
dake (177) *only*
damarimasu, damaru (176) *be silent*
damatte (176) (damatte imashita) *stayed silent (see* damarimasu*)*
dansu (197) (dansu o shimasu) *dance*
dare? (31) *who?*
dare ka (173) *someone*
de (62) *by means of, at*
dekimashitara (184) *when it's ready*
dekimasu, dekiru (208) *be able to*
demashita (160) *left (see* demasu*)*
demasu, deru (110) *leave*
denkiseihin (94) *electrical goods*
densha (132) *train*
denwa (53) *telephone* (denwa o shimasu) *to telephone*
depāto (86) *department store*
deshi (206) *apprentice(s), pupil(s), follower(s) of a master*
deshita (37) *was, were (see* desu*)*
deshō (235) (... deshō ka?) *polite form of* ... desu ka? (sō deshō) *that's (probably) right*
desu, da (irr.) (4) *am, is, are*
dewa arimasen (12) *am not, is not, are not*
dewa (52) *well, then*
dezainā (4) *fashion designer*
disuko (212) *disco*
dō? (28) *how?* (... wa dō desu ka?) *how do you like ...?/how would you like (some) ...?*
doa (222) *door*
dochira? (55) *where, in what direction?*
doitsu (11) *Germany*
doitsujin (11) *German person*

dohyō (193) *sumō wrestling ring*
dōjō (206) *martial arts hall*
doko? (30) *where?*
doko ka (173) *somewhere*
dokushin (144) *single, unmarried*
dokusho (197) *reading (for pleasure)*
dokyumentarii (197) *documentary*
dōmo (37) *thank you (informal)*
dōmo arigatō (28) *thank you (usual)*
dōmo sumimasen (12) *sorry/thank you (expressing indebtedness)*
dōmu (203) (Tōkyō dōmu) *Tokyo dome (name of a stadium)*
donna (197) *what kind of ...?*
dono ...? (30) *which ...?*
doragonzu (202) (Chūnichi doragonzu) *Chūnichi dragons baseball team*
doraibu (114) (doraibu o shimasu) *go for a drive*
dorama (197) (hōmu dorama) *soap opera (lit. 'home drama')*
dore? (30) *which one/ones?*
dorobō (247) *robber*
Doron (11) *Delon*
dosei (215) *Saturn*
dotchi? (65) *in what direction?, where? (short form of* dochira*)*
dōyatte? (274) *in what way?*
doyōbi (114) *Saturday*
dōzo (28) *go ahead!, here you are*
dōzo yoroshiku (12) *please look kindly on me*

e (62) *to, towards*
e (92) *picture(s)*
ē (10) *yes (informal)*
eakon (140) *air conditioning*
earobikkusu (194) *aerobics*
Edo (23) *previous name of Tōkyō*
eiga (197) *movie(s)*
eigakan (116) *cinema*
eigo (117) *English language*
eigyōbu (52) *sales division*
eikoku (272) *Britain*
eki (54) *station*
-en (81) *yen*
enjinia (12) *engineer*
enka (197) *Japanese ballad*
enryo (229) *reserve, 'holding back'*
Erizabesu (4) *Elizabeth*
ēto ... (195) *erm ...*

famikon (211) *home computer (video) game*
firumu (88) *film (for a camera)*
fōdoa (98) *four-door (car)*
Fōrin (224) *Follin*
fuben (na) (89) *inconvenient*
fujinyōhin (94) *women's clothing*
-fun (106) *counter for minutes (also* -pun*)*
furansu (11) *France*
furansugo (208) *French language*
furansujin (11) *French person*
(o-)furo (26) *bath*
furui (89) *old*
furukute (198) *old and ... (see* furui*)*
furusato (146) *home (native home)*
fusuma (32) *sliding screen door*
futari (162) *two people*
futatsu (90) *two (objects)*
futatsume (no) (62) *the second (in a series)*
futon (32) *futon (mattress folded away during the day)*
futsuka (115) *2nd of the month*

305

futsū (132) (futsū densha) *ordinary (local) train*
fuyu (115) *winter*
fuyuyasumi (115) *winter holiday*

ga (30) *but*
ga (137) *particle indicating that the preceding word is subject of the sentence*
gaijin (47) *foreigner (see also* gaikokujin)
gaikoku (74) *abroad*
gaikokugo (272) *foreign language*
gaikokujin (74) *foreigner*
gakkō (36) *school*
gakubatsu (122) *alumni clique*
gakusei (12) *student, pupil*
gaman (200) *patience* (gaman shimasu) *be patient*
ganbarimasu, ganbaru (121) *try hard*
ganbatte (121) (ganbatte kudasai) *try hard! (see* ganbarimasu)
Ganjī (11) *Gandhi*
gasorin (56) *petrol* (gasorin sutando) *petrol station*
-gatsu (114) *counter for months*
gattsu (200) *guts, courage*
gēmu (203) *game (e.g. in baseball)*
genkan (26) *entrance area where shoes are taken off*
genki (na) (16) *well* (o-genki desu ka?) *how have you been?*
genmai (182) *brown (unhusked) rice*
getsuyōbi (114) *Monday*
ginkō (36) *bank*
ginkōin (12) *bank employee*
giri (210) *duty*
go (53) *five*
go (203) (nisshūkan go) *two weeks from now*
go- (35) *an 'honorific' which makes the following word more polite (if the word you're looking for isn't here, look it up under the first letter following* go-)
gochisōsama (deshita) (37) *I enjoyed the meal (lit. 'it was a feast')*
gogatsu (114) *May*
gogo (106) (gogo shichiji) *7 p.m.*
gohan (182) *(cooked) rice/meal*
gomen kudasai! (26) *anyone at home?, pardon me*
goro (106) (rokuji goro) *about 6 p.m.*
gorufā (12) *golfer,* (puro gorufā) *professional golfer*
gorufu (94) *golf*
gozaimashita (226) (arigatō gozaimashita) *thank you very much*
gozaimasu (16) (ohayō gozaimasu) *good morning (lit. 'it is early')*
gozaimasu (87) *very polite form of* arimasu (de gozaimasu) (52) *very polite form of* desu
gozen (106) (gozen hachiji) *8 a.m.*
-guchi (156) *entrance, exit*
Gurafu (11) *Graf*
gurai (116) (sanjikan gurai) *about three hours*
gurē (no) (83) *grey*
Gureggu (11) *Greg*
guriin (no) (83) *green*
Guriin (4) *Green*
guriinsha (136) *first-class compartment (lit. 'green car')*
gyūniku (187) *beef*

ha (240) *tooth*
hachi (53) *eight*
hachigatsu (114) *August*
hadaka (229) *naked*
haha (35) *(my) mother*
hai (10) *yes/'I hear you' (aizuchi)*
haikingu (197) *hiking*
hairimasu, hairu (247) *enter, go into*

hajimarimasu, hajimaru (115) *begin*
hajimemashite (4) *how do you do?*
hako (264) *box*
-haku (142) *counter for nights (also* -paku)
han (106) (goji han) *half past five*
hana (149) *nose*
hanashi (172) (hanashi o shimasu) *talk, speak*
hanashimasu, hanasu (172) *talk, speak*
hanbāgu (169) (hanbāgu sutēki) *hamburger steak*
handokuriimu (88) *handcream*
hansamu (na) (149) *handsome*
hantaigawa (56) *opposite*
happa (240) *leaf*
haragei (271) *'art of the belly'*
haru (115) *spring*
haruyasumi (115) *spring holiday*
(o-)hashi (29) *chopsticks*
hashigo (170) *ladder*
hatachi (120) *twenty years old*
hatsu (132) *departure*
hatsuka (115) *the 20th of the month*
hawai (237) *Hawaii*
hayai (199) *fast, early*
hē (72) *an 'aizuchi' expressing surprise*
hea burashi (88) *hairbrush*
Heian (18) *period of Japanese history (794–1192)*
Heisei (114) *name of the present emperor's 'era' (1989–) (*Heisei sannen) *3rd year of Emperor Heisei, i.e. 1991*
hen (na) (175) *strange*
heta (148) (tenisu ga heta desu) *I'm bad at tennis*
heya (141) *room*
hidari (62) *left (as opposed to right)*
higashi (154) *east*
hikemasu (209) *can play (see* hikimasu)
hiite (247) (sen o hiite) *draw a line! (see* hikimasu)
hikimasu, hiku (209) *play (a stringed musical instrument)*
hikimasu, hiku (247) *draw (a line)*
hiku (80) *minus*
hima (197) (hima na toki) *in your spare time*
hiragana (22) *Japanese script (used for writing words or parts of words for which there are no 'kanji')*
hirugohan (108) *lunch (lit. 'noon rice')*
hito (47) *person*
hitori (162) *one person*
hitotsu (90) *one (object)*
hitotsume (no) (62) *the first (in a series)*
hoēruzu (202) *Taiyō Whales baseball team*
hoka (no) (220) *other, another*
hokusei (154) *north-west*
hokutō (154) *north-east*
hōmen (136) *towards (towards Ōsaka – Ōsaka hōmen)*
hōmu dorama (197) *soap opera (lit. 'home drama')*
hon (89) *book*
honjitsu (184) *today (very polite)*
honne (171) *a person's genuine opinion (vs tatemae)*
hontō (72) (hontō ni) *really*
honya (87) *bookshop*
Hōpu (4) *Hope*
horā (197) (horā eiga) *horror film*
hōru (256) (NHK hōru) *the NHK hall in Tōkyō*
horumon (160) *hormone*
hōsekiya (87) *jeweller's*
hoshi (246) *star*
hoshii (274) (kuruma ga hoshii desu) *I want (to have) a car*

hoteru (141) *hotel*
hotondo (194) (hotondo ikimasen) *I hardly ever go*
hotto (164) *hot (as opposed to iced) coffee (short for* hotto kōhii)
Hōzurii (255) *Horsley*
hyaku (80) *100*
hyakuman (80) *1,000,000*
hyōjungo (19) *standard speech*

Ibu (7) *Yves*
ichi (53) *one (number)*
ichido (117) (mō ichido) *once more*
ichigatsu (114) *January*
ichiman (80) *10,000*
ichinichi (108) (ichinichi ni nikai) *twice a day*
ichioku (80) *100,000,000*
ichiryū (51) *first rank (e.g. company)*
ie (30) *house*
iemoto (207) *'headmaster' system of group organisation*
igirisu (11) *Britain*
igirisujin (4) *British person*
ii (17) *good*
iie (10) *no/don't mention it*
iimashita (174) *said (see* iimasu)
iimasu, iu (174) *say*
iimasu (21) (nan to iimasu ka?) *what's it called?*
ikaga (40) *how? (polite)* (... wa ikaga desu ka?) *how about some ...?/how do you like ...?*
ikanakatta (233) *didn't go (see* ikimasu)
ikanakereba (237) (motte ikanakereba narimasen) *have to take (see* motte ikimasu)
ikanakute (237) (motte ikanakute mo ii desu) *don't have to take (see* motte ikimasu)
ikebana (105) *art of flower arranging*
ikimashita (172) *went (see* ikimasu)
ikimashō (204) *let's go (see* ikimasu)
ikimasu, iku (108) *go*
ikitai (274) (ikitai desu) *want to go (see* ikimasu)
ikura? (85) *how much?*
ikutsu? (120) *how many? (o-ikutsu desu ka?) how old are you?*
ima (106) *now, at the moment*
imashita (173) *was, were (see* imasu)
imasu, iru (36) *am/is/are* (... -te/de imasu) *am/is/are ... -ing*
imōto (35) *(my) younger sister*
imōto-san (35) *(another person's) younger sister*
inaka (146) *countryside*
inakamono (146) *country bumpkin*
indo (11) *India*
irasshaimase (81) *welcome! (very polite)*
irasshaimasu (36) *is/are (very polite form of* imasu)
iremasu, ireru (233) *include, insert*
iro (83) *colour*
iroiro (172) *all sorts of things*
iru (36) *be (see* imasu)
issho (172) (Ueda-san to issho ni) *with Ueda-san*
isu (117) *chair*
itadakimasu (37) *bon appétit! (lit. 'I humbly receive this')*
itaria (83) *Italy*
itashimashite (28) (dō itashimashite) *don't mention it!*
itashimasu (21) (yoroshiku onegai itashimasu) *very polite form of* yoroshiku onegai shimasu
itsu? (173) *when?*
itsuka (115) *the 5th of the month*
itsumo (109) *usually*
itsutsu (90) *five (objects)*
itta (233) *went (see* ikimasu)

itte (62) (itte kudasai) *go! (see* ikimasu)
itte 'rasshai (37) *(lit.) go and come back!*
itte kimasu (37) *I'll be off! (lit. 'I'll go and come')*
iu (117) *say, call (see* iimasu) (... to iu) *called '...'*
iya (na) (17) *horrible*
iyaringu (94) *ear-ring(s)*
izakaya (188) *drinking place serving food*

ja arimasen (12) *am not, is not, are not (negative of* desu)
ja/jā (37) *well, then*
jaiantsu (202) (Yomiuri jaiantsu) *Yomiuri Giants baseball team*
jamu (81) *jam*
jazu (197) *jazz*
-ji (106) *o'clock*
-jikan (116) (nijikan) *for two hours*
jiko (21) (jiko shōkai) *self-introduction*
-jin (11) *person from (name of a country)*
jinja (54) *shrine*
jinjibu (52) *personnel division*
jisho (117) *dictionary*
jitensha (116) *bicycle*
jiyūseki (136) *unreserved seat*
jogingu (197) *jogging (jogingu o shimasu) jog*
jōmu (67) *managing director*
Jon (5) *John*
jōyō (104) (jōyō kanji) *general use 'kanji'*
(o-)jōzu (148) (tenisu ga jōzu desu) *I'm good at tennis*
jugyō (121) *lesson*
jū (80) *ten*
jūdō (155) *a Japanese martial art*
jūgatsu (114) *October*
jūichigatsu (114) *November*
juku (108) *cram school*
jūman (80) *100,000*
jūnigatsu (114) *December*
(go-)jūsho (55) *address*
jūsu (41) *fruit juice*

ka (10) *particle indicating that the sentence is a question*
kachō (66) *section chief*
kachimashita (202) *won (see* kachimasu)
kachimasu, katsu (202) *win*
kado (62) *corner, turning*
kādo (6) *card*
kaerimashita (172) *went/came back (see* kaerimasu)
kaerimasu, kaeru (108) *go/come back*
kagami (243) *mirror*
(o-)kaidokuhin (81) *special offer*
(o-)kaikei (184) *bill*
kaimashita (185) *bought (see* kaimasu)
kaimasu, kau (185) *buy*
kaimono (114) *shopping (kaimono o shimasu) go shopping*
kaiseki (ryōri) (182) *Japanese food as served at expensive restaurants*
kaishain (12) *company employee*
kaisha (36) *company*
kaisoku (132) *type of train*
kaitai (274) (kaitai desu) *want to buy (see* kaimasu)
kakarimashita (269) *took (time) (see* kakarimasu)
kakarimasu, kakaru (116) (nijikan kakarimasu) *it takes two hours*
kakejiku (29) *hanging scroll*
kakemasu (209) *can write, draw, paint (see* kakimasu)
kakimasu, kaku (209) *write, draw, paint*
kamera (89) *camera*
kami-sama (88) *god*

kaminoke (149) *hair*
-kan (145) *(following an expression of time)* for ... *(that period)*
kana (22) *the Japanese sound-related syllabaries*
kanada (11) *Canada*
kanai (35) *(my) wife*
kanashii (166) *sad*
(o-)kane (185) *money*
kangaete (178) *(kangaete imasu) I am thinking about it (see* kangaemasu*)*
kangaemasu, kangaeru (178) *think*
kanji (18) *Chinese characters used in written Japanese*
kankei (187) *relations, relationship*
kankoku (11) *South Korea*
kanojo (172) *she*
kanpai! (166) *cheers!*
kantan (na) (89) *easy*
kāpu (202) *(Hiroshima kāpu) Hiroshima Carp baseball team*
kara (10) *from*
kara (198) *because*
karada (272) *body*
karaoke (178) *music with vocal part removed for singing along*
kare (185) *he*
karēraisu (6) *curried rice*
Kāru (7) *Carl*
karui (89) *light*
kasei (215) *Mars*
kashikomarimashita (220) *very polite equivalent of* wakarimashita
kashimasu, kasu (222) *lend*
kata (40) *shoulder*
katakana (22) *Japanese script used mainly for foreign words*
katamichi (134) *one way (ticket)*
katta (40) *won (see* kachimasu*)*
kawa (75) *river*
kawaii (29) *pretty, cute*
(o-)kawari (37) *second helping*
kayōbi (114) *Tuesday*
(go-)kazoku (35) *family*
keiei (50) *management*
keiretsu (78) *group of companies linked in production, marketing and finance*
keiribu (52) *accounting division*
keisatsu (176) *police (station)*
kēki (6) *cake(s)*
kekkō desu (64) *all right, fine, I've had enough!*
kekkon (144) *marriage (kekkon shite imasu) I'm married*
kekkonshiki (236) *wedding*
kendō (155) *martial art using bamboo 'swords'*
kenka (181) *argument, fight*
keredo (184) *but (very polite)*
kesa (169) *this morning*
keshimasu, kesu (222) *switch off, extinguish*
keshite (223) *(keshite mo ii desu ka?) may I switch off ...? (see* keshimasu*)*
keshōhin (94) *cosmetics*
ki (75) *tree*
ki (225) *(ki o tsukete) take care!*
kiiro (83), kiiroi (84) *yellow*
kikimasu, kiku (110) *listen to, hear*
kimashita (173) *came (see* kimasu*)*
kimasu, kiru (233) *wear*
kimasu, kuru (irr.) (37) *come*
kimi (69) *you (very familiar)*
kin'enseki (136) *no-smoking seat*
kinō (168) *yesterday*

kinsei (215) *Venus*
kinyōbi (114) *Friday*
kirai (148) *(kēki ga kirai desu) I dislike cake*
kirei (na) (29) *pretty, beautiful, clean*
kirimasu, kiru (233) *cut*
kissaten (87) *coffee shop*
kisu (222) *kiss (kisu o shimasu) to kiss*
kita (154) *north*
kitamuki (240) *facing north*
kitanai (199) *dirty*
kite (40) *come!*
kitte (247) *(kitte kudasai) please cut! (see* kirimasu*)*
-ko (81) *counter for small objects*
ko (47) *child*
kōban (54) *police box*
kōcha (41) *black tea*
kochira (65) *in this direction, this/here (polite)*
kochira koso (60) *for my part, too*
kodomo(-san) (36) *child(ren)*
kogaisha (50) *subsidiary (lit. 'child company')*
kōhii (6) *coffee*
kōhōbu (52) *public relations department*
koko (30) *here*
kōkoku (81) *printed advertisement(s)*
kokonoka (115) *the 9th of the month*
kokonotsu (90) *nine (objects)*
kōkō (112) *short form for* kōtōgakkō: *senior high school*
kōkōsei (34) *senior high school pupil (16–18)*
kokugo (272) *national language, i.e. Japanese*
kokunai (74) *within a country, domestic*
kokusaibu (52) *international department*
kokusaika (267) *internationalisation*
(o-)kome (186) *uncooked rice*
komedii (197) *comedy*
komeya (186) *rice merchant's*
kōmuin (12) *civil servant*
konban wa (16) *hello (in the evening), good evening*
kondo (204) *(mata kondo) some other time!*
kongetsu (168) *this month*
konna (199) *this kind of*
konnichi wa (16) *hello (from 10/11 a.m. to dusk)*
kono ... (30) *this ... these ...*
konpyūta (6) *computer*
konsāto (205) *concert*
konshū (168) *this week*
koppu (30) *glass*
kore (28) *this (one), these (ones)*
kōshū (95) *(kōshū denwa) public telephone*
koso (60) *(kochira koso) for my part, too*
kotatsu (28) *low table with heater underneath*
kotchi (65) *in this direction (short form of* kochira*)*
kōto (82) *coat*
kōtōgakkō (112) *senior high school*
kotoshi (168) *this year*
kowai (166) *frightening*
kowakatta (172) *was frightening (see* kowai*)*
kowashimasu, kowasu (242) *break*
ku (53) *nine*
-ku (55) *ward (in Tōkyō and other big cities)*
kudasai (26) *please (give me)*
kudasaimase (184) *very polite form of* kudasai: *please*
kugatsu (114) *September*
kumiai (50) *(rōdō kumiai) trade union*
kumo (240) *spider*

-kun (16) *familiar term for men younger than the speaker*
kuni (11) *country*
kurabu (94) *club*
kurashikku (197) *classical music*
kurisumasu (6) *Christmas*
kuro (83), kuroi (84) *black*
kurofune (150) *the 'black ships' of Commodore Perry*
kuruma (116) *car*
kusuriya (87) *chemist's, pharmacy*
kutsu (82) *shoe(s)*
kutsushita (82) *socks*
kutsuya (89) *shoe shop*
kyabetsu (81) *cabbage*
(o-)kyaku(-san/-sama) (88) *customer, client, guest*
kyō (60) *today*
(go-)kyōdai (36) *brothers and sisters*
kyōiku (104) (kyōiku kanji) *the 960 or so Chinese characters taught at elementary school (lit. 'education kanji')*
kyonen (168) *last year*
kyū (53) *nine*
kyūdō (197) *archery*
kyūjitsu (214) *official rest day*
kyūkō (132) *express train*
kyūri (90) *cucumber*

machimasu, matsu (60) *wait*
mada (148) *still*
made (64) *as far as, until*
mado (117) *window*
mae (56) *in front of*
maemuki (178) (maemuki ni) *positively*
mafurā (237) *scarf*
magarimasu, magaru (62) *turn*
magatte (62) (magatte kudasai) *turn! (see* magarimasu)
-mai (81) *counter for flat things*
mainen (195) *every year*
mainichi (195) *every day*
maishū (195) *every week*
maitoshi (195) *every year*
maitsuki (195) *every month*
mājan (208) *mahjong*
makaroni (204) (makaroni uesutan) *spaghetti western*
māketingubu (52) *marketing department*
Makudonarudo (205) *McDonald's*
makkuro (177) *completely black*
(o-)mamori (246) *lucky charm*
(o-)manjū (264) *doughy dumplings (often with bean paste inside)*
manshon (99) *block of flats (from English: 'mansion')*
maru (100) *zero, circle*
Marukusu (7) *Marx*
-masen (12) *present polite negative verb ending*
-masen deshita (172) *past polite negative verb ending*
-mashita (172) *past polite verb ending*
-mashō (204) *polite verb ending (meaning 'let's ...!') (-mashō ka?) shall we ...?*
massugu (62) *straight on*
-masu (108) *present polite verb ending*
masukara (94) *mascara*
mata (203) *again* (mata kondo) *some other time!*
matcha (206) *green tea used in tea ceremony*
(o-)matsuri (192) *festival*
matte (60) (matte kudasai) *wait! (see* machimasu)
Meiji (18) *name of a Japanese emperor and era (1868–1912)*
meishi (66) *namecard*
Meriru (7) *Meryl*

meron (90) *melon*
(o-)meshiagari (184) (kochira de o-meshiagari deshō ka?) *will you eat here? (very polite)*
midori (no) (83) *green*
migi (62) *right*
migigawa (256) *right hand side*
mijikai (89) *short*
mikan (90) *mandarin orange*
mikka (115) *the 3rd of the month*
mikkusu (162) (mikkusu sando) *assorted sandwiches*
(o-)mikuji (243) *Japanese kind of fortune telling*
(o-)mimai (219) *present given to someone in hospital*
mimashita (172) *saw (see* mimasu)
mimasu, miru (110) *see, look at, watch*
minai (235) *doesn't/won't see (see* mimasu)
minami (154) *south*
minshuku (138) *bed and breakfast*
minyō (209) *traditional Japanese folk song*
misemasu, miseru (91) *show*
misete (91) (misete kudasai) *show me!*
miso (37) *fermented soya bean paste*
mite (222) *look! (see* mimasu)
mitsu (40) *honey*
mitsukete (180) (mitsukete kudasai) *please find*
mittsu (40) *three (objects)*
mittsume (no) (62) *the third (in a series)*
(o-)miyage (137) *souvenir*
mizu (170) *water*
mizugi (237) *swimsuit*
mo (5) *too, as well*
mō (117) *more (mō ichido) once more (mō ippon) one more bottle*
mō (145) *already (mō nishūkan) two weeks up to now (mō kekkō desu) I've already had enough*
(o-)mochi (182) *rice cake*
(o-)mochikaeri (184) *eat out, take away*
mochimasu, motsu (174) *have, hold*
modan (146) *modern*
moderu (12) *fashion model*
mokusei (215) *Jupiter*
mokuyōbi (114) *Thursday*
momiji (14) *maple tree*
monbushō (118) *Ministry of Education*
mōningu setto (162) *set breakfast*
mono (224) *thing*
moraimashita (172) *received (see* moraimasu)
moraimasu, morau (172) *receive*
moshi moshi (52) *hello (on the telephone)*
moshi (247) *if*
mōshimasu (21) (... to mōshimasu) *I am called ... (polite)*
motte (174) (motte imasu) *hold, have (see* mochimasu) (motte ikimasu) *take (lit. 'go holding') (motte kimasu) bring (lit. 'come holding')*
motto (220) *more*
muika (115) *the 6th of the month*
murasaki (no) (83) *purple*
mushiatsui (17) *hot and humid*
musuko (34) *(my) son*
musuko-san (34) *(another person's) son*
musume (34) *(my) daughter*
musume-san (34) *(another person's) daughter*
muttsu (90) *six (objects)*
muzukashii (34) *difficult*

na (17) *word following some adjectives before a noun*
nagai (89) *long*

nagemasu, nage**ru** (241) *throw*
-nai (235) *present plain negative verb ending*
naka (74) *middle, inside*
-nakatta (235) *past plain negative verb ending*
-nakereba (236) (-nakereba narimasen) *must . . .*
nakōdo (105) *go-between*
nakunarimashita (181) *was lost (see nakunarimasu)*
nakunarimasu, nakuna**ru** (174) *be lost, get lost*
-nakute (236) (-nakute mo ii desu) *it's all right not to . . .*
nama (187) (nama biiru) *'live' beer*
(o-)namae (69) *name*
nan? (28) *what?* (nan desu ka?) *what is it?* (with counter: nan . . . desu ka?) *what quantity of . . .?*
nan de? (116) *how?* (i.e. by what means of transport?)
nana (53) *seven*
nanatsu (90) *seven (objects)*
nanban? (53) *what number?*
nanbansen? (136) *what platform?* (lit. 'what number track?')
nangai? (94) *what floor?*
nangatsu? (114) *what month?*
nani? (83) *what?*
nani ka (173) *something*
nani'iro? (83) *what colour?*
nanji? (106) *what time?*
nankai? (94) *what floor?*
nankai? (195) *how many times?*
nanmei(-sama)? (162) *how many people?* (very polite)
nannen? (114) *what year?*
nannichi? (115) *what day (i.e. date)?*
nannin? (162) *how many people?*
nanoka (115) *the 7th of the month*
nanpaku? (143) *how many nights?*
nansai? (120) *how old?*
nansei (154) *south-west*
nantō (154) *south-east*
nanyōbi? (114) *what day of the week?*
narimashitara (184) (o-kimari ni narimashitara) *if you have decided*
narimasu, na**ru** (236) *become*
narimasen (236) (-nakereba narimasen) *must . . .*
naritaku (274) (naritaku arimasen) *don't want to become (see narimasu)*
nasaimasu (184) (nani ni nasaimasu ka?) *what would you like? (very polite)*
natsu (40) *summer*
natsuyasumi (115) *summer holiday*
nattsu (40) *nuts*
naze? (198) *why?*
ne (16) *. . . isn't it? (exclamation)*
nē (195) (sō desu nē . . .) *erm . . ., let me think . . .*
nekkuresu (94) *necklace*
neko (242) *cat*
nekutai (82) *tie*
nemashita (174) *slept, went to bed/sleep (see nemasu)*
nemasu, ne**ru** (108) *sleep, go to bed/sleep*
nen (195) (nen ni sankai) *three times a year*
-nen (114) *counter for years*
neru (108) *sleep, go to bed/sleep (see nemasu)*
nete (111) (nete imasu) *she is sleeping*
ni (53) *two*
ni (36) *in, at (a place)*
-nichi (114) *counter for dates*
nichiyōbi (114) *Sunday*
nigatsu (114) *February*
nigemashita (181) *escaped (see nigemasu)*

nigemasu, nige**ru** (181) *escape*
nigiyaka (na) (146) *lively, exciting*
nihon (11) *Japan*
nihongo (18) *Japanese language*
nihonjin (5) *Japanese person*
nihonjinron (14) *'learned' discussions about the Japanese*
nihonkai (155) *Japan Sea*
nihonshu (182) *'sake', rice wine*
nijikai (170) *second party (in 'ladder drinking sessions')*
nijūyokka (115) *the 24th of the month*
-nin (162) *counter for people*
niku (186) *meat*
nikuya (186) *butcher's*
ninjin (90) *carrot*
ninjō (210) *spontaneity, empathy, humaneness*
nioi (28) *smell*
nippon (23) *Japan (formal)*
niryū (51) *second rank (e.g. company)*
nishi (154) *west*
nishiai (203) *two games (see -shiai)*
nishūkan (145) *for two weeks*
niwaijiri (197) *gardening*
no (12) *of*
nomi (205) (nomi ni ikimasu) *to go out for a drink*
nomimasen (234) (nomimasen deshita) *didn't drink*
nomimashita (169) *drank (see nomimasu)*
nomimasu, no**mu** (110) *drink*
nomimono (164) *drinks*
nonda (233) *drank (see nomimasu)*
nonde (175) (nonde imashita) *were drinking (see nomimasu)*
Nōman (11) *Norman*
noren (188) *curtains at entrance to many small restaurants*
nōto (117) *notebook*
nuketa (240) (nuketa ha) *a tooth which has come out*
nurimasu, nu**ru** (247) *colour in*
nutte (247) (kuro ni nutte kudasai) *colour it black!*
nyūjiirando (11) *New Zealand*
Nyūman (7) *Newman*
nyūsu (197) *news*
Nyū Yōku (10) *New York*

o (90) *particle indicating that the preceding word is the object of the sentence*
o- (35) *an 'honorific' which makes the following word more polite (if the word you're looking for isn't below, look up under the letter following o-)*
o-bā-san (185) *old woman, grandmother*
o-cha (41) *green tea*
o-chaya (186) *tea merchant's*
ōeru (12) *OL, 'office lady' (female office worker)*
ōfuku (134) *return (ticket)*
ohayō (gozaimasu) (16) *(good) morning!*
ohiru (205) *lunch (lit. noon)*
oishi-sō (166) *looks delicious*
oishii (29) *delicious*
oishikatta (166) *was delicious (see oishii)*
ojama shimasu (40) *lit. 'I'm disturbing you' (said when entering a home)*
o-jii-san (185) *old man, grandfather*
o-jō-san (34) *(another person's) daughter*
okaerinasai (37) *welcome back!*
okagesama de (16) *fine, thank you (lit. 'thanks to you')*
okake kudasai (40) *please sit down*
okanjō (166) *bill, check*
o-kā-san (35) *mother*

ōkii (30) *big*
o-kimari (184) (o-kimari ni narimashitara) *if you have decided*
okimasen (110) *doesn't/don't wake up* (*see* okimasu)
okimashita (172) *got up* (*see* okimasu)
okimasu, **okiru** (108) *get up*
oku-san (35) (*another person's*) *wife*
o-machi (52) (shōshō o-machi kudasai) *wait a moment, please* (*very polite*)
omoi (89) *heavy*
omoshiroi (29) *interesting, funny*
omoshirokatta (166) *was interesting* (*see* omoshiroi)
onegai shimasu (12) *please* (*lit. 'I ask a favour'*) (yoroshiku onegai shimasu) *please look kindly on me*
o-nē-san (35) (*another person's*) *older sister*
ongaku (197) *music*
o-nii-san (35) (*another person's*) *older brother*
onna (47) *female, woman*
onsen (139) *hot spring*
ore (5) *I* (*men's Japanese: informal*)
orenji (no) (83) *orange*
Oriento (141) (Oriento hoteru) *Orient hotel*
oshibori (30) *wet handtowel*
oshiemasu, **oshieru** (222) *tell, teach*
osoi (199) *late, slow*
osoku (225) (osoku made) *until late*
Ōsutoraria (11) *Australia*
oto (175) *noise*
o-todoke (184) (o-todoke ni agarimasu) *I will deliver it* (*very polite*)
otoko (47) *male, man*
o-tō-san (35) (*another person's*) *father*
otōto (35) (*my*) *younger brother*
ototoi (168) *the day before yesterday*
otōto-san (35) (*another person's*) *younger brother*
ototoshi (168) *the year before last*
otsukaresama deshita (76) *'you must be tired!', 'well done for working hard'*
otto (35) (*my*) *husband*
owarimasu, **owaru** (115) *end, finish*
oyakata (207) *'father' figure in sumō, yakuza, etc.*
oyasuminasai (16) *good night* (*lit. 'please rest'*)
oyogimasen (194) *don't/doesn't swim* (*see* oyogimasu)
oyogimasu, **oyogu** (194) *swim*

pachinko (160) *Japanese-style* (*upright*) *pinball*
painappuru (81) *pineapple*
paipu (235) *pipe*
-paku (142) *counter for night(s)* (*also* -haku)
pansuto (82) *panty hose*
pantsu (82) *underpants, panties*
pariigu (202) *Pacific baseball league*
pasokon (29) *personal computer*
pen (222) *pen*
Pere (11) *Pele*
piinatsu (137) *peanuts*
pinku (no) (83) *pink*
piza (81) *pizza*
poppusu (197) *pop* (*music*)
Pōru (7) *Paul*
poteto (41) (poteto chippu(su)) *potato crisps*
-pun (106) *counter for minutes* (*also* -fun)
puran (185) *plan*
purēyā (94) (shiidii purēyā) *CD player*
purezento (220) *present*
puro (12) *pro, professional*
puropōzu (185) (puropōzu o shimashita) *proposed* (*marriage*)

pūru (6) (*swimming*) *pool*
rabusutōrii (197) *love story*
raigetsu (202) *next month*
rainen (202) *next year*
raion (255) *lion*
raishū (202) *next week*
raisu (7) *cooked rice, served on a plate, Western-style* (karēraisu) *curry and rice*
rajio (89) *radio*
raketto (94) (tenisu raketto) *tennis racket*
rāmen (160) *a kind of Chinese noodle*
rāmenya (188) *rāmen shop*
Rēgan (7) *Reagan*
reikyūsha (240) *hearse*
remon (162) *lemon*
Renon (5) *Lennon*
repōtā (5) (*TV or radio*) *reporter*
resutoran (60) *restaurant*
retasu (90) *lettuce*
Ringo (7) *Ringo*
ringo (90) *apple*
rinsu (88) (*hair*) *conditioner*
rippukuriimu (88) *lipsalve*
Robāto (4) *Robert*
robii (255) *lobby*
rōdō kumiai (50) *trade union*
rokku (148) *rock* (*music*)
roku (53) *six*
rokugatsu (114) *June*
rōmaji (22) *Roman script*
Ronarudo (7) *Ronald*
Rondon (10) *London*
rōnin (112) (*formerly*) *masterless samurai;* (*now*) *resitting university applicant*
Rōran (7) *Laurent*
rotenburo (263) *outside hot spring pool*
Ruisu (7) *Lewis*
ryokan (138) *Japanese inn*
ryōri (197) *cooking* (ryōri o shimasu) *cook*
(go-)ryōshin (36) *parents*
ryōshūsho (64) *written receipt*

sabishii (146) *lonely*
sadō (105) *Japanese tea ceremony*
-sai (120) *counter for 'years old'*
saijitsu (214) *national holiday*
saizu (184) *size* (*of clothes*)
sakana (37) *fish*
sakanaya (186) *fishmonger's*
sakaya (186) *liquor store*
sakazuki (178) *sake cup*
(o-)sake (148) *alcohol, Japanese sake*
saki (62) *just after*
saki'ika (137) *dried squid*
sakoku (150) *closed country*
sakura (14) *cherry blossom*
-sama (88) *honorific making the preceding word more polite*
samui (17) *cold*
-san (10) *honorific making the preceding word more polite, Mr/Mrs/Miss/Ms*
san (53) *three*
sandaru (237) *sandals*
sando (162) *sandwich* (*short form of* sandoitchi)
sandoitchi (137) *sandwich*
sangatsu (114) *March*

Sanjitto (11) *Sanjit*
sankaku (247) *triangle*
sankuriimu (237) *suncream*
sanpo (197) (sanpo o shimasu) *go for a walk*
sanryū (51) *third rank (e.g. company)*
(o-)sara (30) *plate*
sarada (81) *salad*
saraigetsu (202) *the month after next*
sarainen (202) *the year after next*
saraishū (202) *the week after next*
sarariiman (58) *white-collar worker*
sashimi (87) *raw fish*
sasupendā (82) *braces*
sasupensu (197) (sasupensu eiga) *suspense movie*
sawarimasu, sawaru (242) *touch*
sayōnara (76) *goodbye*
se (149) (se ga takai) *tall*
(o-)seibo (218) *end of year gift, gift-giving season*
seijin (214) (seijin no hi) *coming of age day (15 January)*
seinengappi (127) *date of birth*
seishin (200) *spirit*
seiza (229) (seiza o shimasu) *kneel formally*
(o-)senbei (41) *rice cracker*
senbetsu (219) *going-away present*
sengetsu (168) *last month*
sensei (12) *teacher*
sensengetsu (168) *the month before last*
sensenshū (168) *the week before last*
senshū (168) *last week*
sensu (221) *fan*
sentaku (114) *laundry (sentaku o shimasu) do the washing*
sentō (46) *public bath*
seriigu (202) *Central baseball league*
sērusuman (145) *salesman*
sētā (82) *sweater*
settai (170) *business entertainment*
setto (162) (mōningu setto) *set breakfast*
shachō (67) *company head/chairman of board of directors*
shain (50) *employee*
shakai (50) *society*
shakaijin (70) *working member of society (lit. 'society person')*
shamisen (206) *a Japanese stringed instrument*
shanpū (88) *shampoo*
shashin (34) *photograph*
shatsu (82) *shirt*
shawā (140) *shower*
shi (53) *four*
-shiai (203) *counter for number of games*
shiawase (na) (269) *happy*
shibaraku (16) (shibaraku desu ne) *it's been a long time!*
shichi (53) *seven*
shichigatsu (114) *July*
shichi-go-san (34) (lit.) *'7-5-3': a special day for children aged 7, 5 and 3*
shichū (6) (biifu shichū) *beef stew*
shigatsu (114) *April*
(o-)shigoto (12) *work, job*
shigotoba (121) *place of work*
shiidii (94) *CD (shiidii purēyā) CD player*
shijō (50) *industries and markets*
shikaku (213) *square*
shikashi (174) *but*
shimaguni (2) *island country*
shimasen (121) *doesn't/don't do (see shimasu)*

shimashita (172) *did (see shimasu)*
shimashō (204) *let's do (see shimasu)*
shimasu, suru (irr.) (12) *make, do (… ni shimasu) I'll have …*
shimemasu, shimeru (222) *shut*
shinbō (200) *perseverance*
shinbun (110) *newspaper*
shingō (62) *signals, traffic lights*
shinguru (140) *single (room)*
shinjimasu, shinjiru (246) *believe (in …)*
shinjinrui (259) *'new species of humanity' (a media term for the young generation)*
shinkansen (131) *super-express 'bullet' train*
shinpuru (na) (269) *simple*
shinsen (na) (81) *fresh*
shinshiyōhin (94) *menswear*
shintō (238) *'indigenous' Japanese religion*
shiro (83), shiroi (84) *white*
shiru (37) (miso shiru) *'miso' soup*
shita (264) *under, below*
shitai desu (142) *want to do/make (see shimasu)*
shite (40) (shite imasu) *am /are/is doing (see shimasu)*
shiteiseki (136) *reserved seat*
shitsurei (12) *rude(ness) (shitsurei shimasu) (12) excuse me; (52) goodbye*
shitte (40) *knowing*
shizuka (na) (199) *quiet*
shōbai (170) (mizu shōbai) *entertainment business (lit. 'water trade')*
shodō (206) *calligraphy*
shōgakkō (112) *elementary school (6–11)*
shōgaku (119) (shōgaku ichinensei) *first-year elementary school pupil*
shōgakusei (126) *elementary school pupil*
shōgatsu (138) *New Year, January*
shōgi (208) *Chinese 'chess'*
shōji (29) *wood and paper sliding door*
shōkai (21) (jiko shōkai) *self-introduction*
shokuji (169) *meal (shokuji o shimasu) eat a meal, eat out*
shokuryōhin (94) *foodstuffs*
shoppu (160) (kōhii shoppu) *coffee shop*
shōshō (52) (shōshō o-machi kudasai) *wait a moment, please (very polite)*
shōtengai (87) *shopping street*
Shōwa (114) *name of the previous emperor's era (1925–1989)* (shōwa ninen) *2nd year of Emperor Shōwa (i.e. 1926)*
shū (195) (shū ni yonkai) *four times a week*
shufu (12) *housewife*
'(go-)shujin (35) *husband*
shuppatsu (132) *departure*
sō (10) (sō desu) *that's right (ā, sō desu ka) oh, really*
-sō (166) (oishi-sō) *looks delicious*
soba (56) *very near*
soba (160) *buckwheat noodles*
sobaya (188) *soba shop*
sochira (65) *in that direction, that/there (polite)*
sofā (6) *sofa*
sōji (114) *cleaning (sōji o shimasu) do the cleaning*
soko (30) *there*
sōmubu (52) *administration division*
sonna (198) *that kind of*
sono … (30) *that …*
sorariumu (194) *solarium*
sore (28) *that (one), those (ones)*
soretomo (184) *or (formal)*

soro soro (225) (soro soro shitsurei shimasu) *'gradually I must be leaving', it's time to go*
soshite (121) *and*
soto (27) *outside*
sotchi (65) *in that direction (short form of* sochira)
subarashii (29) *wonderful*
sugoi (29) *amazing*
sugoku (165) *very, really (informal)*
sugu (175) *immediately, at once*
suika (90) *watermelon*
suimasu, su**u** (222) *inhale* (tabako o suimasu) *smoke a cigarette*
suisei (215) *Mercury*
suiyōbi (114) *Wednesday*
sukasshu (197) *squash*
sukāto (82) *skirt*
suki (148) (sushi ga suki desu) *I like sushi*
sukii (94) *ski(s), skiing*
sukoshi (117) *a little*
(o-)sumai (69) (o-sumai wa dochira desu ka?) *where do you live?*
sumāto (na) (149) *slim*
sumi-e (92) *ink painting*
sumimasen (30) *excuse me* ((dōmo) sumimasen (12)) *sorry/thank you*
sumimasu, sum**u** (121) *live (in a particular place)*
Sumisu (7) *Smith*
sumō (148) *sumō, Japanese wrestling*
sunakku (188) *(often expensive) type of bar*
sunde (121) (Tōkyō ni sunde imasu) *I live in Tokyo (see* sumimasu)
suniikā (82) *sneaker(s)*
sūpā (36) *supermarket*
supeingo (208) *Spanish language*
supiido (98) *speed*
supōtsu (94) *sport*
supōtsuyōhin (94) *sportswear*
surippa (82) *slipper*
(o-)sushi (6) *sushi (raw fish on bite-sized lumps of rice)*
sushiya (188) *sushi restaurant*
sutairingu rōshon (88) *styling lotion (for hair)*
sutairu (149) (sutairu ga ii) *has a good figure*
sutando (56) (gasorin sutando) *petrol station*
Sutā (7) *Starr*
Sutefi (11) *Steffi*
suteki (na) (29) *great*
sutēki (169) *steak*
sutemasu, sute**ru** (247) *throw away*
sutete (247) (sutete kudasai) *throw (it) away!*
Sutoraisando (7) *Streisand*
Sutoriipu (7) *Streep*
sūtsu (82) *suit*
suwarimasu, suwa**ru** (222) *sit*
suwarōzu (202) *Yakult Swallows baseball team*
suzushii (17) *cool*
tabako (148) *cigarette*
tabe (204) (tabe ni ikimasu) *go and eat*
tabemasen (234) *don't/doesn't eat (see* tabemasu)
tabemashita (169) *ate (see* tabemasu)
tabemasu, tabe**ru** (108) *eat*
tabemono (240) *thing(s) to eat*
tabetai (274) (tabetai desu) *want to eat (see* tabemasu)
tabete (111) (tabete imasu) *am/are/is eating (see* tabemasu)
tachimasu, tatsu (241) *stand up*
tadaima (37) *I'm back! (lit. 'just now (I've returned)')*
tai (202) (go tai ichi) *5 to 1 (baseball score)*
taigāsu (202) (Hanshin taigāsu) *Hanshin tigers baseball team*

taihen (na) (121) (taihen desu) *it's hard!*
tai'iku (214) *physical education*
taisetsu (na) (174) *important*
taisō (108) *gymnastics* (taisō o shimasu) *do gymnastics*
takai (89) *expensive, high* (se ga takai (149)) *tall*
takaku (149) (se ga takaku arimasen) *isn't tall*
take (185) *bamboo*
takushii (6) *taxi*
tamanegi (90) *onion*
Tānā (11) *Turner*
tandai (112) *short form of* tanki daigaku: *junior college*
tanjōbi (172) *birthday*
tanki (112) (tanki daigaku) *junior college*
tanoshii (166) *enjoyable*
tanoshikatta (172) *was enjoyable (see* tanoshii)
tasu (80) *plus*
tatemae (171) *public (insincere) opinion (vs* honne)
tatami (26) *mats laid into the floor in Japanese-style rooms*
tatemasu, tate**ru** (241) *stand (something) up*
te (175) *hand*
tēburu (117) *table*
tekisuto (34) *textbook*
temae (62) *just before*
tenisu (94) *tennis* (tenisu o shimasu) *play tennis*
tenki (17) *weather*
tennō (214) *emperor*
(o-)tera (54) *temple*
Tērā (11) *Taylor*
terebi (29) *TV (set)*
tii (162) (remon tii) *lemon tea*
tisshu (88) *paper tissue*
to (21) *if, when, particle signifying indirect speech*
to (83) *and*
tō (90) *ten (objects)*
tōchaku (132) *arrival*
(o-)toire (28) *toilet*
toka (197) (rokku toka jazu ...) *rock, jazz, and so on ...*
tōka (115) *the 10th of the month*
tokei (221) *watch*
toki (181) (sono toki) *at that time*
tokidoki (194) *sometimes*
tokkyū (132) *limited express train*
tokonoma (28) *wall alcove, often adorned with a hanging scroll*
tomarimashita (268) *stayed, spent the night (see* tomarimasu)
tomarimasu, toma**ru** (268) *stay, spend the night*
tomatosōsu (81) *tomato sauce*
tomemasu, tome**ru** (62) *stop*
tomete (62) (tomete kudasai) *stop!*
tomodachi (172) *friend*
tonari (56) *next to*
tori (246) *bird*
torii (248) *gateway to a shrine*
torimashita (181) *took away (see* torimasu)
torimasu, to**ru** (181) *take away*
toriniku (187) *chicken*
torishimariyaku (66) *director (of a company)*
tōsutā (94) *toaster*
tōsuto (162) *toast*
totemo (28) *very*
tsuchi (215) *earth, ground*
tsugi (no) (62) *next*
tsugō (204) (tsugō ga warui) *conditions are bad (for meeting)*
tsuin (140) *twin (hotel room)*
tsuitachi (115) *the 1st of the month*

tsukemasu, tsukeru (222) *switch on*
tsukemono (87) *pickles*
tsukete (225) (ki o tsukete kudasai) *take care!, safe journey!*
tsuki (185) *moon, month* (tsuki ni ikkai) *once a month*
tsukue (117) *desk*
tsuma (35) *(my) wife*
(o-)tsumami (41) *snack accompanying alcohol*
tsumaranai (166) *boring, trifling* (tsumaranai mono desu ga ...) *this (present) is just a trifle, but ...*
tsumaranakatta (166) *was boring*
tsume (240) *toenail(s)*
tsunakan (81) *canned tuna*
(o-)tsutome (69) *place of employment* (o-tsutome wa dochira desu ka?) *where do you work?*
tsutomemasu, tsutomeru (121) *be employed*
tsutomete (121) (sūpā ni tsutomete imasu) *I work at/for a supermarket*
tsutsumimasu, tsutsumu (233) *wrap up*
tsuyu (14) *rainy season*

uchi (27) *house, inside* (uchi no Ueda (67)) *Ueda from inside (my company)*
udon (160) *a kind of noodle*
udonya (188) *udon shop*
ue (264) *above, on*
uesutan (204) (makaroni uesutan) *spaghetti western*
Uinsuton (7) *Winston*
Uiriamu (255) *William*
uisukii (175) *whisky*
umi (235) *sea*
uriba (94) *department (in a store)*
urusai (199) *noisy*
ushiro (56) *behind*
utaimasu, utau (209) *sing*
utaemasu (209) *can sing (see utaimasu)*

wa (5) *particle spotlighting the previous word – can be translated as 'regarding ...', 'as for ...'*
wagashi (29) *Japanese sweets*
wakai (149) *young*
wakarimashita (60) *I see, I understand (lit. 'I have understood' – see wakarimasu)*
wakarimasu, wakaru (60) *understand, know*
wanpiisu (82) *dress*
warui (176) *bad*
washitsu (140) *Japanese-style room*
watakushi (5) *I (formal)*
watashi (5) *I*
watashimashita (180) *passed (see watashimasu)*
watashimasu, watasu (180) *pass (something to someone)*

-ya (187) *suffix indicating a shop or restaurant*
yakitori (160) *barbecued chicken*
yakitoriya (187) *yakitori restaurant*

yakizakana (188) *grilled fish*
yakusoku (60) *appointment, promise*
yakuza (207) *Japanese gangsters*
yakyū (212) *baseball*
yama (75) *mountain*
yamemashita (121) *stopped (see yamemasu)*
yamemasu, yameru (121) *stop*
ya ... nado (197) *and so on*
yaoya (87) *greengrocer's*
yappari (181) *as I thought*
yasui (81) *cheap*
(o-)yasumi (115) *holiday, time off*
yatai (160) *street vendor's cart*
yattsu (90) *eight (objects)*
yo (81) *particle, turning a sentence into an exclamation*
yobikō (112) *cram school*
yōguruto (81) *yoghurt*
yoi (17) *good (see also ii)*
yōi (225) (yōi o shimashita) *prepared*
yōka (115) *the 8th of the month*
yokatta (254) *was good (past form of yoi/ii)*
yokka (115) *the 4th of the month*
yokozuna (192) *sumō grand champion*
yoku (194) (yoku ikimasu) *I often go*
yoku (196) (yoku utaemasu) *she can sing well*
yoku (149) (yoku arimasen) *isn't good (negative of yoi/ii)*
yokute (196) *good and ... (see ii)*
yomimashita (173) *read (in the past) (see yomimasu)*
yomimasu, yomu (110) *read*
yon (53) *four*
yoroshiku (12) (dōzo yoroshiku/yoroshiku onegai shimasu) *please look kindly on me/do me this favour*
yoru (106) *evening*
yōshitsu (140) *Western-style room*
yotei (254) *plan*
yottsu (90) *four (objects)*
yoyaku (142) *reservation*
yūbe (169) *yesterday evening*
yūbinkyoku (54) *post office*
yubiwa (246) *ring*
yukata (139) *type of loose-fitting kimono*
yuki (133) (Ueno yuki) *Ueno-bound*
yukkuri (117) *slowly*
yunomi (29) *tea cup*

zaibatsu (78) *pre-war financial clique of banks, companies, etc.*
zannen (204) (zannen desu) *it's a pity*
(o-)zashiki (28) *main living room*
zazen (249) *zen meditation*
zenzen (194) (zenzen ikimasen) *I never go* (zenzen dekimasen) *I can't do it at all*
zero (53) *0 (zero)*
zubon (82) *trousers*

GLOSSARY: ENGLISH–JAPANESE

Use this word list to remind yourself of words you've already studied: since the list only contains words which occur in the book, it is not comprehensive enough to be used as a dictionary. The number in brackets after each Japanese word refers to the page on which it first occurs in the book. If you are unsure how to use the word, you will usually find an example of its use on the page indicated.

about (about 6 p.m.) *goro (106)* (*rokuji goro*)
about (about three hours) *gurai (116)* (*sanjikan gurai*)
above ... *no ue (264)*
abroad *gaikoku (74)*
accounts division *keiribu (52)*
address (what's your address?) (*go-*)*jūsho (55)* (*go-jūsho wa dochira desu ka?*)
administration division *sōmubu (52)*
aerobics *earobikkusu (194)*
after (after the bank) *saki (62)* (*ginkō no saki*)
after (after the lesson) *ato (145)* (*jugyō no ato*)
again *mata (203)*
age (counter for) *-sai (120)*
air conditioning *eakon (140)*
alcove in a Japanese-style room *tokonoma (28)*
all right *daijōbu (204)*
all sorts of things *iroiro (172)*
already (already two years) *mō (145)* (*mō ninen*)
a.m. (8 a.m.) *gozen (106)* (*gozen hachiji*)
am, are, is (see Grammar Sec. 7) *desu, da (4), imasu, iru (36)*
am not, are not, is not (see Grammar Sec. 7) *ja arimasen (12)*
amazing *sugoi (29)*
America *amerika (11), beikoku (187)*
American (person) *amerikajin (4)*
American English *beigo (272)*
and (joining sentences) *soshite (121)* (joining words) *to (83)*
and so on (rock, jazz, and so on) *toka (197)* (*rokku toka jazu toka ...*) (*ya ... nado*)
another *hoka (no) (220)*
anyone at home? *gomen kudasai! (26)*
apartment block *manshon (99)*
apartment, flat *apāto (99)*
apple *ringo (90)*
appointment *yakusoku (60)*
archery *kyūdō (196)*
April *shigatsu (114)*
arrival (what time does it arrive?) (*tō*)*chaku (132)* (*nanji chaku desu ka?*)
as far as *made (64)*
as I thought *yappari (181)*
as well (see Grammar Sec. 8J) *mo (5)*
assorted sandwiches *mikkusu sando (162)*
at (see Grammar Sec. 8G, H) (by means of) *de (62)*
at (a place) *ni (36)*
at once, immediately *sugu (175)*
August *hachigatsu (114)*
Australia *Ōsutoraria (11)*
autumn *aki (115)*

baby *akachan (185)*
bacon *bēkon (81)*
bad *warui (176)*
bad at (I'm bad at tennis) *heta (148)* (*tenisu ga heta desu*)
badminton *badominton (194)*
bag *baggu (82)*

bamboo *take (185)*
bank *ginkō (36)*
bank employee *ginkōin (12)*
bar (Western-style, e.g. in a hotel) *bā (140)* (comfortable and often expensive) *sunakku (188)* (eating/drinking places) *akachōchin (188), izakaya (187)*
baseball *yakyū (212)*
baseball batter *battā (40)*
basement *chika (94)*
bath (at home) (*o-*)*furo (26)* (public) *sentō (46)*
beautiful, pretty *kirei (na) (29)*
because ... *kara (198)*
become *narimasu, naru (236)*
bed and breakfast *minshuku (138)*
beef *gyūniku (187)*
beer *biiru (41)*
behind ... *no ushiro (56)*
believe in *shinjimasu, shinjiru (246)*
below *shita (264)*
belt *beruto (82)*
bicycle *jitensha (116)*
big *ōkii (30)*
bill, check *okanjō (166)*
bird *tori (246)*
birthday *tanjōbi (172)*
biscuit *bisuketto (40)*
black *kuro (83), kuroi (84)*
black (completely black) *makkuro (177)*
black tea *kōcha (41)*
blouse *burausu (82)*
blue (of natural things) *ao (83), aoi (84)* (e.g. of clothes) *burū (no) (83)*
body *karada (272)*
bon appétit! *itadakimasu (37)*
book *hon (89)*
bookshop *honya (87)*
boring *tsumaranai (166)*
boutique *butikku (87)*
box *hako (264)*
bra *bura(jā) (82)*
bracelet *buresuretto (94)*
braces *sasupendā (82)*
Brazil *burajiru (11)*
break *kowashimasu, kowasu (242)*
breakfast *asagohan (108)*
breakfast set *mōningu setto (162)*
bring *motte kimasu, motte kuru* (irr.) *(174)*
Britain *igirisu (11), eikoku (272)*
British person *igirisujin (4)*
brothers and sisters (*go-*)*kyōdai (36)*
brown *chairo (83), chairoi (84)*
bus *basu (116)*
business entertainment *settai (170)*
businessman *bijinesuman (4)*

but (beginning a sentence) *shikashi* (*174*) (connecting clauses) *ga* (*30*)
butcher's *nikuya* (*186*)
butter *batā* (*40*)
buy *kaimasu, kau* (*185*)
by means of (see Grammar Sec. 8H) *de* (*62*)

cabbage *kyabetsu* (*81*)
cake(s) (Western-style) *kēki* (*6*) (made from rice) (*o-*)*mochi* (*182*)
call (what's it called?) *nan to iimasu ka?* (*21*) (I'm called . . .) . . . *to iimasu/mōshimasu* (*21*)
calligraphy *shodō* (*206*)
camera *kamera* (*89*)
Canada *kanada* (*11*)
car *kuruma* (*116*)
card *kādo* (*6*)
care (take care!) *ki o tsukete* (*kudasai*) (*225*)
carrot *ninjin* (*90*)
cat *neko* (*242*)
CD (player) *shiidii* (*purēyā*) (*94*)
Central baseball league *seriigu* (*202*)
chair *isu* (*117*)
chairman of board of directors *shachō* (*67*)
cheap *yasui* (*81*)
cheers! *kanpai!* (*166*)
cheese *chiizu* (*162*)
chemist's *kusuriya* (*87*)
cherry blossom *sakura* (*14*)
chess *chesu* (*208*)
chicken (barbecued) *yakitori* (*160*)
chicken (meat) *toriniku* (*187*)
child(ren) *kodomo/o-ko-san* (*36*)
China *chūgoku* (*11*)
Chinese characters in written Japanese *kanji* (*18*)
Chinese 'chess' *shōgi* (*208*)
Chinese food *chūkaryōri* (*184*)
Chinese person *chūgokujin* (*11*)
chocolate(s) *chokorēto* (*6*), *choko* (*219*)
chopsticks (*o-*)*hashi* (*29*)
Christmas *kurisumasu* (*6*)
cigarette *tabako* (*148*)
cinema *eigakan* (*116*)
circle *maru* (*100*)
civil servant *kōmuin* (*12*)
classical music *kurashikku* (*197*)
cleaning (do the cleaning) *sōji o shimasu, suru* (*114*)
client (*o-*)*kyaku*(*-san/-sama*) (*88*)
close *shimemasu, shimeru* (*222*)
closed country *sakoku* (*150*)
clothing (women's) *fujinyōhin* (*94*)
club *kurabu* (*94*)
coat *kōto* (*82*)
coffee *kōhii* (*6*)
coffee shop *kōhii shoppu, kissaten* (*87*)
cold *samui* (*17*)
colour *iro* (*83*)
colour in *nurimasu, nuru* (*247*)
come *kimasu, kuru* (irr.) (*37*)
come back *kaerimasu, kaeru* (*108*)
comedy *komedii* (*197*)
coming of age day *seijin no hi* (*214*)
company *kaisha* (*36*)
company employee *kaishain* (*12*)
computer *konpyūta* (*6*)

computer (personal) *pasokon* (*29*)
concert *konsāto* (*205*)
conditioner (for hair) *rinsu* (*88*)
convenient, handy *benri (na)* (*29*)
cook *ryōri o shimasu, suru* (*197*)
cool *suzushii* (*17*)
corner *kado* (*62*)
cosmetics *keshōhin* (*84*)
country, nation *kuni* (*11*)
country bumpkin *inakamono* (*146*)
countryside *inaka* (*146*)
courage *gattsu* (*200*)
covered shopping street *shōtengai* (*87*)
cram school *yobikō* (*112*), *juku* (*108*)
crisps *poteto chippu*(*su*) (*41*)
cucumber *kyūri* (*90*)
culture *bunka* (*58*)
curried rice *karēraisu* (*6*)
curtains outside many small restaurants *noren* (*188*)
customer (*o-*)*kyaku*(*-san/-sama*) (*88*)
cut *kirimasu, kiru* (*233*)
cute, pretty *kawaii* (*29*)

dance *dansu o shimasu, suru* (*197*)
date of birth *seinengappi* (*127*)
daughter (my) *musume* (*34*)
daughter (another person's) *musume-san, o-jō-san* (*34*)
day before yesterday *ototoi* (*168*)
day after tomorrow *asatte* (*202*)
December *jūnigatsu* (*114*)
delicious *oishii* (*29*)
department (in a store) *uriba* (*94*)
department store *depāto* (*86*)
departure (what time does it depart?) *hatsu/shuppatsu* (*nanji hatsu desu ka?*) (*132*)
desk *tsukue* (*117*)
diamond(s) *daiya* (*176*)
dictionary *jisho* (*117*)
differ (i.e. be incorrect) *chigaimasu, chigau* (*12*)
difficult *muzukashii* (*34*)
dinner *bangohan* (*108*)
director (of a company) *torishimariyaku* (*66*)
dirty *kitanai* (*199*)
disco *disuko* (*212*)
dislike (I dislike cake) *kirai* (*148*) (*kēki ga kirai desu*)
disturb (I'm disturbing you) *ojama shimasu* (*40*)
division chief *buchō* (*66*)
division (of a company) *-bu* (*52*)
do *shimasu, suru* (irr.) (*12*)
documentary *dokyumentarii* (*194*)
don't have to . . . . . . *-nakute mo ii desu* (*236*)
don't mention it! *iie* (*10*), *dō itashimashite* (*28*)
door *doa* (*222*)
door (sliding, made of wood and paper) *shōji* (*29*)
double room *daburu* (*140*)
drank *nomimashita, nonda* (*233*) (see drink)
draw (a picture, map, etc.) *kakimasu, kaku* (*209*) (a line) (*sen o*) *hikimasu, hiku* (*247*)
dress *wanpiisu* (*82*)
drink *nomimasu, nomu* (*110*)
drinking place serving food *izakaya, akachōchin* (*188*)
drinks *nomimono* (*164*)
drive (go for a drive) *doraibu o shimasu, suru* (*114*)
dumplings (often with bean paste inside) (*o-*)*manjū* (*264*)
duty *giri* (*210*)

early *hayai* (*199*)
ear-ring(s) *iyaringu* (*94*)
earth, ground *tsuchi* (*215*)
east *higashi* (*154*)
easy *kantan* (*na*) (*89*)
eat *tabemasu, taberu* (*108*)
eat/dine out *shokuji o shimasu, suru* (*169*)
eat out, take away (*o-*)*mochikaeri* (*184*)
education *kyōiku* (*104*)
eight *hachi* (*53*)
eight (objects) *yattsu* (*90*)
eighth of the month *yōka* (*115*)
electrical goods *denkiseihin* (*94*)
elementary school (age 6–11) *shōgakkō* (*112*)
elementary school pupil *shōgakusei* (*126*)
emperor *tennō* (*214*)
emperor's official name (1989–) *Heisei* (*114*) (1925–1989) *Shōwa* (*114*)
employee *shain* (*50*)
end, finish *owarimasu, owaru* (*115*)
engineer *enjinia* (*12*)
English language *eigo* (*197*)
enjoyable *tanoshii* (*166*)
enough (I've had enough!) *kekkō desu* (*166*)
enter *hairimasu, hairu* (*247*)
'enthusiastic listening noise' *aizuchi* (*8*)
entrance area of a house *genkan* (*26*)
erm ... *anō* .../ *ēto* ... (*195*)
escape *nigemasu, nigeru* (*181*)
evening *yoru* (*106*)
every day *mainichi* (*195*)
every month *maitsuki* (*195*)
every week *maishū* (*195*)
every year *mainen* (*195*), *maitoshi* (*195*)
excuse me (on making a request) *sumimasen* (*ga* ...) (*30*) (e.g. on leaving/entering a room) *shitsurei shimasu* (*12*)
expensive *takai* (*89*)
extinguish *keshimasu, kesu* (*222*)

family (another person's) *go-kazoku* (*35*)
family (my) *kazoku* (*35*)
fan *sensu* (*221*)
fashion accessory *akusesarii* (*94*)
fashion designer *dezainā* (*4*)
fast *hayai* (*199*)
father (my) *chichi* (*35*)
father (another person's) *o-tō-san* (*35*)
February *nigatsu* (*114*)
fermented soya bean paste *miso* (*37*)
festival (*o-*)*matsuri* (*192*)
fifth of the month *itsuka* (*115*)
fight *kenka o shimasu, suru* (*181*)
film (for a camera) *firumu* (*88*)
film (i.e. movie) *eiga* (*197*)
fine (here is fine (to taxi driver)) *kekkō desu* (*64*)
fine, thank you (lit. 'thanks to you') *okagesama de* (*16*)
finish *owarimasu, owaru* (*115*)
first rank (e.g. company) *ichiryū* (*51*)
first (in a series) *hitotsume* (*no*) (*62*)
first class compartment (lit. 'green car') *guriinsha* (*136*)
first of the month *tsuitachi* (*115*)
fish *sakana* (*37*)
fish (grilled) *yakizakana* (*188*)
fishmonger's *sakanaya* (*186*)
five *go* (*53*)

five (objects) *itsutsu* (*90*)
flat things (counter for) *-mai* (*81*)
flat (apartment) *apāto* (*99*)
flower arranging *ikebana* (*105*)
folk song *minyō* (*209*)
food *tabemono* (*240*)
foodstuffs *shokuryōhin* (*94*)
for ... (for two hours) *-kan* (*145*) (*nijikan*)
for my part, too *kochira koso* (*60*)
foreign language *gaikokugo* (*272*)
foreigner *gaijin* (*47*), *gaikokujin* (*74*)
four *shi* (*53*), *yon* (*53*)
four (objects) *yottsu* (*90*)
fourth of the month *yokka* (*115*)
France *furansu* (*11*)
free (in your free time) *hima na toki* (*197*)
French language *furansugo* (*208*)
French person *furansujin* (*11*)
fresh *shinsen* (*na*) (*81*)
Friday *kinyōbi* (*114*)
friend *tomodachi* (*172*)
frightening *kowai* (*166*)
from *kara* (*10*)
fruit juice *jūsu* (*41*)

games (counter for number of) *-shiai* (*203*)
gangster *yakuza* (*207*)
gardening *niwaijiri* (*197*)
gateway to a shrine *torii* (*248*)
genuine opinion *honne* (*171*)
German person *doitsujin* (*11*)
Germany *doitsu* (*11*)
get up *okimasu, okiru* (*108*)
gift *purezento* (*220*) (for going-away) *senbetsu* (*219*) (mid-year) *o-chūgen* (*218*) (end of year) *o-seibo* (*218*) (to someone in hospital) (*o-*)*mimai* (*219*)
give *agemasu, ageru* (*172*)
glass *koppu* (*30*)
go *ikimasu, iku* (*108*)
go ahead! *dōzo* (*28*)
go and come back! *itte 'rasshai* (*37*)
go and eat *tabe ni ikimasu, iku* (*204*)
go back *kaerimasu, kaeru* (*108*)
go-between *nakōdo* (*105*)
go into, enter *hairimasu, hairu* (*247*)
go out for a drink *nomi ni ikimasu, iku* (*205*)
go to bed/sleep *nemasu, neru* (*108*)
god *kami-sama* (*88*)
going to ... (going to Ueno) *yuki* (*133*) (*Ueno yuki*)
golf *gorufu* (*94*)
golfer *gorufā* (*12*)
good *ii* (*17*), *yoi* (*17*)
good afternoon *konnichi wa* (*16*)
goodbye *shitsurei shimasu* (*52*), *sayōnara* (*76*)
good evening *konban wa* (*16*)
good morning *ohayō gozaimasu* (*16*)
good night *oyasuminasai* (*16*)
good at (good at tennis) (*o-*)*jōzu* (*148*) (*tenisu ga jōzu desu*)
grandfather *o-jii-san* (*185*)
grandmother *o-bā-san* (*185*)
great *suteki* (*na*) (*29*)
green (of natural things) *midori* (*no*) (*83*) (e.g. of clothes) *guriin* (*no*) (*83*)
greengrocer's *yaoya* (*87*)
grey *gurē* (*no*) (*83*)

ground, earth *tsuchi* (215)
guest (*o-*)*kyaku*(-*san*/-*sama*) (88)
guts, courage *gattsu* (200)
gymnastics *taisō* (108)

hair *kaminoke* (149)
hairbrush *hea burashi* (88)
half (half past five) *han* (106) (*goji han*)
hamburger steak *hanbāgu sutēki* (169)
hand *te* (175)
handcream *handokuriimu* (88)
handsome *hansamu* (na) (149)
hanging scroll *kakejiku* (29)
happy *shiawase* (na) (269)
hard *taihen* (na) (121)
hardly ever (I hardly ever go) *hotondo* (194) (*hotondo ikimasen*)
hat *bōshi* (82)
hate (I hate hats) *daikirai* (148) (*bōshi ga daikirai desu*)
have (see Grammar Sec. 7) *motte imasu, iru* (174), *mochimasu, motsu* (174), *arimasu, aru* (55)
Hawaii *hawai* (237)
he *kare* (185)
hear *kikimasu, kiku* (110)
hearse *reikyūsha* (240)
heavy *omoi* (89)
hello (on the telephone) *moshi moshi* (52) (when you first meet someone) *hajimemashite* (4) (in the morning) *ohayō* (*gozaimasu*) (16) (from 10/11 a.m. to dusk) *konnichi wa* (16) (in the evening) *konban wa* (16)
here *koko* (30)
here (polite) *kochira* (65)
here you are *dōzo* (28)
hiking *haikingu* (197)
hold *motte imasu, iru* (174)
holding back, reserve *enryo* (229)
holiday, national one-day holiday *saijitsu* (214)
holiday(s), time off (*o-*)*yasumi* (115)
home *uchi* (27)
home (native home) *furusato* (146)
honey *mitsu* (40)
honorific making the following word polite *o-* (16), *go-* (35)
honorific making the preceding word polite *-san* (10), *-sama* (88)
horrible *iya* (na) (17)
horror film *horā eiga* (197)
hospital *byōin* (36)
hot *atsui* (16)
hot coffee (as opposed to iced) *hotto* (*kōhii*) (164)
hot spring *onsen* (139)
hot spring pool in the open air *rotenburo* (263)
hotel *hoteru* (141)
house *ie* (30), *uchi* (27)
housewife *shufu* (12)
housework, cleaning *sōji* (114)
how? *dō?* (28), *ikaga?* (40)
how? (by what means of transport?) *nan de?* (116)
how? (in what way?) *dōyatte* (274)
how about some ...? ... *wa dō*/*ikaga desu ka?* (40)
how have you been? (lit. 'are you well?') *o-genki desu ka?* (16)
how many? *ikutsu?* (120)
how many nights? *nanpaku?* (143)
how many people? *nannin?* (162)
how much? *ikura?* (85)
how old? *nansai?*/*o-ikutsu?* (120)
humid (and hot) *mushiatsui* (17)
hundred *hyaku* (80)

hundred million *ichioku* (80)
hundred thousand *jūman* (80)
husband (my) *otto* (35), *shujin* (35)
husband (another person's) *go-shujin* (35)
I (usually) *watashi* (5) (formal) *watakushi* (5) (men's Japanese: informal) *boku* (5), *ore* (5)
I enjoyed the meal *gochisōsama deshita* (37)
I see (lit. 'I have understood') *wakarimashita* (60)
I'll be off! *itte kimasu* (37)
I'm back! *tadaima* (37)
if *moshi* (247) ... *to* (241)
immediately, at once *sugu* (175)
important *taisetsu* (na) (174)
in (a place) (see Grammar Sec. 8G) *ni* (36)
in (in two weeks) *go* (203) (*nishūkan go*)
in front of ... *no mae* ... (56)
in this direction *kochira* (65), *kotchi* (65)
in that direction *sochira* (65), *sotchi* (65)
in that direction (over there) *achira* (65), *atchi* (65)
in which direction? *dochira, dotchi?* (65)
include, insert *iremasu, ireru* (233)
inconvenient *fuben* (na) (89)
India *indo* (11)
ink painting *sumi-e* (92)
inn (Japanese-style) *ryokan* (138)
inside ... *no naka* (74)
inside (Ueda from inside my company) *uchi* (27) (*uchi no Ueda*) (67)
insincere opinion of a person *tatemae* (171)
interesting, funny *omoshiroi* (29)
internal, within a country *kokunai* (74)
international department *kokusaibu* (52)
internationalisation *kokusaika* (267)
Ireland *airurando* (11)
island country *shimaguni* (2)
isn't/am not/are not *ja arimasen* (12)
it's time to go *soro soro shitsurei shimasu* (225)
Italy *itaria* (83)

jam *jamu* (81)
January *ichigatsu* (114)
Japan *nihon* (11), *nippon* (formal) (23)
Japan Sea *nihonkai* (155)
Japanese ballad *enka* (197)
Japanese feudal lord *daimyō* (130)
Japanese language (as learned by foreigners) *nihongo* (18)
Japanese language (as studied by the Japanese) *kokugo* (272)
Japanese person *nihonjin* (5)
jazz *jazu* (197)
jeweller's *hōsekiya* (87)
job (*o-*)*shigoto* (12) (part-time) (*aru*)*baito* (111)
jogging (go jogging) *jogingu o shimasu, suru* (197)
July *shichigatsu* (114)
June *rokugatsu* (114)
junior college *tanki daigaku, tandai* (112)
junior high school (age 12–15) *chūgakkō* (112)
junior high school pupil *chūgakusei* (108)
Jupiter *mokusei* (215)
just before ... *no temae* (62)
just past ... *no saki* (62)
just right *chōdo ii* (89)

kiss *kisu o shimasu, suru* (222)
kneel formally *seiza o shimasu, suru* (229)

ladder *hashigo* (170)

last month *sengetsu* (*168*)
last week *senshū* (*168*)
last year *kyonen* (*168*)
late, slow *osoi* (*199*)
leaf *happa* (*240*)
leave *demasu, deru* (*110*)
left (as opposed to right) *hidari* (*62*)
leg *ashi* (*149*)
lemon *remon* (*162*)
lend *kashimasu, kasu* (*222*)
lesson *jugyō* (*121*)
let me think ... *sō desu nē* ... (*72*)
let's ...! ... *-mashō* (*204*) (polite verb ending)
lettuce *retasu* (*90*)
light (as opposed to heavy) *karui* (*89*)
like (I like sushi) *suki* (*148*) (*sushi ga suki desu*)
like very much (I like diamonds very much) *daisuki* (*148*) (*daiya ga daisuki desu*)
lion *raion* (*255*)
lipsalve *rippukuriimu* (*88*)
liquor store *sakaya* (*186*)
listen *kikimasu, kiku* (*110*)
little (a little) *sukoshi* (*117*)
live (in a particular place) *sumimasu, sumu* (*121*) (I live in Tōkyō) *Tōkyō ni sunde imasu* (*121*)
lively *nigiyaka* (*na*) (*146*)
living room (*o-*)*zashiki* (*28*)
lobby (of a hotel) *robii* (*255*)
lonely *sabishii* (*146*)
long *nagai* (*89*)
long time (it's been a long time!) *shibaraku desu ne* ... (*16*)
look at *mimasu, miru* (*110*)
looks delicious *oishi-sō* (*166*)
lose, be lost *nakunarimasu, nakunaru* (*174*)
love story *rabusutōrii* (*197*)
lover(s) *aijin* (*181*)
lucky charm (*o-*)*mamori* (*246*)
lunch *hirugohan* (*108*), *ohiru* (*205*)
lunch box (*o-*)*bentō* (*137*)

mahjong *mājan* (*208*)
make, do *shimasu, suru* (irr.) (*12*)
man *otoko* (*no hito*) (*47*)
management *keiei* (*50*)
managing director *jōmu* (*67*)
map *chizu* (*117*)
maple tree *momiji* (*14*)
March *sangatsu* (*114*)
marketing department *māketingubu* (*52*)
marriage *kekkon* (*144*)
married (I'm married) *kekkon shite imasu* (*144*)
Mars *kasei* (*215*)
martial art (using bamboo 'swords') *kendō* (*155*)
mascara *masukara* (*94*)
mats (laid into the floor of a Japanese-style room) *tatami* (*26*)
mattress (folded away during the day) *futon* (*32*)
May *gogatsu* (*114*)
meal *shokuji* (*169*)
meat *niku* (*186*)
meet *aimasu, au* (*172*)
melon *meron* (*90*)
menswear *shinshiyōhin* (*94*)
Mercury *suisei* (*215*)
million *hyakuman* (*80*)
Ministry of Education *monbushō* (*118*)

minus *hiku* (*80*)
minutes (counter for) *-pun/-fun* (*106*)
mirror *kagami* (*243*)
Miss *-san* (*10*)
model (fashion model) *moderu* (*12*)
modern *modan* (*146*)
Monday *getsuyōbi* (*114*)
money *o-kane* (*185*)
month (once a month) *tsuki* (*185*) (*tsuki ni ikkai*)
month after next *saraigetsu* (*202*)
month before last *sensengetsu* (*168*)
more *motto* (*220*)
more (one more bottle) *mō ippon* (*117*)
morning *asa* (*106*)
mother (my) *haha* (*35*)
mother (another person's) *o-kā-san* (*35*)
motorbike *baiku* (*116*)
mountain *yama* (*75*)
movie *eiga* (*197*)
Mr *-san* (*10*)
Mrs *-san* (*10*)
Ms *-san* (*10*)
music *ongaku* (*197*)
music for singing along *karaoke* (*178*)
musical instrument (a type of) *shamisen* (*206*)
must ... *-nakereba narimasen* (*236*)

naked (as used of an unwrapped gift) *hadaka* (*229*)
name (*o-*)*namae* (*69*)
namecard *meishi* (*66*)
near ... *no chikaku* (*56*)
near (very near) ... *no soba* (*56*)
necklace *nekkuresu* (*94*)
negative verb ending (polite) (present) *-masen* (*12*)
negative verb ending (polite) (past) *-masen deshita* (*172*)
negative verb ending (plain) (present) *-nai* (*235*)
negative verb ending (plain) (past) *-nakatta* (*235*)
never (I never go) *zenzen* (*194*) (*zenzen ikimasen*)
new *atarashii* (*28*)
New Year *shōgatsu* (*138*)
New Zealand *nyūjiirando* (*11*)
news *nyūsu* (*197*)
newspaper *shinbun* (*110*)
next *tsugi* (*no*) (*62*)
next month *raigetsu* (*202*)
next to ... *no tonari* (*56*)
next week *raishū* (*202*)
next year *rainen* (*202*)
night(s) (counter for) *-paku/-haku* (*142*)
nine *kyū* (*53*), *ku* (*53*)
nine (objects) *kokonotsu* (*90*)
ninth of the month *kokonoka* (*115*)
no (don't mention it) *iie* (*10*)
noise *oto* (*175*)
noisy *urusai* (*199*)
noodle (variety 1) *rāmen* (*160*) (variety 2) *udon* (*160*) (variety 3) *soba* (*160*)
north *kita* (*154*)
north-east *hokutō* (*154*)
north-west *hokusei* (*154*)
north-facing *kitamuki* (*240*)
nose *hana* (*149*)
no-smoking seat *kin'enseki* (*136*)
notebook *nōto* (*117*)
not really (I don't really like it) *amari* (*148*) (*amari suki ja arimasen*)

319

November *jūichigatsu* (114)
now *ima* (106)
number *bangō* (53)
nuts *nattsu* (40)

object particle (see Grammar Sec. 8C) *o* (90)
o'clock *-ji* (106)
October *jūgatsu* (114)
of (see Grammar Sec. 8E) *no* (12)
office worker (female) *ōeru* (12)
official rest day *kyūjitsu* (214)
often (I often play tennis) *yoku* (194) (*yoku tenisu o shimasu*)
oh, really *ā, sō desu ka* (10)
OK *daijōbu* (204)
oil (oil painting) *abura* (*abura e*) (209)
old *furui* (89)
old man, grandfather *o-jii-san* (185)
old woman, grandmother *o-bā-san* (185)
older brother (my) *ani* (35)
older brother (another person's) *o-nii-san* (35)
older sister (my) *ane* (35)
older sister (another person's) *o-nē-san* (35)
once (once more, please) *ichido* (117) (*mō ichido onegai shimasu*)
on foot, walking *aruite* (116)
one *ichi* (53)
one (object) *hitotsu* (90)
one person *hitori* (162)
one day *ichinichi* (108)
one way (ticket) *katamichi* (134)
onion *tamanegi* (90)
only *dake* (177)
open *akemasu, akeru* (174)
opposite ... *no hantaigawa* (56)
or (formal) *soretomo* (184)
orange (mandarin orange) *mikan* (90)
orange (colour) *orenji (no)* (83)
order (e.g. given to a waiter) *(go-)chūmon* (184)
other *hoka (no)* (220)
outside *soto* (27)

p.m. (7 p.m.) *gogo* (106) (*gogo shichiji*)
Pacific baseball league *pariigu* (202)
paint *kakimasu, kaku* (209)
panty hose *pansuto* (82)
parents *(go-)ryōshin* (36)
part-time job *(aru)baito* (111)
pass (something to someone) *watashimasu, watasu* (180)
patience (be patient) *gaman* (200) (*gaman shimasu, suru*)
peanuts *piinatsu* (137)
pen *pen* (222)
people (counter for) *-nin* (162)
perseverance *shinbō* (200)
person *hito* (47)
person from ... *-jin* (11)
personnel division *jinjibu* (52)
petrol (petrol station) *gasorin* (56) (*gasorin sutando*)
pharmacy *kusuriya* (87)
photograph *shashin* (34)
physical education *tai'iku* (214)
pickles *tsukemono* (87)
picture *e* (92)
pig *buta* (187)
pinball (Japanese-style) *pachinko* (160)
pineapple *painappuru* (81)
pink *pinku (no)* (83)
pipe *paipu* (235)

pity (it's a pity) *zannen desu* (204)
pizza *piza* (81)
place of employment *(o-)tsutome* (69)
place of work *shigotoba* (121)
place where martial arts are practised *dōjō* (206)
plan (for a building etc.) *puran* (185) (intention) *yotei* (254)
plate *(o-)sara* (30)
platform number *-bansen* (136)
play (a sport) ... *o shimasu, suru* (108)
play (a stringed musical instrument) *hikimasu, hiku* (209)
please (give me ...) *kudasai* (26), *onegai shimasu* (12)
please (do me this favour) *yoroshiku onegai shimasu* (12)
plus *tasu* (80)
police, police station *keisatsu* (176)
police box *kōban* (54)
pop (music) *poppusu* (197)
pork *butaniku* (187)
post office *yūbinkyoku* (54)
potato crisps *poteto chippu(su)* (41)
prepare *yōi o shimasu, suru* (225)
present *purezento* (220)
pretty, cute *kawaii* (29)
pretty, beautiful, clean *kirei (na)* (29)
professional *puro* (12)
programme (TV) *bangumi* (197)
propose (marriage) *puropōzu o shimasu, suru* (185)
public relations division *kōhōbu* (52)
public telephone *kōshū denwa* (95)
purple *murasaki (no)* (83)
put in *iremasu, ireru* (233)

quiet *shizuka (na)* (199)

racket (tennis racket) *raketto* (94) (*tenisu raketto*)
radio *rajio* (89)
rain *ame* (247)
rainy season *tsuyu* (14)
rāmen shop *rāmenya* (188)
raw fish *sashimi* (87)
read *yomimasu, yomu* (110)
reading (for pleasure) *dokusho* (197)
really? (aizuchi) *hē?* (72), *hontō ni?* (72), *sō desu ka* (10)
receipt (written) *ryōshūsho* (64)
receive *moraimasu, morau* (172)
red *aka* (83), *akai* (84)
regarding the other day *kono aida wa ...* (226)
relations, relationship *kankei* (187)
reporter (TV or radio) *repōtā* (5)
reservation *yoyaku* (142)
reserved seat *shiteiseki* (136)
resitting university applicant *rōnin* (112)
restaurant *resutoran* (60)
return (ticket) *ōfuku* (134)
rice (uncooked) *(o-)kome* (186) (brown, unhusked) *genmai* (182) (cooked, served in a bowl) *gohan* (182) (cooked, served on a plate) *raisu* (7)
rice bowl *chawan* (30)
rice cake *(o-)mochi* (182)
rice cracker *(o-)senbei* (41)
rice merchant's *komeya* (186)
rice wine (sake) *nihonshu* (182), o-sake (148)
right *migi* (62)
right (hand side) *migigawa* (256)
ring *yubiwa* (246)
ring in sumō wrestling *dohyō* (193)
river *kawa* (75)

robber *dorobō* (*247*)
rock (music) *rokku* (*148*)
Roman script *rōmaji* (*22*)
room *heya* (*141*)
room (Japanese-style) *washitsu* (*140*) (Western-style) *yōshitsu* (*140*)
rude(ness) *shitsurei* (*12*)

sad *kanashii* (*166*)
safe journey! *ki o tsukete kudasai* (*225*)
sake (rice wine) *nihonshu* (*182*), *o-sake* (*148*)
salad *sarada* (*81*)
sales division *eigyōbu* (*52*)
salesman *sērusuman* (*145*)
sandal *sandaru* (*237*)
sandwich *sandoitchi* (*137*), *sando* (*162*)
Saturday *doyōbi* (*114*)
Saturn *dosei* (*215*)
say *iimasu, iu* (*174*)
scarf *mafurā* (*237*)
school *gakkō* (*36*)
script type (for Japanese words) *hiragana* (*22*) (for foreign words) *katakana* (*22*)
sea *umi* (*235*)
second (in a series) *futatsume* (*no*) (*62*)
second helping (*o-*)*kawari* (*37*)
second of the month *futsuka* (*115*)
second rank (e.g. company) *niryū* (*51*)
section chief *kachō* (*66*)
see *mimasu, miru* (*110*)
self-introduction *jiko shōkai* (*21*)
senior high school (age 16–18) *kōtōgakkō* (*112*), *kōkō* (*30*)
senior high school pupil *kōkōsei* (*34*)
September *kugatsu* (*114*)
set breakfast *mōningu setto* (*162*)
seven *nana* (*53*), *shichi* (*53*)
seven (objects) *nanatsu* (*90*)
seventh of the month *nanoka* (*115*)
shall we ...? ... *-mashō ka?* (*204*)
shampoo *shanpū* (*88*)
she *kanojo* (*172*)
shirt *shatsu* (*82*)
shoe *kutsu* (*82*)
shoe shop *kutsuya* (*89*)
shopping (go shopping) *kaimono* (*114*) (*kaimono o shimasu, suru*)
short *mijikai* (*89*)
shoulder *kata* (*40*)
show *misemasu, miseru* (*91*)
shower *shawā* (*140*)
shrine (building) *jinja* (*54*)
shrine entrance gate *torii* (*248*)
shrine (household Buddhist) *butsudan* (*29*)
signals, traffic lights *shingō* (*62*)
simple *shinpuru* (*na*) (*269*)
sing *utaimasu, utau* (*209*)
single (unmarried) *dokushin* (*144*)
single (room) *shinguru* (*140*)
sit *suwarimasu, suwaru* (*222*)
sit down, please *okake kudasai* (*40*)
six *roku* (*53*)
six (objects) *muttsu* (*90*)
sixth of the month *muika* (*115*)
size (of clothes) *saizu* (*184*)
ski(s), skiing *sukii* (*94*)
skirt *sukāto* (*82*)

sleep, go to bed/sleep *nemasu, neru* (*108*)
sliding screen door *fusuma* (*32*)
slim *sumāto* (*na*) (*149*)
slipper *suripppa* (*82*)
slow *osoi* (*199*)
slowly *yukkuri* (*117*)
small *chiisai* (*28*)
smell *nioi* (*28*)
smoke a cigarette *tabako o suimasu, suu* (*222*)
snack accompanying alcohol (*o-*)*tsumami* (*41*)
sneaker(s) *suniikā* (*82*)
soap opera *hōmu dorama* (*197*)
soba shop *sobaya* (*188*)
society *shakai* (*50*)
socks *kutsushita* (*82*)
sofa *sofā* (*6*)
solarium *sorariumu* (*194*)
some other time! *mata kondo* (*204*)
someone *dare ka* (*173*)
something *nani ka* (*173*)
sometimes *tokidoki* (*194*)
somewhere *doko ka* (*173*)
son (my) *musuko* (*34*)
son (another person's) *musuko-san* (*34*)
sorry (*dōmo*) *sumimasen* (*30*)
soup ('miso' soup) *miso shiru* (*37*)
south *minami* (*154*)
South Korea *kankoku* (*11*)
south-east *nantō* (*154*)
south-west *nansei* (*154*)
souvenir (*o-*)*miyage* (*137*)
spaghetti western *makaroni uesutan* (*204*)
Spanish language *supeingo* (*208*)
speak *hanashimasu, hanasu* (*172*), *hanashi o shimasu, suru* (*172*)
special offer (*o-*)*kaidokuhin* (*81*)
spider *kumo* (*240*)
spirit *seishin* (*200*)
sport *supōtsu* (*94*)
sportswear *supōtsuyōhin* (*94*)
spring *haru* (*115*)
spring holiday *haruyasumi* (*115*)
square *shikaku* (*213*)
squash *sukasshu* (*197*)
squid (dried) *saki'ika* (*137*)
stand (something) up *tatemasu, tateru* (*241*)
stand up *tachimasu, tatsu* (*241*)
standard Japanese language *kyōtsūgo* (*19*)
standard speech *hyōjungo* (*19*)
star *hoshi* (*246*)
start *hajimarimasu, hajimaru* (*115*)
station *eki* (*54*)
stay, spend the night *tomarimasu, tomaru* (*268*)
stay silent, stop speaking *damarimasu, damaru* (*176*)
steak *sutēki* (*169*)
step up *agarimasu, agaru* (*184*)
stew *shichū* (*6*)
still *mada* (*148*)
stop (when in motion) *tomemasu, tomeru* (*62*)
stop (doing something) *yamemasu, yameru* (*121*)
straight on *massugu* (*62*)
strange *hen* (*na*) (*175*)
student *gakusei* (*12*)
study *benkyō o shimasu, suru* (*108*)
styling lotion (for hair) *sutairingu rōshon* (*88*)

subdivision of a 'chōme' (used in addresses) *banchi* (55)
subsidiary company *kogaisha* (50)
suit *sūtsu* (82)
summer *natsu* (40)
summer holiday *natsuyasumi* (115)
sumō grand champion *yokozuna* (192)
suncream *sankuriimu* (237)
Sunday *nichiyōbi* (114)
supermarket *sūpā* (36)
sushi restaurant *sushiya* (188)
suspense movie *sasupensu eiga* (197)
sweater *sētā* (82)
sweets (Japanese-style) *wagashi* (29)
swim *oyogimasu, oyogu* (194)
swimming pool *pūru* (6)
swimsuit *mizugi* (237)
switch off *keshimasu, kesu* (222)
switch on *tsukemasu, tsukeru* (222)

table *tēburu* (117)
table (low with heater underneath) *kotatsu* (28)
take *motte ikimasu, iku* (174)
take (time) *kakarimasu, kakaru* (116)
take away *torimasu, toru* (181)
take away, eat out *(o-)mochikaeri* (184)
tall *se ga takai* (149)
taxi *takushii* (6)
tea (green) *o-cha* (41), tea (black) *kōcha* (41), tea (lemon) *remon tii* (162), tea (made in tea ceremony) *matcha* (206)
tea ceremony *sadō* (105)
tea cup *yunomi* (29)
tea merchant's *o-chaya* (186)
teach *oshiemasu, oshieru* (222)
teacher *sensei* (12)
telephone (n.) *denwa* (53) (vb.) *denwa o shimasu, suru* (53)
television *terebi* (29)
television computer game *famikon* (211)
tell *oshiemasu, oshieru* (222)
temple *(o-)tera* (54)
ten *jū* (80)
ten (objects) *tō* (90)
ten thousand *ichiman* (80)
tennis *tenisu* (94)
tenth of the month *tōka* (115)
textbook *tekisuto* (34)
thank you (usually) *dōmo arigatō (gozaimasu)* (28) (casual) *dōmo* (37) (expressing indebtedness) *dōmo sumimasen* (12)
that (one) *sore* (28)
that (one) over there *are* (28)
that ... *sono* ... (30)
that ... over there *ano* ... (30)
that kind of ... *sonna* ... (198)
that's right *sō desu (ne)* (10)
that's (probably) right *sō deshō* (235)
there *soko* (30)
there (i.e. over there) *asoko* (30)
there is/are ... *arimasu, aru* (55)
these (ones) *kore* (28)
these ... *kono* (30)
thing *mono* (224)
thing(s) to eat *tabemono* (240)
think *kangaemasu, kangaeru* (178)
third rank (e.g. company) *sanryū* (51)
third of the month *mikka* (115)
third (in a series) *mittsume (no)* (62)

this (one) *kore* (28)
this ... *kono* ... (30)
this kind of ... *konna* ... (199)
this month *kongetsu* (168)
this morning *kesa* (169)
this week *konshū* (168)
this year *kotoshi* (168)
those (ones) *sore* (28)
those (ones) over there *are* (28)
three *san* (53)
three (objects) *mittsu* (40)
throw *nagemasu, nageru* (241)
throw away *sutemasu, suteru* (247)
Thursday *mokuyōbi* (114)
ticket (return) *ōfuku* (134) (single) *katamichi* (134)
tie *nekutai* (82)
time (for two hours) *jikan (nijikan)* (116)
time (at that time) *sono toki* (181)
tired (you must be tired!) *otsukaresama deshita* (76)
tissue *tisshu* (88)
to, towards *e* (62)
toast *tōsuto* (162)
toaster *tōsutā* (94)
today *kyō* (60)
toenail *tsume* (240)
toilet *(o-)toire* (28)
Tōkyō (the old name for ...) *Edo* (23)
tomato sauce *tomatosōsu* (81)
tomorrow *ashita* (202)
too (see Grammar Sec. 8J) *mo* (5)
tooth *ha* (240)
touch *sawarimasu, sawaru* (242)
towards (towards Ōsaka) *hōmen* (136) (*Ōsaka hōmen*)
towel (wet, used for wiping hands) *oshibori* (30)
trade union *rōdō kumiai* (50)
traffic lights *shingō* (62)
train *densha* (132)
train type (ordinary) *futsū (densha)* (132) (faster than ordinary) *kaisoku* (132) (express) *kyūkō* (132) (limited express) *tokkyū* (132) (super express, 'bullet') *shinkansen* (131)
tree *ki* (75)
triangle *sankaku* (247)
trifling thing (it's just a ...) *tsumaranai mono desu ga* ... (166)
trousers *zubon* (82)
try hard *ganbarimasu, ganbaru* (121)
Tuesday *kayōbi* (114)
tuna (canned) *tsunakan* (81)
turn *magarimasu, magaru* (62)
turning *kado* (62)
TV *terebi* (29)
twentieth of the month *hatsuka* (15)
twenty-fourth of the month *nijūyokka* (115)
twenty years old *hatachi* (120)
twin (hotel room) *tsuin* (140)
two *ni* (53)
two (objects) *futatsu* (90)
two people *futari* (162)

USA *amerika* (11), *beikoku* (187)
udon shop *udonya* (188)
under, below ... *no shita* (264)
underground shopping street *chikagai* (87)
underground, subway *chikatetsu* (116)
underpants *pantsu* (82)
understand, know *wakarimasu, wakaru* (60)

union (i.e. trade union) *rōdō kumiai* (50)
university *daigaku* (112)
university student *daigakusei* (111)
unmarried *dokushin* (144)
unreserved seat *jiyūseki* (136)
until *made* (64)
until late *osoku made* (225)
urban subdivision (used in addresses) *-chōme* (55)
usually *itsumo* (109)

Venus *kinsei* (215)
very *totemo* (28)
video *bideo* (94)

wait *machimasu, matsu* (60)
wait a moment, please *chotto matte kudasai* (60)
walk (go for a . . .) *sanpo o shimasu, suru* (197)
walk (action of walking) *arukimasu, aruku* (242)
want (to have something) *. . . ga hoshii* (274) (to do something)
     . . . tai desu (274)
ward (in Tōkyō and other big cities) *-ku* (55)
warm *atatakai* (17)
washing (do the washing) *sentaku o shimasu, suru* (114)
watch *mimasu, miru* (110)
watch (i.e. wristwatch) *tokei* (221)
water *mizu* (170)
'water-trade' (evening entertainment business) *mizu shōbai* (170)
watermelon *suika* (90)
wear *kimasu, kiru* (233)
weather *tenki* (17)
wedding *kekkonshiki* (236)
Wednesday *suiyōbi* (114)
week (four times a week) *shū ni yonkai* (195)
week after next *saraishū* (202)
week before last *sensenshū* (168)
welcome back! *okaerinasai!* (37)
well, then *dewa* (52), *jā/ja* (37)
well (I'm well) *genki desu* (26)
west *nishi* (154)
western (type of film) *uesutan* (204)
what? *nan?* (28), *nani?* (83)
what colour? *nani'iro?* (83)
what day (i.e. date)? *nannichi?* (115)
what day of the week? *nanyōbi?* (114)
what floor? *nankai?* (94)
what kind of . . .? *donna* (197)
what month? *nangatsu?* (114)
what number? *nanban?* (53)
what number track? *nanbansen?* (136)

what time? *nanji?* (106)
what year? *nannen?* (114)
when? *itsu?* (173)
where? *doko?* (30)
where? (in what direction?) *dochira?* (55), *dotchi?* (65)
which one(s)? *dore?* (30)
which . . .? *dono . . .?* (30)
whisky *uisukii* (175)
white *shiro* (83), *shiroi* (84)
white collar worker *sarariiman* (58)
who? *dare?* (31)
why? *naze?* (198)
wife (another person's) *oku-san* (35)
wife (my) *kanai* (35), *tsuma* (35)
win *kachimasu, katsu* (202)
window *mado* (117)
winter *fuyu* (115)
winter holiday *fuyuyasumi* (115)
with . . . . . . *to issho (ni)* (172)
within a country, internal *kokunai* (74)
wonderful *subarashii* (29)
work *(o-)shigoto* (12)
work for/at . . . . . . *ni tsutomete imasu, iru* (121)
working person ('member of society') *shakaijin* (70)
wrap *tsutsumimasu, tsutsumu* (233)
wrestling (Japanese-style) *sumō* (148)
write *kakimasu, kaku* (209)

yakitori restaurant *yakitoriya* (161)
year (counter for) *-nen* (114)
year (three times a year) *nen ni sankai* (195)
year after next *sarainen* (202)
year before last *ototoshi* (168)
yellow *kiiro* (83), *kiiroi* (84)
yen *-en* (81)
yes *hai* (10)
yes (informal) *ē* (10)
yesterday *kinō* (168)
yesterday evening *yūbe* (169)
yoghurt *yōguruto* (81)
you *anata* (69), *. . . (person's name) . . . -san* (69)
you (very familiar) *kimi* (69)
young *wakai* (149)
younger brother (my) *otōto* (35)
younger brother (another person's) *otōto-san* (35)
younger sister (my) *imōto* (35)
younger sister (another person's) *imōto-san* (35)
zero *maru* (100), *rei* (100), *zero* (53)